©2021

BANGKOK
UTOPIA

BANGKOK UTOPIA

MODERN ARCHITECTURE
AND BUDDHIST FELICITIES, 1910–1973

Lawrence Chua

University of Hawai'i Press
Honolulu

spatial habitus

Subventions for the publication of this book were generously
provided by the Graham Foundation for Advanced Studies
in the Fine Arts and a Syracuse University CUSE award.

Library of Congress Cataloging-in-Publication Data

Names: Chua, Lawrence, author.
Title: Bangkok utopia : modern architecture and Buddhist felicities,
    1910–1973 / Lawrence Chua.
Other titles: Spatial habitus (Series)
Description: Honolulu : University of Hawai'i, 2021. | Series: Spatial
    habitus: making and meaning in Asia's architecture | Includes
    bibliographical references and index.
Identifiers: LCCN 2020025425 | ISBN 9780824884604 (hardcover) | ISBN
    9780824887735 (adobe pdf) | ISBN 9780824887742 (epub) | ISBN
    9780824887759 (kindle edition)
Subjects: LCSH: City planning—Thailand—Bangkok—History. | City
    planning—Thailand—Bangkok—Religious aspects—Buddhism. | Urban
    ecology (Sociology)—Thailand—Bangkok. | Visionary
    architecture—Thailand—Bangkok. | Architecture—Political
    aspects—Thailand—Bangkok. | Bangkok (Thailand)—Buildings, structures, etc.
Classification: LCC HT169.T52 B3634 2021 | DDC 307.1/21609593—dc23
LC record available at https://lccn.loc.gov/2020025425

Portions of chapters 2 and 5 appeared as "A Tale of Two Crematoria: Funeral
Architecture and the Politics of Representation in Mid-Twentieth-Century
Bangkok" in the *Journal of the Society of Architectural Historians* 77, no. 3 (September
2018).

Design by Nord Compo

For Khru Ben (1936–2015)

CONTENTS

PART III. SYSTEMS

ILLUSTRATIONS

ACKNOWLEDGMENTS

The foundations of this book were built on the advice, support, and friendship of Anne Blackburn, Ngampit Jagacinski, Samson Lim, and Tamara Loos. Along with those of the two anonymous reviewers of the manuscript, their generous and critical comments on early drafts helped transform it into a book. Early in my training as a historian, Medina Lasansky helped shape the ways that I look at the material and rhetorical aspects of architecture.

Ms. Koraphin Taweta, Ms. Nanthaka Pollachai, and the dedicated staff of the National Archives of Thailand, the National Library, the Ho Vajiravudh, the archives of the Association of Siamese Architects, and the General Phraya Phahonphonphayuhasena archives at the National Artillery Center in Lopburi generously helped locate, share, and reproduce important documents from the history of the country. Eric Richter, the archivist at the Carrier Corporation Archives in Syracuse, patiently helped me track down a small but important document that I had been trying to locate since I was a doctoral student.

The publication of this book was supported by generous grants from the Graham Foundation for Advanced Studies in the Fine Arts and Syracuse University's Collaboration for Unprecedented Success and Excellence (CUSE). Fellowships at the Freiburg Institute of Advanced Studies at the Albert-Ludwigs-Universität and the International Institute of Asian Studies at Universiteit Leiden allowed me to pursue an idyllic year of uninterrupted writing and research. In Freiburg, Nikolaus Binder went out of his way not only to help me navigate German bureaucracy but also to introduce me to the pleasures of living in his hometown. Petra Fischer, Bernd Kortmann, Britta Küsst, Johanna Bichlmaier, Roland Muntschick, and the entire administration of FRIAS made me feel immediately welcome and at home. At the IIAS, Philippe Peycam and Paul Rabé facilitated access to many wonderful researchers and resources, including Michel Antelme, who graciously helped me with *khom* inscriptions. Early on, the Asian Cultural Council as well as Dean Michael Speaks and Associate Dean Julia Czerniak at the Syracuse University School of Architecture supported research travel at important moments in the book's development.

I am grateful for the thoughtful and critical guidance of many colleagues and fellow researchers. These include Ida Aroonwong, Chatri Prakitnon-takan, Noa Roei, Jenny Reardon, Catherine McBride, Lorena Bachmaier Winter, Majid Daneshgar, Azar Mir, Oliver Braeunling, Paolo Silvestri, Anne Holzmüller, Onur Yildirim, Henrike Laehnemann, Nancy Campbell, Eva Ambos, Carola Erika Lorea, Bindu Menon, Haydon Cherry, Thomas Patton, Arjun Subrahmanyan, Lee Kah Wee, Jiat-Hwee Chang, Imran bin Tajudeen, Pamela Corey, Nana Adusei-Poku, Nathaniel Walker, and Elizabeth Lacouture; Li Hung-chiung, Huang Li-ling, and the other comrades of the Asia Theory Network; the members of the Critical Asia working group: Arnika Fuhrmann, Sudarat Musikawong, and Wang Zhuoyi; the members of the Urban Humanities working group: Peter Christensen, Samia Henni, Julia Walker, Lisa Trivedi, and Mimi Cheng; and at Syracuse University: Jean-François Bédard, Romita Ray, Mitesh Dixit, Amber Bartosh, and Sou Fang. Barbara Opar, the librarian at the School of Architecture, has been a remarkable research and teaching collaborator since my arrival at Syracuse. My research assistants Tao Shuxiao, Jun Cao, Maureen Yue, Yu Zhixiao, and Alexander Kuhn helped me redraw images and organize the manuscript.

Lisa Miller has been my constant companion, no less during the research and writing of this book; she was the voice at the end of the line who always knew when and where to find me. Paul Pfeiffer, Julie Mehretu, Jessica Rankin, Shu Lea Cheang, John Letourneau, Rachel Carrigan, Brigitte Landou, Tanalap Anantasin and Mana Promnikorn, Jacob Chuah, Francis Chuah, Jimmy Chuah, and their families, and Gwynn Jenkins created spaces for me to think, write, decompress, and escape in Bangkok, New York, Paris, and Penang. I am especially grateful to Lakshmi for the long and clarifying *dérives* through George Town.

Finally, my partner, Timothy Gerken, has been my shelter and my witness throughout the period of researching and writing this book. With Khush, a felicitous recent addition to both our lives, he continues to provide unexpected perspectives on the worlds we have been blessed to travel through together.

NOTE ON TRANSCRIPTION

English-language studies of Thailand have been historically inconsistent in their transcription of Thai words. This book is no exception, since it makes use of vocabulary from not only Thai (Th.) but also Pali (P.), Sanskrit (Skt.), Chinese, and architecture. Although it endeavors to conform to the Royal Thai General System of transcription, it defers to commonly accepted usage for proper names (e.g., Vajiravudh rather than Wachirawut). It makes use of Pali terms for scriptural references (e.g., *Nibbānasutta*), but for terms like *devaraja, chakravartin,* and "mandala," which are part of the political vocabulary of Southeast Asian studies, I have deferred to the more widely used Sanskrit terms. Chinese names and terms are rendered in pinyin except for certain historical proper names (e.g., Sun Yat-sen instead of Sun Yixian).

CHAPTER ONE

INTRODUCTION

The word "utopia" is not often associated with the city of Bangkok, better known for its disorderly sprawl, overburdened roads, stifling levels of pollution, chronic flooding, vivid class disparities, and increasingly violent political landscape.[1] Yet, throughout the twentieth century, pictorial, narrative, and built representations of utopia were a critical part of the transformation of the city into a national capital and commercial entrepôt. When the city was officially founded in 1782 on the banks of the Chaophraya River as the home of the Chakri dynasty, its orientation was based on material and rhetorical considerations that alluded to ideal times and spaces. The construction of palaces, monastic complexes, walls, forts, and canals sought not only to create a defensive network but also to symbolically locate the terrestrial realm of the king within the Theravada Buddhist cosmos.[2] However, as older representations of the universe encountered modern architecture, building technologies, and urban planning in twentieth-century Bangkok, new images of an ideal society attempted to reconcile urban-based understandings of Buddhist liberation and happiness with worldly models of political community like the nation-state.

UTOPIA AND BUDDHIST FELICITIES

The concept of utopia has a long and well-examined historical relationship with modernism—and is often implicated in the failure of modernist architects to provide appropriate settings for civic and private life.[3] However, this book outlines an alternative genealogy of both utopia and modernism in a part of the world that has often been overlooked by scholars of both. Conditions of happiness and forms of salvation have long been expressed as architectural and urban forms in the idealized corpus that historian and Pali literature scholar Steve Collins has called "the Pali imaginaire"—the imagined world of texts written in and sometimes translated into the sacred language of Theravada Buddhism.[4] These felicitous states included various heavens, earthly paradises, the coming Buddha's millennium, and the Perfect Moral Commonwealth of a Good King.[5] Existential conditions were often described through the metaphor of place (*thāna*). Nirvana (P. *nibbāna*) and other Buddhist felicities were often imagined as cities that could be measured in finite distances like the *yojana*.[6] Even before the Chakri monarchs established their capital in Bangkok, Southeast Asian kings—informed by Pali textual culture—lived in palaces and cities modeled on representations of those in the heavens. The centers of dynastic power in early Buddhist and Hindu Southeast Asia were fashioned as models of the central cosmos.[7] Narrative texts as well as buildings, town planning, murals, ornament, and manuscript illustrations linked the unconditioned realm of *nibbāna* with the conditioned worlds of the heavens and the abodes of royalty.[8] In turn, architecture and landscape—along with vernacular compilations of Pali texts, narratives, and other commentaries and translations—played an important part in the transmission of the Pali imaginaire to mass populations without knowledge of Pali.[9]

Although modernity transformed the world of Theravada Buddhism, the narratives and imagery of the Pali imaginaire continued to be relevant in the modern period.[10] However, its civilizational role in Siam changed as the polity reformulated itself into a nation-state with modern borders and entered into a new global order.[11] By examining built forms as well as architectural drawings, building manuals, novels, poetry, and ecclesiastical murals, this book creates an understanding of the encounter between the spatial dimensions of Buddhist felicities such as *nibbāna* นิพพาน, *sri ariya metteya* ศรีอาริย์ เมตไตรย, Uttarakuru อุตตรกุรุ, Mount Meru พระสุเมรุ, and the Himmaphan forest หิมพานต์ and the geometries of the world capitalist system into which Siam was thrust in the twentieth century. It asks why the image of utopia, or an urban reality imagined beyond the time and space of the present, was critical for the development of the city into a major metropolis and nodal point in the global capitalist economy. To answer this question, it looks at the ways architecture has been integral to the production of ideology, the conjoined genealogies of the imagined community of the nation-state and the imaginary community of utopia, and the development of an urban Buddhist modernism that was related to but different from other responses to modernization.

Although frequently overlooked in historical studies of modern architecture and the urban built environment, Bangkok is an important case for scholars of modernism. While modernity, and its cultural expression modernism, has been conventionally associated with disenchantment, scientific reason, the rise of an autonomous bourgeoisie, liberal democracy, and industrialization, in cities like Bangkok it did not occasion a full-scale rejection of Buddhist felicities, older cosmological understandings of space, sociopolitical arrangements, and material approaches to the built environment. Thai architecture was able to accommodate these felicities while responding to the cultural experience of modernity on its own—albeit conditioned—terms as a sovereign nation. This makes Bangkok an excellent but by no means isolated case study for scholars who seek an understanding of how local forms of knowledge and truth claims transformed the new forms, technologies, and expertise of modern architecture. The twentieth century is the historical moment in Thailand when the art of building moved from the domain of the *nai chang* (craftsman), with its attentiveness to divine orientation, rituals, and patrons, to the professional "scientific" expertise of the architect and urban planner, real estate speculation, industrial materials, mass construction, and public space. But building and urban planning did not move neatly from the realm of "magic" to that of technology. The twentieth century saw the lines between the religious and the secular, the royal and the public, Buddhism and modernity, enchantment and reason, interwoven into complex aesthetic regimes. By the twentieth century, Thai architects were able to draw on diverse influences, symbols, materials, and techniques that transgressed orthodox historical and geographical categories to support a utopian form of nationalism.

IDEOLOGY AND THE BUILT ENVIRONMENT

How did architecture come to play such an important role in the formulation of a utopian nationalist ideology? Architecture and landscape are projects of the imagination.[12] They begin as a representation of an idea and acquire form in the material world through complex negotiations with labor, capital, materials, populations, and site. As both a form of representation and material construction, the built environment has historically played an important role in creating and sustaining ideological frameworks.[13] More than a collection of buildings, the built environment is a filter through which human beings engage with the world. Because architecture and landscape interventions can be integrated into the everyday and the natural, they form a critical component of ideology—a comprehensive normative vision of reality that influences the way people think of, act in, and view the material world.[14]

In premodern Southeast Asia, local political actors took to constructing and reconstructing buildings and infrastructural projects to tie together the ideologies of *devaraja* (Th. *thewarat*), or divine kingship, and the *cakkavattin*

(Skt. *chakravartin*; Th. *chakrawadirat*), or the righteous kingship of the universal monarch within the spatiotemporality of lived experience. Bernard Groslier, for example, has pointed out the ways that the construction of Angkor's Vishnuite temples and the hydraulic works that surrounded them underscored the relationship between agricultural cycles and the ideology of state, king, and religion.[15] The construction of Candi Borobudur by Sailendra kings between 760 and 830 CE merged the chthonous cult of kings of the mountain with the Buddha Vairocana, linking the family of the Tathagata with the lineage of the dynasty on Java's fertile Kedu Plain.[16] The Buddhist kings of fourteenth-century Sukhothai created sacred landscape sites not only to make claims to territory and populations but also to articulate a historical relationship between their realms and older sacred centers of prestige and power, like Lanka.[17]

Historian Anne Blackburn and geographer James Duncan have been at the forefront of a considerable body of research concerned with the multiplication of Buddhist landscapes across the Theravadan ecumene that sought to bring Southeast Asian Buddhists "mentally as well as physically" into closer proximity with the geographies of the historic Buddha.[18] More recently, historian Maurizio Peleggi has shown how the replication of Buddhism's sacred geography through architecture and landscape was a practice of cultural memory, or reusing texts, images, and rituals to stabilize and convey a society's self-image.[19] However, little has been written about the ways new sites, technologies, and understandings of space in the twentieth century held this historic landscape in relationship to the modern world. By the nineteenth century in Siam, the monarchy continued to build monuments, palaces, and monastic complexes that signified their sacred authority at the center of a mandala that linked the heavens with the territories they ruled. However, they also commissioned public works like Hualamphong Railway Station, leisure sites like the Sala Chaloem Krung, and new roads like Charoen Krung to position their reign within a modern utopia of railroads, cinemas, and automobiles.

IMAGINED AND IMAGINARY COMMUNITIES

The word "utopia" entered the Thai language as a loan word, just as it entered English as a playful synthesis of the Greek words for "good place" and "no place."[20] Indeed, there is no exact corollary between the felicities of the Pali imaginaire and the utopias of the industrial ecumene. Entry into the great city of Nibbāna, or Mahanakhon Nipphan มหานครนิพพาน, was usually narrated as a singular journey that was intended as a metaphor for right practice. On the other hand, since Thomas More's conception of it, the utopian city was realized collectively, through the reorganization of society and its institutions: not only education, law, and sanctions but the built environment itself. In twentieth-century Bangkok, the felicitous city of *nibbāna* and utopia encountered each other and produced a particular way of understanding the potential of the modern city. Bangkok's utopias, unlike those of the industrial ecumene—such as Charles Fourier's *phalanstère*, Ebenezer Howard's *Garden Cities of To-Morrow*, and Tony Garnier's *Cité industrielle*—were not driven solely by a fantasy of technological progress, but through a dialectical engagement between cosmological thinking and a modern understanding of political community. Because Thailand did not experience direct colonization by a European power but performed a kind of autocolonization in the nineteenth and twentieth centuries, older, cosmologically based ideologies of political legitimation entered into a complex relationship with nationalism as the Siamese monarchy sought to assert their identity as both divine and modern rulers.[21] While historically minded anthropologists like Charles Keyes have investigated the importance of millennial thinking to the *phu mi bun* ผู้มีบุญ (men of merit) rebellions that occurred at the frontiers of the centralizing Siamese state and France's expanding colonial project in the beginning of the twentieth century, little has been written about the historical importance of architecture and its rhetorical qualities in fostering a utopian nationalist ideology during this turbulent period.[22]

Utopian nationalism linked the imagined community of the nation with the imaginary community of utopia.[23] In Siam and later Thailand, it was part of a broader cultural and economic campaign on the part of the Siamese monarchy to assert their relevance in a turbulent urban landscape transformed by extraterritorial laws, migrant Chinese labor, and the rise of new urban classes. The old economic and political machinery of the state was gradually eroded by the integration of Siam into the world capitalist economy, but a new system had not yet fully developed to replace it. In reaching back to an imagined past as well as projecting into a modern future, utopian nationalism filled this caesura, allowing the old regime to revive itself, albeit in an adjusted form.[24] In the mid-nineteenth century, as the old system collapsed and merchant capitalism expanded in Siam, the power of local lords (*khunnang*) decreased because they remained tied to old production relations. The monarchy, on the other hand, benefited from capitalism, which allowed the Siamese state to centralize and, in turn, establish royal absolutism. The king, and later the state, now came to occupy the center of a new urban geometry, no longer defined by the rigid forms of a cosmic mandala. The city continued to be an important part of the formulation of a new, nationalist ideology.

By examining the ways that the new spaces of the city became arenas for modern subject formation, utopian desire, and political hegemony, as well as social unrest, this book outlines a theory of the modern city as a space of antinomy, able not only to sustain heterogeneous temporalities but also to support conflicting worldviews within the urban landscape. Faced with a new understanding of the city as a productive node in the world capitalist economy of the twentieth century, architects, planners, and political leaders as well as workers, migrants, and activists used Buddhist felicities as a platform for imagining and expressing modernity in Bangkok during the twentieth century.

BUDDHIST MODERNISM

The political scientist Marshall Berman famously distinguished between "modernity," "modernization," and "modernism." He described the process of social development that brought the tempest of modern life into being as "modernization." This included discoveries in the physical sciences that transformed our understanding of the universe and our place in it; the industrialization of production, which changed scientific knowledge into technology, created new human environments and destroyed old ones, sped up the tempo of everyday life, and generated new forms of corporate power and class struggle; demographic expansion, upheaval, and migration; the development of increasingly powerful national states, bureaucracies, and an autonomous bourgeoisie; an enormous expansion of mass communication systems that bound together diverse regions, peoples, and cultures; the growth of mass social movements that challenged political and economic rulers and sometimes led to democratization; population explosions and mass migrations; an ever-expanding and volatile capitalist world market; all of which informed rapid and often violent urbanization.[25] "Modernity" described the ways these features had been experienced by the individual, the attitude toward life that was associated with a continuous process of evolution and transformation, and a new temporality that oriented the subject toward a future that was different from the past and the present. "Modernism" referred to the cultural responses toward modernity that were oriented toward the future and the desire for progress. Visions and ideas that represented humans as the subjects as well as the objects of modernization and gave them the power "to make their way through the maelstrom and make it their own" were the focus of modernist movements in the arts, literature, and architecture.[26] While modernity mediated between the processes of socioeconomic development known as modernization and the subjective responses to it in the form of modernist discourses and movements, the experience of it could be notably different when considered from places outside Europe and North America.[27] The architectural historian Sibel Bozdoğan, for example, has pointed out that in countries outside Western Europe and North America, such as Turkey, modernity did not result from the transformation of society into an urban-, industrial-, and (capitalist) market-oriented order but was part of an official program implemented either by colonial governments or by modernizing authoritarian nation-states.[28] In Thailand, architectural historian Chatri Prakitnontakan has called for examining Thai architectural culture and production beyond the categories that have constructed its historical understanding in Europe and North America.[29] This is not an argument for the existence of "multiple modernities" that maintain the primacy of "the West" in the formulation of the modern. Rather, it suggests that urban modernity must be understood as a differentiated and discordant global process that produced new forms of society in diverse locations.[30]

What it meant to be a modern subject in Europe was thus very different from what it meant in places like Thailand, where individual subjectivity also involved questions of being with gods and spirits.[31] In Thailand, as historian Tamara Loos points out in her study of family law in Siam, modernity was never secular but always Buddhist.[32] Studying the ways that Buddhism shaped modern architecture and urbanisms in Thailand opens up an understanding of modernity as a global phenomenon produced through a dialectical engagement between nineteenth- and twentieth-century innovations and beliefs and practices that claimed continuity with the mythic and historical past.[33] Looking at the broader Theravada Buddhist ecumene, in which ideas about modernity circulated in the nineteenth century, Blackburn has similarly argued that new imported discourses and forms of social identification in colonial Sri Lanka did not always displace those that had existed previously.[34] In colonial Cambodge at the turn of the century, Anne Hansen has pointed out that Khmer Buddhists were engaged in articulating modern experience in their own heterogeneous terms but that Buddhism remained the primary means for articulating a new self-consciousness of what it meant to be both Khmer and modern, an experience marked by what she has described as "demythologization without disenchantment."[35] In exploring the legal, institutional, and literary frameworks of Buddhist modernism, these three historians of Southeast Asia have also opened up a path to better understand the material and ideological negotiations between old and new values in the very birthplace of modernity: the city.

By the twentieth century, Bangkok was no longer imagined as the center of a preordained sacred geography but as a designed cosmography that was produced by human labor. Its urban plan was grounded not only in the beliefs of its royal patrons but also in the sometimes conflicting beliefs of new urban classes in the spatial qualities of a new social, political, and economic order. This "spatial imagination" found expression in buildings, landscapes, infrastructure space, building manuals, graffiti, drawings, and the phenomenological experience of the built environment.[36] Investigating these expressions of twentieth-century Buddhist spatial imaginaries illuminates the process through which Bangkok's inhabitants worked out the relation between social and physical phenomena and established links between the physical qualities of the city and its inhabitants, ritual practices, sensory experiences, and nonmaterial ideas and ideals.

METHODOLOGIES AND SOURCES

To examine these links between the material and rhetorical aspects of architecture and the built environment, this book deploys an "urban humanities" approach. "Urban humanities" is a critical interdisciplinary research methodology for scholars of the built environment that combines the analytical and illustrative tools of the design professions with humanities-based modes of historical and literary inquiry to reveal parameters of the lived experience of urban space.[37] Recently, architectural historians like Swati Chattopadhyay and Max Hirsh have used urban humanities methodologies to examine the experiential qualities of infrastructure space by bringing the intentions of designers and planners into dialogue with the spatial practices of its users.[38] This book builds on their work by reading architectural representations of urban space against literary representations of the city in order to develop a deeper understanding of architecture's narrative qualities in the twentieth century.

This book draws on archival and field research completed in multiple state and private archives in Thailand over the course of a ten-year period to better understand architectural and urban narratives. The primary material archive consists of the buildings themselves. These range from leisure gardens and royal palaces to reliquary stupas in monastic complexes to cinemas and stadia. Many of these case studies, like the stadium and the hotel, will be familiar to scholars of architecture working in other parts of the world. Others, like the *phra merumat* (crematorium) are unique to Southeast Asia. Field research at these sites is able to reveal what an image often cannot: how the building is deployed in its material context. The book also draws on secondary, rhetorical archives that include architectural images (plans, sections, elevations, diagrams, and photographs as well as illustrated manuscripts, building manuals, and architectural models) and literary representations (poems, novels, and memoirs as well as proposals, correspondence, funerary volumes, and codes). These secondary archives, primarily in Thai and Chinese, reveal what the primary archive cannot: how architecture has been deployed rhetorically in the cultural landscape.

The story of modern architecture emerged and evolved over the course of the twentieth century as a series of incidents that became historical events by means of a narrative told primarily by European architects and scripted in a series of publications.[39] Just as structures that are particular to Thailand, like the *phra merumat*, expand modern architecture's typological repertoire beyond the factories and housing of this received narrative, the rich idiosyncrasies of Thai-language literature open up our understanding of modernity and the way it has been recorded in architectural history. The three genres of Thai historical writing—*tamnan*, *phongsawadan*, and *prawatisat*—reflect the ways the past was understood as continuous with the modern present in nineteenth- and twentieth-century Bangkok. *Tamnan* were prehistorical narratives that placed Thai polities within the larger world of Buddhism. *Phongsawadan* chronicled dynastic accomplishments and emphasized the place of the Thai within a world of kingdoms. The nineteenth- and twentieth-century *prawatisat* narrative tradition sought to place Siam and later Thailand as a nation-state among other nation-states. The new historical modality, however, was conditioned by earlier spatial and temporal views. This produced what historian Thongchai Winichakul has called "a historiography that was modern in character but based upon traditional perceptions of the past and traditional materials."[40] The cosmological landscape of the *tamnan* informed the *phongsawadan* and the *prawatisat*. Even if the time represented by deities and sages or the Buddha himself was different from the time of monarchs who appear on a historical timeline, they can be understood, as Buddhist studies scholar Donald K. Swearer has suggested, as representing equal parts of a single story in which the divine, demonic, and human interacted on a single stage.[41] Sacred cities appear within these histories as particular episodes within an integrated cosmic, natural, geographic, religiohistorical narrative structure. Following Swearer, this book narrates a history of Buddhist modernism in twentieth-century Bangkok as a "unitary history that has different chapters composed of various episodes."[42]

STRUCTURE OF THE BOOK

This book is organized into three parts, composed of nine chapters. Rather than attempt a totalizing historical narrative about the triumphal rise of modernism in Thailand, it follows a loose chronology from early twentieth-century absolutism, through the paradoxical rise of constitutional democracy and military dictatorship in the middle of the century, to the emergence of a regime of "development" in the postwar period. Together, these three parts mirror the trajectory of ideas in the architect's studio, from their conceptualization as drawings, models, and plans to their material realization in steel, concrete, and glass, to the ways they sit within larger urban, national, and global systems and ultimately engage with their users. It follows the development of representations of ideology into ideological systems.

Chapter 2 of this book examines the interest in cosmological order, strategic defense, and historical lineage that drove the original planning of the city. It examines the *Tamra phichai songkhram* and the *Traiphum phra ruang*, two key treatises that were revised and reproduced in the early days of the city, and establishes a foundation for understanding the twentieth-century shift in the conceptualization of the city as a modern capital, the reorganization of the building trades, and the relationship between the monarchy and the spaces and peoples it ruled over. It is a prelude to the first part of the book, "Tools," which examines the technologies of the nascent architectural profession that were used not only to conceptualize the building in the design process, but also to imagine utopia. During this period (1910–1933), diagrams, models, and the academic plan, section, and elevation sought to articulate a new vision of the cosmos and the place of the ruling class and the populations it ruled over within it. Chapter 3 compares the diagrams of the City of Willows, a paradisiacal enclave of Chinese secret societies loosely based on the Pure Land of Amitābha Buddha, which were intended to guide the building of secret society lodges in Bangkok, with diagrams of Theravadan ecclesiastical architecture modeled on eighteenth-century illustrations of *nibbāna*. These diagrams circulated among two different constituencies via manuals that were intended to inculcate their users with a new sense of communal belonging that drew on older dynastic and religious lineages. Chapter 4 examines the models of the miniature city of Dusit Thani, a queer utopian landscape created by King Vajiravudh in the gardens of two of his royal palaces. This highly detailed miniature city served as a stage where the all-male members of his inner court rehearsed modern political relationships while vying for the favors and attention of the absolute monarch. Chapter 5 looks at the ways the plan, section, and elevation allowed for an updated view of the Buddhist cosmos as well as built space by looking at changes in the funeral pyre modeled after Mount Meru that was used to cremate royalty and, after the overthrow of the absolute monarchy in 1932, commoners who had sacrificed their lives for the state.

The second part of this book, "Materials," examines the period between 1933 and 1957, when modern building materials and technologies like steel, concrete, and air-conditioning allowed for the construction of modern environments that reframed Buddhist felicities. Chapter 6 looks at the ways air-conditioning and steel framing facilitated "sensuous citizenship formation" in the Sala Chaloem Krung cinema by creating a space in which large numbers of audience members could congregate and experience the climate of "civilization" distinct from the tropical realities of the city. The building was conceived of in the last days of the absolutist monarchy but not completed until Siam adopted its first constitution; its ornamental features referred to the pantheon of deities that populated the *Ramakian*, the thirteenth-century Thai version of the epic *Ramayana*, while the building's structural and ventilation systems produced a new kind of technologically driven "magic" that ultimately could not be sustained under the absolute monarchy. The overthrow of the absolute monarchy in 1932 was heralded by the People's Party as the coming of *sri ariya metteya*, the era of the future Buddha.[43] Chapter 7 looks at the ways steel-reinforced concrete produced by the Siam Cement Company was seized upon by architects and ideologues of the People's Party as the material through which this new world of equality could be realized. Just as a religious metaphor was exercised by the People's Party to announce Siam's entry into the modern world of democracy and universal suffrage, contradictory forms of architecture emerged in the capital during this period that sought to reconcile utopianism with militarism.

The third part of the book, "Systems," is composed of a single chapter that returns to the planning of the city, this time during the Cold War era (1957–1973). During this period, Thailand's military dictatorship forged new alliances with private enterprise and the US government, and an emphasis on national "development" and urban planning decoupled utopianism from the democratic ideals of the previous era. Architects and planners participated in emerging systems of governance through the establishment of an automotive transportation network that linked Bangkok with remote provinces during the Cold War. Using the metaphor of the *vimāna*, a literary typology that was both vehicle and palace, this section looks at the ways a "floating paradise" emerged that consisted of both the high-profile hotels and commercial buildings that projected Bangkok as a prosperous, exotic metropolis and the anonymous brothels, bars, and love motels that emerged in its shadows.

While the speculative visions of architects and political actors have often masked the repressive machinations of class society, utopianism continues to be an important motivator of social change. At a moment when the ideological framework of neoliberal capitalism denies that any alternatives are possible, let alone viable, it is important to evoke not just a "glimmer of alternative economic and political possibility."[44] This excavation of utopian thinking from the peripheries of the world capitalist economy lays the foundations not for naïve optimism but for a critical politics of hope that acknowledges the ways dreams and imaginative speculations about the city have been historically conditioned, on the one hand by capitalism and colonialism and on the other by Buddhist felicities concerned with emancipation from suffering. This volume reveals several non-European genealogies of utopia to offer readers an understanding of not only how urban populations historically imagined and inhabited the spaces and temporalities of capitalism in the twentieth century, but also how these spaces were challenged and transformed.

CHAPTER TWO

A HISTORICAL AND COSMOLOGICAL FRAMEWORK

In 1782, King Phuttayotfa founded a new capital and a new dynasty follow-ing the overthrow of King Taksin.[1] The new capital stood on the eastern banks of the Chaophraya River, across from Taksin's capital, Thonburi. Two years later, at Phuttayotfa's second coronation, he anointed the city with its proper name:

> กรุงเทพมหานคร บวรรัตนโกสินทร์ มหินทรายุทธยา มหาดิลกภพ นพรัตนราชธานีบูรี รมย์ อุดมราชนิเวศน์มหาสถาน อมรพิมานอวตารสถิต สักกะทัตติยวิษณุกรรมประสิทธิ์
> The city of angels, the glorious city, where the eminent jewel of Kosin-dra resides,[2] the great city Ayutthaya of Indra, the grand capital of the world endowed with nine precious gems, the town of delight, abounding in enormous royal palaces, the celestial *vimāna*, where reincarnated gods reign, a city built by Viśnukam at the consent of Indra.[3]

The formal name of the city underscored Phuttayotfa's ambitions to create a sanctified, well-fortified, and prosperous city on a bend in the Chaophraya River. The multiple urban models the city aspired to referred to felicitous abodes in the Indic cosmos but also echoed once-powerful cities in the region. The "great city Ayutthaya of Indra," for example, referred to Ayutthaya, the last great polity of the Thai central plains, which was sacked by the forces of the Burmese Kongbaung dynasty in 1767. As a "great city" of the deity Indra, Ayutthaya served as both a physical and a spiritual model for Bangkok. Both Phuttayotfa and Taksin had been raised in families that were a part of Ayut-thaya's cosmopolitan ruling class.[4] At the time of Bangkok's formal naming, Phuttayotfa had already drafted laborers from the provinces to expand the new capital. Some were conscripted to make new bricks, while others brought down old bricks and spolia from the ruins of Ayutthaya. According to the *Phra-ratchaphongsawadan krung rattanakosin ratchakan thi 1* (Dynastic Chronicles of the First Reign), a text written in the nineteenth century by the Siamese minister of foreign affairs Chao Phraya Thipakorawong (Kham Bunnag), when this labor force proved insufficient, Phuttayotfa levied ten thousand Khmers to dig a canal perpendicular to the bend of the river, making the city into an artificial island that mirrored the historical topography of Ayutthaya.[5] Even these new conscripts proved lacking, and so an additional five thousand Lao laborers were corvéed from Vientiane along with others from provinces bordering the Mekong River. These laborers, many of whom stayed to become part of the city's early polyglot population, were tasked with digging the foundations for the walls around the capital city.[6]

The new capital thus made symbolic, strategic, and historical claims through the mobilization of human labor. The city's main canals and walls formed a symbolic plan that alluded to the mountain ranges and rivers that encircled the axis mundi of the Indic cosmos, Mount Meru. They also created a network for public transportation, water supply, and military defense that made the new city a more strategic location than Taksin's capital at Thonburi.[7] Finally, they placed the city within the historic lineage of polities (*muang*) on the central plains by incorporating Ayutthaya's riverine plan and material spolia. In doing so, the new capital made a material as well as rhetorical claim to the lineage of the former polity and reduced Taksin's fifteen-year reign to what Maurizio Peleggi has called "a dynastic interlude."[8] The parameters of the city were further reinforced by the establishment of a network of palaces and forts, with the *lak muang* (city pillar) and the Phra Borom Maha Ratchawong (Grand Palace) at its center. Many of these fortresses, including Fort Phra Sumen and Fort Mahakan, were named after important sites, directions, or figures in the Indic cosmos.[9] The Grand Palace of the king, the Front Palace of the viceroy, and the Rear Palace of Krom Phraratchawang Bowornsathanphimuk (Prince Anurakthewet) not only mapped out the strategic defense of the king's authority but also communicated his central position within the city's political structure.

The founding of the city also marked the establishment of a new ideological order. Historian Nidhi Eoseewong has pointed to the emergence of a new bourgeois mentality and urban worldview stimulated by increased overseas trade during this period.[10] The early Bangkok period saw a remarkably cosmopolitan body of literature constituted through royally sponsored translations and recensions of earlier transregional works. These included the complete Siamese version of the *Ramayana*, the *Ramakian*; the *Romance of the Three Kingdoms* 三國演義; the *Mahavamsa* chronicle of Buddhism in Sri Lanka; the *Ratchathirat* chronicle of the Mon kings of Pegu; the *Dalang* and *Inao* from Java; and the *Duodecagan* cycle of tales from Persia.[11] Phuttayotfa also established a definitive version of the *Tipitaka,* the Pali-language scriptures of Theravada Buddhism, in an effort to enhance an understanding of Buddhism as it was practiced in what he considered the time of the Buddha himself.[12] Most notably, he ordered the recension of two works that would have an important influence on the planning of the city: the *Tamra phichai songkhram,* a purportedly sixteenth-century divination manual for warfare, and the *Traiphum phra ruang,* a treatise on the felicitous realms of the Three Worlds, or Trailokya, cosmology. While the former offered a literal template for the strategic planning of the city, the latter provided the basic orientation of the city as a series of concentric circles surrounding a sacred center. Both of these models can be understood as an attempt to divine the destiny of a new dynasty by integrating the concerns of urban planning with astrological study and fashioning the material terrain into a sacred geography after the rhetorical image of the cosmos.

DIVINATION AND STRATEGY

Although the city's defense may have been of paramount concern to Phuttayotfa, a general who had witnessed the defeat of Ayutthaya and Thonburi, the strategic planning of the city was inseparable from its cosmic positioning. His efforts to create a new capital on the east bank of the Chaophraya River from Taksin's capital at Thonburi were, in part, motivated by defense. He had returned victorious from wars with Cambodia in the east, but the Kongbaung dynasty still posed a threat in the west. If the new capital were on the eastern banks of the Chaophraya, the river itself would form a substantial obstacle to an incursion from the west. The east was furthermore the place of auspicious new beginnings and a direction in which the new city could expand safely.[13] Concern with the strategic positioning of garrisons was intertwined with the correct siting of the city pillar. The anchor of Tai polities, the city pillar marked the axis mundi of the cosmos as well as the symbolic center of the capital.[14] To move the capital to its more strategic location on the east bank of the river required resituating the city pillar at an auspicious place and time. To determine the appropriate site for the pillar and the auspicious moment for its installation, the *Tamra phichai songkhram* was consulted. Multiple versions of the treatise exist, but Thai historians have traced the original version of the Thai manual to 1518, when King Ramathibodi II of Ayutthaya (r. 1491–1529) undertook its compilation.[15] It was later revised under the reign of King Naresuan of Ayutthaya (r. 1590–1605) and entered into modern Thai history shortly after the founding of Bangkok, when Phuttayotfa ordered a recension that drew on translations of a Burmese version of the manual.[16] A later recension was produced in

1825, under the auspices of the viceroy, or the king of the Front Palace, and then printed in 1926 by the Krom Silpakon (Department of Fine Arts).[17]

Manuals like the *Tamra phichai songkhram* were distant relatives of the Indic *śāstra* tradition, likely brought to the court of Ramathibodi II through trade with the Coromandel Coast and the importation of Brahmin priests.[18] The term *śāstra* refers to a written or verbal codification of rules or a body of scientific knowledge that presented largely technical knowledge that was theoretically grounded in Vedic scriptures.[19] Indeed, the *Tamra phichai songkhram* shared similarities with the military segments of the *Arthaśāstra*, the Sanskrit treatise on statecraft and military strategy, such as detailed battle formations and strategies for deceiving the enemy.[20] However, most of the *Tamra phichai songkhram* consisted of illustrated omens and mandalas to predict the outcome of battle and supernatural methods.[21] The omens are read from astrological calculations based on constellations or observations of nature, such as the shapes of clouds and appearance of the sun and moon, but also include strategic formations based on mythical creatures from the Himmaphan forest, which surrounds the axis mundi of the Hindu and Buddhist cosmos, Mount Meru. The *Tamra phichai songkhram* thus integrated a reading of the celestial bodies of the cosmos with terrestrial concerns of strategy and fortification.[22]

The *Tamra phichai songkhram* identified eight symbolic mandalas for the organization of strategic defense. Of these, the most appropriate for the geography of the new city was the *naganam* because it indicated the strategic placement of troops along flowing waterways.[23] The *naganam* was so named because of its resemblance to the chthonic water serpent, or *naga,* and was deemed appropriate for controlling the area close to where canals, streams, and rivers flowed.[24] The *naganam* had both temporal and spatial aspects. It predicted the scheduling of troops based on auspicious signs and determined that the sixth lunar month was the last month that the *naga*'s head would be in the west. Therefore, any auspicious activity in the future would have to be done in the eastern direction. Sunday, it also noted, was the day of auspicious peace and victory in defense.[25] Thus it was on Sunday, 21 April 1782, that a new city pillar was installed with some haste on the east bank of the Chaophraya.[26] Phuttayotfa chose a site for it on an axis with Wat Bang Wa Yai (today Wat Rakhang Khositaram) on the western bank of the river, then the home of the Somdet Phra Sangharat, or the supreme patriarch of Thai Buddhism. The city pillar marked the head of the *naga*, while Wat Bang Wa Yai marked its tail, and the axis between it and the city pillar thus linked the two sides of the river through the body of the water serpent.[27]

Although cited in the Phuttayotfa recension of the *Tamra phichai songkhram* and alluded to in a diagram of the *mangkon phayu kham nam* (dragon procession crossing the water), the *naganam* doesn't appear as an illustration until the 1825 recension (figure 2.1).[28] In the later diagram, nine garrisons (*khai*) spread across both banks of a river and six towers (*ho rap*) at the head of the *naga*. There is an unmistakable similarity to the topography of the city that Phuttayotfa founded. The drawing shows that by the early nineteenth century, the ruling classes of the Chakri dynasty sought to depict the geographical characteristics of Bangkok as a landscape that was in harmony with the *naganam*.[29] Neither the *naganam* nor the *mangkon phayu kham nam*, however, was an urban plan in the modern sense. Instead of strict parameters, they offered a spatiotemporal guide that could be interpreted by court Brahmins, military leaders, and administrators in charge of corvée laborers alike. As an instrument of divination, the *Tamra phichai songkhram* entwined space and time to allow diverse actors to determine an appropriate course of action within the uncertainty of the universe. Bangkok was founded at a turbulent historical juncture in which the dominant polity of the region was destroyed and a complex scramble for power ensued.[30] Within the latter half of the eighteenth century, wars with the Kongbaung dynasty and military expeditions in Vietnam, Cambodia, Pattani, and Laos preoccupied the courts of the Thai central plains.[31] Given the turmoil of the period in which Bangkok was founded, the *naganam* mandala was not just a strategic plan but a model of certainty for the future of the new capital, offering up a diagrammatic parallel between what Paul Wheatley has called "the regular and mathematically expressible regimes of the heavens and the biologically-determined rhythms of life on earth."[32]

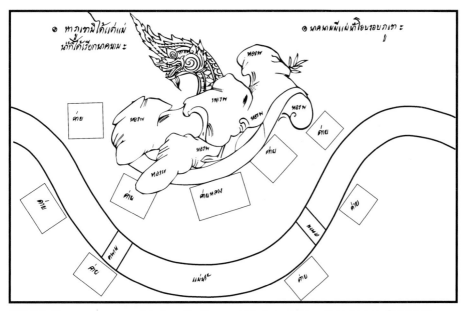

FIG. 2.1. The *naganam* mandala from the *Tamra phichai songkhram,* Department of Fine Arts edition, Krom Silpakon. Redrawn by Alexander Kuhn.

The use of the *naganam* as a template for urban organization can be understood as part of a longer history of mandala-based planning that informed city planning in the Indic world. Although the mandala has a much longer history as an instrument for meditation, insight, and ritually demarcating consecrated space, in Theravada Southeast Asian polities, including those in the Thai central plains, the mandala provided a spatial template whereby the moral precepts of the Pali imaginaire could be replicated in the mundane world of the political capital.[33] It also served as a metaphor for the political organization of Southeast Asian polities.[34] The "mandala polity" is a modern conceptualization of an arena full of petty kingdoms rather than a centralized state. It describes the network of loyalties between ruler and ruled and among rulers, all of whom aspired to be the highest lord of the area over which they claimed sovereignty.[35] Historian Michael Aung-Thwin has noted of the court at Pagan that its structure was founded on the principle of four cardinal points protecting a center, with princes, queens, and ministers distributed across the cardinal points and surrounding the throne at the center.[36] A similar structure informed the design of Phuttayotfa's court.

The Thai term *monthon*, derived from the Pali *maṇḍala*, has at least two principal meanings: an administrative region and a circle.[37] It reflects the multiple meanings embedded within the mandala: more than a symbol, it sought to structure the terrain of the material world after an abstract rhetorical image of celestial space.[38] In theory, the built environment of human and divine habitation in premodern South and Southeast Asian cities was ordered on the geometrical pattern of a place-making mandala, or *vāstu-mandala*.[39] This mandala was generated by an axis mundi, an existentially centered point of transition between cosmic planes.[40] In lived space, the axis mundi was sheltered by a sacred enclave or temple that was oriented to the cardinal directions, assimilating the kingdom to the cosmic order and constructing a sanctified living space within profane space. The ordered cosmos represented in the temple was then amplified axially across the city. While this model was adopted with great success in medieval urban settlements like Pagan and Angkor, it was appropriated with varying results in Bangkok in the eighteenth century. Historian Maurizio Peleggi has noted that the city showed a lack of concern for the correct spatial arrangements associated with Indic town planning.[41]

The historian Edward Van Roy has recently argued that this lack of precision was due to the shifting of the axis mundi as Brahmanical influence on the court of Phuttayotfa waxed and waned. The city pillar was the original axis mundi of the new city, and its installation in 1785 marked the designation of the city's formal name. The pillar was erected equidistant between the city's new west- and east-bank moats. Shortly after, the location of the axis mundi shifted two hundred meters, when the palladium of the kingdom, the Emerald Buddha, or Phra Kaew Morakot, was installed nearby in its own chapel on the grounds of the Grand Palace.[42] It is plausible, as Van Roy argues, that new palladia and symbols that began to accumulate in the city—like the Emerald Buddha, the Sihing Buddha (Phra Phutta Sihing), and the Chinarat Buddha (Phra Phutta Chinarat)—may have anchored axes in Bangkok's early morphology. However, how far these axes extended cannot be accurately ascertained because they were not reinforced visually through roads. What is certain, however, is that the concentric canals and walls that defined the city reinforced the prevailing cosmological model of Mount Meru, and the shifting morphology of the city was due in part to a shift in the new court's ideological direction and its attempt to identify accurate models of the felicitous realms described in the Pali imaginaire.[43] This new ideological direction drew on the "recension" of a purportedly fourteenth-century cosmological text, the *Traiphumikatha* (Sermon on the Three Worlds) or *Traiphum phra ruang* (The Three Worlds According to King Ruang).[44]

THE COSMOLOGY OF THE THREE WORLDS AND THE CONCENTRIC MANDALA

In the first year of his reign, Phuttayotfa convened a meeting of the sangha to prepare a revised version of the *Traiphum phra ruang.*[45] Although the *Traiphum* was the first text in the Theravadan ecumene to describe the cosmology of the Three Worlds, or Trailokya, the concept of the Three Worlds predates Buddhism and has been traced back to the Purāṇas.[46] In its earliest iteration, the Trailokya described a universe that pivoted on Mount Meru, about which the sun, moon, and stars revolved. On the summit of this cosmic axis was the city of the gods, situated in the center of the continent of Jambudvīpa, the abode of men, which was itself surrounded by an alternative series of seven concentric annular oceans and seven concentric annular continents. This model changed over time, so that the concentric oceans became separated by intervening mountain ranges and were in turn surrounded by a cosmic ocean. In the *Traiphum* version of the Trailokya, four continents were arranged in this ocean in the cardinal directions. The continent of the south was Jambudvīpa (Th. Chomphutawip), which human beings inhabited. All variants of the Trailokya, however, were surrounded by mountain walls that defined their bounds within a void. They were used as paradigms for the spatial organization of temple, capital, and state.[47]

The cosmos of the *Traiphum* was organized into thirty-one domains across three planes of existence or universes: the sensuous plane (*kammaphum*), the corporeal plane (*rupaphum*), and the incorporeal plane or (*arupaphum*) (figure 2.2). The *Traiphum* described the three universes as disks or "inverted alms bowls."[48] The world of desire was the only part of the universe that could be visualized, since the worlds of form and formlessness were aerial planes located above the heavens that belonged to the world of desire. The surface of the sensuous plane was the land of human beings, the space above the disk was heaven, and the thickness of the disk was the subterranean space of hell.[49] All three universes, however, were in the same pattern. The *Traiphum* described the space of the cosmos in quantifiable terms and was lavishly illustrated in concertina-folded manuscripts (*samut phap*) throughout the eighteenth and nineteenth centuries. For instance, distances within the Three Worlds were measured in *yojana*, a premodern standard unit used in the Indic ecumene with varying modern equivalents.[50] As chapter 3 reveals, *nibbāna* was frequently represented as a city, Mahanakhon Nipphan, which surpassed the perfection of heaven and was located outside the universe. The center of the sensuous plane was Mount Meru, the vertical axis of the universe, encircled by sixteen mountain ranges and oceans that functioned as walls and moats.[51] However, the *Traiphum* did more than simply articulate in written form the desires of the monarch to be legitimate in the eyes of his subjects. It contextualized social hierarchy as an integral part of the natural order by encoding class distinctions within an understanding of both real and imagined space.

At the peak of the sacred mountain was the *vimāna* of Indra, or the castle Phaichayon Prasat. The *vimāna*, a literary typology examined in greater detail in chapter 8, has been translated as "vehicle," "palace," and "city." It was composed of "gem palaces and gem *prangs*" and "a great many places for play and amusement," all surrounded by a wall of gems with one thousand gates.[52] The identification of the king with Indra was appropriated by Buddhist kings so that the terrestrial palace of the king was considered a model of Indra's abode on Mount Meru.[53] This relationship was underscored by the incorporation of Indra into the formal name of Phuttayotfa's capital. The concentric rings of rivers and mountains that surrounded Mount Meru in the *Traiphum* influenced the circling of walls and moats around Bangkok's Grand Palace, even if it didn't provide a literal model for urban planning.

The *Traiphum phra ruang* is generally considered to have been composed from more than thirty Buddhist doctrines by the king of Sukhothai, Phya Lithai (Maha Dhammaraja I) in 1345, when the central Thai polity was still a significant political, economic, and cultural center on the Southeast Asian mainland.[54] Indeed, many features of the *Traiphum* support these claims.[55] However, several notable historians have questioned these origins as suspect because of the lack of a secure transmission of the manuscript from the fourteenth to the eighteenth century. They have suggested that the text as it is currently known was likely to have been composed sometime between 1776 and 1778, after the fall of Ayutthaya and the founding of new capitals along

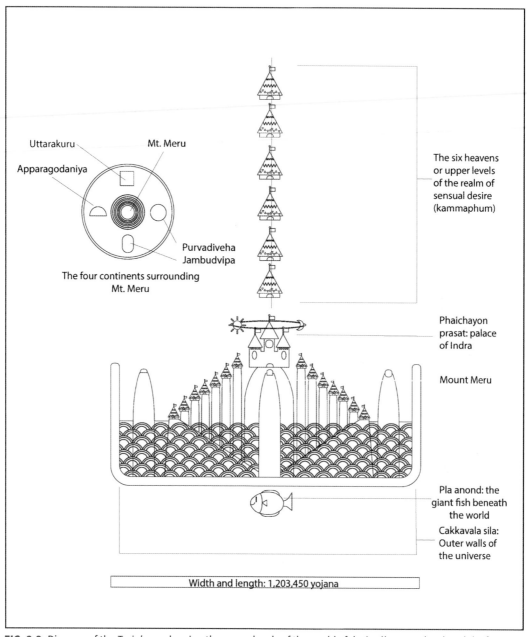

Uttarakuru

Apparagodaniya

Mt. Meru

The six heavens
or upper levels
of the realm of
sensual desire
(kammaphum)

Purvadiveha
Jambudvipa

The four continents surrounding
Mt. Meru

Phaichayon
prasat: palace
of Indra

Mount Meru

Pla anond: the
giant fish beneath
the world

Cakkavala sila:
Outer walls of
the universe

Width and length: 1,203,450 yojana

FIG. 2.2. Diagram of the *Traiphum,* showing the upper levels of the world of desire (*kammaphum*) and the four continents surrounding Mount Meru. *Nibbāna* sits above the upper levels. Illustration by Jun Cao, based on a drawing by Suthida Atput.

the Chaophraya River.[56] Because no complete copy of the text is believed to have survived the sacking of Ayutthaya in 1767, multiple attempts were made to produce an authoritative version of the text.[57] The versions that emerged at this time became key texts in the creation of a dynastic patrimony that linked first the Thonburi and then the Bangkok court with Ayutthaya and Sukhothai and served as a textbook of both Siamese Buddhism and Southeast Asian kingship. The royal scholars who were convened by Phuttayotfa at the beginning of his reign used remnants of the *Traiphum* to create what was essentially a new text, the *Traiphum lokwinitchai*, or the *Trailokawinitchai* (Treatise on the Three Worlds).[58] The new text included much of the same information as extant versions of the *Traiphum* but emphasized the cycle of the universe, the origins of the world, mankind, and righteous government. Earlier versions of the *Traiphum* included this information at the very end, but in the *Traiphum lokwinitchai* this was moved to the beginning. Perhaps the most important change was the description of the center of the cosmos. In the *Traiphum lokwinitchai*, the first territory that emerged from the waters prior to the origin of the world is the Bo Tree Throne, or Throne of Enlightenment, on the Jambudvīpa continent, on which the Buddha would sit and attain enlightenment.

This had important resonances for thinking about the state and kingship. It underscored the merging of Khmer-derived understandings of the *devaraja* (Th. *thewarat*), or "god-king," with the Buddhist concept of the *chakravartin* (P. *cakkavatti*; Th. *phra cakraphadirat*), or righteous "Universal Monarch," that was in earlier versions of the *Traiphum*.[59] It elaborated the ten duties of the righteous king, aligning the worldly ruler with the bodhisattva, or Buddha-to-be.[60] The Universal Monarch of the *Traiphum* acted as an exemplar of kingly conduct, with the "desire to lead all creatures beyond the ocean of sorrows of transmigration."[61] In the early Bangkok period, laws frequently mentioned that the foundation of royal authority lay in the *duties* of the king, rather than in his deva- or god-like attributes.[62] This forged a relationship between the Theravadan Buddhist clergy, or sangha, and the institution of the monarchy, whereby the sangha legitimated the king's authority as consistent with Buddhist values and the king defended and patronized the monastic order.[63]

During the nineteenth century, Siam transitioned from a "mandala polity" to a nation-state that placed the capital at the center of a new geo-body.[64] This change accompanied a shift in the spatial imagination that drew on both the spatial qualities of a new social, political, and economic order and older ideas about cosmological space. Architectural historian Dell Upton has described the "spatial imagination" as a synthetic process that attempted to translate nonspatial goals and categories, such as nationalism, into spatial terms.[65] A modern Buddhist spatial imagination was forged as contact with new philosophical traditions engendered a redefinition of the position of the *chakravartin* and the felicitous worlds of the *Traiphum* in the face of Western "science."[66] The Siamese monarchy had inherited an Indic-derived theory of kingship with an urbanistic focus that was being assailed in the nineteenth century by new ways of thinking about the space of the cosmos. It needed to continue to assert its primacy at the center of the Indic cosmos while participating as a modern sovereign power among other nation-states.

In 1872, Chao Phraya Thipakhorawong, the author of the *Dynastic Chronicles* mentioned earlier, published the *Kitchanukit*. The first book produced under Siamese supervision, it used empirical methods of applied science to explain social hierarchy. "If one reflects on the evidence one concludes that men are born unequal, differing from one another," he wrote.[67] At the same time, he reaffirmed Buddhist values and underscored the rational qualities of the religion. Buddhist cosmography wasn't dismantled but reworked and refined so that it could coexist with other constructions of reality.[68] The *Kitchanukit* separated the natural world from the moral world, using the physical sciences to explain natural phenomena while attributing others to moral actions. For example, although the text dispelled the notion that rain fell because rain-making deities ventured out of their homes, it supported the idea that variations in human difference were due to the merit that beings had accumulated in previous lives.[69] Although the *Traiphum* was inadequate in describing the natural world, in Thipakhorawong's analysis it could explain the consequences of immoral acts. The *Kitchanukit* was thus a renovation of the cosmological view, a way of restating its vitality in the new world of reason, maps, and machines. The *Traiphum*, which had guided urban planning and represented the king at the center of the Three Worlds, now needed to adjust to other methods and tools of representing and organizing space.

The analysis of the *Traiphum* in the *Kitchanukit* reflected the antinomies of modernity in nineteenth- and twentieth-century Bangkok. Just as the *Kitchanukit* could hold in tension the cosmology of the *Traiphum* with a scientific understanding of the world, the modern Buddhist spatial imagination could accommodate both Buddhist felicities and new approaches to architecture and planning. By the end of the nineteenth century, these antinomies could be seen in a map of the city where two patterns dominated the patchwork morphology of the capital (figure 2.3). One was the older concentric mandala with the accumulated palladia of state marking the metaphorical center of the cosmos and radiating outward from the grounds of the Grand Palace. The other was a modern grid unfolding to the north in the new royal suburb of Dusit centered on the classical revival form of the Ananta Samakhom Throne Hall, the equestrian statue of Chulalongkorn,

and the open plaza that bound the two of them.[70] The Grand Palace and
Dusit were linked by a modern thoroughfare that began construction in
1899: Ratchadamnoen Avenue. This thoroughfare, with its wide carriage-
ways, shady footpaths, and concrete bridges spanning the concentric canals
that separated the grid from the mandala, was hailed by foreign commentators as "the finest boulevard in Bangkok."[71] Political power was no longer
displayed exclusively through monuments like the city pillar or the chapels
dedicated to palladia like the Phra Kaeo Morakot or Phra Phutta Sihing,
but through infrastructural interventions and public spaces. The Buddhist
spatial imagination was likewise no longer exclusively represented in divination treatises and mandalas but, as the following chapters reveal, through
tools like mass-produced manuals, models, plans, sections, elevations, popular literature, urban planning proposals, and graffiti. The modern Buddhist
spatial imagination of twentieth-century Bangkok could still accommodate
the enchantment of the previous era while responding to the cultural experience of modernity. It no longer envisaged the city as the center of a preordained sacred geography but as a designed cosmography that was produced
through human labor. Part I places the new spatial imagination and its tools
of expression within the historical reorganization of the building trades
and the transition from master craftsman (*nai chang* นายช่าง) to architect
(*sathapanik* สถาปนิก) as chief purveyor of built works. An influx of migrant
construction labor from southern China, the patronage of architectural
and engineering experts trained in Turin's Beaux-Arts-oriented Accademia
Albertina di Belle Arti and the School of Application for Engineers,[72] and
the translation of the words "architect" and "architecture" into the Thai
language by King Vajiravudh (r. 1910–1925) himself, ushered in new modes
of construction, ways of understanding the building process, and the founding of schools of architecture and professional associations. As large-scale
intraregional migration coupled with the expansion of European colonialism, extraterritorial laws made legal and cultural identification with a particular state increasingly salient to Bangkok's ruling class. As the following
chapters reveal, these events produced a form of nationalism that reimagined the bonds between the Siamese ruling class and its subjects as partici-
pants in a shared utopian project.

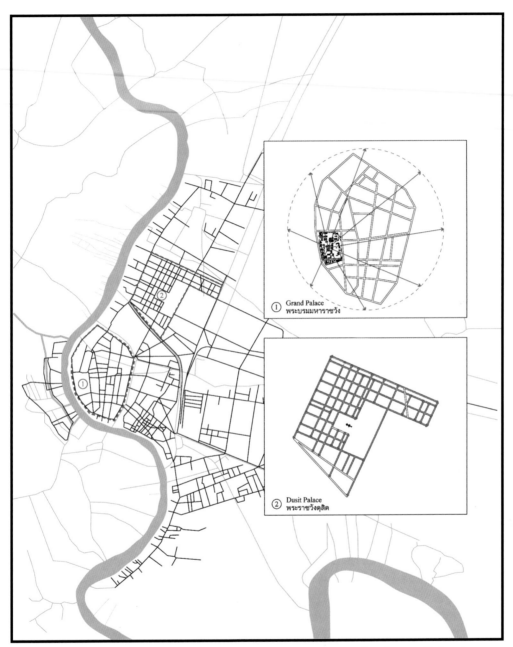

FIG. 2.3. Map of Bangkok, ca. 1900, showing the concentric mandala centered on the Grand Palace in Rattanakosin Island and the new gridded suburbs of Dusit. Illustration by Sou Fang.

Inside the map, the insets are labeled:

① Grand Palace
พระบรมมหาราชวัง

② Dusit Palace
พระราชวังดุสิต

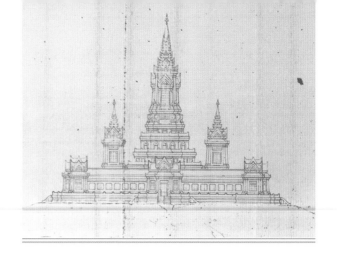

PART I

TOOLS

CHAPTER THREE

DIAGRAMMING UTOPIAN NATIONALISM

Nibbāna and the City of Willows

In May 1910, a general strike of Bangkok's migrant labor force brought the Siamese economy to a standstill for five days before it was suppressed by armed force. Migrant laborers from the south and southeastern coast of China had become indispensable to the building of the Siamese monarchy's public works after the abolition of slavery and the gradual phasing out of corvée labor from 1874 to the early years of the twentieth century.[1] The strike was a critical obstacle in the transformation of the city from the courtly center of a mandala polity into the modern capital of a sovereign nation-state and a nodal point in the world capitalist economy. The Siamese government blamed the unrest on the growing political influence of secret societies (*hongmen* 洪門) on the city's migrant labor population and sought to expel the strike's most offensive agitators from the country, including those who claimed extraterritorial protection as subjects of European colonial powers.[2] The Siamese Ministry of the Interior compiled a list of those who were to be deported.[3] In addition to describing the nature of their offenses, the list assigned to each member of this group a number, a name, and a "race."[4] In place of a family name, the names of the accused were all preceded by the appellation *jin* (Chinese). Among Jin Ngoen, Jin Ha, Jin Wae, and Jin Theng was number 28, Jin Fong (Chinaman Bubbles). Bubbles was racially identified in the registry of deportees as *khae* (Hakka), and he confessed to inciting violence by hurling a brick at a rickshaw puller and intimidating him into ceasing work.[5] Reports of violence during the general strike were not uncommon. The ministry's index listed several others who confessed to similar acts of physical and verbal coercion. All the accused were of different "racial" origins: Hakka, Teochew, Hailam, and Cantonese, but in the register the police reduced them all to a broader taxonomy: Chinese.

URBAN CONFLICT AND UTOPIAN IMAGINAIRES IN EARLY TWENTIETH-CENTURY BANGKOK

The register demonstrates the importance of nationality to the administrators of the growing capital as a way of indexing its diverse, polyglot population.[6] It suggests that regional linguistic and cultural identities like Hakka, Teochew, and Cantonese, which had heretofore been ways that migrant laborers had identified themselves and one another, were in the process of being subsumed into national categories like "Chinese" as the Bangkok-based monarchy sought to legitimate its rule over an increasingly fractured urban population. The secret societies that flourished in Siam during the nineteenth century not only were the primary organizers of the country's growing urban labor force but also became a critical vehicle for the development of a Chinese national identity as the Bangkok-based monarchy mobilized a Siamese national identity. New systems of classification not only redrew the boundaries of human membership in the imagined community of the nation but also reconstituted the built environment in which these new national identities could be performed. Two manuals published in the early twentieth century reimagined architecture as an integral part of speculative nation-building projects while drawing on older cosmological narratives and pictorial conventions: the *Tamra ang yi* ตำราอั้งยี่ (lit. Secret Society Textbook) and the *Baeb nawakam* แบบนวกรรม (lit. The Styles of Nawakam Kowit). These manuals depicted two utopian imaginaires as sites that could be rebuilt in lived space: the Muyang Cheng (City of Willows) and Mahanakhon Nipphan (Great City of Nibbāna). Although the term "manual" refers to a book of instructions for learning a subject or operating a machine, comparative terms in Thai are not as distinct. The terms *tamra, khu meu,* and even *kham pi* share overlapping semantic meanings and are often used interchangeably whether or not they refer to a textbook, a handbook, or a treatise.[7] The *Tamra ang yi* was compiled by the police for the purpose of gathering criminal intelligence, even though its materials originated in the secret societies and circulated in other formats before the twentieth century. It was intended as a narrative guide to the symbols, codes, behavior, and spaces of the secret societies that centered on the revival of the last Han ethnic dynasty, the Ming, in a secret, mythical city. The documents in the *Tamra ang yi* instructed society members in a ritual in which new society members were inculcated in the history of the organization and its symbolism and made to swear thirty-six oaths. Inductees followed a ritual path that was meant to mirror the historical flight of the society's five founders and their ultimate arrival in a utopian enclave known as the Muyang Cheng 木楊城 (City of Willows). The *Baeb nawakam* was produced by the Ministry of Religious Affairs under the auspices of the supreme patriarch of the Buddhist religion in Siam. Although not strictly a construction manual, it was the product of research into the building forms of the Bangkok region and codified the correct grammar of monastic complexes in Siam. Its publication was driven largely by the Siamese ruling class's fear that Bangkok was being built in the image of the migrant laborers' imagined homeland. In spite of their differences, both can be considered part of the broader taxonomic category of manuals because they disseminated knowledge, in this case about space and community, in a systematic way and established a set of normative rules and hierarchies associated with that knowledge. Both manuals reveal the ways that nationalism emerged out of the cultural systems that preceded it: the dynastic realm in the case of the *Tamra ang yi* and the religious community in the case of the *Baeb nawakam*. The felicitous realm of *nibbāna* and the moral utopia of the City of Willows at the center of these manuals can be understood as part of the warp and weft of not only state nationalism but other ideologies of national community as well. In early twentieth-century Bangkok, two forms of nationalism, both utopian in character, converged and competed with each other as the city was reimagined and rebuilt into a modern capital.

THE WARP AND THE WEFT OF MANUAL KNOWLEDGE

Benedict Anderson has famously pointed out the ways that technologies like the census, the map, and the museum produced a warp and weft of the colonial state's domain: a totalizing classificatory grid that could be applied to the diverse peoples, regions, cultures, and architecture under its rule as well as a series of reproducible plurals that inhabited this modern world.[8] As the Bangkok-based monarchy deployed colonial methods to create a nation-state, diagrams, technical drawings, and models that circulated through manuals during the period combined the warp of the image with the weft of the written word to produce an important tool of knowledge production and statecraft.[9] Historian Craig Reynolds has traced the origins of manual knowledge in Thailand to the premodern oral transmission of knowledge that was formatted to facilitate practical use. Reynolds argued that these were local forms of knowledge and, although strategically important for royal courts and unevenly distributed, were not limited in use to the upper classes alone.[10] In the nineteenth and twentieth centuries, manual knowl-edge in Southeast Asia began to be disseminated more widely in the form of grammars, cosmologies, medical and astrology manuals, manuals on the art and science of warfare, and manuals on how to behave properly and how to be modern.[11]

The emergence of these popularized forms of the manual can be placed at the collision of five global historical developments in late nineteenth- and early twentieth-century Bangkok. The first is the movement toward man-ual training in the centers of the industrializing world. In the nineteenth century, manuals became a tool of vocational education to supplement more classically oriented, text-based pedagogy.[12] Manuals like the *Tamra ang yi* and the *Baeb nawakam* assumed a greater significance in Siam as the Bangkok-based monarchy became increasingly preoccupied with projecting itself as a modern state. Another movement was the use of building manuals in British colonial environments of the same period as a means of instruct-ing officials and builders in the colonial Public Works Administration in incorporating regional idioms into their designs as "native" details.[13] Such guides to imperial identity served the nationalist project in Siam as well, as the Crown drew on colonial models to exert its political, cultural, and jurid-ical authority over an increasingly diverse territory.[14] A third genealogy can be traced back to at least twelfth-century China through the use of *tu pu* 圖譜, a sequence of rubrics in which graphic illustrations were paired with an explanatory text.[15] The *tu pu* were of critical importance to trades in China like skilled carpentry, which used manuals like the fifteenth-century *Lu Ban jing* 魯班經.[16] The *Lu Ban jing* distinguished itself from modern manuals by combining knowledge about technique with mythopoetic narratives about the origins of the profession, its rituals, divination practices, and the correct uses of "building magic." In lieu of trade unions, such manuals were instru-mental not only in communicating the craft and technology of the trade, but also in protecting its practitioners, who would have had singular access to "supernatural" powers that could produce either auspicious or harmful domestic environments.[17] A fourth historic tendency was the production of illustrated manuscripts between the seventeenth and nineteenth centu-ries of the *Traiphumikatha* ไตรภูมิกถา (The Sermon on the Three Worlds) or *Traiphum phra ruang* ไตรภูมิพระร่วง (The Three Worlds According to Phra Ruang).[18] Reynolds considered the *Traiphum* a kind of manual because it classified and ranked all animate existence on the basis of merit and estab-lished normative "rules" for social hierarchy in premodern times. It also articulated the aesthetics of what was superior and socially dominant.[19] Texts like the *Traiphum* were originally disseminated as a special genre of *samut phap,* or concertina-folded illustrated manuscripts made of paper pre-pared from the inner bark of the *khoi* or *sa* tree that could be opened up as large maps that depicted the material characteristics of the Theravadan Buddhist cosmos.[20] Some of these manuscripts integrated local geographic features into cosmological diagrams, representing the confluence of both sacred and profane spaces.[21] Although illustrated manuscripts continue to be produced today, their prevalence ended around the same time as the first printing of the *Traiphum* as a cremation volume, in 1912.[22] In the early twentieth century, Bangkok was not only a place in which these literary trajectories converged but also where the powers of the "magician-technician" (*fang shi* 方士) and the experience of the master craftsman (*nai chang* นายช่าง) came into conflict with the technological knowledge of the expert architect and the energies of the unskilled laborer.

UTOPIAN NATIONALISMS IN EARLY TWENTIETH-CENTURY BANGKOK

Both the *Tamra ang yi* and the *Baeb nawakam* can be understood as instructional manuals that sought to represent a new form of political belonging for this new labor force while drawing on older conceptions of community and spatial representation. While the *Tamra ang yi* emerged from the language of the dynastic realm and the *Baeb nawakam* drew primarily from the imaginings of the religious community, both can be read against each other as instruments of a new form of community in the twentieth century. Premodern local manual knowledge in Southeast Asia often drew on divine provenance (the physician of the Buddha or Viṣṇu, for example) and supported the sacred, almost magical value that some kinds of technical knowledge held.[23] In the nineteenth and twentieth centuries, the languages of the dynastic realm and the religious community were reformulated in architectural tools like the manual and the diagram as well as replicable built forms like the *hongmen* lodge and the Thai wat that could address the reorganization of labor in the building trades.

While both the *Tamra ang yi* and the *Baeb nawakam* sought to instruct their readers through the use of image and text, they used different illustrative and narrative approaches. The *Tamra ang yi* paired diagrams with a regressive mythological narrative on the origins of the secret societies and the mystical, utopian enclave at their center. The *Baeb nawakam*, on the other hand, used schematic conventions like the plan and section to represent an older cosmological view that could exist in the present. Juxtaposing their images and the narratives they supported offers a new way to understand the utopian character of nationalism that developed amid the reorganization of the building trades as new transregional migrations of construction labor (between the southern coast of China and Bangkok) and architectural expertise (from Turin to Bangkok by way of St. Petersburg and Istanbul) intersected in early twentieth-century Bangkok.[24]

The term "utopian nationalism" describes the early twentieth-century ideology that used an imaginary community or utopia as an engine for the imagined community of the nation.[25] In Siam, utopian imagery—in the form of not only literature but also diagrams, technical drawings, models, and built works—was used to reimagine the bonds between the Siamese ruling class and its subjects under the banner of a new national identity. Utopian nationalism was part of a broader cultural and economic campaign on the part of the Siamese monarchy to stem the rising political power of recently migrated Chinese labor and urban merchant classes. The old machinery of the state, the premodern *sakdina* system of social hierarchy, was already obsolete, but a new one had not yet fully developed. In reaching back to the imagined past of the religious community and the dynastic realm as well as projecting into a modern future, utopian nationalism allowed the old regime to continue, albeit in an adjusted form.[26] By bringing together familiar pictorial conventions, narratives about an ideal community, and regional precedents, the images of the *Tamra ang yi* and the *Baeb nawakam* played a crucial role in not only defining this utopia for a broader public but also persuading them that it could be built in the present.

Key to the transition from the *sakdina* system to a new political economy was the massive influx of migrant labor to Siam in the nineteenth century brought about by the abolition of slavery and the repeal of corvée labor.[27] In the mid-nineteenth century, King Chulalongkorn (Rama V) funded the hiring of migrant workers to build a canal from Bangkok to Ayutthaya in order to avoid the "vexation, misery and compulsion" of impressing Siamese labor.[28] The monarchy increasingly came to depend on an expanding migrant workforce to develop Bangkok's infrastructure: cutting canals, building roads and railways, and constructing commercial buildings along the new thoroughfares. These workers came largely from treaty ports on the southern coast of China and were a polyglot group divided among five regional language groups that were sometimes unintelligible to one another. They were further organized into clans, trade guilds, and *hongmen* or *ang yi*.[29] The *hongmen* were introduced to Siam in the seventeenth and eighteenth centuries to protect traditional occupations against intruders.[30] At least six different *hongmen* of great power existed in Bangkok by 1889, and laborers had to belong to at least one of them to secure employment in the city.[31] By 1906, the number had increased to thirty, including thirteen Teochew, eight Cantonese, seven Hailam, and two Hakka societies.[32] All Bangkok's *hongmen*, however, were variants of the Tiandihui 天地會, or Heaven and Earth Society, a society with origins on the south China coast that exerted a strong influence over Chinese communities throughout Southeast Asia in the nineteenth-century.

DYNASTIC PATRIMONY

The 1910 strike made clear the growing potential of the *hongmen* to organize across speech groups and national borders. For the Siamese monarchy, migrant labor was indispensable to the project of nation building, but the potential of the migrants' having their own class or national allegiance was disturbing. Secret societies had already been banned in 1898, and in 1907 a new unit of the police department (Kong Trawaen Phanaek Jin) was formed to monitor criminals in the migrant communities. The force collected many of the hand-colored Chinese-language documents that circulated among secret society members during this period. These documents provide a vivid description of the origins of the *hongmen* and their secret rituals, symbols, documents, and hierarchies. Similar documents and diagrams were collected by colonial officials across Southeast Asia in the nineteenth and early twentieth centuries.[33] Although these sets were often incomplete and varying in the use of codes, illustrative detail, language, and characters, they share a prolific use of architectural imagery as a method of educating the desires of the migrant members of the *hongmen* by simultaneously projecting backward into an imagined dynastic past and forward toward a speculative national future.

The *Tamra ang yi* traces the origins of the society back to the seventeenth-century South Shaolin Monastery in Fujian Province.[34] When the Qing Empire was attacked by a nomadic polity from the northwest, the Shaolin monks went to meet the invaders and repelled them. The Kangxi emperor rewarded the monks, but disloyal officials in his court conspired to destroy them and convinced the emperor to send an expeditionary force to attack the monastery. The imperial army burned the monastery and killed all but five of the monks. These five monks founded an anti-Qing resistance movement that sought to restore the Ming dynasty. Five grand lodges and five minor lodges were established in various provinces in China, each with their own banners, passwords, and seals. This narrative is consistent with the accounts of other offshoots of the Tiandihui by colonial officials in diverse locations and periods, but historians have noted the difficulty of separating the history of the *hongmen* from the legends surrounding their origin and disseminated in texts like the *Tamra ang yi*. Recent scholarship suggests that this origin narrative is inaccurate and that the Tiandihui was likely founded in 1767 by the monk Hong Er 洪二 at the Guanyin temple 觀音亭 in Gao Xi Xiang 高溪鄉, Fujian Province.[35]

FIG. 3.1. Illustration of the Ghee Hin secret society lodge in Singapore, detailing spatial arrangements for the initiation ceremony rites, ca. nineteenth century. From the collection of William George Stirling, National Museum of Singapore, National Heritage Board.

The *Tamra ang yi* can be understood not only as a narrative account of the *hongmen*'s origins but also as a manual that allowed for this narrative to be spatially replicated in new locations as a replica of the City of Willows. The re-creation of sacred Buddhist landscapes has a long history, but the *Tamra ang yi* is notable in that it can be read as a detailed illustrated manual for the serial reproduction of this landscape across diasporic networks.[36] Its annotated diagrams are models of the gates, bridges, and landmarks of the City of Willows that was to be constructed at varying scales within the society lodge (figure 3.1). Throughout Southeast Asia, *hongmen* lodges took many forms. Before the *hongmen* were outlawed in Malaya, for example, the Singapore headquarters of the Ghee Hin Society were in a shop house on China Street.[37] Lodges in the Dutch East Indies, meanwhile, could be rudimentary affairs, cobbled together from masonry and timber and finished with rammed earth or wattle. Others might be hidden deep in the jungles, to avoid detection by colonial authorities.[38] There is little, if any, record of the material characteristics of the lodges belonging to the Bangkok *hongmen*, but it is likely that their lodges existed in both the developing urban and peri-urban conditions of the city at the time.[39] The nineteenth-century Dutch Sinologist and naturalist Gustaaf Schlegel noted that the design of lodges in the Southeast Asian colonies of the Netherlands was usually based on the form of a square within a circle.[40] Not only would this geometry have symbolically represented the enclosure of earth within heaven and the universality of the brotherhood; it would have also mapped out the relationship between the three characters of the Tiandihui's name. *Tian* 天 (heaven), represented by the circle, encompassed *di* 地 (earth), represented by the four cardinal directions of the square, at whose center was a righteous *hui* 會 (society).

REMAKING THE CITY OF WILLOWS

The main chamber of the lodge had four symbolic gates at each of the cardinal directions, inscribed with verses that associated the gate with one of the four elements, but also directing the visitor in the correct path that the founders of the society had taken when they fled the Shaolin Monastery for the refuge of the City of Willows. The North Gate, for instance, was inscribed with the following couplet:

> North of Wang Gui the water rises to the heavens (and is difficult to cross)
> (But) in Yunnan and Sichuan there is a road by which you can travel.[41]

Beyond the cardinal gates were the Great Hong Gate, the Gate to the Hall of Fidelity and Loyalty, and then finally the Gate to the City of Willows (figures 3.2 and 3.3). Drawn in the *Tamra angyi* as facades, they are immediately identifiable by even the most amateur aficionado of architecture as Chinese. Facades like these have long functioned as diagrammatic shorthand for China and can be seen in early Buddhist caves at the outer edges of Tang dynasty China.[42] In tandem with the couplet, they served to identify the City of Willows within the known landscape of China's provinces and gestured to a national identity beyond the regional linguistic and cultural bonds that tied together most migrant laborers in Bangkok.

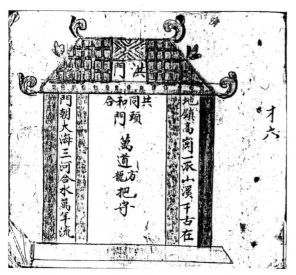

FIG. 3.2. Diagram of the Hong Gate, one of the three gates initiates had to pass through to be inducted into the *hongmen. Tamra ang yi,* 55. National Archives of Thailand.

The lodge might be understood as a scale model of the capital of this speculative empire, the City of Willows. Described at length in the induction rituals, the city had a genealogy. It was founded in the Tang dynasty and was "the seat of universal peace."[43] It was presided over by the Amitabha Buddha of the Pure Land, but the city had a distinctly material character:

> In the City of Willows we manifest
>   our loyalty
> In the center of a palace of gold,
>   pearls, and precious stones
> Our ancestor Buddha sits
>   enshrined.[44]

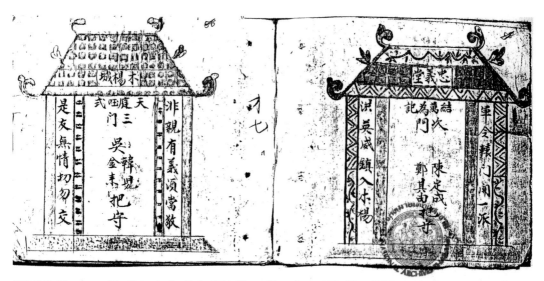

FIG. 3.3. Diagrams of the Gates to the Hall of Fidelity and Loyalty and the City of Willows, the last two gates that inductees passed through on their way to the main altar of the lodge. *Tamra ang yi,* 56–57. National Archives of Thailand.

The city was as "high as the eye can see" and "as broad as two capitals and thirteen provinces."[45] Like all classical Chinese cities, the City of Willows was a walled city, but its grandeur was suggested by the five broad concentric double walls that surrounded it. Each of the walls was emblazoned with slogans composed of four large characters. In order from the outermost wall were written:

United with Heaven Hong Flourishes
Obey Heaven and Act Righteously
Heaven's Courts Are a Plan for the Empire
Overthrow the Qing and Restore the Ming
The Heavenly Cloud Is Beneficial to All[46]

These slogans place the city within the intersection of heavenly, terrestrial, and social spheres and legitimate the society's mandate to restore the Ming dynasty. These relationships between a celestial and political model of the city are further reinforced in the city's design. The city had three temples, dedicated respectively to Guan Yin 觀音, the Bodhisattva Avalokitesvara worshipped as the Goddess of Mercy, Guan Di 關帝, the deity name of the historic Eastern Han dynasty general, Guan Yu 關羽, who was worshipped as the God of War, and Gao Xi 高溪, the place in Fujian where the five founding members of the society first took an oath to overthrow the Qing and restore the Ming. A model of this latter temple would sometimes be placed within the lodge. The city also had three pagodas, the highest of which had nine stories (figure 3.4).[47] The city's infrastructure is also highly symbolic. The five wells of the city were positioned in the cardinal directions plus the center and each filled with a primary element (wood, fire, metal, water, and earth). Only the central well, dedicated to the element of earth, had drinkable water for the initiate. It was so plentiful that its levels were described, curiously, as "reaching into heaven." The city's seventy-two fields yielded two crops a year and were supplemented by five orchards growing peaches, plums, rushes and willows, firs and cedars, and bamboo.[48] Although the largest of its three main streets were filled with 108 shops with names like Peace United, Patriotism United, and Myriads United, selling fabric, fruits, and dry goods, red rice was considered the most precious commodity in the city.[49] In the diagram of its main gate in the *Tamra angyi* (figure 3.3), couplets on both sides of the gate announce a new social order: "Though not a relative, if just, they are worthy of respect" 非親有義須當敬 and "A friend, if without honor, should be rejected" 是友無情切勿交.[50] These couplets and the gate they decorate describe to the initiate a new form of kinship and loyalty that was rooted in ethical, urban fraternity. In the *Tamra ang yi*, only 5 of the city's 108 homes are occupied. The rest are reserved for society members once the Ming dynasty is restored. The city was a utopia that would be realized upon the completion of the society's mission.

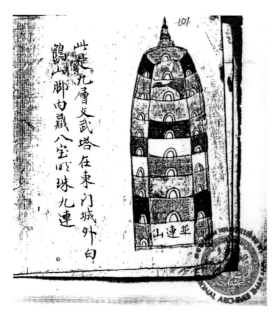

FIG. 3.4. Diagram of the nine-story pagoda in the City of Willows. *Tamra ang yi,* 102. National Archives of Thailand.

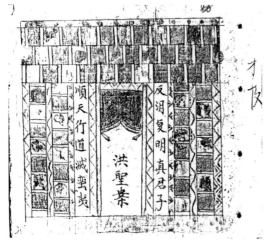

FIG. 3.5. Diagram of the main altar at the heart of the City of Willows and the *hongmen* lodge. *Tamra ang yi,* 81. National Archives of Thailand.

Its realization was the ultimate goal of all *hongmen* and their members.

At the center of the lodge, and the symbolic center of the city, would have been placed the main altar. A diagram depicts the appropriate couplets flanking the center of the altar (figure 3.5). On the right, a coded verse calls on brothers of the *hongmen* to "Overthrow the Qing and restore the Ming, that is what a person of noble character should do." The character for the Qing dynasty is encoded to avoid detection by the authorities. On the left is posted another anti-Qing verse: "Obey heaven and perform the righteous acts to extinguish the barbarians." These couplets suggest that the project of the *hongmen* was tied up in the return to a mythic dynastic past, of which the City of Willows was the capital. In fact, the association of the *hongmen* with a mythological past was integral to their claim to a long, unbroken tradition. The invocation of the past was a characteristic shared by both colonial powers and nationalist movements in the following two centuries, who could reach back to an imagined past to legitimate claims to historical continuity even if none existed. Diagrammatic maps of the lodges, collected and sometimes drawn by colonial officials in Malaya, suggest that these images formed a cosmic map of the society's past, but also instructed initiates in how to navigate their way in a treacherous present so as to build a righteous future.

FREEMASONRY AND THE *HONGMEN*

Nineteenth-century interest in the *hongmen* was also related to the import of secret societies on colonial intellectual development. Chief among these societies was the order of Freemasons, whose contemporary history begins in the Grand Lodge of England in 1717, although its ideals and rituals can be traced back to an earlier period of cathedral building from the tenth to sixteenth century.[51] Just as the *hongmen* in Bangkok functioned to protect skilled tradesmen and laborers, the Freemasons were born out of the need to organize traveling stoneworkers but became purely social societies after the decline of cathedral building. The movement spread to the European continent and the Americas afterward and began to take on political and military overtones. When European colonial civil servants—some of them, like W. G. Stirling and Georges Coulet, Freemasons themselves—encountered the *hongmen* in Asia, they were impressed by the similarities between the two secret societies.[52] Freemasons developed a theory about the similarities between the two organizations, claiming a common mythic ancestor.[53] Although these myths have long since been disavowed, several similarities remain striking. Both were all-male orders that, at least rhetorically, sought to level social inequity through invoking fraternal belonging. They were organized into autonomous subunits but shared common rituals and symbolism. Their symbolism drew on geometries that had their origins in the building trades. Just as Freemasonry was used by European revolutionaries in the early nineteenth century to recruit new members, the *hongmen*—their networks, rituals, and imagery—were used by Chinese revolutionaries to organize overseas communities of migrant laborers.[54]

Like the Freemason societies of the black Atlantic that produced universal human networks transcending the boundaries of national community, the *hongmen* of nineteenth- and twentieth-century Bangkok demonstrated the potential of such secret societies in organizing an exclusively male form of community that was not based on blood kinship.[55] The *hongmen*, like the Freemasons, spread with colonization and the new economic order that it brought across a transregional network of treaty ports. However, capitalism also changed the *hongmen* into a vehicle that sought to align its utopian ambitions with the needs of Bangkok's new urban proletariat. Their diagrams served an important purpose for inculcating the values of the organization to new members, reminding them of not only their ethical and political obligations but also their racial belonging and the future society they were building. Writing about the use of diagrams in early Siamese police work, historian Samson Lim has noted that some diagrams do more than represent what is real; they help people create and operate on reality in the way a timeline allows for an understanding of time as a progression. Lim uses examples like the *duang chata,* a diagram used by fortune-tellers and astrologers to predict possible future outcomes as well as explain past events. One doesn't need to know anything about the movement of the stars or their cosmological context. The diagram helps to articulate unseen relationships through an assortment of lines, circles, and symbols, to connect what is considered "fiction" or "myth" to real life.[56] Immediately familiar to even an unskilled worker in the building trades as symbols of the land the migrants had left, the diagrams of the *Tamra angyi* similarly became symbols of the distinctive identity of the new migrants and of the architectural forms that they could produce in a new urban landscape. They were one in a replicable series that created a historical depth of field.[57] The actual place and the time of the City of Willows was not as important as the fact that this utopian city could exist in the new world in which the migrants found themselves.

THE *BAEB NAWAKAM* AND THE RACIALIZATION OF ARCHITECTURE

The use of these serial images in creating a link between the present and a dynastic lineage among an urban population was not lost on the Siamese monarchy, who formulated a competitive spatial imaginary that was also based on race. The 1910 strike also signaled a shift in official attitudes toward the Chinese labor that had built the Siamese monarchy's public works throughout the nineteenth century. The racialization of Siam's nascent working class was part of a larger world spatial division of labor. Immanuel Wallerstein has written of the emergence of racial categories in tandem with the expansion of a Europe-centered capitalist world economy. Along with an occupational hierarchy, Wallerstein noted an "ethnicization" of the workforce within a given state's boundaries.[58] In Bangkok, the ability to produce certain architectural forms became associated with distinct races. Alien idioms were separated out from a national vocabulary. This represented a marked shift from the deployment of diverse techniques, ornamentation, and forms in court-patronized monastic complexes of the eighteenth and early nineteenth centuries, like Wat Chetuphon (Bangkok, 1788–1804).[59] Here, earlier migrations of primarily Teochew craftsmen had brought not only their building skills to the construction of *chedi* (pagodas) and *sum* (entrance arches), but also new forms and techniques, like the *teng* (Chinese-style pavilion) and *jian nian* 剪黏, the setting of ceramic shards around metal armatures. These innovations were integrated into the architecture of palaces and royal monasteries along with Khmer and Sinhalese idioms.[60] However, in the twentieth century, as new waves of migration swelled the construction industry, the court began to patronize European draftsmen and a new vision of modernity emerged. "Chinese" forms were still consumed, but in a way that emphasized their difference from "Thai" forms.

While earlier generations of craftsmen had produced hybrid forms like the *chedi* at Wat Chetuphon, the monarchy was now concerned that the Chinese-dominated building trades would produce a replicable architectural language that was not consistent with their ambitions to create a nation on par with European powers. Between 1912 and 1917, the supreme patriarch of the Buddhist religion, Prince Wachirayan, a half brother of King Vajiravudh's father, King Chulalongkorn, made a tour of upcountry wat (monastic complexes) to investigate their architecture, religious practices, financial management, and educational practices. Wachirayan's tour can be understood as part of the larger centralizing reforms of the 1902 Sangha Act, which he promulgated and which sought to control the practice of Buddhism in the country.[61] In addition to observing the diversity of practice across the kingdom, he also noted that the monks didn't have any idea about proper craftsmanship, having entrusted building to migrant Chinese carpenters.[62]

> The monks hired Chinese craftsmen to restore the wat and gave them samples of things to be followed, but the Chinese couldn't do them in the Thai style. For example, a cho fa (finial) with naga (mythical serpent) heads became a finial with dragon heads and they couldn't draw or sculpt a good Buddha image or the base of a statue. The Prince saw that if the situation were to be left as such without any intervention, Thai designs would disappear completely.[63]

To remedy this, Wachirayan ordered the Ministry of Religious Affairs to copy the design of different royal wat in Bangkok and publish them as a construction manual known as the *Baeb nawakam*, named after the author and illustrator Phra Nawakam Kowit. Prince Wachirayan selected small and less elaborate details from monastic complexes in Bangkok that could be copied by provincial wat that did not have access to a lot of financial resources or skilled labor. The simplified forms of royally patronized wat in Bangkok, an erstwhile regional architecture, were held up as a new national standard, to be taken up by monastic complexes in rural areas, regardless of their historical and environmental appropriateness.[64] These drawings, like the one of the *uposot* (ordination hall) of Wat Chan in Phetchaburi Province (figure 3.6), however, were consistent with images of *nibbāna* from eighteenth- and nineteenth-century illustrated *samut phap* manuscripts of the *Traiphum phra ruang*. A possibly early nineteenth-century illustrated manuscript that is archived in the British Library depicted the levels of the Three Worlds of sensual desire, form, and formlessness using a formal vocabulary similar to that in the *Baeb nawakam*.[65] The manuscript included both a text from the Abhidhamma Pitaka of the Pali canon, the *Dhammasangani*, written in *khom* script, and a description of the *Traiphum* written in a combination of Thai and *khom*.[66]

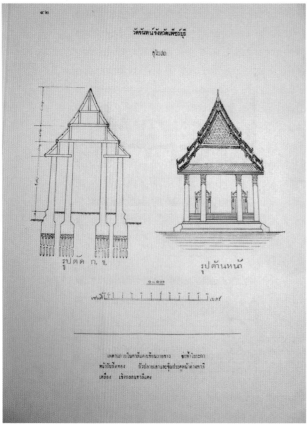

วัดจันทน์จังหวัดเพชรบุรี

กุฎิ:อุโบสถ

รูปตัด ก. ข.

รูปด้านหน้า

เลขานุการในรากลื่นดคเขียนลายยชาว   ชนที่โบกฺปกา
หน้าบันปิดทอง   บัวปลายเสาและฐชุบประคนหินำต่างๆทาสี
เหลือง   เชิงกลอนทาลินดง

FIG. 3.6. Nawakam Kowit, drawing of the *uposot* of Wat Chan, Phetchaburi Province, in the *Baeb nawakam.* Suksapan Organization.

However, the striking images, attributed to "Nai Sun," depicted the Three Worlds of the *Traiphum.* The very first image of three pavilions represented the highest level of the world of formlessness or *Nevasañanâsaññāarūpabrahma* (figure 3.7). Images like this were consistent with images of Mahanakhon Nipphan, or the Great City of Nibbāna, depicted at the pinnacle of the Three Worlds in *Traiphum* manuscripts. A comparison of *bai sema,* or markers denoting the sacred space around the *uposot,* and an illustration of the Great City of Nibbāna from the 1776 Thonburi *Traiphum* manuscript that was commissioned by King Taksin reveals similarities in the organization of the facade and its staging on a redented base, but the *Baeb nawakam* diagrams are notably simplified (figure 3.8).

THE CITY OF NIBBĀNA

The metaphor of the City of Nibbāna figured prominently in numerous canonical and para-canonical Theravada Buddhist suttas.[67] In the *Saddhar-maratnāvaliya,* the thirteenth-century Sinhala translation of the *Dhamma-pada Atthakathā,* the commentaries on the *Dhammapada* that Pali literary scholar Charles Hallisey has called "an instructional aid to those on the way to the city of Nibbāna," the walls of the city are made of Morality, the moat made of restraints Fear and Shame, a city gate of Wisdom with lintels of Effort, a protective column of Faith, and watchmen of Mindfulness. It had a nine-storied palace of the Nine Spiritual Attainments, four roads of the Fourfold Path going in four directions, the Hall of Justice named the "Rules of the Monastic Order," and a royal boulevard called "the Path of Mindfulness." There were markets selling the flowers of Higher Knowledge, perfumes of Moral Conduct, and the Fruits of the Path.[68] A similar description

FIG. 3.7. Nai Sun, illustration from the *Traiphum/Dhammasangani* manuscript. Or 15245, fol. 1r, British Library.

of "The Blessed One's City of Dhamma" is found in the *Milindapañha*, a discourse between King Milinda and the monk Nagasena.[69] In a translation and commentary on a Thai or Khmer non-canonical sutta called the *Nibbāna-sutta*, Charles Hallisey notes that the metaphor refers not only to the buildings of the city but also to the flocks of birds (i.e., the living things that are attracted to the city) and can be understood also as something that protects, shuts out, and provides security.[70]

> The great city of Nibbāna has an encircling wall, a gate, a watchtower, a moat, streets, a bazaar, a pillar, an interior (place), a bed, a couch, the brightness of lamps, a lake filled with cool water and sand; it is frequented by bees and by flocks of geese, cakkavāka birds, pheasants, cuckoos, peacocks, and heron. What is that encircling wall? The wall of virtue. What is that gate? Knowledge is the gate. What is that watchtower? The watchtower of concentration. What is that moat? The encircling ditch of loving kindness. What are those streets? The streets of the forty meditation topics. What is that bazaar? The bazaar of the constituents of enlightenment. What is that pillar? The pillar is effort. What is that interior (place)? The interior place of the books of the Abhidhamma. What is that bed? The bed of renunciation. What is that couch? The couch of release. What is that brightness of lamps? The brightness of the lamps of the

FIG. 3.8. The Glorious City of Nibbāna (Die erhabene Stadt Nibaphan), from the *Traiphum* manuscript, allegedly commissioned by King Taksin, ca. 1776. Mss II 650 F4–5V. Museum für Asiatsiche Kunst, Staatliche Museen zu Berlin.

vision that comes with liberating knowledge. What is that lake? The lake of meditation. What is that cool water which fills it? It is filled with the cool water of compassion. What is that sand? The eighteen kinds of Buddha-knowledge are the sand. What are those bees that frequent it? Those who are free from the cankers are the bees which frequent it. What are the flocks of geese, cakkavāka birds, pheasants, cuckoos, peacocks, and heron which frequent it? Buddhas, arahants, and those who are free of defilements and faults are the flocks of geese, cakkavāka birds, pheasants, cuckoos, peacocks, and heron which frequent it. Thus the great city of Nibbāna is peaceful, a refuge, the topmost, and thus the final goal.[71]

This vivid description of *nibbāna* shares many of the physical characteristics of the City of Willows but also elucidates the city as a metaphor for the mind of the practitioner on their journey to awakening.

The images in Nai Sun's *Dhammasangani/Traiphum* manuscript further support the idea of the city as the destination of the righteous practitioner.

Devoid of human presence, the architectural facades draw on parallel perspectival conventions rather than linear perspective. While linear perspective creates the illusion of distance on a single visual plane by making people, places, and things appear as if they are viewed from a single vantage point, parallel perspective renders objects, whenever represented, in the same size so that the sides of structures are arranged in parallel fashion and don't disappear at the vanishing point. The manuscript images share a similar but more elegant approach to the didactic drawings of the *Baeb nawakam*, which render the new national standard in cruder lines in order to reveal construction methodology and measurements. Most notably, they introduce the orthogonal language of the plan, section, and elevation as a way of understanding the built environment. By rejecting shading and projecting from the ground plan rather than from a fixed, distant perspective, the *Baeb nawakam* drawings present buildings not as they might appear to the eye, but by calculated standards that could be read and understood by unskilled laborers.[72]

THE BIRTH OF THE *SATHAPANIK*

We cannot know with any certainty how the *Baeb nawakam* was received. The Department of Public Instruction of the Ecclesiastical Government published one thousand copies of the manual, but there is no record of how it was distributed.[73] Yet, the publication of the *Baeb nawakam* reveals much about the importance of architecture to the project of nation building. Its publication can best be understood as part of a larger reorganization of the building trades undertaken by the Crown during this period. As part of this effort, King Vajiravudh founded the Siam Cement Company in 1913 with significant investment from the Privy Purse Bureau. As we shall see in chapter 6, the company played an important role in the dissemination of a cheaply and easily reproducible national architectural vocabulary throughout the country. Vajiravudh also translated the words "architect" and "architecture" into Thai during this period. The Association of Siamese Architects credits the king with translating the word "architecture" into Thai during an audience with the architect Mom Chao Ithithepsan Kridakon. Ithithepsan asked the king how to properly translate the English term "architecture" into Thai.[74] The king wrote down the English words "architecture," "arch. science," "architect," and "arch. drawing" with their Thai translations: *sathapatayakam*, *sathapathayawet* or *sathapatayasat*, *sathapok*, and *sathapathyalek*. The root of all of these terms, *sathapat*, derives from the *Sthapaka* and *Sthapatya Veda*, treatises that provide unique attention to the topics of Hindu art and architecture.[75] The original Sanskrit term, *sthapatya,* has been variously translated as "building," "erecting," and "establishment." In Hindu temple construction, the priest was referred to as *sthapaka* and the builder as *sthapati.*[76] As chapter 4 further elaborates, Vajiravudh's use of Sanskrit terms to define the new profession of architect was consistent with his erudite interest in both classical and modern literature.

Commenting on the later translation of these terms in Thai-language lexicons, Ithithepsan reflected that although the Thai translation deviates from the English in that it emphasizes "the art and science of construction," the word connotes much more and should really be defined as "expertise in the Art and Science of Construction that gives rise to artistic characteristics."[77] Through "artistic characteristics," and not simply expertise in construction—something the city's new wage-labor force were tasked with—the architect could produce the utopian spaces of the Siamese nation in lived space and, in turn, "make people love their homeland."[78]

Ithithepsan reached back to the eighteenth-century English architect Christopher Wren to demonstrate this relationship. Wren's role in the rebuilding of London after the Great Fire of London in 1666 as well as his membership in Parliament served Ithithepsan's argument well. Like Ithithepsan, Wren was an architect enmeshed within networks of royal power whose work proved that urban planning was the work of the architect and not just government bureaucrats. "Sir Christopher Wren has said, 'Architecture is useful in politics. It establishes a stable nation, persuades people and commerce to come together as one, and makes people love their homeland, which is a love that greatly establishes beauty and goodness to public property.'"[79]

One of the ways architecture could accomplish this, Ithithepsan believed, was through what he called "civic aesthetics" (*arayawichitsastr* อารยวิจิตรศาสตร์). This term, with its roots in Pali and Sanskrit, points to the importance of the city in formulating the concept of citizenship as well as the utopian responsibilities of the architect. Urban planning was the province of the architect who grasped that order was as much a political concern as an aesthetic one. While it was true, Ithithepsan wrote, that the city was built by human labor, the city also shaped human behavior. Orderly and beautiful cities, created by knowledgeable architects, produced well-behaved citizens who worked, played, and lived together in convenience, joy, and safety. Poorly planned cities, he believed, produced narrow-minded, corrupt, exploitative, and lazy citizens. Architecture, he reasoned, was in the business of establishing civilization and progress. The civilized city was the leader for the rest of the country to follow.[80]

It was critical, then, that the architecture of this city be unique and not derivative of the homeland of the migrant laborers who were transforming

Bangkok. The drawing of oppositional relations between Chinese labor and Thai architectural design was an integral part of the creation of a nationalist aesthetic during the early twentieth century. The manual not only identified certain forms as "Thai" and "pure," but also linked these to the race of their builders. Modern Chinese craftsmen could not accomplish what ancient Thais had, it suggested. It created a divide between craftsmanship and design that would be exploited through the establishment of the Department of Fine Arts and the invention of the architectural profession during Vajiravudh's reign.[81] A key motivation for the department and the architectural profession was to "preserve" the imagined continuity of the dynastic past.

Prince Wachirayan undertook his research during the consolidation of state and ecclesiastical power at the turn of the nineteenth century. He drew on both British colonial models of art history and early twentieth-century tendencies in architectural discourse that sought to eschew "primitive" ornamentation in favor of forms that reflected modern forms of construction like steel-reinforced concrete. He was the first supreme patriarch in Siam who had real power in managing the administration, education, and properties of the Buddhist clergy. His work focused on both integrating a formal educational structure into provincial areas and monastic standardization, using Buddhist practices from the region around Bangkok as a model.[82] The publication of the *Baeb nawakam* was part of this attempt to centralize authority in the institutions of the Bangkok court by creating an aesthetic vocabulary that aligned racial purity, national sovereignty, modernity, and the economic investments of the Crown. It consolidated the "purity" of "Thai" forms in relationship to the foreign influence brought by "Chinese" craftsmen. This conflation of the physical and intellectual capabilities of the Chinese "race" can be read in Prince Wachirayan's depiction of Chinese craftsmen who were capable only of reproducing Chinese forms and the collapsing of multiple regional and historical influences into a binary opposition between "Chinese" and "Thai" forms.[83]

Prince Wachirayan's creation of an architectural manual mirrored nineteenth-century British colonial attempts to codify South Asian architecture in similar books, like Samuel Swinton Jacob's *Jeypore Portfolio of Architectural Details.* These books built on attempts by Victorian historians to depict Indian architecture as a perpetual decline from ancient greatness, and privileged art that could be linked to an origin in the West. Certain architectural idioms were considered "Mughal" and of value, while other local idioms were considered "Hindu" or "Buddhist" and "defective," as the governor of Madras in 1870, Lord Napier, pointed out.[84] Indian society was perceived as static in relationship to a dynamic, modern Europe, and the elements of its architecture were deemed similar and interchangeable. The volumes weren't arranged chronologically or by region of origin, nor were the illustrations presented to illuminate the structures of which they were a part. Instead they were arranged topically: copings and plinths, capitals, brackets, arches, doorways. The result was a kind of "pattern book" that architects and builders could freely borrow from without concern for context or history.[85] British imperial architects used tools like these to incorporate certain "native" features into their work in a way that showed they fully understood, and thus controlled, their colonial subjects. Wachirayan similarly sought to privilege Thai design over Chinese craftsmanship and control the labor that was employed to produce monastic architecture, making it easily reproducible by untrained craftsmen (figure 3.9). Just as the British cast themselves as the inheritors of the glorious Mughal past, seeking to reestablish it in their own Raj, the *Baeb nawakam* cast the Siamese monarchy as the protectors of an older cosmology.

In early twentieth-century Bangkok, two manuals emerged that depicted the architectural forms of a utopian "homeland." The *Tamra ang yi*, a collection of diagrams and accompanying written explanations, sought to instruct the migrant members of Bangkok's secret societies in not only the history of their organization but its architectural forms as well. The *Baeb nawakam*,

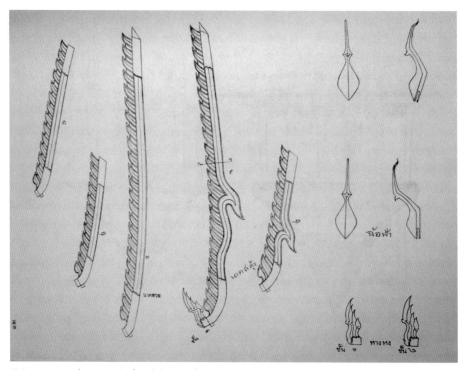

FIG. 3.9. Nawakam Kowit, finial designs from the *Baeb nawakam*. Suksapan Organization.

a collection of technical drawings of ecclesiastical architecture, sought to instruct provincial monastic complexes in the proper construction of a Thai wat. While the *Tamra ang yi* excavated an imagined dynastic past to produce speculative images of a restored Han utopia in the City of Willows, the publication of the *Baeb nawakam* went a step further, identifying the architectural methods and techniques through which a utopian Thai community based on an image of *nibbāna* might be built.

The diagrams of the *Tamra ang yi* and *Baeb nawakam* are crude enough that they purge regional details in favor of a shorthand for a new national identity and detailed enough to allow viewers to project a personal affinity onto them. Their simplicity suggests that this potential world not only is able to be built but also is infinitely reproducible. Benedict Anderson has persuasively argued that nationalism emerged when three cultural conceptions lost their grip on the human imagination: a particular script—like Chinese or *khom*—offered privileged access to ontological truth because it was inseparable from that truth; the belief that society was naturally organized around and under high centers, like the monarch at the center of the mandala, a node of access to being around which human loyalties were organized in a hierarchical and centripetal fashion; and a concept of temporality in which cosmology and history were so closely linked that the origins of the world and of men were the same. In early twentieth-century Bangkok, these ideas didn't lose their hold on the imagination so much as they were reformulated through architecture. The *hongmen* initiate could be assured that at the same time his rituals were being performed in a Bangkok lodge, the same rituals were being undertaken in more or less the same kinds of spaces throughout East and Southeast Asia. The Thai Buddhist making merit in the wat could also be assured that the same acts of devotion were happening in similar halls all over the kingdom. Anderson argued that print capitalism precipitated the search for a meaningful way of linking fraternity, power, and time in a new way. But how did print capitalism impact those members of the urban population who did not have access to the written word? What allowed the illiterate Teochew laborer to claim ancestry with the Ming? The language of architecture was a way of transmitting ideas about communal belonging that exceeded the written word, allowing growing numbers of people to think of themselves and their relationships to others in new ways, united in the goal of creating a utopia in the city.

In early twentieth-century Bangkok, the diagrams of the *Tamra ang yi* and *Baeb nawakam* offered a series of reproducible plurals that could inhabit the totalizing classificatory grid established by developing states in China and Siam to order and control the diverse peoples, regions, cultures, and architecture under its rule.[86] Reading these images as part of a larger history of utopian imaginings both expands and reorients the history of a literary genre that is conventionally narrated as the displacement of older notions of paradise in a different temporal zone to a new humanistic order in the same historical moment. The utopias of early twentieth-century Bangkok suggest that older conceptions of ideal societies continued to permeate modern political thought and the cultural imagination.

As a tool of the architect, the diagram is a simplified figure that is intended to convey essential meanings.[87] In the case of the diagrams in the *Tamra ang yi* and *Baeb nawakam*, that essential meaning is the nation-state. The diagram becomes an accessible language that can absorb things, events, and experiences of the world as it exists around us.[88] By extracting the salient features of utopia in the form of its component parts—gates, roofs, walls, and finials—the diagrams and their accompanying narratives no longer form a cosmological map but a plan for the nation-state. The manuals demonstrate that the diagram is more than simply a technical tool and can operate as an instrument of speculative imagination. They reveal not only the close relationship between religious illustration and architectural drawing but also the conjoined genealogies of modern notions of selfhood and architecture. The diagrams in these two manuals are figures removed from ground. Their lack of shadow and light suggests that these are not images of nature "as it really is" but of the world "as it could be." Although they may have drawn on real-life precedents, these are structures that are not representations of things that existed in the real world. They existed in the image, waiting to be liberated into the present through the labor of construction and the materials of the modern world. As we shall see in chapter 4, images of a modern society without the troublesome presence of a working class and their needs could be expressed through the architectural model.

CHAPTER FOUR

MODELING QUEERTOPIA

But the queerness of their features was more than
counterbalanced by other advantages.

—King Vajiravudh, "Uttarakuru: An Asiatic Wonderland"

In early May 1918, as the hot season reached its peak in Bangkok, King Vajiravudh decamped to a coastal retreat on the Gulf of Siam with his favorite
male courtiers. Over the following days, the king and his retinue of handsome young men would retire to the beach at Bang Thalu and build elaborate cities out of sand.[1] After returning to the royal residence at Dusit Palace
in the new northern suburbs of Bangkok, the king ordered a miniature city
built in the palace gardens and named it Dusit Thani: Muang Prachathipatai, which might literally be translated as "City of the Tusita Heaven: The
Democratic Polis." This highly detailed utopian landscape occupied a little
under four thousand square meters and was composed of more than three
hundred miniature structures including fully electrified private houses, theaters, cinemas, banks, palaces, a regularly convened bicameral parliament,
as well as a constitution, a police force, a fire department, a tax system, and
three newspapers (figure 4.1).[2] Although this was not the first attempt by the
king to carve out a utopian enclave within the city, it was the longest-lived
and most influential one. When the king decamped to Phya Thai Palace in
1919, he took his model utopia with him. There, as urban model, mediated
landscape, and theatrical stage, it became the center of a queer aesthetic
regime that linked the king's prolific endeavors in architecture, literature,
theater, fashion, and visual art with the training of a modern ruling class.

FIG. 4.1. Dusit Thani: Muang Prachathipatai, the miniature city of King Vajiravudh in Dusit Palace, ca. 1918. National Archives of Thailand.

QUEERNESS AND IMAGINED COMMUNITIES

The term "queer" here operates at multiple levels in describing the ways that the miniature city's appearance often disguised deeper internal contradictions. In its turn-of-the-century historical context, "queer" suggests the dislocated atmosphere of a Bangkok dominated by migrant workers and extraterritorial laws as well as the unusual *Alice in Wonderland*-like spatial and temporal scales at play in Dusit Thani.[3] The scale model was both political tool and speculative play toy for Vajiravudh. He was attentive to the worldwide decline of monarchies but thought that a parliamentary system of government could not yet be introduced at the scale of the nation.[4] It needed to be developed in a smaller, metropolitan context first, and Vajiravudh considered Dusit Thani the model for a modern municipal government in which a new generation of leaders, drawn from the ranks of the newly emergent urban classes in Bangkok, could be trained. Vajiravudh's prolific literary and artistic output can best be understood not only as a personal expression of his estrangement from the temporal context in which he was born but also as part of a larger project to distance himself from the older families associated with the monarchy and cultivate a modern ruling class to replace them.

The early twentieth-century evolution of the term "queer" can also be used to refer to the ways that the intra-male relations of the king's inner court disrupted the polygynous heteronormative atmosphere of earlier iterations of the royal palace. The model city can be seen as part of the development of a larger project undertaken after Vajiravudh's ascension in which he "gutted" the Inner City of the Grand Palace and rejected key aspects of Siamese political culture such as engaging in extensive marital alliances, employing male kin in positions of power, and displaying his masculine virility through the accumulation of wives and the production of children.[5] While Vajiravudh's father, Chulalongkorn, had framed his reign as an attempt to fuse "old" and "new" tendencies and develop a system of government that was both modern and appropriate for Siam, in many respects he simply layered Europeanized styles over local practices, preserving the core social relationships of the ancien régime.[6] As a ruler who grasped the importance of aesthetics to political rule, Vajiravudh sought to further transform the city—not only in appearance, but in its social relationships as well. The model city was an important instrument in training Vajiravudh's new ruling class in not only the machinations of running a modern city but also the proper taste, dress, and behavior of its citizens.

Finally, the use of the term "queer" gestures toward the homosocial and homosexual bonds of nationalism that were cultivated by Vajiravudh at Dusit Thani.[7] While assertions of the king's homosexual relationships remain speculative and cannot be corroborated by historical evidence, the leisure activities of the king and his inner court that centered around Dusit Thani sought to generate passionate sentiments for both the monarch and the nation he represented. The historian Chaem Sunthonwet remarked of Dusit Thani that "one couldn't find a single housewife there," largely because men were expected to set up households together.[8]

In its most instrumentally political capacity, Dusit Thani functioned as the model hub of a new system the king created in which ambitious courtiers from common or obscure backgrounds could ascend the ranks by developing close bonds with the absolute monarchy. Getting an audience with Vajiravudh was difficult, but it was much easier if one had a home at Dusit Thani since he frequently spent time there.[9] Situated deep within the inner sanctum of two royal palaces, however, Dusit Thani was also a utopian canvas that allowed Vajiravudh to experiment with modeling a form of nationalism based on queer social and spatial relations. The models, drawings, and landscape interventions produced for the miniature city sought to make the homosocial relations of Vajiravudh's nationalism appear natural. They did this by situating an eclectic collection of architectural forms associated with the burgeoning concept of *siwilai* (civilization) within a picturesque landscape.

When Vajiravudh returned to Bangkok as a crown prince after nine years of education in England, he was dissatisfied with the city he encountered.[10] Bangkok was transforming into a modern capital but still did not offer the diversions of an imperial metropolis like London. A prolific writer, he expressed his discontent most clearly in his novels, plays, poems, and essays. In the epistolary novel *Hua chai chai num* (Heart of a Young Man), the king, writing under the pen name Ramachitti (the wisdom of Rama), expresses the dislocations of the capital through the experiences of Praphan, a young Thai man returning from his education abroad in England. The novel was first published in *Dusit samit*, one of Dusit Thani's three newspapers. Early in the novel, he complains that Bangkok's one weakness was that it lacked entertainment venues on par with London's. Praphan noted that although there were a few European hotels in the city, there were far more Chinese hotels ("they are just choc full of *Chinks*," he writes).[11] Throughout the novel, Praphan is preoccupied with not being mistaken for Chinese. His anxiety begins even before he has reached Bangkok. Stopping in Singapore, he is refused a room at a European hotel when the front desk assumes he is Chinese. When he corrects them, a room is made available to him. Finally, after arriving in Bangkok and seeing his younger brother Prapha again, he becomes even more self-conscious. "I must say that I got quite a shock to see Prapha for he has grown to look like a *real chink*! Prapha said that everyone tells him he looks more like me every day, which so depressed me that when I got home I rushed to look in my bedroom mirror. While it is true that Prapha does rather resemble me, I don't have the face of a Chinaman at all, so why should my younger brother?"[12] Praphan was certain that a civilized subject lurked under his skin and was concerned that, although his family members shared his outward appearance, they did not share the rhythms of his modern heart.

Like his protagonist, Vajiravudh must have felt similarly disoriented upon returning to the royal suburbs surrounding Dusit Palace. The area looked similar enough to contemporary suburbs that he would have seen in European cities, albeit surrounded by tropical vegetation, paddy fields, and fruit orchards. After all, the grid of new roads and canals that defined the new suburb was created by European-trained engineers Carlo Allegri and Octave Fariola de Rozzoli and obliterated the irregular lines of old paddy fields that had previously occupied the three square kilometers of plantations and farms.[13] These broad rectilinear roads and the facades of fin de siècle fenced-in villas like Bang Khun Phrom were part of an attempt by Vajiravudh's father, King Chulalongkorn, to fuse "old" and "new" tendencies and develop a physical and political infrastructure that was both modern and appropriate for Siam.[14] The reality, however, was that these architectural and planning interventions hid local practices like polygynous marriage that sustained political ties between the monarch and his supporters behind Second Empire and Baroque revival facades.[15]

A primarily Italian architectural coterie left their imprint on the city by the early twentieth century. Nearly all of them had been trained in the Accademia Albertina delle Belle Arti in Turin and went on to make a name for themselves serving faltering monarchies in locations as diverse as St. Petersburg and Istanbul before arriving in Bangkok in the nineteenth century, where they were employed by the Public Works Department.[16] Architects, engineers, and artists like Mario Tamagno, Annibale Rigotti, Cesare Ferro, and Carlo Allegri worked under the supervision of Siamese princes or nobles such as Krom Phraya Narisara Nuwattiwong (Prince Naris; 1893–1898; 1899–1905), Phraya Suriyanuwat (Koed Bunnag; 1905–1906), Chao Phraya Yommarat (Pan Sukhum; 1906–1907), and Krom Luang Nares Voraridhi (1907–1912). The working relationship between Siamese administrators and Italian staff was far from smooth, however. Phraya Suriyanuwat remarked in a report to Chulalongkorn that "it is very obvious that the architects are simply recent graduates who immediately came to Bangkok to work right after their final exams. They have textbook knowledge, but no practical and detailing experience. Any experience they have is received from the Chinese carpenters here in Bangkok. . . . Mr. Allegri, who is in charge of the Europeans, has only civil engineering knowledge but no architectural expertise. It is very obvious that all of them do not understand the European standards of fine carpentry and masonry."[17]

The Ananta Samakhom Throne Hall, begun in 1905 but not completed until the early years of Vajiravudh's reign, is an excellent example of the results of these contentious collaborations between older members of the court, steeped in the conventions of the *nai chang* (master builder), and members of the architectural profession (figure 4.2). Originally, King Chulalongkorn had requested that Kon Hongsakul, the fifth-generation royal master builder, build a new audience hall, named after one that had been built in 1854 in the Grand Palace. He wanted the hall built in a "traditional Siamese style," but because Kon Hongsakul was unable to complete the project in the time required, the project was reassigned to the Italian architects and engineers of the Public Works Department.[18] Annibale Rigotti, a graduate of the Turin Accademia, who had worked with Raimondo D'Aronco in Istanbul before moving to Bangkok in 1907, collaborated with a fellow graduate of the Accademia, Mario Tamagno, on the throne hall.[19] Although the facade presents itself to the visitor as a fairly academic approach to classical revival composition, a study of the plan reveals that the conventional symmetry and cruciform arrangement of a basilica has been broken up into three symbolic spheres, suggesting the continuing cosmological influence of the *Traiphum phra ruang.*

FIG. 4.2. Mario Tamagno and Annibale Rigotti, Ananta Samakhom Throne Hall, Bangkok, 1907–1915. National Archives of Thailand.

Vajiravudh returned to a court that acknowledged the importance of modernization but still held fast to older belief systems like the *Traiphum.* For example, the northern suburbs of Dusit that Chulalongkorn created may have been patterned after modern colonial cities like Singapore and Batavia, but he named it after one of the six upper levels of the *Traiphum*'s *kammaphum,* or world of desire, the Abode of Contented Devas or the Tusita heaven where the future incarnation of the Buddha, Metteya, resided.[20] Located between the Yama heaven and Nirmarnarati heaven, time ran differently in the Dusit heaven. A full day was equivalent to four hundred years in the world of men, and the life span of the resident deities, or devas, was four thousand heavenly years or 584 million earthly years.[21] As a man of letters and a young ruler, Vajiravudh was concerned with understanding the ways these older relationships between celestial and natural time and space played out in the twentieth century. He turned his critical attention to Uttarakuru, one of the continents that lay in the shadow of Mount Meru.

AN ASIATIC WONDERLAND

In 1912, some six years before the founding of Dusit Thani, Vajiravudh published an English-language essay in the *Siam Observer* based on some earlier diary entries about Uttarakuru, one of the four continents surrounding Mount Meru in the *Traiphum*. The description of Uttarakuru in the *Traiphum* contrasted with that of Jambudvīpa, the continent in which human beings dwelled. Uttarakuru was an idyllic society, populated by a race of people with square faces and life spans of one thousand years. They ate a kind of rice that grew by itself and had no chaff. They did not suffer disease and lived with an inexhaustible wishing tree known as the Kalpapreuk, which provided them with enough wealth that they had no need of private property. They practiced vegetarianism and did not kill animals. They also engaged in a kind of free love, in which there was no dowry. When women gave birth, the offspring were left by the side of the road to be cared for by Uttarakuruns in common.[22] Reading the *Traiphum* at the beginning of the twentieth century, Vajiravudh pronounced Uttarakuru a utopia that pre-dated Thomas More's.[23]

Vajiravudh recognized the potential of class critique latent in the *Traiphum*'s description of Uttarakuru and poked fun at the idea that a classless society might be realizable. However, he also recognized the ideological importance of such utopian models in articulating the relationship between morality and manners. "Like all ancient authors he had to represent his ideas about social reforms under the cloak of religion, and explained that such blessings enjoyed by the people of Uttarakuru were the results of past and present merit principally because the Uttarakuruans had kept and still kept within the limits of Five Moral Virtues," Vajiravudh wrote of King Lithai. "He also stated, at the end of the chapter on Uttarakuru, that 'those who are born in the continent of Jambu are never reborn in any of the other three continents.' This sentence was apparently put in to discourage people from seeking after the unattainable. But the seeds of discontent with their present lot once sown were not easy to eradicate."[24]

Discontent was prevalent throughout the world Vajiravudh knew. By the time the young prince ascended the Siamese throne, colonial powers had either overthrown neighboring rulers, as in Burma and Aceh, or consolidated them within the colonial bureaucracy, as in the Dutch East Indies, British Malaya, and French Indochina. Later constitutionalist revolts in Persia and the Ottoman Empire ended their absolutist regimes. Most significantly for the Siamese Crown, the Qing dynasty was overthrown in China in 1911, the year Vajiravudh was made king. The same year he published his essay on Uttarakuru, Vajiravudh had to suppress a coup d'état inspired by these republican stirrings. It is of little surprise, then, that Vajiravudh's essay is a denunciation of contemporary republican and socialist ideals wrapped in a critique of utopia. It seems odd that an aesthete like Vajiravudh, who named his model city after the abode of the future incarnation of the Buddha, Metteya, would be so critical of the concept of utopia. In fact, Vajiravudh was motivated by more earthly affairs. Political scientist Kasian Tejapira has pointed out that by lumping together utopian and scientific socialism, Vajiravudh was able to dismiss any ideology that challenged private ownership of the means of production as a fanciful objective that would be impossible to achieve.[25] The text—and, as chapter 3 indicated, Vajiravudh's early reign—was haunted by the specter of the 1911 Xinhai revolution in China, which he denounced in *Uttarakuru: An Asiatic Wonderland* as a modish intellectual fad. "The Chinese Revolt against the Manchus succeeded not from any inherent merit of the rebel cause, nor did it succeed because the Chinese People really understood anything about it, or that the change was absolutely necessary for the welfare of the Nation, but rather because it was a manifestation of 'Unrest Fever' and 'New Mania' combined, which made the 'Revolution Plague' so virulent, that the Manchu 'doctors,' with their antiquated appliances were incapable of coping with it."[26] He was critical not only of Sun Yat-sen 孫逸仙, the first president and chief ideologue of Republican China, but particularly of Kang Youwei 康有為, the Qing court reformer who wrote the utopian polemic *Da Tong Shu* 大同書. Published in 1902, the book was based on the Confucian ideal of the Da Tong, or Great Unity, a global society with a single, centralized government and no borders.

A QUEER FAMILY: VAJIRAVUDH'S *NAI NAI*

Vajiravudh was critical of the idea of collective child-rearing in Uttarakuru, an idea shared by Kang's *Da Tong Shu*.[27] Each person, having no family ties, would devote the whole of their attention to the community rather than have to take care of their offspring. The idea that the family unit would be eradicated sat uneasily with Vajiravudh. While Vajiravudh rejected the older polygynous relations that had sustained the inner court, he advocated for a new conception of familial ties. In the models of modern domesticity that Vajiravudh would rehearse with his male courtiers at Dusit Thani, a queer formulation of the family was necessary for the production of a nationalist ideology that positioned the king as "daddy" to his sons.

The men of the inner court, or *nai nai,* were Vajiravudh's invented, if not biological family. He spoke about *chup liang,* "raising them," and told them, "I regard you as my children, and you must think of me as your father."[28] When he rose in the morning, he announced, "Daddy is up and awake now!"[29] At the same time, Vajiravudh rejected the polygynous practices of his forefathers and sought to avoid the production of what Tamara Loos has wryly described as "mutinous biological offspring."[30] While political power had been associated with the number of wives in previous reigns, King Vajiravudh sought to transform this model.[31] Excluding women from the inner court cut many older families out of new business relationships built around the Crown and instead allowed a group of men who were mostly commoners to profit from the king's attention.[32]

Dusit Thani became the hub of a new system the king created in which ambitious—and handsome—male courtiers could ascend the ranks by developing close bonds with the absolute monarch through participating in activities at Dusit Thani rather than by engaging in extensive marital alliances.[33] To build a home in Dusit Thani required the permission of first the king and then an official in charge of public works. Homeowners invested time and money in decorating their model homes in order to win contests and ultimately to catch the eye of the king. Those who couldn't build their own houses rented shop houses (*hong thaew*).[34] Rents as well as water and electricity bills were collected to improve the miniature city's infrastructure. Leftover money was sent to the Royal Navy.[35] Rama VI's rationale was that a male courtier's allowance was traditionally frittered away on vices like gambling or prostitution and so Dusit Thani modeled a new form of domestic behavior that benefited the state.[36]

MODELING A QUEER UTOPIA

Although Dusit Thani was notable in the ways it integrated life-size human beings into a scaled-down model of an ideal city through media, finance, and political administration, the miniature city was striking in its attention to material details. The small buildings that lined its manicured streets were thoughtfully articulated and highly decorated. They were illuminated at night with electrical lighting, and the landscape in which they were set was carefully manicured. Citizens of Dusit Thani were part of a privileged circle of the inner court who had secured permission from the king to build their symbolic homes within the miniature city. Plans were presented to an official in charge of public works after royal permission was secured. Only after the plans had been approved could a house be built. As the city grew, homeowners tried to outdo one another designing their model homes in order to catch the king's eye. Some houses had miniature tennis courts. Others planted miniature persimmon trees in antique ceramic pots they had specially ordered from China.[37] This contest was supported by a royal decree and reinforced by a committee who inspected the miniature city for maintenance and cleanliness.[38] While the increasing attention to detail projected an image of elegance (*khwam ru ra*), it also created a rise in house prices. While a modest teakwood house in the early years of Dusit Thani cost 130 baht, toward the end of the Sixth Reign a minister's teakwood house was more than 3,000 baht.[39] Courtiers who participated in Dusit

Thani as landowners soon came to understand the ways value could be produced from land speculation and real estate investment even at the reduced scale of the model city.

The architectural model has historically augmented political meaning and symbolized achievement and ownership. Models representing captured cities, for instance, were featured in Roman triumphal processions.[40] France's King Louis XV's collection of models of fortified towns took on almost magical properties and became for him "objects of prestige" that embodied the power and wealth of his kingdom as much as they were "princely toys."[41] In the seventeenth century, King Prasat Thong of Ayutthaya built Prasat Nakhon Luang, "The Holy Imperial Metropolis," a palace based on the scaled-down dimensions of Angkor Thom on the banks of the Passak River.[42] Nearly three centuries later, perhaps inspired by his legacy, King Mongkut used a scale model of Angkor Wat to make a claim about the spatial dimension of his realm and the historical legitimacy of his reign. The model still occupies a popular corner of the Grand Palace in Bangkok. In the final year of his reign, some seven years after Henri Mouhot led his first expedition to Angkor, Mongkut sent his own surveying expedition to the region to see whether any of the temples could be moved back to Bangkok. When the expedition reported that all but one of the temples were too large to move, Mongkut then ordered another expedition to disassemble and move Ta Prohm to Bangkok, requiring the conscription of men in Battambang and Siem Reap. Shortly after, he also sent a court official to survey Angkor Wat and take its measurements so that a model of it could be copied in Bangkok.[43] The expedition to disassemble Ta Prohm did not fare as well, however, and was attacked by three hundred locals who killed the court representatives and scattered the Khmer conscripts into the forest.[44]

Unlike his grandfather, Vajiravudh used the model to do more than just stake a symbolic historical claim to a territory, such as Siem Reap, or to a dynastic lineage, like the kings of Ayutthaya or the Khmer *devaraja*. It was also a pedagogical instrument that was used in an elaborate political theater that engaged the lives of his courtiers. Dusit Thani married the masculine attributes of the model as an exercise of spatial dominance in the urban field with the feminine character of the Victorian dollhouse as a model of the domestic sphere. The emphasis on municipal hygiene, order, and appearance was an extension of the private, inner sanctum of the modern home. Yet, women were absent from the primary unit of the household at Dusit Thani. In reforming the polygynous institution of the inner court, Vajiravudh redefined the heteronormative domestic conventions of Victorian culture. The homosocial relationships at Dusit Thani formed the backbone of Vajiravudh's utopian nationalism, in which passionate feelings for the king could be projected onto the nation. It created a new spatial model for the nation, in which the authority of the king was no longer confined to the ritual geometry of the mandala but extended inward to the domestic space of his subjects and outward to the "natural" landscape.

MANDALA GEOMETRIES AND NATIONAL LANDSCAPES

As discussed in chapter 2, pre-eighteenth century Southeast Asian polities such as Angkor, Sukhothai, and Ayutthaya imagined themselves as the center of complex geometric mandalas. The borders of the modern nation-state required a different formal approach. At Angkor Thom and Angkor Wat, the center of the mandala polity was the *devaraja* (celestial monarch), whose authority radiated out from the formless world at the center of the inner shrine through the world of form into the palace complex, and in turn influenced the sensual realms of the city, the polity, and nature. The new landscape suggested by Dusit Thani began with the picturesque artifice of the house and its male owners, situated within a newly bounded "nature" where pea-gravel roads with historically evocative names like Ayutthaya Rangsan (Ayutthaya Creates) and Siam Chana Seuk (Siam Victorious at War) meandered along miniature canals, cutting through bogs, hills, and small islands, tying these features into not only a picturesque form but also a historically coherent political unit. Dusit Thani proposed a model of the city in which the monarchy was no longer confined to the sacred cella at the center of the temple, as at Angkor Wat, but could be present everywhere in nature. The political order of the mandala now competed with modern conceptions of the landscape.

Vajiravudh divided the city into five political districts whose names drew on their topographical characteristics. Amphoe Khao Luang (the Royal Mountain District), for example, was elevated on a small hill, and Amphoe Bungphraram (Rama's Swamp) was sited in the marshier terrain of the garden. In fact, Dusit Thani presented itself as more of a leisure garden than an organized metropolis. The garden was the ideal unifying form for Vajiravudh's aesthetic experiments in design, theater, and politics and can be understood as a corporeal intervention that sought to engage all the senses and reproduce certain sentiments, like pleasure, in the bodies of its visitors. Both the plan of the city and its political and media culture sought to integrate life-size human bodies with the 1:20 spatial scale of the miniature built environment. Perhaps the most obvious indication of this is that the streets were large enough for human beings to walk through. The historian Bua Sochisewi recalled playing at Dusit Thani as a child, after the city had been moved to Phya Thai Palace. In those days, the miniature city had fully taken on the ambience of an amusement park and was known by associates of the court as *ban lek muang noi*, or "little city of small houses."[45] Citizens of Dusit Thani took on the role of tour guides to the model city.

It was not only the members of the court and bureaucracy who walked these paths, but the palace grounds staff as well. Charged with the city's upkeep, these workers cut grass, repainted and repaired structures as needed, and often had to clear the small animals that took up residence in the buildings of the miniature city.[46] Toads, in particular, found the small buildings ideal domiciles, much to the dismay of Dusit Thani's "citizens" and groundskeepers, who had to clean up their bodies after they started to decompose. Caricatured in the pages of *Dusit samit*, the event underscored the constant upkeep required to maintain not only the "natural" appearance of the miniature city but its property values.[47]

The play on human and nonhuman scales at Dusit Thani reflected the dissonant relationships between labor, nature, and capital in the new urban society of the early twentieth century. The manicured gardens of Dusit Thani served as a tool for working out these relationships in space. The attempt to fit hierarchical planning within a garden setting underscored the historical relationship between urban planning and landscape design that had become increasingly central to both European capitalist development and architectural theory since the Enlightenment.[48] Widely taken up in nineteenth-century Europe, the naturalizing of urban conditions through the conventions of the picturesque reduced the city and its economic functions to a natural phenomenon. As cities like Bangkok grew with populations that left the familiar economic relations of the countryside, where values were produced through the agricultural husbandry of nature, they encountered a new urban economic environment, where values were driven by the speculative principles of industrial and mercantile capitalism. At Dusit Thani, the integration of life-size human bodies into a picturesque landscape of miniature houses produced a utopian disguise for the encounter between Siam's formative urban capitalism and the *sakdina* economies based on precapitalist or feudal exploitation of the land. The human-managed countryside as well as the less-cultivated forests that supported rural life throughout Siam during the late nineteenth and early twentieth centuries were rapidly being centralized, enclosed, and marked by canals, roads, mines, and plantations as part of the boom in real estate speculation and nation building as well as the squeezing of commodities like rubber, tin, and rice out of the land to fuel Siam's recent entry into the world capitalist economy. Dusit Thani allowed the court to reimagine their growing empire as a picturesque utopian political community in which an urban-based civilization (*siwilai*) was framed as a part of the natural landscape.

SIWILAI AND THE STYLES OF CIVILIZATION

The approximately three hundred structures at Dusit Thani belonged to no single style or architectural appearance. In many ways, the city's eclectic approach to materials, idioms, and construction methods built on the interventions of Chulalongkorn at Bang Pa-in, the summer palace outside Ayutthaya where Vajiravudh's father had peppered the landscape with a Gothic revival wat, various Second Empire palaces, and Khmer revival monuments as a collection of novel buildings that reflected Siam's entry into a changing global political landscape. The diverse building types and styles of Dusit Thani, however, were driven not only by an interest in discerning the appropriate architectural form of a civilized nation among other nations, but also by the transitional nature of Siam's construction industry and architectural profession in the early twentieth century. While most of the model buildings were constructed of wood, others were made of brick, mortar, and even concrete, which had become a strategic building material to the Crown after the establishment of the Siam Cement Company in 1913. This eclectic historicism saw itself play out across all four types of building at Dusit Thani: royal and religious, government, entertainment and leisure, and private homes. Both the Mahakhiriratchapura Throne Hall and another unnamed throne hall were reported by the newspaper *Dusit samai* to be built out of concrete. The concrete throne halls, the newspaper reported, were much more beautiful than other structures.[49] Other buildings, like Wat Thammathipatai (figure 4.3) and

FIG. 4.3. Wat Thammathipatai, original model from Dusit Thani installed in the Vajiravudh Hall, National Library Complex, Bangkok. Photo by author.

the Royal Palace (figure 4.4), were built in historicist and regional idioms that referred to the polity of Ayutthaya rather than that of Athens or Rome. Building two of the most important royal and religious structures at Dusit Thani with multitiered gable-hipped roofs and extended finials further established the idioms of the central region of Siam as standardized national forms. Their inclusion in a collection of colonial-style buildings suggested a certain equivalence between Siamese and European historicism. Other buildings, like the mansard-roofed Theoatchamthan Throne Hall (figure 4.5), were a pastiche of historicist styles that were more difficult to ascribe to one geographic locale. Its mix of Italianate, Gothic, and Second Empire elements was indicative of both the global trajectory of the architectural profession and construction labor in the late nineteenth and early twentieth centuries.

The eclectic approach to modernism was an experiment in progress. When individual citizens sought to reproduce the same connections to an imagined past in their homes, they faced criticism in Dusit Thani's press. A commentary in the *Dusit Recorder* of March 1918 titled "Khlai wihan" (Like a *Vihara*) critiqued a house in the miniature city because it wasn't harmonious (*mai kleun kan*) with its surrounding buildings. "It looks like a wat was built in the house," the anonymous critic commented, remarking with some degree of resignation that today buildings often resemble the form of a Buddhist monastic complex.[50] The comment suggests that while older, regional styles were appropriate for religious buildings, domestic architecture required a new form.

FIG. 4.4. The Royal Palace at Dusit Thani, original model from Dusit Thani installed in the Vajiravudh Hall, National Library Complex, Bangkok. Photo by author.

FIG. 4.5. Theoatchamthan Throne Hall, original model from Dusit Thani installed in the Vajiravudh Hall, National Library Complex, Bangkok. Photo by author.

Just as the classical revivals were used in nineteenth-century European metropoles and colonial entrepôts to articulate a political legacy that could be traced back to a largely imagined ancient Rome and Athens, the new eclecticism strove to define a new kind of utopian political community based on the idea of civilization. The question of what a civilized society looked like occupied Vajiravudh and the citizens of Dusit Thani. An article in the *Dusit Recorder* written under the pseudonym "Royal Page" remarked that the term had been heard often lately at court and that those who were called "civilized" were people who had a good reputation (*mi naa mi taa*), while those who were "uncivilized" were considered barbarians. The word was defined in the dictionary as "the change in customs that is in order with other countries," but Royal Page found this definition too constricting. Who, he wondered, decided which customs to change, and whether what was popular for people in the whole world, or in one country, or in one individual, was good for another country?

Dusit Thani sought to define the appearance of the civilized city and the tastes of its modern citizens through architecture and landscape design. Three approaches to building design reinforced the picturesque presentation of the landscape, somewhere between the exotic and the familiar: Siamese historicist, European historicist, and what Thai historians have called *romaentik*, a play on transliterating the English words "Roman" and "romantic." Distinctly regional forms like Wat Thammathipatai were interspersed among a variety of Gothic revival and Second Empire buildings (such as the Phra Ratchawang Angkrit, or English Palace, and the Theoat-chamthan Throne Hall) to suggest a certain equivalence not only between Siamese and European historicism but between the colonial practices of Bangkok, London, and Paris in Southeast Asia. The king would have been familiar with these eclectic forms of architecture not only from his journeys to colonial entrepôts like Singapore but also from his tenure as a student in England during a period in which the "Indo-Saracenic," like the Tudor and Gothic revivals, was seen as a national alternative to a Mediterranean-derived classicism. They were often seen as interchangeable and could be used together to secure a "picturesque" effect that projected the nation into the "natural" landscape.[51] The flourishes of many of these model buildings likewise reflected the Bangkok court's self-image as a participant in the colonial enterprise as well as their imagined distance from the people, culture, and lands that they colonized, even if many of them were within the city limits.

DUSIT THANI'S IDEOLOGICAL LANDSCAPE: MEDIA, THEATER, AND PERSUASION

The publication of Royal Page's article on the meaning of *siwilai* suggests not only that the court wrestled with the appropriate appearance of modernity in Siam but that Dusit Thani was a highly mediated experience as well. Three life-size newspapers circulated among its citizens and members of the court, but the impact of the newspapers extended far beyond the walls of the king's palaces. On the one hand, these newspapers were utopian tracts, published during the flourishing of Thai mass-print culture. They provided an opportunity for an imagined national community to read about its exploits and endeavors and place itself within the everyday life of the court, creating a "confidence of community."[52] Citizens could rest assured that their personal exploits were a part of the larger story of Dusit Thani as it unfolded on the pages of its newspapers. These newspapers were also a guide to appropriate political behavior. The newspapers were the clearest indication of Dusit Thani's ambitions to train Vajiravudh's *nai nai* into modern subjects. As might be expected of media that covered a miniature utopian city with a citizenry only in the hundreds, Dusit Thani's newspapers did not have a lot of news to report. They often resorted to gossip about the citizens of the municipality to fill their pages.[53] That most articles were signed with the names of avatars rather than the real names of courtiers compounded this problem. Because Dusit Thani's newspapers wielded influence far beyond the miniature city, citizens became concerned that the newspaper would expose them to other members of the court and, inevitably, the king, if they behaved inappropriately.

Dusit samai was a daily and was first printed at the royal printing house on 1 November 1919. Another daily, *Dusit sakkhi,* began publication a little more than two weeks later. The newspaper later changed its name to the *Dusit Recorder* but maintained its Thai title. A third, *Dusit samit,* was published less frequently and sometimes edited by the king himself. *Dusit samit's* name came from the English word "smitten" and was edited by either the king or his closest courtiers, Chao Phraya Ramrakhop, Phraya Anirutthewa, and Mom Luang Pin Malakul, among others. There were 390 subscribers, more than half members of Dusit Thani.[54] First published on 7 December 1919, *Dusit samit* often featured the king's own writings and caricatures.

In a short illustrated skit in *Dusit samit* entitled "Showing the History of Debate" (Sadaeng tamnan kan to top), Vajiravudh traced the idea of political persuasion back to the beginning of the world, when two monkeys debated, through to the present, when two women vendors argued. Chaem Sunthonwet considered the short, amusing article as a critique on the primitiveness of debate in the press at the time. A cartoon drawn by the king that accompanied the skit (figure 4.6) depicted a tortoise and a human figure in Chinese costume in conflict. Uniformed courtiers restrain both figures. The jovial countenance of the courtiers suggested that there was an entertaining element to this kind of argument, but the citizens of Dusit Thani were expected to engage in more civilized forms of debate and persuasion.

Dusit Thani was a stage for a new form of political behavior and a living exhibition of a model city. The importance of the theater and exhibitions as instruments of instruction in the ways of the modern world is suggested by both the internal world of Dusit Thani and its placement within the palace grounds. The pages of the *Dusit Recorder* were filled with frequent announcements of exhibitions like the one of Vajiravudh's pictures of young men and women in colorful costumes at the Dusit Nawit Somoson social club or the one of international fashion and costumes from the international theater.[55] Several model buildings themselves were entertainment halls and exhibition galleries that served as political spaces. An indication of the importance of these sites can be seen

FIG. 4.6. Vajiravudh, "The History of Debate," *Dusit samit,* Vajiravudh Hall, National Library of Thailand.

in the grandiose appearance of the Khonthapnatsala Theater in Amphoe Bang Trai district of Dusit Thani (figure 4.7). The theater was a solid mass of circular forms organized around a central rotunda. The Khonthapnatsala was one of several theaters and part of an infrastructure of leisure at Dusit Thani. There was a cinema next to the Bang Trai market, a theater called

FIG. 4.7. Top, Phraratchawang Angkrit (the English Palace) at Dusit Thani. Bottom, Khonthapnatsala Theater at Dusit Thani. National Archives of Thailand.

Dusit in the Sanam Luang or royal field of Tambon Bang Trai district, and a bath house in Amphoe Khao Luang district, as well as a bowling lane, billiards rooms, and exhibition spaces.[56] In March 1918, the Nakhon Sala (Town Hall) was enlarged and took over the billiards room of the old Hotel Metropole, suggesting the interchangeability of political and leisure spaces in the utopian city.[57] The preoccupation of the city's urban plan and media with exhibitions and entertainment suggests that leisure, display, and spectacle were part of a larger political culture of aesthetic persuasion.

When Vajiravudh moved to Phya Thai, Dusit Thani was placed on the fringes of the palace grounds. Between it and the king's abode, an Italianate garden (called the "Roman garden") was built around a long pool. Vajiravudh is said to have sometimes used the pool to bathe in, but it was also the setting for theatrical productions in the evening.[58] Steps at the western edge of the pool led to an elevated stage with two arbors and a small pavilion that served as a stage (figure 4.8). One can imagine Vajiravudh, when he was not acting on the stage, observing the Roman garden from his balcony, with Dusit Thani comprising an even larger garden in the background. The adjacency of his bedchambers, the Roman garden, and Dusit Thani suggest that these were all settings in which the king could exercise the political authority and command the kind of respect as a sovereign that he often lacked in the real world.

FIG. 4.8. Pavilion in the Roman garden, Phya Thai Palace, Bangkok, ca. 1920. Photo by author.

MODELING A MODERN RULING CLASS

The modern culture of persuasion that Vajiravudh sought to teach his *nai nai* was reinforced not only at the miniature scale of Dusit Thani but in the human scale of the court. For example, on 27 October 1918, Vajiravudh called a meeting of the citizens of Dusit Thani and explained voting to them. The citizens, however, were confused by the concept, as they knew that the real power to appoint officials resided with the absolute authority of the king.[59] Shortly after, however, on 7 November 1918, a constitution was created for Dusit Thani. The parliament required by the constitution, the Sala Rataban (Government House), was installed on 9 July 1919.[60] On the surface, these political innovations in Dusit Thani are difficult to reconcile with the political legacy of Vajiravudh, who is conventionally framed as an absolutist monarch.[61]

However, they are consistent with Vajiravudh's concern for training a modern ruling class, an interest that emerged in the nineteenth century, as a new bureaucratic class emerged in Bangkok. These bureaucrats were largely commoners who had been educated up to the level where they were no longer indentured as *phrai* (corvéed freemen) in the premodern *sakdina* system of social hierarchy.[62] The emergence of this new class was an unexpected result of the modernizing reforms undertaken by King Chulalongkorn. The ancien régime had not intended to create a new social class and were concerned only with extending and modernizing the existing ruling class (*nai*). Below them were the Chinese mercantile class and at the bottom were the *phrai*. When the new bureaucratic middle classes made their presence felt, however, the monarchy had difficulties in placing them within the existing *sakdina* social order since they were neither *nai* nor *phrai*.[63] A new centralized bureaucracy staffed by *kharatchakan* (lit. "servants of the king") was graded on merit and replaced the decentralized *sakdina* society, in which status was determined by birth. Training this new class how to behave as political administrators and modern subjects required a new system of education. Traditional Buddhist codes of conduct before the reform of monastic education and administration at the turn of the century sought to perfect one's practice in order to achieve a better rebirth in a future incarnation or the ultimate goal of *nibbāna*. A new code was introduced in the early years of the twentieth century that intended to inculcate this new class of royal officials with a set of behavioral norms that would support the administration of the absolutist state.[64] Manuals like *Sombat khong phu di* (Qualities of a Gentleman, 1901), by Mom Ratchawong Pia Malakul, Vajiravudh's appointed guardian during the early years of his English tutelage, helped to codify a set of manners and morals for this new class. Divided into ten sections, the book is organized according to ten virtues and the actions (*kam*) that students were required to practice in order to achieve them: conduct of the body (*kayakam*), conduct of speech (*wachikam*), and conduct of the mind (*manokam*). Pia's use of the term *kam*, the Thai spelling of the Pali term *kamma* (Skt. *karma*), suggests the importance of a Buddhist foundation to his conception of the modern subject. Pia's methodology similarly drew on Buddhist practices of disciplining the body, speech, and mind but wed them to a Victorian concern for etiquette. Like Pia's text, Dusit Thani also reflected the continuing influence of Buddhist thinking and the import of new bourgeois ideals that were derived from Victorian England in producing a model citizen and a model society.[65] Dusit Thani can be seen as a part of this larger *mission civilisatrice*, extending the training of *phu di* (refined people) to not only the behavior and appearance of the individual, but the spaces in which they lived as well.

Maintaining a city at the scale model of Dusit Thani proved easier than managing one at the urban scale of Bangkok. By 1929, an estimated 702,544 people lived in a city that was continually expanding due to real estate development initiated by members of the royal court, the titled bureaucracy, and the monarchy itself.[66] The infrastructure of the city lagged far behind. An estimated 150 tons of rubbish were produced daily, and newspapers remarked on how dirty the city was. The garbage in Sampheng, particularly, was piled several feet higher than the street. The stench penetrated even the walls of Phya Thai Palace, where Vajiravudh complained that he had to sit under mosquito nets all day to counter the flies that had gathered in the city. When Vajiravudh's former chaperone Chao Phraya Yommarat (Pan Sukhum) proposed building a large incinerator to burn the garbage, the king criticized the idea because it didn't address the larger lack of civic-mindedness among Bangkok's citizens. They did not exhibit the appropriate manners of modern urban citizens. Besides, the government would have to absorb the cost of the incinerator and Vajiravudh thought it more appropriate that the people who benefited from the city's order and cleanliness be taxed.[67] Chao Phraya Yommarat had worked for Vajiravudh's father and was a citizen of Dusit Thani. He informed the king that implementing a municipality in the gardens of Phya Thai or Dusit Palace was one thing, but doing it at the scale of the growing capital was quite another. There were three important and related obstacles that needed to be overcome. One was that the population of the city needed to be trained in understanding their responsibilities as citizens and not just their rights to interfere with the government. Another was that the municipal revenue that was generated by taxing Thai citizens of Bangkok wasn't enough to support the efficient care of the city. Related to that was the problem of extraterritoriality and the Chinese, who didn't generate tax revenues. If they increased the taxes for the poor of the city, they would have to sell their homes to pay their taxes, and that would create resentment against the government. In a speech given at the opening of Dusit Thani's miniature parliament, Vajiravudh hoped that the model city would set the precedent for the rest of the country but admitted that this would take time, as "there are some obstacles."[68]

Yet, in spite of Chao Phraya Yommarat's enumeration of the external obstacles to the implementation of Dusit Thani's utopian plan, the largest obstacle to its success was embedded within the model itself. In architectural practice, the model is a tool that is made to understand space and give instructions, a sort of memorandum. At Dusit Thani, these formal aspects of the model overshadowed its critical intentions. In spite of its democratic pretensions, Dusit Thani was more of a formal utopia than a practicing parliamentary democracy. Its citizens admitted confusion when asked to make political decisions but developed rigorous systems for maintaining the city's order and hygiene in order to please the king. Motivated by a regime of appearances, Dusit Thani's citizens created a convincing formal utopia that had the appearance of a modern metropolis and all the institutional evidence of a municipal democracy, but which functioned politically as an absolutist city-state.

Dusit Thani sought to reconcile the relationship between urban utopia and picturesque landscape as a scale model in which men towered over both "nature" and the city. It transformed the feminine character of the Victorian dollhouse and garden as models of the civilized domestic sphere and nature into a masculine exercise of spatial dominance in the landscape. The emphasis on municipal hygiene, order, and appearance was an extension of a domestic space that was both modern and homosocial. Vajiravudh sought to distance himself from the powerful families who had formed marital alliances with the monarchy in previous reigns by both reforming the polygynous institution of the inner court and grooming a modern ruling class from among the new urban classes of the early twentieth century. In doing so, he also redefined the domestic conventions of the Victorian ecumene in which he sought to participate. The homosocial relationships at Dusit Thani became the backbone of a utopian nationalism in which romantic associations could be projected onto the king and the imagined community of the nation he represented. A model of utopia around which Vajiravudh's ideal of the nation-state developed, Dusit Thani was queer both in its inversion of the social reality of the city around it and in the homosocial relations it cultivated.

The social and moral order expressed in Dusit Thani negated the temporality of the urban social process while ensuring social stability through a fixed spatial form.[69] In comparison to the vast changes to the urban plan undertaken by his father, Chulalongkorn, Vajiravudh did relatively little to transform Bangkok or seek profitable investment through road extension. The Privy Purse Bureau paid little attention to investment in land and row houses during his reign, and no records exist of large-scale row-house construction during this period.[70] Vajiravudh's focus was the utopian model of the city rather than the city itself.[71] The manicured gardens, democratic games, and eclectic structures of Dusit Thani were walled off from the unrest and public life of the city growing up outside the palace walls. Yet Dusit Thani's modern political culture could survive only by draining the land and labor around it.

When Vajiravudh died, Bangkok continued to expand, but the model city was dismantled. Vajiravudh's successor, Prajadhipok, gave some of the model houses to the governor of Lamphun, who exhibited them in the provincial museum. Phya Thai Palace itself underwent a transformation into first a hotel and later a hospital.[72] As we shall soon see, Vajiravudh's utopian ideals would also take on a curious afterlife. The most important reincarnation was Siam's first national constitution, introduced fourteen years after Dusit Thani's by a small group of foreign-educated military personnel and civil servants, including one of Vajiravudh's former royal pages, who overthrew the absolute monarchy.[73]

CHAPTER FIVE

PLANNING KAMMATOPIA

The Politics of Representation and the Funeral Pyre

On 24 March 1926, the remains of King Vajiravudh, the last king of Siam to complete his reign as an absolute monarch, were cremated in an elaborately ornamented thirty-five-and-a-half-meter-high structure on Bangkok's royal parade grounds, Sanam Luang (figure 5.1). Since its inception in the mid-eighteenth century, this open field in front of the Grand Palace had been reserved for ritual royal ceremonies that glorified the authority of the monarchy and its claims to divine legitimacy. Vajiravudh's cremation was no exception. The event lasted for several days and was attended by large local crowds and visiting foreign dignitaries.[1] The splendor of the cremation ceremony sought to shore up support for Siam's embattled monarchy, which was struggling to assert its political authority during the worldwide decline of monarchism and the encroachment of European colonialism in the region. It could not, however, prevent the overthrow of the absolute monarchy in 1932. A year later, the royal sanctity of Sanam Luang was violated in a massive display of military fanfare and popular support when the bodies of seventeen commoners who had died suppressing a royalist rebellion led by Prince Boworadet (1877–1947) were cremated in an unornamented, flat-roofed, open-plan structure (figure 5.2). This was the first time that nonroyal bodies had been accorded this honor. The architecture of the soldiers' and policemen's crematorium was a defiant gesture on the part of the new state toward the institution of the monarchy. The center of both spectacles was the monumental structure known as the *meru*, or *men*.[2] A symbolic representation of the center of the Indic and Buddhist universe, Mount Sumeru,

FIG. 5.1. Narisara Nuwattiwong, crematorium of King Vajiravudh, Bangkok, 1925. National Archives of Thailand.

FIG. 5.2. Crematorium of the soldiers who sacrificed their lives defending the constitution, Bangkok, ca. 1934. General Phraya Phaholphayusena Archives, Artillery Center, Lopburi.

or Mount Meru, the *phra men* was the site from which the physical bodies of powerful, meritorious people were traditionally dispatched to the upper echelons of the cosmos. Although their radically different appearance reflected two seemingly oppositional political ideologies—absolutism and constitutional democracy—together the two crematoria can be understood historically as complementary transitional structures that allowed older cosmological approaches to space and politics to not only survive but also flourish in an era of turbulent social upheaval. Key to this continuity was the deployment of new modes of architectural representation, such as the plan and section, that had been cultivated under the absolutist reign of Vajiravudh. Associated with the nascent architectural profession and the rational representation of space, these tools supported a modern worldview that drew on premodern social hierarchies. Understanding this relationship is critical in comprehending the conjoined genealogies of militarism and utopianism in the formation of a modern state and its public spaces.

During the twentieth century, the absolutist court and the constitutionalist regime that succeeded it deployed funeral architecture and its symbolic forms to articulate new ideas about national belonging, civic sacrifice, and political power in urban public space. The crematorium was transformed from an exclusive ritual space for members of the royal family and the titled bureaucracy to a public space for the performance of political spectacle. Just as important, the palatial image of Mount Meru in the Thai Buddhist imaginaire from which the *men* took its form became closely identified with that of a modern utopia as the nation-state took the place of the absolute monarch as the symbolic object of veneration.[3] The first declaration made by the People's Party after the 1932 change in government, for example, announced the arrival of the felicitous Buddhist realm of *sri ariya metteya*.[4] What this new utopia would look like, however, was unclear to the architects and ideologues of the period. As Siam moved further from a constellation of diffuse regional political allegiances, or a "mandala polity" that revolved around a divinely appointed monarch, into a centralized nation-state with recognizable geopolitical borders, architectural methods of representing space, such as the plan and elevation, played a significant role not only in producing the architectural form of this utopia but also in perpetuating the hierarchical social relations of the past by ensuring the continuity of spatial conceptions in which those relations were performed.[5] The *men* played an important role in representing new forms of national belonging that were consistent with older conceptions of social hierarchy that were articulated in temple murals and manuscript illustrations. The *men* of the twentieth century operated not only as propaganda but also as larger-than-life representations of a world that could be inhabited by human beings. By the time the crematorium for the soldiers and policemen who died suppressing the Boworadet rebellion was built, the *men* could accommodate older worldviews within a modern representational framework that sacralized the nation-state rather than the body of the king.

The *phra men* derived its primary spatial organization from the *Traiphum phra ruang,* which is discussed in greater detail in chapter 2. Understanding the influence of this text on the philosophical orientation of eighteenth- and nineteenth-century Siamese court literature and ecclesiastical murals opens a view into the ways that Siamese architects and craftsmen sought to map out these idealized social and spatial relations in historical space and time in the twentieth century using new tools and technologies of representation. Literary scholar Namphueng Padamalangula has pointed out that the *Traiphum* is a text that plays with the concept of boundary and the alternation between the logic of exclusion and participation.[6] Embedded within the *Traiphum* was a commentary on the boundaries of political power and hierarchy, and of social inclusion and exclusion. The righteous Universal Monarch (*chakravartin*) was an example of someone who had performed meritorious deeds in a previous life. Although such meritorious people were usually reborn in the heavens, they were also sometimes reborn as nobles and lords in the human domain, surrounded by an almost infinite number of attendants. Such a monarch was righteous and just and did not cause his subjects to lose their respect for him.[7] Those who had divine right had been people who were virtuous in the past.[8] The *Traiphum* had an enormous influence on the worldview of Siamese society and also shaped city planning, architectural design, symbolism, and ornamentation. The Buddhist monastic complex, or wat, was oriented in harmony with the *Traiphum,* which in turn were responses to Pali scriptural materials on which the *Traiphum* drew. In the ordination hall (*uposot*) of most wat, a mural of Mount Meru is painted as the backdrop for the main altar, creating a visual affinity between the image of the Buddha and the center of the cosmos. Kings used symbols from the *Traiphum*, like the mythical bird with human characteristics (*garuda*), to show they were on par with the celestial beings who inhabited the sacred mountain and also to brand the monastic complexes, palaces, and public works that they built, most notably on the gable end.[9] The sumptuary code of the Siamese court was closely related to not only the symbolism expressed in the *Traiphum* but also the specialized construction skills needed to render them in lived space.[10] Knowledge about construction and ornament was passed down from royal craftsmen (*nai chang*) who were descended primarily from three families. Within these families, pattern books and architectural manuscripts were scarce and closely guarded.[11] The royal code of architectural elements (*thananusakdi nai ngan sathapatayakam*) that the *nai chang* developed was part of a larger code in which certain symbolic designs were limited to the monarchy.[12] Violating these codes amounted to committing lèse-majesté. Built forms adorned with royal paraphernalia, seals, and emblems, including the *phra merumat*, not only announced royal power but also enforced social stratification. Their appearances set an aesthetic norm for lower ranks in the social hierarchy to emulate, but never achieve.[13]

In nineteenth-century Siamese society, the knowledge on which these hierarchies were established was changing. Just as Chao Phraya Thipakorawong offered a renovation rather than a dismissal of the cosmological view of the *Traiphum*, as described in chapter 2, an adjustment to rather than a rupture with aesthetic codes and institutional spaces that the *Traiphum* represented also occurred. This allowed Siamese architects to ensure that older social hierarchies remained consistent, albeit in a modern form. One can see this by comparing representations of *phra men* in murals and poetry of the early seventeenth and eighteenth centuries with twentieth-century renderings of the crematorium in the architectural language of the plan, elevation, and section.

LITERARY AND VISUAL REFERENCES TO THE *PHRA MEN*

Court poetry and temple murals were important sources of information about the *phra men* for early twentieth-century architects and political patrons. These sources are largely from the seventeenth and eighteenth centuries, a period that covers the eclipse of Ayutthaya as the dominant polity in the region and the rise of new dynasties in the vicinity of contemporary Bangkok: Taksin's Thonburi and the Chakri dynasty's Bangkok. Examining these epigraphical and visual sources reveals not so much what the *phra men* of the period might have looked like, but their ideal representations as well as the relevance of funeral architecture to early modern Southeast Asian urban societies. Representations of funeral architecture in poetry and on the murals of wat walls sought to persuade worshippers of the moral consequences of their actions and endowed liturgical narratives with an easily apprehended and vivid realism. More important, they depicted where one fit in the cosmos.[14] In particular, the poetry and murals of the eighteenth century reveal the ways that royal cremations made legible the aesthetic codes of social hierarchy to clergy, courtiers, and common people. This was accomplished in three ways: through public displays of mourning that demonstrated the emotional status of the king as "Lord of Life" to his subjects; through the use of lavish and rare materials in the construction of the pyre and even in the burning of the corpse; and through public displays of common, royal, and exotic entertainments. In contrast to their European counterparts, the funeral architecture of Siam's absolutist monarchs was the focal point of spectacular displays of popular entertainment and celebration. Although the intended audience of these ritual entertainments was the spirits of the deceased, they acted as cultural-cum-political means for the new rulers to assert and publicize their authority. Popular entertainments, like the architecture that housed them, may have been intended as abstract models of the paradisiacal pleasures that lay on the other side of the pyre for the deceased, but they also created a shared sense of belonging to a public community, even if this community was socially and spatially stratified.[15] While the crematorium, as a model of Mount Meru, occupied the symbolic center of the funeral complex, outlying structures included halls and open spaces for acrobatics, masked theater, Chinese opera (ngiw), puppet theater, boxing, and exotic displays of human endurance such as lying on nails and spears.[16] In *Nang utai*, an eighteenth-century poem, the author vividly describes the entertainment at the cremation ceremony.

When everything is ready	Royal servants tell the king
Serfs shave their hair	The royal corpse is moved to the site
The royal parasol and entertainment	Both dancers and flowers
Pour lustral water	A windmill of fireworks
Flower-shaped explosions	cry out and reverberate loudly
Fireworks dot the sky	Resembling stars
Drama and songs	Some dance and some sing
Go into the ring	Go up the pole and somersault[17]

Far from being exclusively somber rituals, royal cremations showcased varied entertainments that created a lively public event and may have helped to assuage some of the grief associated with the funeral. Another later poem commemorating a royal funeral ceremony in the early eighteenth century described the role of these entertainments in navigating the grieving process.

Civilians young and old	And middle-aged
Dress up and look sharp	Step elegantly
Observe	Celebrate and preen
Delighted, intent on	Plucking off sorrow, being happy[18]

The attention to realist details in these poems signified a shift away from mystic and ritual purposes in the literature and arts of the court.[19] Artists and intellectuals began to put human beings, rather than the Buddha or mystical creatures, at the center of their thinking and to focus on the present, rather than the next life.[20] The interest in the everyday can also be discerned in religious murals in monastic complexes built during the eighteenth century in Thonburi and Bangkok. While the Buddha and other mystical creatures continued to be important elements in these murals, they increasingly came to share space not only with royalty but also with slaves and serfs performing daily rituals. In depictions of the funeral ceremony for the Buddha, commoners engaged in daily life occupy the same pictorial frame as royalty and celestial beings.

While these groups shared the same field, they were separated in different spatiotemporal fields. Murals of scenes from the life of the historic Buddha Sakyamuni in the *uposot* of Wat Thongthammachat in Thonburi show how ideas about hierarchy were communicated through depictions of the *phra men* and the cremation ceremony. The lives of deities, aristocrats, and common people are juxtaposed with one another in parallel but unequal dimensions. The murals also reveal the ways that, though they occurred within the same temporal space of the cremation ceremony, the entertainment spectacles reinforced social order by depicting acceptable comportments for different classes. Wat Thongthammachat was reported to have been built sometime during the Ayutthaya period (1351–1767) but had fallen into disrepair by the time Bangkok was established in the eighteenth century. The wat was renovated several times during the nineteenth and twentieth centuries, most notably in 1915 by order of Vajiravudh. While there is no way of knowing for certain when the murals in the *uposot* were executed, some sources suggest that they date from the period of the Third Reign (1824–1851).[21] This is highly possible, given both the use of light colors to depict landscape and the lack of linear perspective, a technique that became popular for only a brief period during the Fourth Reign (1851–1868).[22] While it is possible that early twentieth-century conservators added their own details to the scenes, the use of parallel perspective has survived repeated restorations of the murals to the present day.

Bay ten uses these techniques to depict the Buddha's ascension to nirvana, his *mahaparinibbāna* (figure 5.3). The images on these bays demonstrate not only the importance of leisure and entertainments in the cremation ceremony, but also that the public nature of these entertainments was part of a larger spectacle that reinforced the spatial and social hierarchies of the cosmos through architecture and ritual. On the left of bay ten is the Buddha's *phra men,* with five spires *(yod),* representing the sacred mountain's five peaks. On the altar of the *phra men* is an elaborate urn *(kot),* which holds the remains of the Buddha. Adjacent to the *phra men* is a ritual space for monks and nobles. Outside the ritual area is a stage for celebratory entertainments. At the top of bay ten, acrobats perform what was known at the time as *yuan hok,* a type of acrobatic theater thought to have originated in Vietnam.[23] Common audiences are depicted nursing, carousing, smoking, fondling, and vomiting from overindulging. Members of the royal family are seen engaged in more refined activities, such as the procession of a royal lady and courtiers entering the ritual compound to pay their respects to the remains of the Buddha. The figures' comportment is markedly different from the behavior of the large crowd that has assembled in front of a puppet play. The audience members push, fondle one another in a sexual manner, and jockey for space in a way that contrasts sharply with the mannered distances between figures inside the ritual area of the cremation ceremony. By making these behaviors visible within discrete spaces in a public context like the monastic complex, the murals not only reflected the comportment of audiences

FIG. 5.3. *Mahaparinibbāna,* or the ascension of the Buddha to *nibbāna,* bay ten, Uposot Hall, Wat Thongthammachat, Thonburi, ca. eighteenth century. Photo by author.

during the period but also imparted a certain expectation of class-based behavior to their viewers.

This can be seen clearly in bay eleven, which depicts the lighting of the funeral pyre of the Buddha (figure 5.4). The central focus of the mural is a redented *phra men*, which contains the remains of the Buddha, encircled by a high white wall and surrounded by small *chedi* (stupa). On either side of the ritual area, large crowds have assembled to watch not the cremation ritual, from which they have been excluded, but theatrical performances. On the right of the enclosure, a stage has been set up for a performance of a scene

FIG. 5.4. Cremation of the Buddha with various leisure entertainments, bay eleven, Uposot Hall, Wat Thongthammachat, Thonburi, ca. eighteenth century. *Muang boran.*

from the "Kraithong," a folktale. The crowd is rowdy and common, and some of the figures are even engaging in coitus as the drama is performed on the stage. Three figures are seen at the edges of the crowd, entering the walled enclosure. Their crouching, deferential posture as they leave the space of popular entertainment and enter the ritual precincts of the cremation suggests that appropriate behavior was relative to different parts of the ceremonial field.

Drawing on literary and anthropological examples, the historian Nidhi Eoseewong wrote that premodern ideas of space in Thai culture were based on the idea that space was divided into spatiotemporal "parts" (suan) rather than discrete units with clearly demarcated borders situated within universal time. Each suan had its own temporality and rules of behavior, which were different from others. In order to move from one suan to another, it was necessary to change oneself. People of noble birth were considered to be able to enter more suan than ordinary people because they had what Nithi called itthireut, or "potency" or "super-natural power."[24] In order to enter "paradise" (suannakhot), for instance, it was necessary to change one's personality. This view is consistent with the Buddhist view that attaining nibbāna, understood as either a place or a state of liberation from suffering, was possible through transforming oneself through the Noble Eightfold Path. Sites that were potent served as reminders of three things and their relationship to one another: the possibility of change in oneself; the superiority of the aristocracy; and the organization of space into suan that required different behaviors. Hence, the mural became a medium for mediating and broadcasting ideas about how power was enacted within social spaces where different classes encountered one another.

Parallel perspective was employed in temple murals to draw out the supernatural power of noble-born beings to move from one temporal space to another in a way that commoners could not. They could ascend into the higher realms of the Traiphum cosmos in a way that common people, tied to mundane desires, were unable. Murals like the ones at Wat Thongthammachat made visible social and political relations in a way that linear perspective could not. As an integral part of the architecture of the monastic complex, they served to inculcate the simultaneous, hierarchical spaces that comprised the cosmos of the Traiphum in the daily ritual practices of temple visitors. In these murals, the higher realms of the Traiphum could exist alongside profane space, but commoners rarely had access to them in the ways that royalty did. Just as the Traiphum itself underwent a reevaluation when confronted with the methodologies of European rationalism, visual representations of space underwent a transition when they encountered newer scientific methods of rendering space introduced by the nascent architectural profession in Siam: the plan, section, and elevation.[25]

THE *PHRA MEN* OF KING VAJIRAVUDH

The design of Vajiravudh's *phra men* is credited to Krom Phraya Narisara Nuwattiwong (Prince Naris) and was executed by the Department of Fine Arts under the direction of the Ministry of the Royal Household.[26] Prince Naris was active during an extraordinarily long and eventful period from the mid-nineteenth century to the mid-twentieth century. He was the son of King Mongkut and his consort Panarrai, and his architectural accomplishments include the renovation of Sanam Luang, most of the significant structures of Wat Benchamabophit, and the monument to King Phuttayotfa at the Memorial Bridge.[27] He also served as minister of war and minister of the treasury during the late nineteenth century. His political and artistic career bridges the shift from *nai chang* (craftsman) to *sathapanik* (architect).[28] He oversaw much of the work undertaken by the largely Italian coterie of engineers and architects that came to Bangkok in the late nineteenth century to design the city's public works and palaces.[29] An autodidact, Prince Naris learned to draw by studying the work of both Siamese muralists and Italian painters who were employed by the Siamese court in the nineteenth century.[30] Early in his career, he was tasked with improving the charnel grounds of Wat Saket and introducing lavatories in the royal residence by his half brother King Chulalongkorn.[31] He continued to play an influential role in the design of the urban built environment even after the 1932 change in government from an absolute monarchy to a constitutionalist regime. This long career and noble origins suggest much about the aesthetic continuities of the Thai built environment during this period.

The *phra men* that Prince Naris designed was erected at Sanam Luang, the central field or royal plaza that alternated use as a stage for political spectacles and a site for leisure activities like kite flying and other sports. The field began its life in the eighteenth century as the Thung Phra Men, an open area outside the walls of the Grand Palace dedicated to royal cremations but also where *phrai* and prisoners of war would catch lizards to eat.[32] During the Third Reign, rice was cultivated on the field as a symbolic gesture to show the Vietnamese court that the Bangkok court was so prosperous that rice grew even within the royal precincts.[33] It was during the reign of Mongkut (1851–1868), however, that Sanam Luang began to be used as a site for staging political spectacles in earnest when it was given its present name.[34] The field was walled in, suggesting that the intended audience for these spectacles was not the broader public. This changed during the reign of Chulalongkorn (1868–1910), when the field was used as a military parade ground, as the site of the country's first national exhibition, and, most significant, as a site where acts of obeisance to the monarch (*jong rak phak*) were publically performed. To accommodate this new spectacular use of the field, King Chulalongkorn ordered Prince Naris to widen the area to its contemporary dimensions.[35] This enlargement took place after the Front Palace of the viceroy, or Wang Na, was removed, indicating Chulalongkorn's consolidation of absolute power. The transformation of the field into a public space took place during the transformation of Bangkok's royal precincts into a self-consciously modern capital on par with European metropoles and was part of the larger self-fashioning of the monarchy's image as a "civilized" institution equivalent to European monarchies.[36] Although Sanam Luang was used throughout its history for leisure activities, it was never considered a place for commoners. By the Fourth Reign, it was considered to be the sacred place where the spirits of kings were sent to the heavenly echelons of the cosmos.[37] In fact, the entirety of Rattanakosin, the old city in which Sanam Luang was located, was also deemed sacred, and commoners could be cremated only outside its walls.[38]

The *phra men* for Vajiravudh stood in the center of a square about an acre in size. It was enclosed by a lattice fence, which was decorated at intervals with multitiered royal parasols, or *chattravali* (Th. *chatri*), and ornamented posts. Galleries and pavilions ran along the inside perimeter of the fence, to accommodate nobles, monks, and officials. The new king's pavilion was set apart from these and was the most lavishly decorated. At each of the four corners of the compound were towers that were built at ground level.[39] Each tower accommodated a party of four monks, who chanted on the day of cremation. The frame of the *phra men* in the center was built of four enormous teak trunks that were taken from teak forests in the north and floated down to Bangkok on the Chaophraya River.[40] They were driven into the ground thirty feet deep at an incline so that they formed a truncated pyramid with a square base. They were then joined at the top by a roof, on top of which was built a *yod,* crowned by a *chattravali.* The tip of the topmost tier of the *chattravali* was thirty-five and a half meters above the ground, a more modest level than those of previous royal *phra men.*[41] The upper part of the spire was fashioned to represent the four faces of Brahma and then tapered into Vajiravudh's royal crest and namesake, the *phrawachira* (Skr. *vajra*), or celestial thunderbolt.[42]

Prince Naris's elevation and plan of the *phra men* represented a new form of rendering space and social relations in Siam (figures 5.4 and 5.5). Although the design is credited to Prince Naris, the drawings were undertaken by Phra Phromphichit (U Laphanon), a young architect who had been appointed to the Department of Fine Arts in 1912 and continued to develop a prolific portfolio of built works for the constitutionalist government after 1932. Designs for royal *phra men* were not usually drawn on paper, as the scale was too large. They were drawn, instead, on the temple floor of Wat Mahathat, the monastic complex adjacent to Sanam Luang.[43]

While architectural drawings such as Phra Phromphichit's were intended to communicate the dimensions of the *phra men* to the workers who would build it in real, lived space, they were also indicative of a rationalist tendency that sought to measure the world in quantifiable, scientific terms. The hierarchical worlds of the *Traiphum* thus entered into the rational discourse of modern time and space through the tools of the architect. Phra Phromphichit's drawings can also be understood as the consolidation of Vajiravudh's concept of nationalism, based on the three pillars of the nation, the Buddhist religion, and the monarchy, or *chat sasana phra mahakasatri*. Like this formulation, Prince Naris's drawings tied together older concepts of divine legitimacy with the modern concept of the nation. The English-educated king would have been familiar with the British nationalist trinity of God, king, and country, and his version of these three pillars was a way of amalgamating older belief systems into a new form of nationalism that identified the dynastic state with the nation.[44] The early years of Vajiravudh's reign had been marked not only by the political power of migrant laborers and European colonial interests, but also by an abortive coup in 1912. The class of bureaucrats that had developed under Chulalongkorn's reign questioned the authority of the monarch, whose legitimacy no longer derived from the heavens (*devaraja*) but from the people. In a series of lectures delivered between 26 May and 4 July 1911 to the Wild Tiger Corps, the paramilitary organization he founded, Vajiravudh made clear that only by working in the national—and thus royal—interests could an individual satisfy their sense of being.[45] In these lectures, Vajiravudh linked the use of the term *chat*, originally understood as "birth" or "life," to the concept of the national community (*chat banmuang*).[46]

> If I am willing to sacrifice my pleasure, my body, and my life for the benefit of the nation and if you are willing to sacrifice just the same then we can be certain that the Thai nation will be secured. But if you do not make a resolution to make such a sacrifice then I do not see how the Thai nation can survive and escape from disaster. Therefore, I ask you to keep it in your minds that you and I are in the same boat and cannot be separated or escape from each other. If we sink, we sink together; if we survive, we survive together. . . . If it is our *kamma* not to make it across the ocean then do not try to escape, let us die together.[47]

The concept of *kamma* (action) has multiple associations in South Asian philosophy. Buddhism radically transformed older concepts of *kamma* to affirm that liberation was not limited by birthright social status. Rather than attribute their position to previous lives, it held that human beings were accountable for their actions in the present. In the Pali intellectual corpus, reincarnation has been described as the end of a process, which provokes another process that has structural similarity to the first.[48] The fifth-century Theravada Buddhist commentator Buddhaghosa compared reincarnation to the ways a disciple repeats a text recited by his teacher or to the flame of a lamp lighting the wick of another lamp.[49] By the twentieth century, however, Vajiravudh could appropriate the Buddhist conception of *kamma* and instrumentalize it for the nation. The *phra men* played an important role in transforming the critique of tribalism implicit in early Buddhist thought into a rationale for the shared habitation of national space. Rather than emphasize the social critique implicit in the Buddhist conception of *kamma*, Vajiravudh linked it with *chat* to underscore the idea that the actions of the sovereign and his subjects were inextricably linked. By transforming the heretofore private sanctum of the *phra men* into a public spectacle, Vajiravudh's pyre connected not only his life to those of his subjects, but his afterlife as well.

The attempt to link the *kamma* of the nation-state and its citizens with that of the king can be discerned in the elevation of Vajiravudh's *phra men* (figure 5.5). Rendered in ornate, fine lines that appear animated, ornament and structure are integrated in this drawing. There is no discernable difference between the pillars that support the structure and the finials that mark it as a royal project. Lightly rendered clouds emanate from the upper right corner of the drawing, as if the structure is the product of a burst of wind from another world rather than terrestrial human labor. Four terraced flights of stairs run from the ground to the platform underneath the main pavilion, or *busabok*. Easily visible to the crowd, these staircases were accessible to only a small circle of nobility.[50] One staircase was reserved for the exclusive use of the heir to the throne. All the stairs and terraces were decorated with tiered *chattravali* and heavenly figures (*devata*) holding large sunshades. These stairs led to a smaller tiered structure that terminated in a truncated top, made of iron with gilt overlay.[51] They operated as stages for the ascension of the heir to the throne and were the symbolic route from the lived spaces of the nation through the levels of the Buddhist cosmos to the conceptual power of the absolute monarch. The receding hierarchies of social space can be seen in Prince Naris's plan of the *phra men* (figure 5.6). Each level accommodates fewer people, but the broad steps that link them serve as a stage for the crowds that assembled at the peripheries of the cremation ceremony. The most restricted levels could thus still be seen by those who were excluded from them, reminding viewers of their coexistence in the same space, if not the same *suan*. A cosmic mandala rendered in the language of the plan, these drawings mark the historical moment in which the funeral pyre moved beyond a purely symbolic function and was represented as a form of modern public space.

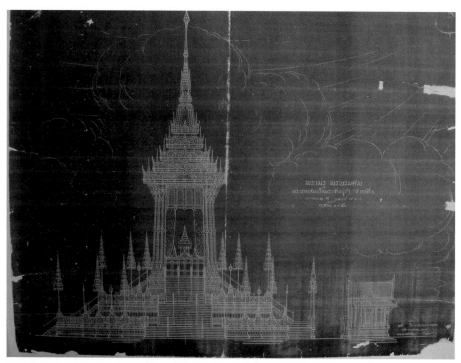

FIG. 5.5. Elevation of the crematorium (*phra merumat*) of King Vajiravudh, ca. 1925. Designed by Narisara Nuwattiwong, the drawing was undertaken by Phra Phromphichit. National Archives of Thailand.

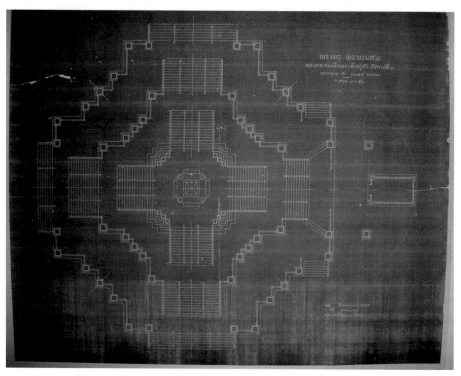

FIG. 5.6. Plan of the *phra merumat* of King Vajiravudh, ca. 1925. Designed by Narisara Nuwattiwong, the drawing was undertaken by Phra Phromphichit. National Archives of Thailand.

Although elaborate, the *phra men* was a self-consciously modern abbreviation of previous versions, like that of King Mongkut, which featured lesser pavilions on the lower platforms surrounding the *busabok*. The cremation itself was an abbreviated and more public version of earlier royal cremation rituals in which the ceremony itself took the place of popular entertainments. The ceremony was divided into two parts, one in the morning and one in the evening, so as to avoid the hottest part of the day and to accommodate the large numbers of people who assembled to pay respects to the *kot*.[52] In the morning, the golden *kot* containing the remains of Vajiravudh was paraded on a gun carriage and circumambulated the pyre three times, followed by King Prajadhipok and his entourage. It was then placed on the eastern stairway and raised by pulleys up the inclined plane. When it reached the highest platform of the pyre, it was installed at the center and wreathed with the red, white, and blue tricolor that had been adopted as the national flag under the Sixth Reign (1910–1925) and symbolized Vajiravudh's triple values of Buddhism (white), the king (blue), and the nation (red for the blood the people were expected to sacrifice in its defense). At the front of the urn was a pedestal with a golden bowl that held the late king's field marshal's helmet. Behind this was his admiral's hat. A garland of flowers decorated the base of the urn. In the afternoon, the golden *kot* was replaced with one made of sandalwood and a curtain was drawn around the upper platform. It was not until evening, however, when Prajadhipok ascended the long stairway and lit the pyre from a lamp containing a sacred fire.[53] The ignition was attended by artillery fire, a fanfare of trumpets, and the playing of the national anthem. The structure was illuminated by electric lamps and the fire tended throughout the night by attendants who ensured that none of the bones escaped the fire. By morning, consecrated water was poured on the hot cinders and, after further rites, the relics of the former king were placed in a small golden urn and carried in state to the Grand Palace.[54]

The funeral ceremony has been described by historians as the most important ceremony of the court, on par with the king's coronation.[55] In an earlier period, it was a way of testing the loyalty of polities surrounding the dominant court. Those who didn't attend revealed themselves as politically suspect, while those who did demonstrated their fealty to the new "Lord of Life."[56] Vajiravudh's cremation adjusted to reflect not only the Bangkok court's new position within a global network of nation-states but also the king's position within a newly sacralized triumvirate that could be broadcast to a national public. The nationalist trappings of the cremation—the exhibition of the tricolor, the playing of the national anthem, and the sacralization of military insignia—framed the body of the deceased king for a new political community as the leader of a nation and not only the divinely appointed ruler of a premodern polity. The political significance of Vajiravudh's *phra men* during the worldwide decline of monarchism and the country's growing financial crisis in the 1920s was suggested by H. G. Quaritch Wales's observation:

> It is particularly important that a Royal Cremation should be celebrated with the greatest possible pomp, because death is the greatest danger that the idea of divine kingship has to combat. It strikes right at the roots of the whole conception, and instills doubt into the minds of a people who, until recently, had not dared even to contemplate the possibility of a king suffering from any mortal infliction; and now, with the spread of western education, modern skepticism, and the shadow of communism, the Royal Cremation plays an even bigger part than formerly in impressing on the people that the king is not dead, but has migrated to a higher plane, where he will work out his destiny as a Bodhisattva for the good of all beings.[57]

Vajiravudh's crematorium was not simply the central prop in a theatrical display of military and religious power, however. It was a structure through which the material and rhetorical spectacle of absolute power could be performed in a way that included the Siamese public in its making. Both the materials and the ritual deployment of the structure re-inscribed the position of the monarchy at the center of both a modern political and ancient spiritual universe. The *phra men* was where the "real," lived world of the body politic met the divine, literary world of the *Traiphum phra ruang.* The *phra men* was a model of the home of the gods as well as the place where the late king could ascend to that sacred mountain. Most important, it was the place where this transcendent power could be made visible for a mass audience in a way that it had not before Vajiravudh's cremation. The public space of the *phra men* became even more pronounced after the absolute monarchy was overthrown on 24 June 1932 by a coalition of civilian and military leaders known as the People's Party.

UTOPIA AND THE PEOPLE'S PARTY

Founded in Paris on 5 February 1927, the People's Party was initially comprised of military, legal, and science students as well as a lawyer and a deputy at the Siamese mission in Paris. The group formulated a six-point program that advocated national sovereignty, public safety, economic planning, equal rights, and universal education that built on a rising tide of popular sentiment against royal absolutism that had been cultivated in the Bangkok press. The founding law student among them, Pridi Phanomyong, would become the group's intellectual leader and an advocate for the controversial collectivization of the Siamese economy. As a student in Paris, Pridi had been exposed to utopian ideals by professors Auguste Deschamps and Charles Gide.[58] The confluence of utopian socialists such as Pierre Proudhon and Buddhist felicities can be discerned in the first statement made by the People's Party after the group overthrew the absolute monarchy in a bloodless transition on 24 June 1932.[59] "Everyone will have equal rights and freedom from being serfs (*phrai*) and slaves (*kha, that*) of royalty. The time has ended when those of royal blood farm on the backs of the people. The things which everyone desires, the greatest happiness and progress which can be called *sri ariya* will arise for everyone."[60] Here, *sri ariya* referred to the temporal period when Metteya (Skt. Maitreya), the successor to the historic Buddha Gautama, would arrive to teach the *dhamma*. The image of Metteya became popular in nineteenth-century Siam through the narrative of Phra Malai, a monk who traveled to multiple realms in the *Traiphum*. The narrative has many forms, versions, and recensions, but consistent in them is the rebirth of Metteya from the Tayatimsa heaven to the human realm after the decline of the Buddhist religion.[61] Upon his ushering in of the period of *sri ariya*, wish trees would grow to provide humans with all that they required for material sustenance (similar to the Kalpapreuk of Uttarakuru described in chapter 4).[62]

To realize the wish trees of *sri ariya* in the twentieth century, Pridi proposed collectivizing land under the auspices of the state, the nationalization of industries, and cooperative farming. Pridi's utopian ambitions, however, were premature. His plan would have dispossessed the monarchy and its institutions of valuable real estate and industrial assets accumulated over the past generation through its use of political power and tax revenues.[63] The proposal thus brought tensions latent within Siamese society to a simmering point. Pridi was denounced as a communist and exiled. Soon thereafter an anticommunist act was passed that defined communism as any theory that advocated the total or partial abolition of private property.[64] Another military coup, however, allowed Pridi to return from exile, which inspired royalists in the army under Prince Boworadet to stage their own countercoup on 11 October 1933. Boworadet, a former minister of defense and ambassador to France under the absolutist regime, charged then prime minister and general Phraya Phahon Phonphayusena with lèse-majesté and of allowing commoners to offend the monarchy.[65] Together with senior military officials, Boworadet led royalist troops from the eastern region of the country to Bangkok, where they encountered fierce resistance from troops loyal to the People's Party. The constitutionalist government was ultimately victorious, but seventeen government soldiers and policemen died suppressing the revolt.

THE CREMATORIUM OF THE CONSTITUTION'S DEFENDERS

From 17 to 19 February 1934, the Siamese constitutionalist government held cremation rituals for the defenders of the constitution on Sanam Luang. The People's Party believed that the revolt was supported by Prajadhipok and even more so when he refused to return to Bangkok during the rebellion. Whether the monarchy was involved in the rebellion is a subject beyond the scope of this chapter, but the suppression of the rebellion marked the decline of the institution of the monarchy and Prajadhipok's eventual abdication.[66] Tensions between the government and the Crown can be discerned in an exchange of correspondence between the Office of the Prime Minister and the Ministry of the Palace regarding the cremation of the seventeen government soldiers and policemen at Sanam Luang.[67] In a memo dated 4 January 1934, Chao Phraya Woraphong of the Ministry of the Palace informed the prime minister, "I have asked His Majesty and His Majesty has instructed me to inform you that if you can choose another spot, for example, Lumphini Park or the Phya Thai field, it would be more appropriate."[68]

Neither of these alternatives, both public parks without the royal imprimatur of Sanam Luang, were deemed appropriate by the prime minister's office. The next day, the Office of the Prime Minister wrote again, entreating the king to reconsider their request. This time they suggested another part of Sanam Luang as a compromise: the area in front of the Soldier's Memorial designed by Prince Naris in 1919 to commemorate the Siamese soldiers who fought in the European theater of World War I. This site symbolically faced away from the Grand Palace.[69] Finally, on 6 January 1934, the Ministry of the Palace relented in a curtly worded memo: "Whereas it is His Majesty's command that if the government intends to have this affair at Sanam Luang, His Majesty will not object, but please understand that the royal opinion is not as such. He has already discussed this matter with Mom Chao Wanawaithayakorn Woraworn."[70]

This terse exchange indicated the tensions between the Crown and the government and the symbolic importance of Sanam Luang as a site for cremation. It also called into question the conflicting uses of public space during the 1930s. A royal space by virtue of its location next to palaces and royally patronized monastic complexes, Sanam Luang had been used to stage spectacles like the funeral of Vajiravudh for a public audience. As the lines between state and Crown were redrawn, the choice of Sanam Luang not only proclaimed the ideological triumph of the new government over conservative royalists but also signaled the reshaping of the political landscape by the People's Party.

The form of the crematorium was also controversial. The constitutionalist government required a new form for the pyre that did not aggrandize the institution of the monarchy. Like the other buildings in the complex, it replaced the royal signifier of the *yod* and *chattravali* with a flat roof and the national tricolor (figure 5.7). The only ornamental element was the national tricolor, which flew on top of the *men*. Three other buildings were erected as part of the cremation ceremony: a long pavilion, a smaller hall dedicated to a merit-making ceremony known as the *rong kongtek*, and a pavilion for entertainments, or *rong mohorosop*. All of these eschewed the royalist ornamentation typically associated with such buildings and drew instead on recognizably "modern" forms. These vaguely neoclassical forms embraced a new tendency in Thai architecture that has been described by architects of the period as *khwam riap ngai* (simplicity) or *sathapatayakam samanchon* (an architecture of the common people). The use of modern architecture by the People's Party to convey the zeitgeist of *sri ariya* can be compared to the use of modernist forms by the republican government in Turkey during the 1920s and 1930s. Sibel Bozdoğan has trenchantly pointed out that modern architecture in such "non-Western" contexts was more of a *representation* of modernity than the outcome of a process of modernization.[71] Its top-down characteristics underscored the relationships between political power and formal concerns. The simple geometries of the crematorium of the soldiers who had died defending the nascent constitution can be seen as a self-conscious attempt to abandon the hierarchies of the previous era, but these geometries did not completely eschew the symbolism of the absolutist period.

Inside the crematorium, the coffins of the soldiers were arranged to radiate from a large post with a gold offering tray holding the constitution, or *phan ratthathammanun*. The constitution was represented by a box that

FIG. 5.7. Flat-roofed crematorium of the soldiers who sacrificed their lives for the constitution, Bangkok, 1933. General Phraya Phaholphayusena Archives, Artillery Center, Lopburi.

was traditionally used to store concertina-folded palm-leaf and mulberry manuscripts. The gold tray upon which it rested was of the kind used to make offerings to royalty or monks so as not to profane them, and it framed the constitution as an aesthetic object (figure 5.8). The first public use of this symbol dated back to 30 December 1932, when a "permanent" constitution was displayed at the Ananta Samakhom Throne Hall, which the People's Party had occupied as their headquarters after overthrowing the absolute monarchy (figure 5.9).[72] The display of the constitution followed a ritual inside the throne hall during which the king signed the constitution on a gold offering tray. This "permanent" version of the constitution gave back many of the extensive powers that had been stripped from the absolute monarchy in a previous charter. Its inauguration positioned it as a grant from the throne.[73] The gold tray thus became a vessel that linked the celestial worlds of the monarch and the *Traiphum* with the profane, political modern world. While sacralizing the constitution as a document that was as sacred as the form of the illustrated manuscripts of the *Traiphum*, it also embodied an irreconcilable contradiction.[74] If the constitution was a charter of the democratic and universal rights of all the citizens of a Siamese nation state, why would the touch of commoners profane it? This symbol would appear repeatedly throughout the tenure of the People's Party in numerous public buildings and monuments throughout Thailand. It continues to be a symbol of political movements in the twenty-first century, even though the constitution itself has been rewritten many times since 1932.[75] It crowned

FIG. 5.8. Thailand's first constitution on a gold offering tray (*phan ratthathammanun*). Ludexvivorum: Creative Commons License.

FIG. 5.9. Public exhibition of the "permanent" constitution on a gold offering tray (*phan ratthathammanun*) in front of the Ananta Samakhom Throne Hall, designed by Mario Tamagno and Annibale Rigotti and built between 1907 and 1915. This was the first public display of this symbol, and it framed the constitution as an aesthetic object bestowed upon the people by the king. National Archives of Thailand.

the monument where the remains of the soldiers, encased in empty artillery shells, would eventually be interred (figure 5.10).[76]

While the People's Party sought to create a new aesthetic language of equality through its use of simple geometric shapes and lack of ornamentation, the contradictions embedded within the form of the *phan ratthathammanun* suggest that rather than displace the inequalities of the previous era, it rationalized them through modern technologies of spatial representation, like the plan, and construction materials, like concrete and steel. These continuities between the absolutist and constitutionalist regimes can be discerned in the cremation ceremony itself, which took place at Sanam Luang from 17 to 19 February 1934. In spite of the "modern" appearance of the crematorium, the ceremony bore many of the same trappings as that of Vajiravudh. The bodies of the soldiers were ritually consecrated by members of the Buddhist clergy and their coffins wrapped in the national tricolor, which had also carried over from the absolutist period.[77] The procession accompanying their bodies to Sanam Luang was believed to have been the largest procession of commoners in the history of Thailand. Although exact figures of the crowd cannot be ascertained, photographs and news reports

FIG. 5.10. Monument to the Defense of the Constitution, Bang Khen, 1936. The remains of the soldiers and policemen cremated on Sanam Luang in 1934 are interred in the base of the monument. The structure is crowned with a sculpture of the *phan ratthathammanun*. Photo by author.

of the event confirm that it was well attended.

The continuities between Vajiravudh's crematorium and that of the soldiers who died defending the constitution is underscored by the role of Prince Naris, who ascended the pyre to light the initial sacred fire and lay wreaths and candles on the seventeen coffins. Prime Minister Phraya Phaholphayusena then lit the actual pyre from the fire Prince Naris had lit, ritually passing on the sacred flame lit by a member of the royal family to the bodies of common soldiers. While Prince Naris's presence may have been a necessary concession on the part of the People's Party to involve the royal family, it was within a visual and symbolic space that was stripped of absolutist imagery. Nonetheless, Prince Naris's participation suggested that in spite of the modern appearance of the crematorium, its organization of space was consistent with earlier iterations during the absolutist period. Just as Buddhaghosa likened the *kammic* inheritance to the wick of a lamp being lit by another, a nobleman initiated the cremation and a commoner, albeit one bolstered by the power of the military and the state, symbolically kindled it into a larger fire.

The crematoria of the absolutist regime and the constitutionalist government that overthrew it were produced through an encounter between seemingly conflicting architectural approaches and worldviews. Built during a period in which not only positivist science and empirical reasoning encountered Indic cosmologies and Buddhist truth claims, but also the modern profession of the architect and architectural techniques encountered the techniques of the master craftsman (*nai chang*), the modern crematorium reconciled older cosmologies with a new rational understanding of the world. The use of the plan, section, and elevation to articulate the modern forms of the crematorium drew not on the development of linear perspective but on the long history of parallel perspective that informed temple murals. The use of the open plan, flat roofs, and cubic geometries associated with modern architecture to accommodate the hierarchies of the *Traiphum* suggests the afterlife of seemingly archaic concepts like *nibbāna* and absolutism in the twentieth century. Modernity did not erase these older cosmological associations and ways of thinking about space but was itself transformed in the encounter. Rather than displace one another, two competing intellectual tendencies could be sustained within the forms of the funeral pyre. While modernity in architectural history is conventionally framed as a rupture with the past, the crematoria of Vajiravudh and the defenders of the constitution suggest a different understanding of modernity as antinomy. One approach did not simply yield to another. Rather, the structure of the modern *men* not only could sustain heterogeneous and discordant temporalities—the past, present, and future—within a single structure, but could also support conflicting philosophical and political views as well as literary and artistic views.

Although the two crematoria were constructed by seemingly oppositional political approaches, they shared a common source. Both drew on the cosmological structure of the *Traiphum* and linked it with the geo-body of the nation. Sacrificing one's life for the new nation was framed within the crematorium as something meritorious and beautiful. The crematorium allowed for the conceptual reincarnation of Vajiravudh's absolutist nationalism as a new form of nationalism that linked the nation and its subjects through shared *kamma*. The pyre of the soldiers in 1934 demonstrated to a nascent Thai public that the common-born citizens of the nation could also be glorified, just as Vajiravudh had been. This violent sacrifice required of Siamese citizens was aestheticized in order to naturalize it as an ideology of loyal service to the state.[78] The result was that the public, and not only the military, furnished the social energy necessary for hierarchical order.[79] The new potency of the *men*, beginning with Vajiravudh's careful staging of the cremation as a nationalist ritual, lay in its placement at the center of a public space.

The remains of the soldiers were treated as if they were sacred relics, similar to those of Vajiravudh. However, instead of being enshrined in a *chedi* under the royal spire representing Mount Meru, they were placed within artillery shell casings, underscoring the use of human beings as fodder for the militarized nation-state, and interred in a political monument under the symbol of the *phan ratthathammanun* in Bang Khen. This northern settlement is today a suburb of Bangkok but was then a peri-urban area where the People's Party chose to build several monuments, including Wat Phra Sri Mahathat, which is discussed at greater length in chapter 7. The Monument for the Defense of the Constitution, or Anusawari Phithak Ratthathamma-nun, framed the historicist idioms of the dynastic past within new materials to produce a nationalist architecture that could reconcile seemingly contradictory impulses.

Designed by Lieutenant Colonel Luang Naruemitr Laekhakarn (Yuean Bunsen, 1890–1955), a faculty member of the army's cadet school, the monument was unveiled in 1936. Its form integrates the symbolism of both utopia and militarism.[80] Its octagonal base is oriented in the eight cardinal and subcardinal directions that surround Mount Meru. The shaft of the monument resembles both a bayonet and a tower-like spire, or *prang*, on top of which sits the *phan ratthathammanun*. A plaque with the names of the seventeen soldiers and policemen who were killed in defense of the constitution adorns the west side of the shaft. On the south side is a frieze of a model Thai family with the father holding a scythe, the mother holding a sheaf of rice, and the son holding a rope. A *dhamma* wheel is fixed to the north side, and facing east is a poem written by Vajiravudh, *Siam anusati*.[81] The final lines of the poem are a clear indication of the shared *kamma* and responsibility of Siamese citizens to the nation:

หากสยามยังอยู่ยั้ง   ยืนยง
If Siam still abides
เราก็เหมือนอยู่คง   ชีพด้วย
We will also endure
หากสยามพินาศลง   ไทยอยู่ ได้ฤๅ
If Siam perishes, can the Thai still endure?
เราก็เหมือนมอดม้วย   หมดสิ้นสกุลไทยฯ
We will also end with the extinction of the Thai

While tombs of unknown soldiers in European and American metropoles allowed modern nation-states to identify themselves as timeless polities through their monumental permanence, the *men* were the spectacular evidence of a secular transformation of fatality into continuity. The representation of utopia through the tools of the architect became key to the formulation of a national space in which a self-conscious public could constitute themselves. In the twentieth century, the *men* were transformed into ephemeral constructions that linked the imagined community of the nation to an afterlife. While human beings, even royal ones, had mortal bodies, the concept of the nation embraced multiple lifetimes and extended well beyond the present.[82] It bound both commoner and monarch together in the perilous voyage across the maelstrom of the mid-twentieth century. In the timber and concrete spaces of modernity's first nationalist funeral pyres, citizens learned to recognize their fellowship as part of a sacred community with seemingly endless incarnations. In the period that followed 1932, until the revival of the political power of the monarchy in 1957, modern materials and building technologies supported the construction of more permanent utopias within the Thai capital. As the following chapters reveal, steel framing, concrete, and air-conditioning permitted architects and their patrons to articulate ideas about national belonging in lived space, creating a closer relationship between urban and architectural features and individual subjectivity.

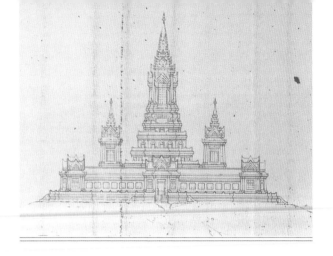

PART II

MATERIALS

CHAPTER SIX

ORDER AND ODOR

Sensuous Citizenship Formation and the Architecture of the Cinema

In 1931, to commemorate the approaching 150-year anniversary of the founding of Bangkok by his great-great-grandfather, King Prajadhipok (r. 1925–1935) made a last-ditch effort to stimulate popular support for the absolute monarchy by commissioning three public works.[1] Sited within close proximity to one another, they were built between the predominantly Chinese district of Sampheng and the royal precincts of Rattanakosin.[2] One was a bascule bridge that traversed the Chaophraya River, the Saphan Phra Phuttayotfa (Memorial Bridge); another was a memorial statue to the founder of the city and the Chakri dynasty, King Phuttayotfa, with a significant open plaza in front of it; and the third was a cinema, the Sala Chaloem Krung (figure 6.1). While all these projects deployed materials and techniques of modernity in the public sphere, the Sala Chaloem Krung integrated both infrastructural and symbolic approaches and brought together modern technologies like air-conditioning and materials like steel-reinforced concrete to produce a new kind of public space in which the experience of citizenship was manipulated through architectural design. Although discussions of indoor climate control have been framed as part of twentieth-century regimes of comfort and hygiene, this chapter repositions the history of air-conditioning within the history of modern mass politics and public space. It integrates a reading of the "visible politics," or architecture, with the invisible technologies that sustain it to better understand architecture's role in the formation of modern identity.[3]

SENSUOUS CITIZENSHIP FORMATION AND THE CINEMA AS A UTOPIAN SITE

The cinema had been a popular site of public entertainment in early twentieth-century Bangkok and was increasingly a place not only where members of the urban public developed an awareness of one another's physical presence, but also where they were able to express their political discontent. Although Prajadhipok's building campaign did little to stem the overthrow of the absolutist system, it was instrumental in the formation of the image and behavior of an ideal citizen, something that would be taken up throughout the constitutionalist period. Both the unseen infrastructural interventions and the visible symbolism of the cinema were the locus of "sensuous citizenship formation," as the city's cinemas were transformed from louche arenas of class conflict and unregulated play into utopian movie palaces that regulated the perceptual experience of the theater and produced a new sense of spatial order. The regulation of experience took place through the use of invisible networks that drew on technologies of sanitization and standardization like air-conditioning and steel-reinforced concrete. However, it also deployed visible ornamental features of the building that aligned the new technology of cinema with older narratives like the epic *Ramakian* and masked theatrical dance forms like *khon* to produce a multisensory narrative of modernity that, like the funeral architecture of chapter 5, could accommodate the hierarchies of the past while admitting new citizens into its telling. While modernist architects frequently subordinated ornament to order, the architecture of the Sala Chaloem Krung suggests that the two were intimately connected in the production of new narratives, perceptual experiences, and public spaces in the twentieth century.

Film historian Sophia Siddique Harvey has used the term "sensuous citizenship formation" to describe the ways that cinematic effects like sound and experimental narrative reconfigure an audience's way of perceiving the world around them. She has argued that the multiple perspectives that the cinema encourages layer the space of the city with an emotional structure that engages with the city's complex cultural milieu. As film reconceptualizes the audience member's sensory systems by opening up new ways of seeing, hearing, and feeling, the audience member leaves the cinema with a transformed sense of the city as a place.[4] Harvey's concept builds on the work of several scholars in film and politics, notably political scientist Davide Panagia, who has described political life as a perceptual exercise.[5] Although many historians and political thinkers writing about the mid-twentieth century have investigated the importance of aesthetics to the development of mass politics, Panagia has extended this conversation by considering the instability of the relationship between our sensory organs and acts of

FIG. 6.1. Samaichaloem Kridakon, Sala Chaloem Krung cinema, Bangkok, 1932. National Archives of Thailand.

perception. In particular, he has drawn attention to the ways human beings condition appearances to the perceptual expectations of readability or adapt the world around them into narrative forms. He has called this privileging of narrative "narratocracy."[6] The film historian Laura Marks, to whom Harvey's idea of sensuous citizenship formation is also indebted, has pointed out that cinema is not fundamentally verbal and does not carry out lines of reasoning in the way that written theory does. It exists on the threshold of language.[7] Although none of these authors was concerned directly with architecture, their work allows us to better understand the unique ways that the architecture of the cinema was not just a static envelope for new technologies, but was itself a narrative form that communicated larger ideas about the world and humanity's place in it through both order and ornament. To claim that the architecture of the cinema was a critical component of "sensuous citizenship formation" is not to suggest that the cinema in Bangkok was a factory that extruded model citizens from the raw material of naïve audience members. Rather, by emphasizing the ways that both visible and unseen characteristics of the cinema's architecture disrupted the certainty of the relationship between human sensory organs and acts of perception, the building reveals itself as a form of political speech as well as a utopic public space in which encounters between diverse members of an urban public could be persuasively narrated as part of an imagined national community rather than simply a gathering of members of diverse races and classes. Just as the funeral pyres discussed in chapter 5 were transformed into a new kind of public space that narrated political belonging in the twentieth century, the cinema became a site where the meaning and experience of being part of a modern political community were framed through design. The transformation of the architecture of the cinema can be understood as part of a civilizing process that sought to change the experience of the city through a modern hygienic regime. Historian Constance Classen has noted that the deodorization of cities like London and Paris was part of the institution of regulations that sought to manage its exponential growth in the nineteenth century.[8] In nineteenth- and twentieth-century Asian cities like Bangkok and Bandung, the suppression of odors was part of a colonial civilizing process, but it also demonstrated the ways architecture could intervene on sensory perception, disrupting the certainty of the senses to persuade audiences they were in a utopian environment that was different from the city in which they lived.

Examining the early cinema as a place of sensory engagement and confusion opens up a deeper understanding of the ways that mass politics operated in the mid-twentieth century. Changes in the materials, structure, and symbolism of the cinema took place alongside the emergence of new forms of political community such as nation, race, and class. The cinema in Bangkok transformed from a chaotic den of subversion and iniquity where moving images of a modern world were screened for diverse and unruly audiences to a palace of sensory order where modern life could be physically experienced in a way that it could not in the outside world. Originally accommodated in timber-framed warehouses, by the 1930s cinemas like the Sala Chaloem Krung could boast steel framing, concrete, and air-conditioning. In Bangkok, early timber-framed cinemas juxtaposed the spaces of other realities against the local tropical climate. In letters published in cinema magazines of the time, audience members described the darkened theater as a libidinal space in which audience members of different races and classes often jostled, fondled, smelled, heard, and tasted one another and felt at ease to express their ambivalence toward the institutions of the state. While the illusory images of primarily imported films in the early years of the Bangkok cinema offered audiences a rare glimpse of "civilized" temporalities and spaces, eventually architects could draw on modern technological innovations like steel framing and air-conditioning to design spaces that reflected a utopian order.

EARLY CINEMA IN SIAM

The first projection of a film in Thailand was recorded by the *Bangkok Times* on 10 June 1887 in a hall (*rong*) belonging to the nobleman Mom Chao Alangkan.[9] However, the first permanent cinema was built by a Japanese promoter named Watanabe Tomoyori in November 1905 in the Nakhon Kasem area of Bangkok on land owned by Wat Chaichana Songkhram. The theater was made of timber with a corrugated iron roof and screened popular Western films such as those from the Pathé Frères Company in Paris.[10] Because of Watanabe's patronage, motion pictures were known in Thai as *nang yipun,* or Japanese shadow theater, a reference to the tradition of shadow puppets (*nang*) that proliferated in premodern island Southeast Asia and the Malay peninsula.[11] Using local theatrical forms to describe the new technology of moving pictures framed it within a different historical trajectory than in Europe and was likely helpful in popularizing it among Siamese audiences. In 1910, during the transition between the reigns of Chulalongkorn and Vajiravudh, there was a surge in the construction of movie theaters and companies in Bangkok. These were largely Chinese-run companies, and their theaters often took the names of Chinese diasporic cities and colonial entrepôts like Penang, Singapore, and Hong Kong. Watanabe's cinema provided the prototype for most of these early cinemas in Bangkok. They resembled warehouses or godowns, as seen in a plan of the cinema of Nai Adrin, a Frenchman in Phrapradaeng Province, just across the river from Bangkok (figure 6.2) or the Sala Chaloem Thani in Nang Loeng, a thriving Bangkok neighborhood (figure 6.3). Methods of representing the space of the cinema became more elaborate, as seen in a plan of a cinema in Minburi from 1928 (figure 6.4). The attentiveness to structural systems and the placement of seating within the Minburi cinema suggest that the architecture of the cinema was increasingly seen as more than simply an envelope for the consumption of moving pictures.

The commercial opportunities of the new entertainment technology were not lost on the monarchy. In 1925, the last year of Vajiravudh's reign, the king decreed that Chao Phraya Ramrakhop establish a Thai film company, the Siam Niramai Company, to compete with Chinese businesses.[12] During Prajadhipok's reign, the king considered closing the Department of Courtly Entertainments (Krom Mohorosop) as a result of the debts accrued by his predecessor.[13] The department was temporarily suspended and eventually folded into the Department of Fine Arts, with many government officials who had been dismissed finding work in the film business.[14] Court preferences for theater and court patronage of dance and dramatic performances also declined as the cinema became the preferred entertainment of both royalty and commoners.[15]

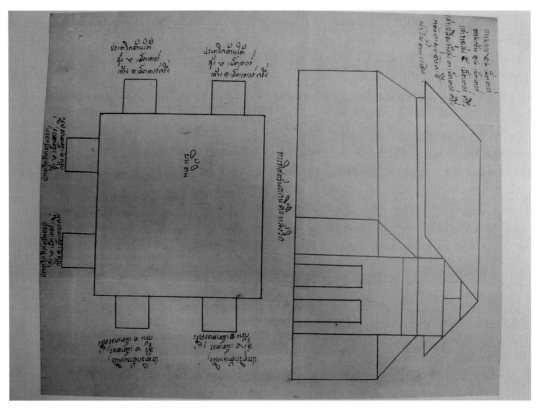

FIG. 6.2. Construction plan for Nai Adrin's cinema in Phrapradaeng, 1916. National Archives of Thailand.

Early cinemas were widely seen as popular dens of impropriety and subversion but also as spaces for inculcating behavior. "Cinemas are the best schools for criminal behavior," opined one Thai journalist in 1923:

> One can see examples of all kinds of stealing in these cinemas. Boys in Bangkok who become "bad" (*tong sia pai*) learned it in the cinema first. It's said that the cinema makes children become bad and not just children in Bangkok. There are quite a large number of upcountry children who come to visit Bangkok once in a while and go "bad" because of cinemas. If you want to see evidence for this, look at the children who are sent by the courts to juvenile delinquent facilities (*rong rian dad san dan*) or who are sentenced to jail terms. These children are most likely children who received a lot of schooling from the cinema.[16]

While cinemas were seen as having a negative pedagogical influence, they were also attractive to the moneyed and educated sectors of Bangkok society, for whom the consumption of modern forms of leisure was part of the formulation of a cosmopolitan image of the urban classes.[17]

FIG. 6.3. Sala Chaloem Thani cinema in Nang Loeng, built in 1918. Photo by author.

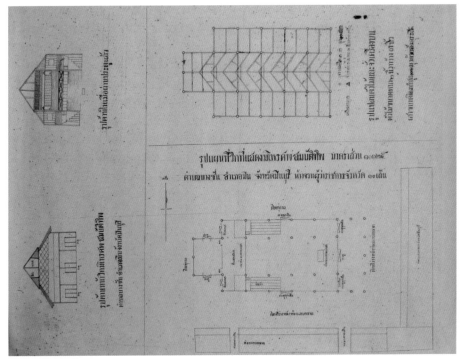

FIG. 6.4. Elevations, plan, and sectional drawing of Sombathip theater of Nai Kao Klinchampi in Minburi, 1928. National Archives of Thailand.

An article in the *Bangkok Daily Mail* of 21 October 1930 reported that audiences had repeatedly failed to "give proper attention and due respect to His Majesty the King" when the "King's Anthem" was played. "It has been noted that when the band strikes up [the "King's Anthem"] some persons seem to pay little attention to it, while others walk out of the hall, quite oblivious to the patriotic custom."[18] The custom, the writer neglected to mention, was a recent innovation and borrowed from the British invented tradition of standing at attention for the playing of the national anthem. In Siam, the police were instructed to remind the public of their obligations when the tune was being played and to take down the names of any offenders who were government officials or members of the military. The article reveals the widespread popular ambivalence toward the institution of the monarchy in the years leading up to the 1932 change in government. Whether this ambivalence was intentional or simply ignorance of how royalty wished to be respected is not clear. What is certain, however, is that the monarchy recognized the political importance of the cinema as a public space for both educating behavior and narrating political sentiment.

The cinema became a place that linked crime, disobedience, political subversion, intimacy, and new forms of technology in the early part of the twentieth century. It was full of inconveniences and irritations due largely to the heterogeneous—in terms of both race and class—audiences that it drew. The cinematic apparatus was an imported modern technology, which made it attractive to the monied and educated sectors of Bangkok society. But its cost was within reach of all but the poorest. The cheapest ticket was 2 *saleung* (a quarter of a baht) and the most expensive was 10 baht.[19] While the cinema was an entertainment that was much more expensive than other diversions—such as folk games—economic statistics of the period suggest that the cheapest tickets were still affordable to the growing middle strata of urban society.[20] In comparison, older sites of entertainment like playhouses and Thai folk drama (*likay*) and Chinese folk opera (*ngiw*) halls were divided along lines of class and race: playhouses were frequented by wealthier, bourgeois customers, while the *likay* and *ngiw* saw largely less well-to-do Siamese and Chinese audiences, respectively.[21] At the cinema, differences in seating prices and seating arrangements may have divided wealthy from poor in principle and permitted avoiding physical intimacy. In practice, as in cinemas everywhere in the world, this was far from the case.[22] The darkened hall provided the cover of anonymity for patrons to touch one another, and even at a distance, smells and sounds traveled in ways that could not be controlled. Members of the Siamese bourgeoisie found themselves, even in their private boxes, assaulted by the presence of lower classes and other "races."

PHAPHAYON SAYAM PALIMENT

A rich source of information about the tactile interactions of audience members with one another and the space of the cinema was the letters section in *Phaphayon sayam*, a popular Thai-language cinema magazine of the early 1920s that was published by Siaosonguan Sibunreuang, the Thai-born Chinese founder of the Siam Cinema Company and a leading figure in the early motion picture industry in Siam. The section was called Phaphayon Sayam Paliment, or Siamese Film Parliament. In a period in which Siam lacked a parliamentary form of government, the name is revealing of the ways in which the modern leisure space of the cinema was coupled with modern political concepts like democracy but also suggests a moving away from the image of the cinema as a site of subversion to a more respectable outlet for political expression. The historian Scot Barmé first introduced these letters to English-speaking scholars in order to understand the socio-cultural dynamic that characterized Bangkok life as the Siamese capitalist economy developed.[23] A closer look at these letters in this chapter demonstrates that a new, class-conscious, and racially coded form of aesthetics developed in which a community of subjects was both linked and divided not only through a common visual language but through shared sensorial feeling as well. These letters also demonstrate the ways that sensory perception was embedded within larger cultural and political frameworks and was not simply a matter of cognitive processes or neurological mechanisms located in individual subjects.[24]

Throughout the 1920s, letters to the column often complained of the unsanitary and smelly conditions in many of Siao's theaters. His most popular theater, the Nang Loeng Cinema (later known as the Patthanakon Cinema) was described as both the largest and most prestigious cinema in the capital, but it was also considered a filthy, smelly place. A letter in the 9 March 1922 issue related the writer and his party's inability to sit in the seats that they had purchased because they were too dirty.[25] A letter from "Dek Dunang" (Film-Viewing Child) complained about the Phatthanakon Cinema. "Even though the theater is the biggest in Siam, its floor is filthy and stained with betel juice," the writer remarked.[26] At the Banglamphu Cinema, a writer detailed the flow of urine across the floor and the smell of children's feces.[27] In all these accounts, the writers expressed frustration at the caesura between the expectations of their fellow audience members and the reality of their behaviors. The writers expected the cinema to be a progressive, civilized space but were disappointed with the messy urban reality that confronted them in its darkened interior. The unseen sensorial experience of the darkened cinema was markedly different from the utopian images projected on the screen. In the 1920s, the images audiences would have seen were largely of Parisian and Hollywood stage sets or the limited landscapes of newsreel programs.[28]

The complaints of the writers in Phaphayon Sayam Paliment extended not only to the physical limitations of the space of the cinema, but to the people that it accommodated as well. One prolific writer named "Mangkon Thong" (Golden Dragon) wrote to ask, "Do cinemas breed beggars?" The letter complained of a young Chinese boy who went around the theater begging from audience members and called on the company to forbid anyone who wore filthy clothing from entering the theater.

> If the company reconsiders other citizens who are the majority and who don't like this, and the company itself perhaps doesn't want to let these derelicts come in and trample on the cinema because they disturb the good citizens who watch films, spread infectious diseases, and breed begging. When the company sympathizes with this group of good audience members, they should totally prohibit low class people from trampling into the cinema. Otherwise the cinema will become a fount of nuisances, infectious diseases, and begging.[29]

Mangkon Thong's pointed use of the term "citizen" (prachachon) in his letter suggests that his critique is about not simply the proper etiquette in a cinema, but who had the right to be seen in a public space. Mangkon Thong's letters would continue to grace the pages of Phaphayon Sayam Paliment over the next few years, referring to the poor as "stinking hordes" (phuak men sap) and demanding corporate policies to control their behavior and admission into the theater.[30]

A writer named "Mangkon Ngoen" (Silver Dragon) took offense at Mangkon Thong's characterizations and countered by criticizing not the "stinking" poor, but "new people who wear too much perfume and still smell bad." "If Mangkon Thong and N.S. still detest these people," he wrote, "they should go abroad because this is Thailand."[31] The writer signed himself Mai Khamloei (Not At All Amused) and took particular offense to Mangkon Thong's characterization of the masses as smelly, asking whether these were not the same people who had brought progress to the Siam Cinema Company.[32]

Mangkon Thong rebutted by arguing that the real public were not the smelly hordes but cleaner types. He suggested, perhaps by way of rapprochement, that there were two kinds of cinema: the type that are like halls or palaces and the ones that are not. He thought it within reason that the palatial types, like the Phatthanakan, had some sort of controls in place over who could enter. As for the other types, like the Phatthanarom and Chua, "If I watched films in a theater like that, I would not call for the company to make laws for control."[33] The public, he believed, should behave in keeping with the demands of a modern civilized space, but older, dirtier cinemas could remain unregulated spaces.

THE CINEMA AS MODERN PALACE

It would be nearly a decade before Mangkon Thong's dream of a cinema palace would be realized. On 4 July 1930, King Prajadhipok and Queen Ramphai Phani visited the Ming Muang market at the edge of Sampheng district to lay the cornerstone of what would become the city's first modern cinema, the Sala Chaloem Krung. The cinema was intended as part of a trio of projects that glorified the Chakri dynasty but instead became something else. Architectural historian Chatri Prakitnontakan has described the three projects as the last monuments to the absolute monarchy, but the Sala Chaloem Krung's import in the formation of a new kind of citizen would be felt long after the 1932 change in government.[34] One of the most important urban innovations of the building campaign was the creation of public space. While earlier government building campaigns had focused on creating a modern image of the monarchy, as in the case of the Ananta Samakhom Throne Hall, or transportation infrastructure, such as the cutting of Charoen Krung Road, the 150-year centenary campaign was concerned with accommodating a new urban public under the symbolic aegis of the monarchy. This is most obvious in the open plaza created in front of the monument to King Phuttayotfa but is also a latent component of the Memorial Bridge and the Sala Chaloem Krung. The bridge connected Thonburi with Bangkok and not only knit communities on both sides of the river into a coherent urban form but also united the spirits of the older capital with the newer one. The Sala Chaloem Krung brought together cinema audiences in a large interior space. In all these projects, the symbolism of the past worked in tandem with new materials like steel and concrete to produce a new narrative about the modern role of the monarchy in bringing together a fractured urban public that was becoming cognizant of its political power.

The building campaign was undertaken during tense economic and political times. There were crop failures in May 1930, and the following month, rice exports and tin prices slumped. In December, the government issued a communiqué that concluded that the economic situation was "serious" and that the government planned to exercise a "rigid economy."[35] However, under the management of the Bangkok Company, 9 million baht was spent on the three-year-long construction of the Sala Chaloem Krung, suggesting the importance of these projects to the regime. So important were these built works to the institution of the monarchy that Prajadhipok, in discussing a proposed trip to the United States, concluded that he had to return in time for the April 1932 ceremonies. In a telegram he sent to the Thai ambassador in Washington, DC, regarding eye surgery, he wrote, "It is very probable that I shall have great difficulties in using right eye in 1932 which means that the operation should be performed before that year which is fixed for opening memorial bridge."[36]

Between the time that Prajadhipok laid the cornerstone of the Sala Chaloem Krung and the opening ceremony of the cinema three years later, on 2 July 1933, the absolute monarchy was overthrown by a coalition of military and civilian members of the bureaucratic bourgeoisie. The work of the cinema's architect, Mom Chao Samaichaloem Kridakon, sought to reconcile competing tendencies that had emerged not only in the royal court but in the capital itself: on the one hand, the desire to preserve the absolute monarchy, and on the other, the inclination to live in a democratic society. These two tendencies can be seen most immediately in the ways that Samaichaloem framed the design of the four-story theater as a mix of traditional symbolism and modern building technologies. Samaichaloem's design strategy, the ways that he sought to integrate ornament and order, however, is usually overlooked by historians. The theater is often described as a "Western" exterior wrapped around a "Thai" interior.[37] A careful examination of both the visible and unseen infrastructural components of the space, however, suggests that Samaichaloem undertook more than simply creating a modernist envelope for a traditional core or hybridizing the design of the theater. Samaichaloem used steel to frame the building both structurally and symbolically: creating a space for the sensory experience of modernity by a public body. He used this structural framework to support a nationalist ideology that drew on the symbolism of historic narratives like the *Ramakian.* This design allowed him to address the structural needs of an interior public space that, in turn, allowed audience members to see themselves as modern subjects with a distinct historical legacy.

Influenced by his training in the École des Beaux-Arts, Paris, Samaichaloem designed a hierarchical and symmetrically ordered public building along major, and then minor, axes. To create the large open gathering spaces necessary for a public program, Samaichaloem used new technologies like a steel-frame structure to support the weight of the building rather than load-bearing walls.[38] Off the main axis of the lobby were smaller rooms that helped support the weight of the structure. The result was a theater with large open spaces that doesn't need visible columns to support it. The steel framing also showcased another significant, although less widely acknowledged, architectural intervention of the early twentieth century.

AIR-CONDITIONING AND ITS DISCONTENTS

The Sala Chaloem Krung was the first movie theater in Southeast Asia to use air-conditioning.[39] The "chilled water system" was purchased from the Carrier Corporation of Syracuse, New York. Theaters in the United States had only recently started to discover the financial rewards of installing this new technology in the larger, more ostentatious "picture palaces" that were being built in the 1920s and 1930s. These "picture palaces" were a change of venue from the more rudimentary nickelodeons that were similar in experience to Bangkok's timber-framed theaters. The new cinemas were fitted with gilded balustrades and moldings, luxurious restrooms, massive chandeliers, lush seating, full orchestras and pipe organs, and deferential uniformed ushers. Historian Marsha Ackerman, in her study of the rise of air-conditioning, noted that these new sensory environments included not just image and, later, sound, but also a cool darkness that allowed audiences to forget the time of day or the season of year. Like these new "palaces," the Sala Chaloem Krung was a place for audiences—who could afford slightly more expensive tickets—to escape the world outside, as long as they were willing to behave in keeping with the ambience that surrounded them.[40]

The installation of centrifugal refrigerating apparatuses in movie theaters was becoming increasingly popular at the time of the Sala Chaloem Krung's opening. The system distributed a cooled air supply downward, recirculated some of the return air, and bypassed some supply air around a cooling coil.[41] Innovations in air-conditioning design allowed for cleaned, cooled, and dehumidified air to be blown into the theater without causing drafts. This was achieved through a system of bypass downdraft air distribution, where the air flowed through outlets located in the ceiling, diffused slowly downward, and then entered return grilles in the floor.

The idea to air-condition the Sala Chaloem Krung occurred only after King Prajadhipok approached the Carrier Corporation in an effort to secure air-conditioning for his palaces. A representative of the company was on a round-the-world tour and made a detour to Bangkok to visit the royal palaces. While there, he learned of the Sala Chaloem Krung project and persuaded the king of the financial and hygienic advantages of air-conditioning. On a visit to the United States, Prajadhipok visited the Carrier and Lyle plants in New Jersey on 15 July 1931 and placed an order for air-conditioning systems for the cinema as well as his personal apartments.[42] The corporation had just started to market its wares to movie theaters. Willis Haviland Carrier, the founder of the corporation, later noted,

> Movies closed during hot weather or showed to such small audiences that
> they operated at a loss. Even on cool days the inside of the theater was hot

if there were many people in the audience. The heat from the people was enormous. A ventilating system did not help much. We argued that, with air conditioning, the theater need never be dark and would do a box-office business in summer because people would go there to cool off—to be comfortable. With our air conditioning, we believed we could sell the theater market without much resistance.[43]

The first centrifugal refrigerating apparatus with downward draft (from ceiling to floor) and recirculation of air to be installed in any theater was the one at the Palace Theater in Dallas in the summer of 1924.[44] This was similar to the system installed in the Sala Chaloem Krung almost nine years later.

Air-conditioning did not figure prominently in the Siamese economy during the 1930s. While machinery is prevalent in the advertising of the period, there seems to have been no attempt at marketing air-conditioning or even cooler environments to the general public. In fact, the few complaints about thermal comfort in Siam's tropical climate came mostly from European travelers. The early twentieth-century Italian journalist Salvatore Besso summarized the general European attitude toward Siam's climate by noting, "But what heat! What an atrocious heat!"[45] The missionary N. A. McDonald observed that the temperature fluctuated between 64 and 98 degrees Fahrenheit (17.78 and 36.67 degrees Celsius, respectively) and found the heat "trying to the constitutions of Europeans."[46] The hottest month of the year, April, was considered also the unhealthiest by Dr. H. Campbell Highet, a fellow of the Royal Institute of Public Health and its principal medical officer.[47] A Swedish prince who traveled to the coronation ceremonies of King Prajadhipok reported that one day the temperature went up to 106 degrees Fahrenheit (41.1 degrees Celsius), but that "one gets used to anything, as the proverb says, and after a few days of fearful perspiration we were able to apply it to ourselves."[48]

It is not surprising, given the "fearful" attitudes of Europeans toward the climate in Bangkok, that air-conditioning became part of a larger discourse on climate and the civilizing mission of colonialism in the twentieth century. In his 1920 article "The Coldward Course of Progress," the sociologist S. Colum GilFillan, inspired by Ellsworth Huntington's 1916 book, *Civilization and Climate*, linked human achievement to cold climates. GilFillan argued that advances in culture pushed the leadership of world civilization farther north, into colder climes.[49] "Hot weather, by increasing the body's chemical action and hence its surplus energy, along with a bad emotional state, has been shown to increase obstreperousness, crime, suicide, assaults, insanity and revolutions," he wrote.[50] In short, native responses to colonialism could be blamed on the climatic conditions of the tropics rather than state violence and disenfranchising political, economic, and cultural policies.

Although this was a familiar colonial discourse, the difference was that now technology could repair this tropical malady. The public-health physician C. E. A. Winslow would play a central role in the success of air-conditioning by affirming the safety and desirability of mechanical cooling. "If the conclusions drawn by Prof. Ellsworth Huntington in his striking book are confirmed by future study, countries whose natural climates do not conform to the ideal he has worked out may find it possible to produce and maintain on an extensive scale those artificial conditions of coolness and changeableness which he finds necessary to stimulate the highest human efficiency," he wrote.[51]

Colonial officials were greatly interested in the possibilities of this new technology. In the Dutch colonial city of Bandung, in the Netherlands Indies, an institute for "technical hygiene and sanitation" was founded in 1935 that soon became primarily concerned with researching climate comfort and air-conditioning. Historian Rudolf Mrázek has pointed out that air-conditioning was an intrinsic component of modern living in the late-colonial Indies. At a 1938 conference in Bandung sponsored by the institute, cinemas were the only places frequented by natives that were considered for air-conditioning because it would bring the colony "closer to the European level."[52] In Hong Kong, C. A. Middleton-Smith, a professor of engineering at the University of Hong Kong, noted that the twentieth century "would be famous in history for the civilization of the tropics" and believed air-conditioning would make tropical colonies more healthy and prosperous.[53]

Indeed, the colonial discourse on modern living was very close to the concept of "civilization" that dominated late nineteenth- and early twentieth-century Siamese thought. The terms *siwilai* and *arayatham* were used to describe this ideal to which the nation aspired. Thongchai Winichakul argued that the quest for *siwilai* was an attempt by various aristocratic and bourgeois groups, including urban intellectuals, to attain and confirm the relative superiority of Siam, once a traditional imperial power in the region, in a new world order of modern nations.[54] It was a term used by both supporters of the absolute monarchy and its detractors to describe the ideal to which Siam aspired. To the anti-absolutists, the institution of the monarchy was a hindrance to becoming *siwilai*. On 27 December 1932, six months after the change in government, Prince Bhidayalongkorn, the head of the Royal Institute of Siam, gave a special lecture called "What Are the Conditions Called *Siwilai*?" The meanings of words like *siwilai*, taken from the English, and *arayatham*, taken from the Sanskrit, the prince asserted, were slippery, no matter how either pro- or anti-absolutists tried to use them.[55] The meaning of *arayatham* in the dictionary, he said, was "progress with good traditions," but what made something a tradition or good was a subject of debate.[56] He pointed out that the term was largely used as a tool for asserting one's superiority over others, as seen in World War I and in certain colonial contexts.[57] Bhidayalongkorn rejected cleanliness, clothing, and poverty as accurate measures of civilization, reasoning that even though Europeans bathed less than Thais, wore unhygienic clothing, and also experienced poverty, they were still considered more civilized. By the end of the speech, the prince remained unclear about what, exactly, *arayatham* meant, but he knew for sure that Siam wanted it because it was a tool for happiness, even if this quality remained elusive to countries and groups throughout the world.[58]

The Sala Chaloem Krung's architect, Mom Chao Samaichaloem Kridakon, used the word *araya*, or "civilized," in a way that attempted to reconcile an absolutist past with the technology of a "modern" present in keeping with the prince's definition of "progress with good traditions." In an undated article that was reprinted in his cremation volume, the architect wrote:

> The construction of large buildings in our country should receive the cooperation of the construction sector, the fine arts sector, and the archaeology sector in order to not create conflict between these sectors. Each sector should compromise for the good of aesthetics in the country. For example, the prang of Wat Arun is an ancient site and a site of artistic value. It gives a great deal of beauty to the country. If a modern building is built next to it, it will lessen the value of this artistic place a lot. We must find a way to leave the areas around ancient places wide enough to make these artistic places distinct. One shouldn't build anything to conceal them or build next to them. All civilized nations (arayaprathet) have taken on preservation acts like this, because they believe ancient sites and artistic sites are signs of civilization and archaeological value. We must not be subject to preservation restrictions to the point that it obstructs the development of the country. If something can be torn down, it should be torn down.[59]

This seemingly contradictory statement spoke to the paradoxical strategy of the Siamese Crown. Seeking to project themselves as a power on par with *siwilai* modern European states required not only projecting an autonomous national identity but also enacting an internal form of colonialism to compete with European imperial ambitions in the region.[60] In its twilight years, the Siamese Crown sought to project an architectural image of itself as *siwilai:* with both a modern outlook and a reinvention of its historical past as unique. Siam needed to progress and construct large new buildings, but it also needed to render distinct the older aspects of its culture by framing them with modern architecture. The theater Samaichaloem designed used materials like steel, concrete, and air-conditioning as not only a structural but also a conceptual frame that linked the symbolism of a mythical past with new construction technologies and in a building that could accommodate large audiences in modern comfort.

Although Prajadhipok did not attend the opening ceremony, he sent a proxy, Chao Phraya Siriphiphat (Mom Ratchawong Mun Darakon), to officiate.[61] After Siriphiphat anointed the main entrance, the committee of the theater switched on the electricity to open the curtain and revealed a portrait of the king projected on a screen as the orchestra struck up the "King's Anthem." The newspaper *Sri krung* reported that the crowd for the opening ceremony was so big that traffic stopped temporarily on the surrounding streets. The newspaper reported that the crowds stood silently both inside and outside the theater as the "King's Anthem" was played. After a light show, Samaichaloem got up and was applauded for his design. This was followed by the showing of a Tarzan movie, *The Dive of Death*.[62]

The opening night confirmed Samaichaloem's design intentions of creating a space meant to accommodate large crowds of people in comfort and safety under the auspices of the monarchy. An estimated two thousand people could be sheltered within the theater's four floors.[63] The importance of accommodating these large numbers of people in a modern environment is suggested by the foregrounding of crowd safety in the designs of Samaichaloem. The journal of the Association of Siamese Architects, *ASA*, noted with some satisfaction that the continuous series of double-hinged doors around the facade's ground floor allowed for the quick evacuation of large numbers of people in case of emergency.[64] As seen in both a drawing of the auditorium by Samaichaloem and an early photograph of the original auditorium, the steel structure allowed for the removal of load-bearing posts inside the auditorium (figures 6.5 and 6.6). For audiences, this opened up unobstructed views of not only the screen, but also one another and the symbolic ornamentation of the hall.

The steel framing allowed for the insertion of royal emblems that were also self-consciously updated to suggest an equivalent modern image of the monarchy as the patrons of the arts. The exterior of the theater was branded by two royal emblems: a *garuda* that hangs over the main entrance and three interlocking circles over the side entrances. The *garuda* that was originally made for the Sala Chaloem Krung was intended to have the characteristics of an American eagle, and a foreign artist was said to have designed it, although the artist's name does not appear on any documents.[65] The original was made of bronze and was stolen.[66] The one that graces the facade of the theater today is made of gold-painted teak and dates from 1971 (figure 6.7). The three interlocking circles are an abstraction of Prajadhipok's royal seal (figure 6.8).[67]

The three lights at the top of the facade are further allusions to the relationship between the monarchy and the heavens (figure 6.9). The perforated copper screens are images of the head of a demon, monkey, and hermit and

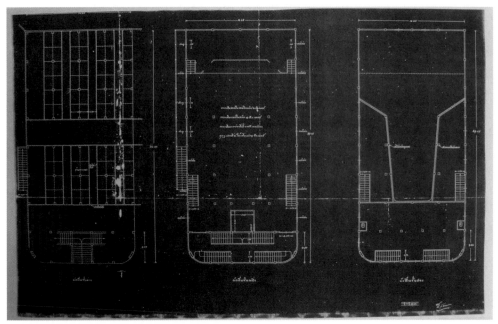

FIG. 6.5. Plan of the auditorium of the Sala Chaloem Krung, showing the steel-frame structure that allowed for an unobstructed view of the screen.

FIG. 6.6. Interior of the Sala Chaloem Krung auditorium. From Samaichaloem Kridakon, *Ngan satapathayakam mom chao samaichaloem kridakon* (The architectural work of Mom Chao Samaichaloem Kridakon) (Bangkok: Phrachan, 1967).

FIG. 6.7. A royal *garuda* guards the entrance to the Sala Chaloem Krung. Photo by author.

FIG. 6.8. An abstract version of King Prajadhipok's royal seal, the *phrasaengson,* above the entrance to the Sala Chaloem Krung. Photo by author.

FIG. 6.9. Perforated copper light screen of Hanuman, a key protagonist in the *Ramakian,* on the facade of the Sala Chaloem Krung. Photo by author.

were designed by Phrathewaphinimmit.[68] These are figures from the *Ramakian,* the Thai reworking of the Ramayana epic that chronicles the exploits of Rama, the mythological namesake of each monarch of the Chakri dynasty.[69]

The *Ramakian* can be understood as a text about statecraft and the fealty of members of the extended royal family (Phra Lak in the *Ramakian*) to the king (Phra Rama).[70] Its invocation at the Sala Chaloem Krung reinforced the historical relationship between politics and aesthetics. The legend of Nang Sida's abduction by Thotsakan and her subsequent rescue by Phra Rama existed in the region since before the thirteenth century and there is archaeological evidence in the ruins of Wat Phra Rama at Ayutthaya. Most written versions of the story were destroyed in the sacking of Ayutthaya and various remnants survived, but a complete Thai version of the story did not reappear until it was commissioned by King Phuttayotfa, the founder of Bangkok, in 1797. Phuttayotfa's version was written for *khon* performances and is the source of all major versions of the Thai story except one written later by Mongkut and another recension by Chulalongkorn. Vajiravudh wrote one as well, which differed from earlier dynastic versions since it was based on an English translation of the Sanskrit original.

Inside the theater, the relationship between the aesthetics of the *Ramakian* and modern politics is further suggested by the perforated copper screens of the three patron deities of the arts that were hung above the stage.[71] By the entrance to the stairs were more screens of Thai dancers, *devas*, and a four-faced image of Brahma (figure 6.10). On the mezzanine, next to a special lounge called the Hong Mekhla, were six perforated copper panels with images of Mekhla, the goddess of lightning and the seas. The goddess's name derives from the Pali words *maṇī* (jewel) and *mekhalā* (girdle) and conjures beauty out of the terrifying experience of lightnings and storms. The dedication of this special lounge to Mekhla points to the ways Samaichaloem's framing of the mythical past articulated the power of modern technologies like electricity as part of a much older, local narrative. It suggested the power of the monarchy to tame the forces of nature and modernity in order to transform them into a pleasurable aesthetic experience.

The Sala Chaloem Krung was intended as a site where a narrative that linked the modern world of steel framing, concrete, air-conditioning, and electricity to the mythical worlds of Rama, Sida, and Mekhla could be disseminated to a broad public. Ticket prices reflected the mass clientele the cinema hoped to draw. The lowest entry fee was 7 *satang* to sit in the row in front of the screen, but box seats were available for 40 *satang* for those who wanted to be secluded from the general public. Students got a special

FIG. 6.10. Perforated copper light screens of characters in the *Ramakian* in the lobby of the Sala Chaloem Krung. Photo by author.

discount: ten got in for the price of nine. Films were screened twice daily at first and then, due to growing demand, four times per day. On holidays, another screening was added.[72] Compared to the annual income of a rural farmer of the period, the price of the cheapest ticket was only marginally less than the price of the cheapest ticket in an ordinary theater during the preceding period.[73]

Accessible to a broad sector of the urban population, the Sala Chaloem Krung attracted audiences who were prone to distraction, albeit in a more refined manner. This is suggested by a passage in M. R. Nimitmongkol Navarat's *The Dreams of an Idealist,* a semiautobiographical utopian novel written in the period after the 1932 change in government:

> One evening while watching a Tarzan film starring Johnny Weissmuller at the Sala Chaloem Krung, Rung could no longer restrain his feelings for her. Perhaps because Somsuan was lovelier than ever, and perhaps, too, because of the alluring fragrance of her perfume, Rung took hold of her hand, tentatively touching the back of it at first, and then encouraged by the fact that she had not withdrawn it, holding it more firmly. She trembled like a young bird caught in a hunter's net, startled even though it was the net of love. He did not let go of her hand, which remained cold and limp in his until the lights went on. When the lights went off, he took her hand again. He had no idea of what the movie was about. Nor did she, as she later admitted. From that night on, they became lovers.[74]

In striking contrast to the letters written to Phaphayon Sayam Paliment about their experience of early timber-framed cinemas, Nimitmongkol describes a scene in which the scent of perfume and the furtive caress of innocent lovers have displaced the odor of feces and the jostling of beggars and thieves.[75]

Under the supervision of the Siamese-German United Cinema company between 1933 and 1936, the Sala Chaloem Krung spawned a number of other related cinemas in the city: the Sala Chaloem Nakhon, the Sala Chaloem Thani in Nang Loeng, and the Sala Chaloem Muang in Banglamphu. The original Sala Chaloem Krung went through several permutations after its opening. Although it was designed as a movie theater, the Sala Chaloem Krung was transformed briefly into a stage theater and enlarged during World War II when Hollywood imports were curtailed.[76] Because of its reputed structural strength, the theater was popular as a bomb shelter during this period as well.[77] After the end of the war, because Western films had not yet returned, local production of Thai films increased. Producers used the Sala Chaloem Krung as a stage to showcase their work, and the theater became known as the center of the Thai film industry, even earning the wishful moniker "the Hollywood of Thai cinema."[78]

The profits of the theater began to slow down in the late 1950s, due to the development of other movie palaces in different parts of the capital. There were plans to turn the Sala Chaloem Krung into a shopping center, but in the end it reverted to its previous use as a stage theater, this time featuring *khon* performances. In 1993, the newly formed Sala Chaloem Krung Monitat Company leased the land for thirty years for 106 million baht, renovated the appearance of the theater, and gave it a new name, the Sala Chaloem Krung Royal Theatre.[79] The transformation of the cinema into a *khon* theater suggests the success of Samaichaloem's strategy of framing "traditional" symbolic elements with modern technologies. It allows for contemporary performances of *khon* to take place on an unabashedly modern stage, with LED teleprompters explaining the intricacies of the narrative spectacle for audiences unfamiliar with the *Ramakian,* from which most of the performances are drawn. The theater's architecture has thus become an integral part of the theatrical narrative.

From its inception, the cinema was a place of radical uncertainty and sensory confusion. Early in its shadowy rooms, audiences groped, smelled, and listened to one another as images of a modern world flickered uncertainly on the screen. While the story of audience members fleeing the cinema during the screening of a Lumière brothers film of a locomotive approaching La Ciotat station has been largely debunked as an unsubstantiated myth, an 1896 poster advertising the film depicts the rails extending beyond the screen and into the cinema.[80] The image suggests that even at this early juncture in the history of the modern built environment, the architecture of the cinema was an integral part of the perceptual experience of the moving image. It joined multiple techniques of modernity that reshaped the perceptual sphere and produced a multisensory experience that transcended the purely visual ways human beings apprehended and understood their surroundings. In Bangkok, for example, the large auditorium of the Sala Chaloem Krung, which lacked visible supports, as well as its flat roof, appeared to defy gravity.[81] Likewise, the air-conditioned interior of the cinema was markedly different from the tropical climate. The "chilled water system" also suppressed the odors of the city's "stinking hordes," which early cinema audiences had found so unsettling, thus creating a perceptual break with the lived experience of the city. Early audiences at the Sala Chaloem Krung reported that just being able to experience the coolness, the elaborate decoration, the music, and the lighting once they entered the door of the cinema was itself worth the price of admission.[82]

As an exceptional, modern space within a growing city, the architecture of the Sala Chaloem Krung was an integral part of a process of "sensuous citizenship formation," in which citizens came to recognize one another as part of the same imagined community. The history of the Sala Chaloem Krung is a reminder that the use of air-conditioning and steel-frame construction in cities like Bangkok was not a universalizing process.[83] At the Sala Chaloem Krung, technologies like air-conditioning and materials like steel and concrete took on different sociocultural meanings and became integrated in different spatial and temporal systems than in Western Europe and the United States. The Sala Chaloem Krung, then, can be understood as a new unfolding of older narratives like the *Ramakian*. In the same way that King Phuttayotfa rewrote the Indic narrative as a *khon* drama for the nascent Siamese court, the Sala Chaloem Krung brought the characters of this classic tale of statecraft into contact with the narratives of modernity. They were deployed along with the materials and technologies of the twentieth century in order to frame the sensorial experience of modernity for urban audiences who were becoming cognizant of their political power as citizens.

CHAPTER SEVEN

CONCRETOPIA

Material and Hierarchy in the Age of *Sri Ariya*

Immediately after the overthrow of the absolute monarchy in 1932, the People's Party boldly declared, "The time has ended when those of royal blood farm on the backs of the people. The things which everyone desires, the greatest happiness and progress which are called 'sri ariya,' will arise for everyone."[1] As examined in chapter 5, the term *sri ariya*, or *sri ariya metteya*, referred to the era of the next incarnation of the Buddha, Metteya (Skt. Maitreya). The new utopian political narrative, in which Siam had finally entered a future era of abundance and equality, needed to be articulated not only in policy but also in the built environment. Modern institutions like public universities and a supreme court as well as older ones like Buddhist monastic complexes sought to announce a new society in which commoners (*samanchon*) were—at least symbolically—the equals of royalty. These new institutions were fashioned largely out of steel-reinforced concrete and sought to translate the new values of the period into architectural form. Formulating the vocabulary of this new architecture of *samanchon* was not a unidirectional ideological operation in which political concepts were rendered into symbols; the institutional architecture was also shaped by the material properties of concrete and the autarkic economic policies of the period.

The use of concrete in Siam had been a nationalist endeavor since the inception of the Siam Cement Company as a royal enterprise in 1913. It was stimulated, in part, by concrete's associations with modernity as well as the continued control of timber by foreign logging companies.[2] While concrete allowed for the rapid construction of new buildings, often at a monumental scale, and allowed the monarchy to develop a stable economic base, it could not easily sustain the sumptuary code that had long governed royal and religious architecture. This code, or *tananusakdi nai thang sathapathayakam*, made Siamese social and political hierarchies legible within the built environment and was produced largely in timber, plaster, and masonry. For example, the walls surrounding the Grand Palace of the king were allowed to have ramparts (*choeng thoen* or *tai tia*) and bastions (*bai pom* or *bai pang*), whereas those of the viceroy's Front Palace could not. The homes of nobles were permitted to have elaborate finials, or *cho fa* (sky tassels), adorning their roofs, while those of commoners, even those of titled bureaucrats, had to make do with less elaborate upturned ends on the barge boards of the gable end, known as *ngao pan lom* (figure 7.1).

Because early twentieth-century concrete did not immediately lend itself to many of these ornamental flourishes, it was used primarily for commercial and residential buildings during the absolutist period. It was not until after 1932, when a new political order was announced, that concrete was deployed widely for government buildings and monuments and a new design language needed to be formulated.[3] The paradox of Thai architects reformatting the hierarchies of the past in the interests of a new civil society developed out of three contradictions that had come to a head in Thai society by the mid-twentieth century. The first of these was Siam's

FIG. 7.1. *Cho fa* finials on the roof of Wat Phra Sri Rachanaddaram, Bangkok. Photo by author.

MATERIALS

assertion of itself as a sovereign nation that required a projection of itself as a modern state with a sovereign historical past that could be traced back to earlier regional polities through an invented hieratic lineage. Another was the simultaneous birth of democratic government and military dictatorship in 1932, when the absolute monarchy was overthrown by a coalition of civilian and military leaders. The third was the aesthetic relationship between the universal and the local. Architects, builders, and patrons had long consumed foreign influences as exotic commodities, but by the 1930s, they sought to place their built works within a larger international discourse while retaining national characteristics. Architecture was an ideal medium for working out these paradoxes, since its very success depends on reconciling seemingly contradictory material characteristics. In the hands of an accomplished architect, for example, extremely heavy materials like steel and concrete can be made to appear almost as if they are floating.

The new paradoxical architectural vocabulary drew on historical regional forms like the *prang,* the towerlike spire that has its origins in Angkor, and *chedi,* the reliquary that can be traced back to the stupa of Vedic South Asia, and used them to amalgamate ecclesiastical, political, and commercial typologies and programs.[4] By bringing together both sacred and profane meanings, the new architectural vocabulary also resulted in the production of new forms of symbolic monument and public space, which, while announcing the important role of commoners in the political life of the nation, also created a troubling affinity between utopianism and militarism. During this period, concrete became a metaphor for the resilience of the masses in making sacrifices for the nation-state.

PHRA SRI ARIYA

The concept of *sri ariya* is said to have derived from the *Anagatavamsa* (The Chronicle to Be), an extra- or post-canonical Pali sutta that reportedly originated in the twelfth century CE. It described the capital of the new society as a city with beautiful lotus ponds, full of fragrant, clear water. The ponds would be accessible to the people at all times. Seven rows of palm trees and walls of seven colors, made of jewels, would surround the city. In squares at the gates of the city, there would be shining wishing trees: one blue, one yellow, one red, and one white.[5]

However, the coming of *sri ariya* is more widely known in Thailand through illustrated manuscripts and folklore that recount the monk Phra Malai's journeys to the lower hells and the upper heavens of the realm of sensual desire or *kammaphum.* Toward the end of his journeys, Phra Malai traveled to the Tayatimsa or Dusit heaven to worship the hair relic of the

Buddha in the Chulamani Chedi, a heavenly stupa believed to contain a relic of the Buddha. There he encountered the bodhisattva Metteya, who had descended from his abode in the Dusit heaven to worship the relic (figure 7.2). Metteya informed Phra Malai that Buddhism would deteriorate five thousand years after the Sakyamuni Buddha's teachings had been on earth. Human nature would degenerate, both physically and morally, and the life span would decrease to ten years. Incest, promiscuity, chaos, and violence would be commonplace. A cataclysmic war would occur in which almost everyone would die save for a handful of wise people who had retreated to the forest to hide in caves. After seven days, they would emerge and create a new society, or *sri ariya*, based on mutual goodwill and a commitment to morality. Following a period of intense rainfall, the earth would flourish with vegetation and villages would be repopulated. The surface of the earth would become as smooth as a drumhead, rice would husk itself, people would be handsome and without physical disabilities, spouses would be faithful to one another, and all beings would live in harmony. At this time, Metteya would be born in the human realm and attain enlightenment.[6]

The story of Phra Malai might be understood as one of social promise, in that it acknowledges human suffering in the present while gesturing toward the future possibility of a new felicitous moral order.[7] Chapter 5 of this volume revealed the utopian ideals that informed the intellectual formation of civilian leaders of the People's Party like Pridi Phanomyong in Paris.[8] The description of *sri ariya* in the Phra Malai tale gave the People's Party a base vision of popular futurity from which to suggest that after 1932 a complete overturning of society had occurred and that a new moral era could emerge.

FIG. 7.2. Manuscript illustration of *Phra Malai* (1868) depicting Phra Malai conversing with Indra in front of the Culamaniya Cetiya (left) and Metteya descending with entourage from the Tavatimsa heaven (right). Or 6630, fol. 56, British Library.

Not long after the People's Party seized power, they set about building the institutions of this new civic society. For example, the country's first institution of higher learning open to commoners, known today as Thammasat University, was built at the edge of the royal parade ground, Sanam Luang. A supreme court, designed by Sarot Sukhyang, was built on the opposite side of the field. The Democracy Monument and the Victory Monument not only symbolized the values of the new era but also created new public spaces and thoroughfares. Steel-reinforced concrete was the material of choice for these new buildings for two primary reasons: it was economically expedient—it allowed for rapid construction that did not require skilled labor and it contributed to the national economy since it was produced by a state-owned company—and it had a modern appearance.

THE SIAM CEMENT COMPANY

The primary manufacturer of concrete in Siam was the Siam Cement Company. Established by royal decree of King Vajiravudh in 1913, the company played an instrumental role in the creation of a modern image for the Thai monarchy and, after 1932, the Thai state.[9] It also produced an important economic base for both and helped to secure a steady source of income while limiting the economic influence of primarily Chinese contractors that had emerged during the modern divisions of labor in the building trades. Vajiravudh and his father, Chulalongkorn, were familiar with the uses of ferroconcrete in European architecture and its associations with modernity through their own travels and the country's participation in international exhibitions.[10] Writing in the Siam Cement Company's fifty-year-anniversary commemorative publication, former prime minister Kukrit Pramoj noted that during the era of colonialism the monarchy sought to give the country the appearance of a Western nation. "No complete change was contemplated, however—that would have been ridiculous—but just enough to impress on the *farangs* that the Thai people were not barbaric, that they were indeed quite 'civilized' and deserved to be left alone."[11] Kukrit's observations are in keeping with the attitudes of King Chulalongkorn and his court, which, as noted in earlier chapters, employed European architects and engineers and embraced European revival styles (like the Second Empire revival of the Baroque and the Gothic revival in the collection of throne halls at the royal summer retreat in Bang Pa-in). However, concrete was not initially deployed in high-profile buildings like palaces and royally patronized monastic complexes, but in the modest shop houses (*hong thaew*) that lined the new roads built through the areas of Bangkok that had been predominantly settled by migrants from the south China coast.

Largely Cantonese-speaking workers were employed in the construction of most of Bangkok's early shop houses.[12] Between 1892 and 1932, the Privy Purse Bureau was the largest owner of shop houses, which were constructed along both sides of newly cut roads. The rapid construction of shop houses was closely related to land investment on the part of the Privy Purse Bureau and was undertaken along major roads in migrant-dominated districts like Sampheng, as well as Phahurat, Charoen Krung, and Fuangna.[13] The Siam Cement Company was able to capitalize on this surge in development. To finance the company initially, Vajiravudh decreed that the Privy Purse buy one-third of its shares, although its actual investment in the company was much larger. By the twenty-first century, the Crown Property Bureau, which emerged out of the Privy Purse Bureau, remained the largest shareholder in the Siam Cement Company.[14]

Initial shares of the company were officially distributed among the Privy Purse Bureau, Chao Phraya Yommarat (Pan Sukhum), and the Danish naval commander, W. L. Grut. Grut invested one-third of the initial capital for subsequent redistribution among the public. He became the second chairman of the board of directors, a position he held until the early years of World War II. Chao Phraya Yommarat's shares were purchased with money loaned to him from the Privy Purse Bureau. This was likely to satisfy some of the company's earliest regulations that three-quarters of its shares were owned by Siamese nationals. However, for the first sixty-one years, Siam Cement was managed by Danish general managers, and it was not until 1974 that the company had its first Thai general manager.[15] Foreign involvement in the company, notably Danish, was strong from the beginning, with the Danes supplying much of the machinery and training for the company's factory in Bang Sue. Denmark was one of several monarchies that the Siamese court sought to develop political and economic relations with throughout the twentieth century. Economic historian Porphant Ouyyanont has noted that this was an attempt on the part of the Siamese Crown to dilute the growing influence of the British or the French in the region.[16]

The importance of the company in helping secure not only permanent built works but also stability for the institution of the monarchy in a changing world economy is suggested by a letter written on 8 April 1919 to Vajiravudh by Chao Phraya Yommarat. A commoner who was a minister under both Vajiravudh and his father, Chulalongkorn, Chao Phraya Yommarat was commissioned by the former to establish the Siam Cement Company. His letter points to two important contributions the company made to the social order. It provided continuity in social relations, as evidenced by Chao Phraya Yommarat's observation that the company would inspire his progeny to work for the state. It also offered an opportunity for civil servants in the government bureaucracy to profit from changes in Bangkok's rapidly expanding construction industry.

> Everyone knows that without royal patronage, the establishment of the Siam Cement Company would have been impossible. On my part, Your Majesty must have realized how I have gone through much suffering and anxiety to work for its establishment. Because of Your Majesty's might and augustness and the merit of my loyalty and gratitude to Your Majesty, this company has prospered. I myself have received the benefits from this prosperity. It has given me encouragement and has facilitated my work in the royal service and my maintenance of the honour Your Majesty have bestowed on me. If this situation continues, it will also provide encouragement for my sons to serve Your Majesty in the civil service for another generation. As a matter of fact, if anyone in the government service depends on salary alone and has no other legitimate sources of income, he cannot fully maintain his honour, especially if he is a high-ranking official. And if he is a minor official with small salary, we will suffer more. Therefore, my wife, my children and I feel that we owe Your Majesty a great debt of gratitude and we always prostrate before your Majesty. We felt that Your Majesty not only has been kind to pay us the salaries, but also has given your support by providing us with a special means of earning our living. Your Majesty's kindness is more than that of our parents. I always think of repaying, in due course, all the 220,000 baht principal which is the money of the Privy Purse Your Majesty has kindly loaned me to buy cement shares.[17]

Concrete was an ideal material for the new shop houses. It allowed for fast construction and, as a result, fast rentals. The new structures also gave migrant-dominated parts of the city like Sampheng and Bangrak a standardized appearance of permanence. The shop house was a popular regional typology and an example of the kind of architecture that emerged in the concession areas that were created by the unequal treaties made between European powers and China during the nineteenth century. It defined most of the southern Chinese port cities as well as the colonial ports of Southeast Asia that were heavily populated by Chinese migrants, such as Singapore, Penang, and Batavia. Bangkok's early shop houses shared many of the same characteristics as these examples of comprador architecture in the region. Comprador houses, offices, and godowns combined the symmetry of classical Greek architecture and forms like the arch, pilaster, and colonnade with Chinese roofing, building materials, and construction techniques. The historian David Kohl has speculated that Chinese emigrants passing through these treaty ports may have had an influence on later architectural practices in the region.[18]

The appearance of Bangkok as a treaty port, however, did not complement Vajiravudh's plans to create a sovereign national community. A new architectural vocabulary developed in the following years that could both make use of ferroconcrete and impart a new identity to Bangkok as the capital of a nation that did not equate modernity with the West. Over the course of the next fifty years, the state sought to simultaneously destabilize independent Chinese construction labor and nationalize the Thai economy. It did this by enacting policies that favored non-Chinese companies and the development of an architectural aesthetic that sought to both distance itself from an imitative Eurocentric modernism and eliminate all traces of Chinese modernity.

As concrete became increasingly important for the construction of government buildings and monuments after 1932, its promotion took on increasingly nationalist tones. While up until the 1930s, European companies retained exclusive licenses to timber concessions in the two-thirds of Siam that were covered with forest, these were revoked after the 1932 change in government and concessions were issued to Thai companies.[19] In spite of this, concrete became the preferred idiom of nation building during the constitutionalist period. After the 1932 change in government, the assets of the Siam Cement Company were nationalized and transferred to the Crown Property Bureau. Annual sales of concrete rose significantly, from 50,000 baht to more than 130,000 baht between 1935 and 1940.[20] Part of this was due to the permanent and economic qualities of ferroconcrete construction, but another part had to do with the material's rhetorical deployment during the period. This deployment took two forms. The state appealed to nationalist biases to promote concrete as a nationally produced material, and it further developed a streamlined architectural aesthetic that underscored a new political era of democracy.

During the Second World War, companies in the construction industry like Siam Cement underscored their relationship to the nation-state and reaffirmed their relevance to the project of nation building. Nationalism, in short, became a convenient way of selling materials, services, and technologies. A memo circulated to the Architecture Division of the Fine Arts Department during this period is indicative of this approach. Issued by the Thai Niyom Company, a company established in 1939 that conducted all import and export transactions in connection with state enterprises and also set up a network to facilitate the marketing of state products within Thailand, the memo made explicit the need for government departments to cooperate with the corporation as a matter of nationalism.[21] Although the company's prices were higher than those of Chinese-owned companies, the Thai Niyom Company guaranteed their quality in ways their competitors did not.[22] The memo appealed to the various government bureaus doing business with Chinese-owned companies by giving two examples of why it made better business sense to buy higher-priced goods from the Thai Niyom Company.[23]

> The first example, when fulfilling a bid for an order from the government, suppose the market price of the goods that are being bid on is four baht per unit, but some non-Thais dare to give a bid of only 3.80 baht. Upon cursory examination, we can see that they must lose .20 satang on each unit and that included other expenses. But in the end, they still make a profit and can do it. This is because they replace one good for the other or lower the quality of the goods, or they send goods that have a value of only 3.40 baht instead. So, even if they send something that is priced .20 satang lower, they will still have a profit of another .20 satang. Or there is another method: if there is a committee or staff that is strict about the real quality of goods, lessen the amount of goods that they actually send. For instance, only 80% of goods are really sent, but they submit a receipt for delivery of 100% of the goods. This isn't to condemn the committees that the government has established, but because of the enormous amount of work that's left in their hands, they might not be able to look after everything.[24]

In this way, the writers of the memo neatly acknowledged widespread corruption in the construction industries while placing the responsibility for these practices on the shoulders of Chinese-owned companies. In the language of the memo, the Thai civil servants who ostensibly engaged in these practices were free of any responsibility. The racialized nature of the memo becomes even more clear as the memo continues.

> The second example is a very important example of how these companies erode Thai cultural traditions like merit-making, or ordination, or cremation. Those non-Thai peoples make the *pha trai khrueng thon* [the undergarment that monks wear to bathe] which have no use on their own [as they are part of a set of three robes that are usually offered to monks by laymen] and sell them at a cheap price for consumers to take to alms-giving ceremonies. The buyer bought it to help the host, the host received it and offered it to the monks, the monks receive the offering and can't use it because there are only half the robes. It's as if we Thai people are cheating ourselves because all three parties [the consumer, the host, and the monks] didn't get any benefit from this exchange. But in the end, the good results and profit fall into the hands of only the non-Thai peoples.[25]

The company argued that this would contribute to the decline of Buddhism in the country and was the reason it should have a monopoly on selling all kinds of military and consumer goods as well as building factories, mills, and canneries for the government. The memo goes on to admit that some of its products during the Second World War may have been poorly made for a short period of time because of war shortages, but that this problem had been corrected at the time the memo was issued. The memo appealed to the nationalist sentiment of its potential clients to overlook the company's own inconsistencies in quality in favor of the higher good of the nation and the race. In fact, during the Second World War, material shortages forced the company to suspend manufacture of its higher-quality Elephant brand for short periods.[26] The importance of concrete during this period was not only for economic reasons. It also allowed the government to standardize a nationalist architecture that could be built in diverse locations throughout the country without being subject to the idiosyncrasies of regional labor, craft, or aesthetics.

ARCHITECTURAL STANDARDIZATION: A STATE MANUAL FOR CONCRETE ARCHITECTURE

While the publication of Prince Wachirayan's *Baeb nawakam* in 1919, discussed in chapter 3, sought to standardize central regional forms as a national idiom, it also simplified their construction. However, the impact the *Baeb nawakam* had on architectural production during the early twentieth century is difficult to gauge, as it was not widely published. The idea of a monastic architectural manual was revived in 1940 by the government of Field Marshal Phibun Songkhram. He ordered the Artisan Division in the Department of Fine Arts under the direction of People's Party ideologue Luang Wichit Wathakan and the architect Phra Phromphichit to delineate the standard drawings for ordination halls. As with the *Baeb nawakam*, the standard plans drew on simplified versions of central regional monastic complexes, but they became more streamlined (figure 7.3). Local contexts were abandoned in favor of a classification system that pragmatically suited the national economy: small-, intermediate-, and large-scale plans were available to copy depending on the financial situation of each monastic complex. These plans were distributed more widely than the *Baeb nawakam*, thanks to a national network of ecclesiastical officers and abbots under the auspices of the Ministry of Public Instruction.

The dissemination of a single new national blueprint for monastic architecture was accompanied by new bureaucratic rules concerning permission to build. Local abbots were more inclined to replicate royal monastic complexes in Bangkok rather than use local architectural qualities because it was easier to get permission to build them.[27] In many ways, this contributed to the decline of the local character of Buddhist monastic architecture and led to homogenous construction throughout Thailand. These changes were not merely cosmetic but were part of a larger attempt on the part of the new state to transform the landscape of potency and popularity, turning popular attention away from charismatic rural monks and their monastic complexes, to the centralized authority of the state sangha and its wat.

Phra Phromphichit's manual continued the project of the *Baeb nawakam*. Just as Prince Wachirayan's manual had framed "traditional" forms as disappearing in the face of cheap Chinese labor, Phra Phromphichit's manual considered an imagined dynastic past in need of preservation. Phra Phromphichit wrote that his impetus for creating a standardized manual of Buddhist architecture was that "if I should not share my knowledge with others to the benefit of my country and my nation, I too should be, like the ancients, letting my knowledge die with me."[28] That such forms had persisted in the twenty-one years since the *Baeb nawakam*'s publication suggests that this may not have been much cause for alarm. What seems more likely is that with the growth of concrete production, deploying the new material in the monastic context presented challenges for architects and builders, particularly for re-creating the refined ornamentation of "traditional" forms that had originally been made out of wood or plaster.

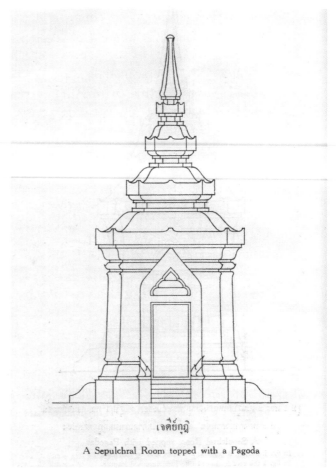

เจดีย์กุฎิ

A Sepulchral Room topped with a Pagoda

FIG. 7.3. Phra Phromphichit, sepulchral room topped with a pagoda, from *Phutta silpasathapatayakam phak ton,* a manual produced by the Department of Fine Arts in 1940. Department of Fine Arts, Thailand.

THE SAWASDISOPHA GATE AND THE HIERARCHIES OF THE *PRANG*

Phra Phromphichit sought to imbue the modern material of ferroconcrete with national characteristics that could be identified as "Thai," but he drew on older regional forms to do so. His Sawasdisopha gate (1936) at the Grand Palace is hailed as a landmark design by historians of Thai architecture because it weds the "modern" with the "traditional" (figure 7.4).[29] Although built during the reign of Phuttayotfa, the plaster and masonry gate was in serious disrepair by the twentieth century, and Phra Phromphichit renovated it using concrete. Situated strategically across from the Ministry of Defense and adjacent to the Phadetdatsakorn bastion, it marks the entrance to the Chapel of the Emerald Buddha within the Grand Palace complex. As

FIG. 7.4. Phra Phromphichit, the Sawasdisopha gate at the Grand Palace, Bangkok, 1936. Photo by author.

such, it connected both sacred and political realms within the city. The *prang* on the top of the gate consists of seven receding terraces topped by a four-tiered spire, or *yod*, and crowned with an iron trident. The form has its origins in Khmer architecture, where it was constructed largely out of laterite or laterite and masonry.[30] Laterite could be sculpted when wet and allowed craftsmen to weave together courses into redented blocks, creating a chiaroscuro effect that made the *prang* appear as if it were a dynamic, rather than sedentary form.[31] Phra Phromphichit's achieved the same redentation using concrete.

The *prang* was used by the Chakri monarchs as a kind of monument to mark the site of important Buddha images as well as the images of former kings. However, it wasn't used to mark the spaces living royalty inhabited.[32] During the reign of King Nangklao, Chinese artisans decorated the *prang* of monastic complexes like Wat Arun and Wat Pho using a technique of gluing ceramic shards around metal armatures known as *jian nian* 剪黏 (figure 7.5). The foreign technique was subordinated to the form of the *prang* in a clear hierarchical relationship. In the Sawasdisopha gate, Phra Phromphichit eschewed any such decoration in a clear articulation of the redented forms of the *prang*. The terraces of the Sawasdisopha gate might be understood as symbolic representations of the realm of human beings at the base and the six ascending upper realms of the *kammaphum,* or realm of sensual desire. The *yod* symbolized mastery of these forms and the four levels of the *rupaphum,* or realm of form. At the Grand Palace, the Sawasdisopha gate is well integrated into the existing walls of the palace, but its squat geometrical lines differ markedly from earlier gates.

ANUSAWARI THAI: A *PRANG* HONORING THE SACRALIZED STATE

The fusion of religious and political ideas in Phra Phromphichit's Sawasdisopha gate stimulated speculation about the possibilities of a concrete architecture that could embody the new constitutionalist state's ambitions to create a modern, democratic nation. Architects who had operated under the absolute monarchy were pressed into service by the Department of Fine Arts to create a nationalist vocabulary that eschewed the royal symbolism of the absolutist past but asserted the sovereign identity of the nation. An unintended consequence of their experiments was the production of an architecture that sacralized the nation. In 1939, the director of the Department of Fine Arts under the direction of Luang Wichit Wathakan issued a memo calling for the construction of a new monument to Thai sovereignty that celebrated the new regime's values of democracy and progress while

FIG. 7.5. The Phra Maha Chedi Song Sri Suriyothai at Wat Phra Chetuphon (Wat Pho), Bangkok, ca. 1859. Photo by author.

enshrining the continuous historical values of the country's imagined past. Thai Monument (Anusawari Thai) was to be built at Pak Nam, the seaport where the Chao Phraya River empties into the Gulf of Siam. Three designs for the monument were drawn up by Phra Phromphichit. Two were in the shape of a *prang* (figures 7.6 and 7.8), while the third placed an elongated, upward-sloping Lao spire at the center (figure 7.7). The more elaborate of the designs (figure 7.8) was to be a concrete monument to secular political power, with an interior that housed a hotel, an economic museum, a dance hall, a restaurant, and a conference center, surrounded by a botanical garden.[33] Wichit sought to make the monument the most important monument not only in Thailand, but also in the world. It was to be one hundred meters high. The base was square and each side was to be one hundred meters in length. The lower floor was ringed by a gallery that was to be an economic museum. "Foreigners who came to see it would feel immediately how much abundance our country has." The first floor was a restaurant / dance hall / theater. The second and third floors were hotels. The fourth floor was a conference room. Formally, the composition consists of two redented squares nestled within each other and surrounding a multitiered redented octagonal tower that supports a square cella.

Wichit wrote:

If this Thai monument is built it will not only be the most important permanent monument in Thailand but can be "One of the Wonders of the World," which can show off the history of Thai architecture to the world. We still don't have people or royalty who can do this, but if we build this monument in our time it will honor us eternally. King Rama VI (the late king) invested five million to build the Ananta Samakhom Throne Hall. It

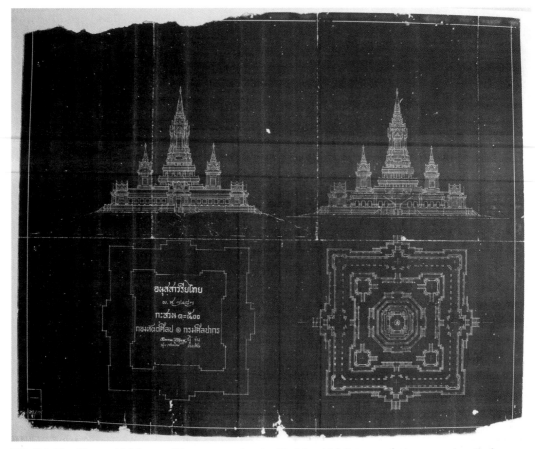

FIG. 7.6. Phra Phromphichit, one of three proposals submitted, in which the *prang* features prominently, for Anusawari Thai (Thai Monument), an unrealized project of the Department of Fine Arts under Luang Wichit Wathakan. National Archives of Thailand.

didn't do anything to honor the country at all. This monument, however, will honor the country and us greatly.[34]

Wichit tied the monarchy's neglect of its duties to the nation directly to what he saw as the failure of the Ananta Samakhom Throne Hall to serve as a convincing monument to Siam's greatness. The Ananta Samakhom Throne Hall was initially commissioned by King Rama V and designed by Mario Tamagno in 1908 as a throne hall in Dusit Palace. It was intended as a monument to the modernizing impulses of the Siamese monarchy. Construction was not completed until 1915. Implicit within Wichit's critique of the hall is a critique of the monarchy's emulation of "Western" architectural forms as the sine qua non of modernity. The proposed Thai monument would address that by impressing modern materials like concrete into a hierarchy that privileged distinctly "Thai" forms like the *prang*.

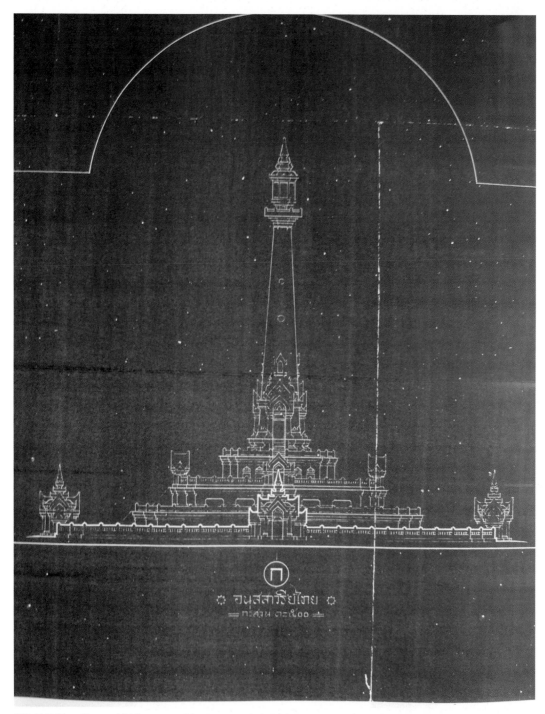

FIG. 7.7. Phra Phromphichit, proposal for Anusawari Thai (Thai Monument), in which the central form is an elongated Lao *that,* crowned by a lighthouse in the form of a sepulchral chamber. National Archives of Thailand.

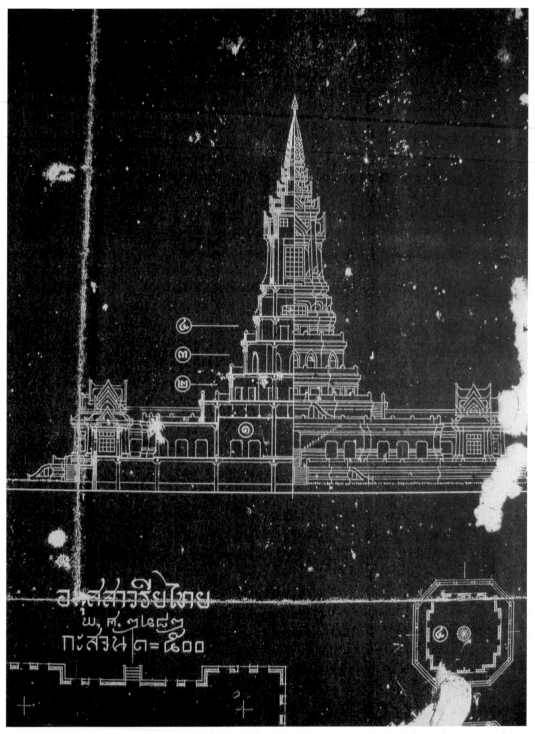

FIG. 7.8. Phra Phromphichit, third proposal for Anusawari Thai (Thai Monument), which shows the location of the dance hall, restaurant, museum, and conference center within the monument. National Archives of Thailand.

Phra Phromphichit's conflation of commercial and political programs within a religious typology was indicative of a new kind of monumentality that developed in Siamese architecture after 1932. While earlier monuments to political power had incorporated religious forms, the new approach to monumentality represented by the plans for Anusawari Thai sought to both align the nation with the religious forms of its imagined past and incorporate a racialized national public into its aesthetic order.

With a budget that was over 2.5 million baht, Anusawari Thai was never realized, likely because of material shortages during the Second World War that interfered with the building of other structures. However, Wichit's memo and Phra Phromphichit's drawings demonstrate that concrete construction technologies stimulated ideas about the scale at which the new regime could build. While monastic complexes in Thailand's central plains never achieved the monumental scale of the temples of Angkor, concrete offered, at least in theory, a means to build at a larger scale. This new scale also permitted older ecclesiastical typologies to accommodate new mass political and commercial programs. Anusawari Thai anticipates the fusion of temple and hotel architecture that dots the contemporary urban landscape of Bangkok.

MONUMENTS TO DEMOCRACY AND DICTATORSHIP

Although a form that is historically associated with Khmer polities centered around Angkor, the *prang* has been used consistently throughout the history of architecture in Thailand. Its deployment in the proposed Anusawari Thai as a symbol of the new Thailand took place amid the government's intensified irredentist claims. Wichit emerged as the intellectual leader of the movement to recover the territories Siam had "lost" to France's Lao and Cambodian colonies.[35] He built on long-standing sentiments among certain political sectors in Siam that saw France's Cambodian protectorate as being historically a part of Siam.[36] In Wichit's 1937 musical, *Ratchamanu*, about a military commander who was reported to have been instrumental in suppressing Khmer attempts to overthrow King Naresuan in sixteenth-century Ayutthaya, the eponymous protagonist reminds his soldiers that the Khmers are "Thais like us! . . . All of us on the Golden Peninsula are the same . . . [but remember] the Siamese Thais [the Thais from Siam proper] are the elder brothers."[37] Wichit noted in the introduction to a printed version of the play that, using principles employed by historians to determine race, "such as the shape of the face and skull, the type of food eaten, common diseases, indigenous literature, music and song . . . it is clear that the Khmers of the present day are Thai."[38]

In the final chapter of the book *Thailand's Case,* Wichit uses a number of European ethnographic and anthropological sources to support his claim for a Thai race. This race includes the Cambodians, a "new" race distinct from the old Khmer race because they have 90 percent Thai blood.[39] Even the Chinese have Thai blood, and he uses a 1923 English source to support this.[40] In a later play, *Chaoying Saenwi,* he made similar claims about the racial relationship between the Shan in northern British Burma and the Thai in Siam.[41] But perhaps the clearest articulation of Wichit's views on race came in a newspaper article in which he extolled the racial ideology of German minister of propaganda Joseph Goebbels, which divided the world on the basis of "race, language, and culture" and pointed to Germany's Anschluss of Austria as an example of how this ideology could achieve lasting peace for Thailand.[42]

Wichit succeeded in mobilizing large numbers of people into the streets to demonstrate their allegiance to the nation and the irredentist cause in October and November 1940. These public spectacles purported to draw on citizens from all sectors of Thai society, including university students, workers, merchants, civil servants, and members of the Chinese and Muslim communities. Members of the aristocracy and bureaucratic bourgeoisie were also motivated. Barmé points out that the Royal Palace Bureau called on their employees to donate 10 percent of their royal annual salary to the minister of defense for the purchase of arms. Given the estrangement between the monarchy and the constitutionalist government, this indicates the extent to which Wichit's campaign of fostering a racially based understanding of national belonging was successful. Skirmishes ensued and escalated in January 1941. The Thai army advanced into western Cambodia, but the Thai navy was defeated off the coast of Sichang Island, resulting in the loss of more than eight hundred lives. At the end of January, negotiations in Tokyo eventually yielded a compromise agreement whereby the French returned two enclaves opposite Luang Prabang and Pakse and the province of Battambang and parts of Siem Reap and Kompong Thom Provinces.[43] The Thai government paid France an indemnity of approximately 1 million pounds sterling and accepted the demilitarization of the Thai-Indochina border. The Thai part of Siem Reap was renamed Phibun Songkhram Province, after the prime minister, and a monument commemorating Thailand's "victory" was designed by Mom Luang Pum Malakun and erected in Bangkok on 24 June 1942 (figure 7.9). A stark obelisk surrounded at its base by sculptures representing each division of Thailand's armed forces, Anusawari Chai Samon Phum (Victory Monument) was said to have been modeled after the bayonet of a soldier's gun. In keeping with government policy, the monument was completed using only materials that had been manufactured in Thailand.[44] This purity of construction was underscored in the rhetorical deployment of the monument as a victory of racialized national community. Like the cession of Indochina's Cambodian provinces, it was largely a paper victory. Khmer, Lao, and Malay members of this community were hierarchically subsumed into the category of Thai under the central Thai.

THE CONCRETE MASSES

The search to reform the symbolist ornamentation of the past informed the construction of the Victory Monument and the Democracy Monument, designed by Jitrasen Miw Aphaiwong and Silpa Bhirasri (né Corrado Feroci) and erected in 1939 (figure 7.10). While nineteenth- and early twentieth-century monuments had used the figure of the king's body as the focal point, the new monuments of the People's Party reimagined this

FIG. 7.9. Victory Monument, designed by Pum Malakun and erected in 1942 commemorated the 1941 "victory" of Thailand over France that resulted in the loss of more than eight hundred Thai lives. Photo by author.

hierarchy. Abstract symbolic forms like the soldier's bayonet or the enshrined constitution along with an idealized form of the commoner's body achieved prominence during this period, replacing the body of the king as the focus of veneration. Although state ideologues extolled these new forms as the representation of a new ideal of equality and democracy, they lent themselves easily to the celebration of virility and imperialism. The durability and strength of concrete became symbolic of the idealized character of the masses as Siam aligned itself with the Axis powers during World War II. The cultural tendency of the period celebrated war and identified the family unit with the nation-state.

A new movement in sculpture was spearheaded by Silpa Bhirasri, who was head of the newly formed Department of Fine Arts under Luang Wichit Wathakan. Silpa sculpted the figures on the base of Victory Monument but considered the monument itself unsuccessful and referred to it at the time of its completion as "the Victory of Embarrassment."[45] Art historian

FIG. 7.10. Jitrasen Miw Aphaiwong and Silpa Bhirasri, Democracy Monument (Anusawari Prachathipatai), Bangkok, 1939. Photo by author.

Apinan Poshyananda considered this evidence of a "half-hearted and unresolved attempt to be modern through the combination of abstract form (the shaft of the sword) and realism (the depiction of the war heroes)."[46] If measured against developments in Thai architecture, however, the relationship between symbolism and realism suggests something else: representations of the human body and political power during this period sought to distance themselves from prior associations with the monarchy and its values. Yet, the new monuments of the constitutionalist period sought the same aura as those of the absolutist period. They were not merely symbols but living embodiments of political power.

In "Human Revolution," a lecture delivered at the Ministry of Defense Club on 15 November 1939, Wichit argued that the history of Thai culture was rooted in the lionization of the weak, slender bodies of aristocrats who had never worked.

> The literary story of the Ramakian that we have critically admired is a thing that has influenced and changed our characteristics incorrectly from our original characteristics since ancient times. The hero of the Ramakian is Rama, who is the most delicate person. He has never worked hard with anybody. Going off to battle, when the character Phiphek tells him, "Today the destiny of the commander-in-chief of the enemy

to die will be difficult, so send someone else to battle; until the time it's easy, you don't have to do anything except raise your Brahma-arrow." Rama does everything like this. The author can make the reader believe that Rama is a person from a high class. He is a meritorious and superb person. The Ramakian is an example of our epic poetry that has continued into many other stories. Our heroes in almost every story are greedy by not wanting to do anything. These stories often praise people who sleep well as people who have merit and speak of people who must work until they are tired as people who have sin. Our poems often sculpt an image of the hero as a person who is thin and delicate. Even if he has to work at something for a little bit, he is described as suspicious. . . . The bodies of our heroes (in these old stories) are supposed to be slender, so that they aren't quite able to even walk. This is contrary to foreign and Chinese epics in which the hero must be someone big, sturdy, and strong who can fight things and kill dragons or can shoulder logs.[47]

Wichit's use of Rama as an example of a hero who looked as if he couldn't quite walk was a barely disguised attack on the monarchs of the Chakri dynasty. Barmé noted that this provided a conceptual framework for participating in the growing market economy by developing a fusion of a bourgeois-type work ethic, religion, and national identity.[48] Wichit went on to argue that a revolution in the very image of the human body was necessary.

I would like to use this lecture as a call to all of our writer friends to help us for a while. Those who write stories, entertaining stories, plays, or any stories at all, please draw a picture of the protagonist in your stories as a strong, sturdy person who is diligent and hard-working, who loves work, who works hard through difficulties. Please don't give us stories of "laziness-but-got-lucky" anymore. Fairy tale books, magic stories, or any fanciful stories where striking a gong once will get three castles, or stories about just lying around and then the royal chariot comes and transforms you into a king: I want to burn all of those stories. Let us show the citizens that laziness and weakness are wicked and lethal things that destroy oneself and the country. Dreaming of windfalls that will come without investing labor is the way people who have lost their minds think. This is not the aspiration of good people. Writers have great influence on society. They are people who have helped train the people of this country. Let us train them in this way. If we all do it together, in only five years, we would be proud that we could build delightful results in our country.[49]

Wichit's call to train the nation into a disciplined labor force through the arts can be discerned in the sculpture and architectural detail of the period. Artists working under Silpa in the Fine Arts Department, like Sitthidet

Saenghiran and Phiman Mulpramuk (figure 7.11), sought to glo-
rify the bodies of laboring Thai
citizens.[50] The musculature of the
two *garuda* that nest in the top corners of the main entrance to the
General Post Office on Charoen
Krung Road in Bangkok (figure
7.12) attest to the depth to which
Wichit's sentiments had perme-
ated the imagination of artists and
architects. The *garuda,* a mythological animal that had become a
state symbol through the absolute
monarchy, became a hypermascu-
line emblem of the new constitutionalist state. Far from heroizing
the workingman or extolling the
labor process, the idealized body
in sculpture, architecture, and
mass media of this period became
a symbol of the state's virility.
Implicit in these exaggerated bodies was a critique of materialism, a
call to a form of spiritualism that
demanded living sacrifices to the
nation and the heroization of war.

FIG. 7.11. Phiman Mulpramuk, maquette for *Warrior,* 1937.
Photo by author.

The nuclear family, as the ideal primary unit of the new economy, came to figure prominently in the iconography of the period (figures 7.13 and 7.14). The
father of the ideal family was now a soldier in the service of the state, and his
wife a woman who dressed following the conventions of state cultural mandates (*rathaniyom*).[51] Their infant child attested to their success in reproducing
the labor force and contributing to the war economy.

CONCRETE, REVOLUTION, AND LIGHT

Shortly after drawing up plans for Anusawari Thai, Wichit and Phra
Phromphichit began working on another project that sought to articulate
a new Thai identity through the construction of a modern monastic complex. Initially, the Fine Arts Department under Wichit wanted to call this
project Wat Prachathipatai (Democracy Wat).[52] The wat was to be an ideal

FIG. 7.12. *Garuda* on the facade of the General Post Office, Bangkok. The building was designed by Jitrasen Aphaiwong and built in 1939. The *garuda* were designed by Silpa Bhirasri. Photo by author.

FIG. 7.13. The ideal family poses in front of their modern home, ca. 1941. National Archives of Thailand.

example of building a monastic complex that established a standard in Thai architecture.[53] It was intended as a symbol of the political change to a democratic system, but after the government sent a special mission to India to request Buddha relics for the new wat, the government decided to give the new complex a more conventional name, denoting it as a Buddha-relic temple: Wat Phra Sri Mahathat. The change in the wat's name, however, did not change the original intention of its patrons, which were to have a *national* place to honor the Buddhist religion and to give the national Thai sangha an opportunity to have a place for both Royal Reform Sect (Thammayut) and Commoner Sect (Mahanikai) monks to live together.[54]

While the wat played an important role in the centralization of state authority throughout the Theravadan Buddhist world, it was more than simply a tool

FIG. 7.14. Sitthidet Saenghiran's maquette for a sculpture of an ideal Thai family, showing the head of the household as a soldier and his wife as a modern woman who dressed according to the conventions of the state cultural mandates (*ratthaniyom*), 1940. Photo by author.

with which the state legitimized its rule and exercised hegemony over its citizens. The wat was subject to the influence of other agents who could collude with or oppose the state. From the perspective of the sangha, for instance, the wat was important for making religious discourse tangible to large numbers of people. In the parlance of Donald Swearer, wat made the Buddha present.[55] In the case of sites that housed relics of the Buddha, they were literal proof of his physical existence. But the character of his body and the potency of the sites that constituted it were subject to the ministrations of religious and political agents. The Buddhist sangha, as holders of a certain kind of ideological power, could cooperate with those who held political, military, and economic power as well as challenge them. For example, it could justify extraction of tribute by the aristocracy, but it could also confront those aristocrats with values, like asceticism, that they could not share.[56] Most important, the wat was historically an important instrument

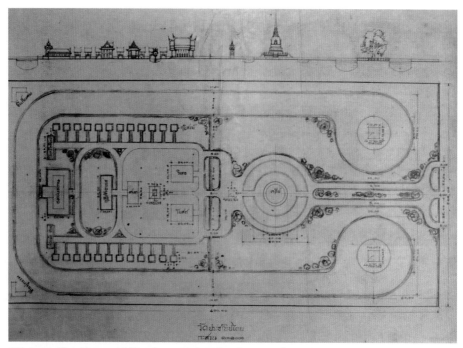

FIG. 7.15. Phra Phromphichit, plan and elevation drawing of Wat Phra Sri Mahathat (then Wat Prachathiptai), ca. 1939. National Archives of Thailand.

of community making. Not only had it long sustained ecclesiastical programs, but it had also served as a community center, hospital, school, and fairgrounds. Like Anusawari Thai, the design of Wat Phra Sri Mahathat integrates both religious and public programs, with the wat's public aspects clearly highlighted in both the larger plan of the wat and the Buddha relic *chedi* that anchored the larger composition.

Phra Phromphichit drew on Beaux-Arts design principles of symmetry, ornamentation, and staging in his use of the *chedi* as a center of gravity. The influence of the French academy on Phra Phromphichit is not surprising. In the early twentieth century, he was an art student in the Ministry of Public Works during the period when Italian engineers and architects like Carlo Allegri and Mario Tamagno held great influence in Bangkok. These architects had trained at the Accademia Albertina in Turin, where the curriculum was similar to that of the École des Beaux-Arts in Paris. Several of Phra Phromphichit's contemporaries studied at the École des Beaux-Arts as well.[57] The distinct approach of the École des Beaux-Arts can be seen in the hierarchy of an early plan of the site of Wat Phra Sri Mahathat (then Wat Prachathipatai) (figure 7.15). The central axis that runs from east to west orders the complex. The central axis telescopes from the main entrance to a *chedi*, where the Buddha relics are enshrined, and then expands into a series of smaller buildings, including the *uposot, haw trai* (scripture hall), *sala* (pavilion), *kuti chao awat* (abbot's residence), and *kuti* (monastic cells). The integration of the complex along the central axis in Phra Phromphichit's plan achieves the unified gestalt that Beaux-Arts design demanded. However, if we examine the elevation of the complex at the top edge of the drawing in relation to this plan, we can clearly see how the main feature of the composition is the *chedi.*

The *chedi*, in the form of a bell (*chedi song rakhang*), acts in a manner similar to monuments in successful examples of Beaux-Arts urban planning.[58] For example, in the 1901 McMillan Plan for the renovation of Washington, DC, the city's two intersecting axes are anchored along a monumental core. In similar fashion, the *chedi* of Wat Phra Sri Mahathat anchors the central axis and provides the overall composition with a comprehensive order. Although amendments were made to the plan before and during construction, the *chedi* remained the dominant feature of the wat. Aerial views captured by British photographer Peter Williams-Hunt shortly after the Second World War reveal a monumental white pagoda sitting directly across from a mass of gable-roofed buildings (figure 7.16).[59] It is composed of three main parts: a substructure supports a bell, which is crowned by a spire, or *yod.*

FIG. 7.16. Peter Williams-Hunt, aerial view of the *chedi* at Wat Phra Sri Mahathat. National Archives of Thailand.

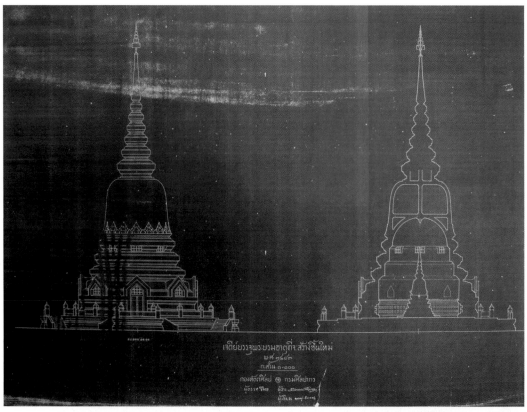

FIG. 7.17. Phra Phromphichit, elevation and section of the *chedi* of Wat Phra Sri Mahathat, 1940. National Archives of Thailand.

The most remarkable aspect of Phra Phromphichit's design, however, was that the *chedi* was a monument that commoners could enter (figure 7.17). The *chedi* has historically been a solid structure, and this gesture, particularly in a *chedi* that housed relics of the Buddha, was particularly radical. The substructure is punctuated with four entrances. The entrances are topped by gable windows. The gable windows are repeated around the base four more times. On top of this are stacked three discs, radial protrusions that are often curved, but here are flattened.[60] The diameter of each disc diminishes progressively upward. Eight clerestory windows punctuate the grooves beneath the third protrusion. The bell sits on top of this superstructure. On top of the bell sits the spire, which is crowned by a multitiered parasol, or *chattravali*.

Light enters Wat Phra Sri Mahathat's *chedi* in a way that it does not in other *chedi*. It trickles in through two series of clerestory windows and illuminates the interiority of the structure (figure 7.18). Here there is a smaller *chedi*, containing the relics of the Buddha. This is the central core of the *chedi* and the site of primary worship. However, the worshippers are surrounded

FIG. 7.18. Light from clerestory windows illuminates the interior of the *chedi* of Wat Phra Sri Mahathat. Photo by author.

FIG. 7.19. Crypts of leaders of the People's Party in the wall of the *chedi* of Wat Phra Sri Mahathat. Photo by author.

by the outer wall of the *chedi*, which contains 112 spaces for the remains of figures connected to the revolution and their wives. These include the primary leaders of the People's Party and three former prime ministers, two of whom were field marshals and one of whom was a civilian lawyer: Phibun Songkhram, Pridi Phanomyong, and Phraya Phaholphayusena. The plaque of former prime minister Field Marshal Phibun Songkhram is prominent on this wall today and continues to be a space of veneration (figure 7.19). In a memo dated 22 April 1941, Luang Wichit argued for the need for such a memorial tomb. He offered a brief comparison of similar tombs for the leaders of European nations that included Westminster Abbey, the Roman Pantheon, Charlottenburg Palace, and the Panthéon. He concluded that the Panthéon, designed by Jacques-Germain Soufflot and his student Jean-Baptiste Rondelet in Paris and built between 1758 and 1790, was the most appropriate model, given that it housed the remains of figures of aesthetic and scientific as well as military and political prominence.[61] The interior of the *chedi* is based on the shape of a dome and recalls the basic structure of the Panthéon. Luang Wichit's proposal was a defiant gesture against the sacred power of the monarchy. No member of the royal family, much less a commoner, would have their remains enshrined within a *chedi* containing Buddha relics.[62] It was more common to have satellite *chedi* built around the main *chedi* to enshrine royal remains. The *chedi* that enshrined Buddha relics was a sort of anchor around which the remains of monarchs orbited.

Light figures in the design of the *uposot* in a more symbolic way. On the gable end of the *uposot* is an image of Arunthepbut (Skt. Aruṇa) (figure 7.20), the charioteer of Surya, the sun, and the brother of the *garuda*. Arunthepbut's duty was to drive the chariot of the sun around Mount Meru, ushering in the first rays of sunshine.[63] While this symbol drew on the cosmological narratives that guided ecclesiastical and royal architecture, it did so in a way that disrupted the spatial relationship between the sangha, or clergy, and the monarchy. Texts like the *Traiphum phra ruang* and *Ramakian* positioned the monarchy as key protagonists in the origin and development of the universe and served to legitimate the ideal of divine right.[64] Those who had divine right had been people who had done good deeds and built great virtue in the past.[65] As we have seen throughout this book, kings used symbols from the *Traiphum*, like the *garuda*, to show they were on par with celestial beings and also to brand the monastic complexes, palaces, public works, and even cinemas that they built, most notably on the gable end.[66] The pediment of Wat Benchamabophit, for example, bears the seal of the king who ordered it built, Chulalongkorn. This symbol, the *phra kieo* or *phra chulamongkut*, is a royal crown resting on a pillow. Concrete offered a solid, permanent base for the new state to brand with its own national symbolism. The choice of Arunthepbut as a substitute for royal branding was a political choice. It was a potent political symbol that was being used in important built works of the period by the People's Party. The same details can be found on Democracy Monument, over the doors of the base that supports the offering bowl that holds the constitution as well as in political propaganda of the period (figures 7.21 and 7.22).

FIG. 7.20. Gable end of the *uposot* hall at Wat Phra Sri Mahathat with figure of Arunthepbut. Photo by author.

FIG. 7.21. Arunthepbut on the lintel of the Democracy Monument. Photo by author.

In architecture, hierarchy establishes a visual and spatial order, privileging certain sequences, axes, and elements above others to create a unified whole. In Siam, this order has historically reflected prestige associated with birthright and political station. The royal sumptuary code reserved certain architectural forms and symbols for royalty and others for nonroyal classes. The 1932 change in government sought to transform Siam into a democratic society in which all its members would be equal, regardless of birth. The new government hailed this historical moment as the dawn of *sri ariya,* the era of the Buddha Metteya, and set about building new public institutions that reflected their utopian ambitions. Their material of choice was steel-reinforced concrete.

Concrete opened up new possibilities for the national building economy, new aesthetic hierarchies, and ultimately the narration of urban public space. It had been an important base for the national economy under the absolutist monarchy, and after 1932 it became even more important as it fulfilled an important aesthetic role as well. It allowed not only for rapid construction that employed unskilled construction labor, but also for the appearance of a modern and stable city. Although the national production of concrete was established in 1913 under the auspices of the absolute monarchy, it was

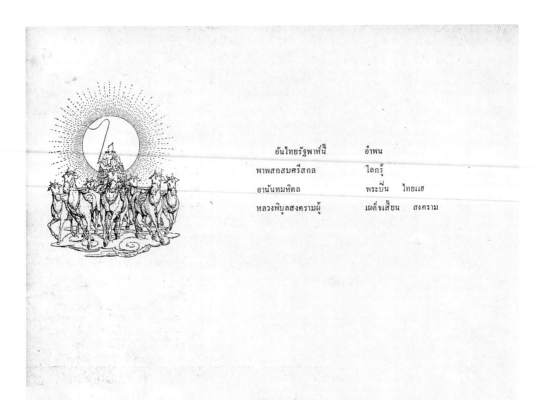

อันไทยรัฐพาห์นี้   อำพน

พาพสกสมศรีสกล   โลกรู้

อานันทมหิตล   พระปิ่น   ไทยแฮ

หลวงพิบุลสงครามผู้   เผด็จเสี้ยน   สงคราม

FIG. 7.22. Page from *Muang thai* magazine, depicting the ceremony at the Democracy Monument on Constitution Day, 1941. Department of Public Relations.

largely used for commercial and housing types because it did not easily sustain the historical language of the Siamese architectural order. However, the 1932 change in government called for building new public institutions that reflected a new national hierarchy. After the architect Phra Phromphichit successfully used concrete to repair the *prang* form of the Sawasdisopha gate, an important gate in the Grand Palace, concrete began to be used in national building programs that mixed religious and political symbolism and programs. The body of the common man assumed a new importance in Thai architecture. Monuments constructed by the People's Party rejected the king's body as the primary focal point and deployed idealized forms of the human figure to idealize both virility and imperialist war. The construction of a new relic *chedi*, Wat Phra Sri Mahathat, reinforced the new hierarchies of the period by placing the bodies of common people in unprecedented proximity to the material remains of the Buddha but under the auspices of the state. Like the funeral pyres of chapter 5 and the Sala Chaloem Krung cinema of chapter 6, such spaces combined both ecclesiastical and political programs, forging a concrete link between the felicitous spaces of the Buddha and the territory of the nation.

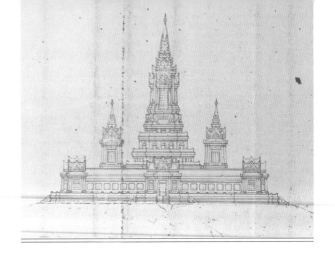

PART III

SYSTEMS

CHAPTER EIGHT

THE FLOATING PARADISE

Infrastructure Space and *Vimānas* of the Cold War Era

In the short story "Wiman loi" (The Floating Paradise), the writer Ta Tha-it (a pseudonym for Chusak Rasijan) describes a journey to a brothel on a boat moored in Khlong Saen Saeb. The *khlong* (canal), one of the few remaining man-made waterways that comprised Bangkok's early transportation infrastructure space, is where a number of enterprising sex workers have set up workstations.[1] The narrator of the story is a *kai phi*, or "ghost guide," an unlicensed guide who shepherds foreigners through the seductive informal economies and leisure spaces of Cold War–era Bangkok. In this case, he takes two American service-men on R & R from Saigon to what they call in English "floating whore boats." The term is a play both on the Floating Market, the English name for the well-known tourist destination at Damnoen Saduak, and on the celestial associa-tions of the term *wiman* (paradise). One of the servicemen, however, tells him, "Don't think you're our guide, Ta. Your work hours have already ended. Think of this as us friends going out together. It's OK." Ta responds unashamedly, "It might be possible to be friends, but it will be difficult for me to go out playing around with you because you use dollars and I use baht."[2]

THE *VIMĀNA* AND THE FLOATING PARADISE

The short story, published in a 1975 collection called *Talui ke khlap* (A Visit to the Gay Club), illuminated not only the shadows of Cold War–era Bangkok's tourist economy and infrastructure space, but also the limits of equality that haunted the development of the city into a "floating paradise." The term "paradise" occurs frequently in Ta's writing about Bangkok.[3] The Thai word *wiman* derives from the Pali and Sanskrit term *vimāna*. It appears in epics like the *Mahabarata* and in later parts of the Pali canon as a "palace-chariot" or a "divine mansion." It is thus both a divine vehicle and a celestial abode. Steve Collins has noted that the *vimāna* appears in the Pali canonical collection *Vimāna-vatthu* as a material reward for merit making and is described in distinctly sensual terms.[4] It may have come to Thai through its Khmer iteration ("celestial palace" or "palace" or "temple"). The *vimāna* was a part of the city's identity from its inception. We learned in chapter 2 that one of the names King Phuttayotfa gave to the city he founded was *phiman* พิมาน, another derivative of the term *vimāna*. In the *Traiphum*, the *wiman* of Indra on the summit of Mount Meru is full of not only palaces and *prang* covered with jewels but places for play and amusement as well.[5] As Thailand entered the Cold War period, the historic image of Bangkok as a *vimāna* was transformed by the language of development. As Ta's use of the Thai term suggests, the new image of the city conflated a celestial abode with a consumer paradise.

The development of the city into a modern *vimāna* was sustained by the two floating populations profiled in Ta's short story: a migrant labor force and visitors drawn to the country's burgeoning international tourist industry. As a result, the city appeared unburdened by the need for housing or public space to accommodate these floating populations and instead focused on developing an infrastructure of roads and hotels that could move these populations into and out of the city cheaply and efficiently. The floating paradise was not based on a moral image or a felicitous state like Uttarakuru, *sri ariya metteya*, or *nibbāna*, but on a free-market utopia that linked happiness to global economic development, tourism, and consumerism. The official emphasis on development accorded a new importance to foreign planning experts and seemingly "freed" professional architects in Thailand from the political implications of social transformation that were implicit in the project of urbanization. While the early twentieth century was marked by intellectual and political interest in "civilization" and modernization, Cold War-era discourse emphasized a narrative that linked national and individual "development" with the goals of comprehensive urban planning.[6] As state priorities became decoupled from the mid-twentieth-century modernist project of social equality, the architectural profession in Thailand turned its attention from "public" monuments, monastic complexes, schools, and stadia to new commercial typologies that were integral to the image of a "developed" city: hotels, banks, and office buildings.[7] This commercial architecture was indicative not only of the emergence of powerful new business conglomerates, but also of a new tendency in the architectural profession, which could pursue an agenda that was seemingly free of political responsibility and pragmatically respond to the demands of corporate clients.[8] Significantly, the emphasis on "development" and commercial architecture changed the concept of leisure from a form of public activity and eroded older conceptions of public space. Public space didn't disappear, however. It was transformed into both commercialized arenas of social, and sexual, intercourse, and unexpected nodes within the city's developing infrastructure space. The floating paradise, however, was haunted by shadow narratives, spaces, and economies like that of the floating brothel in Ta Tha-it's story. This contrast can be seen by excavating utopian images implicit in comprehensive urban planning proposals like the *Greater Bangkok Plan 2533*, popular literature like the *Kai phi* series, and graffiti left behind on the infrastructure spaces of the city. Within these narratives, architecture played an important but self-consciously subordinate role to market forces in shaping the morphology of the city.

THE "AMERICAN ERA" AND TRANSPORTATION INFRASTRUCTURE: ORGANIZING THE FLOATING POPULATION

Under the military regimes that ruled Thailand in the decades following the end of the Second World War until the beginning of the country's three-year experiment in civilian democracy in 1973, development discourse produced an economic and urban narrative that saw the creation of a national transportation infrastructure as the conduit of both political stability and personal fulfillment. Infrastructure became the symbolic, universal measure of the country's place in the global capitalist economy. It not only secured the country against the threat of communism and supported a burgeoning international tourist economy; it transferred migrant laborers into the city's growing industrial and service sectors without permanent settlement. Its definitive characteristic was its facilitation of movement and its patterning of social form.[9] It simultaneously weakened older politicized forms of public space, like the public park, while creating new, privatized opportunities for social congress. The infrastructural networks that were built by the state in collaboration with private business interests and the US military were not only functional tools that circulated people, commodities, and capital in a manufacturing and service-oriented economy; they "organized life" by creating an urban pattern of subject and shadow that defined the way residents of the city saw themselves within a new political, economic, and social order.[10] Bangkok's new commercial districts, office buildings, and high-profile hotels towered over a shadow city of slums, brothels, and "love motels." This dual image of the city, as both floating paradise and floating brothel, positioned Bangkok as part of a universal cultural and economic system and yet lagging behind it.

While urban planning and infrastructure building had been politically instrumentalized by the monarchy since the inception of the city, the city's expansion in the nineteenth century focused largely on developing an infrastructure of canals and roads that further stimulated real estate development.[11] Although the roads facilitated new means of transportation including carriages, rickshaws, trams, and automobiles, which were owned largely by the monarchy and the titled bureaucracy, they developed as a closed system, disconnected from automotive transportation in the rest of the country. Before the 1960s, for example, a motor vehicle could travel no farther than twenty miles from the center of Bangkok.[12] In 1941, the social scientist Virginia Thompson described the city as existing in a state of "vehicular isolation."[13] Although there were major plans to construct highways that linked Bangkok with other regions in the 1930s, these were delayed due to the worldwide economic depression and instability during the Second World War.[14] As late as 1940, there was not a single trunk road that linked the capital with other provinces. The city was an isolated patchwork of gridded zones and circular mandalas. Just as its residents relied on a multilayered system of canals, trams, and roads to navigate its zones, connections with provincial destinations were made through a loosely coordinated system of waterways, railroads, and local roads.

The highway network that came to connect the capital to the rest of the country began to develop in earnest after the Second World War. It expanded tremendously under the regime of Field Marshal Sarit Thanarat, who staged a coup against Phibun Songkhram in 1957 and subsequently seized power by staging another coup on 20 October 1958. The expansion would continue under Sarit's political heirs, Thanom Kittikachorn and Praphat Charusathian, but Sarit's five-year rule marked a turning point in Thai political, economic, and cultural history that was the beginning of what Benedict Anderson and other scholars have called the "American era" (1958–1973).[15] It signaled the reinvention of the institution of the monarchy as a key protagonist in political life, a turn toward a paternalistic form of military rule and violent domestic repression in the name of anticommunism, the elimination of the fifty-*rai* (approximately twenty-acre) limit on permissible landholding that laid the legal foundation for large-scale land speculation, the dismantling of state enterprises, the smashing of trade unions, enforced low wages, favorable conditions for the repatriation of corporate profits, and unhindered access to the country's natural and labor resources for foreign, mainly American, capital.

In the late 1950s and 1960s, large reserves of underutilized labor from rural Thailand's vast poor and seasonally vulnerable regions found work not only in Bangkok's factories and organized services industries but in the city's informal sector and the sexual services industry as well. As most farming depended on monsoon rains and lasted only half the year, many laborers sought employment elsewhere for the other half. By the late 1970s, 1.5 million people were estimated to be moving between village and city in seasonal flows.[16] They could be transferred into the capital without permanent migration due to the transportation infrastructure built during the Cold War. Because there were few attempts to provide state housing for this floating population, the architectural profession focused its attention on privately funded projects like hotels, banks, and office buildings. The mobility of the floating population would prove crucial to the model of development that Thailand pursued under the regime of Sarit Thanarat.

DEVELOPMENT, *PHATTHANA*, AND HAPPINESS

Sarit was a populist who sought to cultivate a rural base of support. His various political campaigns in the Thai countryside strengthened his belief that the rural population had two basic needs: water and roads.[17] In 1960, Sarit made clear the central role of infrastructure in national development and consensus building: "Our important task in this revolutionary era is development, which includes economic development, educational development, administrative development, and everything else. . . . [Regarding] community development, I have noticed with great satisfaction that both government officials and the public have shown cooperation and unity, even in projects involving human labor such as digging, building, and repairing roads, digging and dredging canals, and improving and maintaining the cleanliness of the country."[18] The construction of physical networks linking the capital with the countryside resulted not only in creating an image of a unified, developing nation but also in binding remote parts of the countryside into a new political, economic, and cultural territory centered on Bangkok.

The terms *pattiwat* and *phatthana* were distinctive terms of the Sarit era that are usually translated as "revolution" and "development," respectively. However, Sarit's use of these terms reveals very different understandings of the concepts than the English words suggest. Scholars have recently traced the global narrative of development to an eighteenth-century interpretation of human history as a story of social progress through material change and the expansion of economic relationships. Any nation could develop, the narrative claimed, by improving land, manufacturing, and trade. However, success depended on the "luck" of geography and resources.[19] Political scientist

Thak Chaloemtiarana has pointed out that Sarit's *pattiwat* encouraged political atavism and was aimed at maintaining boundaries between hierarchical sectors. *Phatthana* was meant to extend the regime's paternalism and ensure that change did not undermine the traditional hierarchies of the political system.[20] The difference between *phatthana* and development is suggested by the ways Sarit's policies aligned with general American military and economic interests in the region but departed from many specific recommendations of American "experts."

Sarit restructured the National Economic Council established by Phibun Songkhram's administration in 1959 into the National Economic Development Board.[21] As its new name suggested, it was tasked with drafting Thailand's first comprehensive development scheme. Making liberal use of the World Bank's research undertaken on behalf of the Thai government in 1959, the National Economic Development Board presented its first proposals more than a year later.[22] The first major development goal of the plan stated, "The primary objective of the National Economic Development plan is to raise the standard of living of the people of Thailand. This succinct statement appears to suggest a purely material goal, without regard to social, cultural, and aesthetic values. But while material well-being may be an end in itself, it is also, and more importantly a means to a further end in so far as it enables all citizens to lead fuller, more creative and happier lives. 'Raising the standard of living' must, therefore, be construed in this wider sense."[23]

The plan thus linked the pursuit of happiness, creativity, and aesthetic value with systemic development. It further connected happiness to the overall increased output of goods and services by the private sector. It clearly limited the role of the Thai government to providing infrastructural support in the form of irrigation works, roads, other means of transport, and the provision of inexpensive electrical power to enable happiness through increased productivity by 6 percent per annum.[24] While the plan lacked many specific details, such as employment targets and programs of planned population transfer from rural to urban areas, it influenced the future development of the city by establishing a model of development in which personal fulfillment could be measured through quantitative data.[25]

The plan departed from World Bank recommendations only in advocating for greater spending on irrigation. This discrepancy suggests that the Thai government saw the importance of not only strategic roads and communications infrastructure, but rural development and social welfare projects as well.[26] In reality, however, the two were inseparable and most of the *phatthana* that occurred in the "American era" was accompanied by massive US military buildup in the region.[27] American development projects surged not only in Thailand but also in tropical regions in general after World

War II as part of a new technological confidence and neo-imperial vision. US president Harry Truman said, "Our imponderable resources in technical knowledge are constantly growing and inexhaustible. . . . We should make available to peace-loving peoples the benefit of our store of technical knowledge in order to help them realize their aspirations for a better life."[28] As Thailand became the pivot of American expansion in Southeast Asia, the United States established eight major military bases and minor ones scattered throughout the country, largely in rural areas.[29] By 1961, community development programs in Thailand shifted their emphasis toward rural "security" based on the growing influence of American capital and technocratic advice.[30] The construction of roads and irrigation projects was based more on the need for government access to "insecure areas" than on local needs. The government began building highways for security in 1963 with the cooperation of US Operation Mission and the Office in Charge of Construction. Although Thak has noted that road planning was sparse and scattered between 1961 and 1970, nine routes, known as "security roads," were established by the Royal Highways Department (Krom Thang Luang) during this period, with a total of 817.6 kilometers in the north, northeast, and central regions.[31] By the end of the 1960s, an additional fifty-five projects were initiated by the department in "terrorist-infested areas" with a total of 3,504 kilometers.[32]

Both rural development and strategic road building also sought to control the migration of rural workers into the city and bolster the agricultural economy. Sarit's urban policies appeared at first glance to be scattered and confusing. However, understanding them within the history of mid-twentieth-century urban renovation as well as the context of both rural development and military strategy reveals both strong aesthetic as well as economic motivations. As the previous chapter demonstrated, the People's Party sought to transform Bangkok into a city that was on par with international capitals by not only embarking on urban renovation projects like the lining of Ratchadamnoen Avenue with egalitarian facades but also regulating the dress and appearance of its citizens in public space so that they appealed to universal standards of modern taste. However, Sarit's regime had a more complex approach to urban planning and the behavior of Thai citizens that sought to ameliorate the more troublesome characteristics of modernity—such as democracy—in order to construct a pastoral vision of Thai identity, or *khwampenthai*. For example, on 31 December 1959 he banned pedicabs, or human-powered *samlor*, from the streets of Bangkok.[33] The superficial reason was that they were crude forms of vehicular transportation that were not fit to be seen in a modern city. However, the intended effects of the ban went much deeper. In a speech to his cabinet in 1960, Sarit reflected,

It was a small matter that the pedicabs obstructed traffic and were eye-sores in the capital. The major consideration involved was the question of young men from the rural areas numbering in the ten thousands who had left agricultural productivity in favor of the unproductive profession of pedicab driving. This was detrimental to our national economy. Further-more, the pedicab profession destroyed health: according to the Interior Ministry, pedicab drivers in the end become opium addicts in large num-bers. It is widely held in political science theory that the advent of rural population movements into the capital is a sign of social deterioration.[34]

While the urban interventions of the People's Party were driven by an aesthetic appeal to universal values like modernity and democracy, Sarit's urban aesthetics—piecemeal as they were—were tied to the *phatthanakan* (development) of a national economy that depended on migrant labor in the developing urban service and industrial sector as well as agricultural pro-duction in the countryside. Mired in the city during the peak farming season, the pedicab drivers were a drain on the agricultural economy and contrib-uted little to the urban fabric. In fact, the pedicabs hindered circulation in the city because of their slow speed, lack of maneuverability, and vulnerabil-ity.[35] Returning their drivers to the countryside facilitated both agricultural production and urban transportation. The prime minister sought to further integrate former pedicab drivers back into the rural economy by organizing rural community organizations (*nikhon chonnabot*) to help their transition.[36]

SPECULATIVE NARRATIVES AND THE CITY'S FIRST MASTER PLAN: BANGKOK 2533

While Sarit pursued isolated attempts at formulating urban policy, a coher-ent master plan for the city was left for specialist foreign consultants and overseas-trained Thai technocrats to formulate. A government bureau for urban planning was inaugurated as early as 1935, but planning responsibil-ities shuttled around between different departments until a City Planning Section was established in the Bangkok municipality in 1956.[37] The follow-ing year, an American city planning consultant with the International Coop-eration Administration, Harold E. Miller, recommended various measures to begin a master planning program for Bangkok, and the following year, an agreement was signed between the Ministry of the Interior and the US Operations Mission to Thailand initiating the project. Litchfield, Whiting, Bowne, and Associates of New York City and their associated city planning consultants, Massachusetts Institute of Technology professors Frederick J. Adams, John T. Howard, and Roland Greeley, were commissioned to prepare the *Greater Bangkok Plan 2533* between March 1958 and August 1960. Notably, this was the team's first and only international planning project.

Master plans do not usually project 575 years into the future, and a misreading of the Buddhist-era year 2533 as a Gregorian calendar year would suggest that the plan was not just a work of speculative planning, but an example of utopian literature. Indeed, the plan, like so many master plans of the period, required the same imaginative leap as science fiction writers took to speculate on the "secondary" impact of changes in the urban fabric. As science fiction author Robert Heinlein reflected, "Many people correctly anticipated the coming of the horseless carriage . . . but I know of no writer, fiction or non-fiction, who saw ahead of time the vast changes in the courting and mating habits of Americans which would result."[38] In an attempt to speculate on the social significance of its proposed changes, the Adams, Howard, and Greeley consulting team deployed quantitative "scientific" methodologies reflective of systems thinking to produce graphics that would support qualitative analytical findings about the city's future. For example, the team used test vehicles to measure travel distances at regular five-minute intervals. This field research resulted in the production of isochrone maps of travel times and distances that supported the plan's argument for the creation of a more livable city through the implementation of a new rational system of roads that was convenient, safe, economical, and swift.[39]

The new image of the city was distilled in the plan's map 13 (figure 8.1). Here, the concentric circle mandala that focused on the Grand Palace and was identified in chapter 1 of this book was expanded and updated to include inner and outer concentric rings with a gridded zone at the center. This new centrifugal plan integrated the two geometric approaches of mandala and grid that had emerged at the end of the nineteenth century, refocused attention on the earliest royal precincts of the city in Rattanakosin, and privileged automotive transportation.[40] Freeways divided the city into a checkerboard pattern of zones. The center of the composition was occupied by institutional buildings. Surrounding this were commercial zones. Suburban residential zones surrounded that, and at the very peripheries were agricultural areas. The larger network of roads would link developed mid-density residential "fingers" (denoted by the dark yellow areas on the map) that would grab at lesser-developed areas. Urban planning scholar Apiwat Ratanawaraha has recently observed that this decentralized plan reflected a strategic tendency of defensive dispersal in postwar urban planning.[41] This approach was spearheaded by Tracy B. Augur, a veteran planner who had served as a planning consultant on the development of Oak Ridge, the secret Manhattan Project "atomic city" built in Tennessee to support the manufacture of atomic bomb components.[42] In 1948, Augur argued that a dispersed pattern

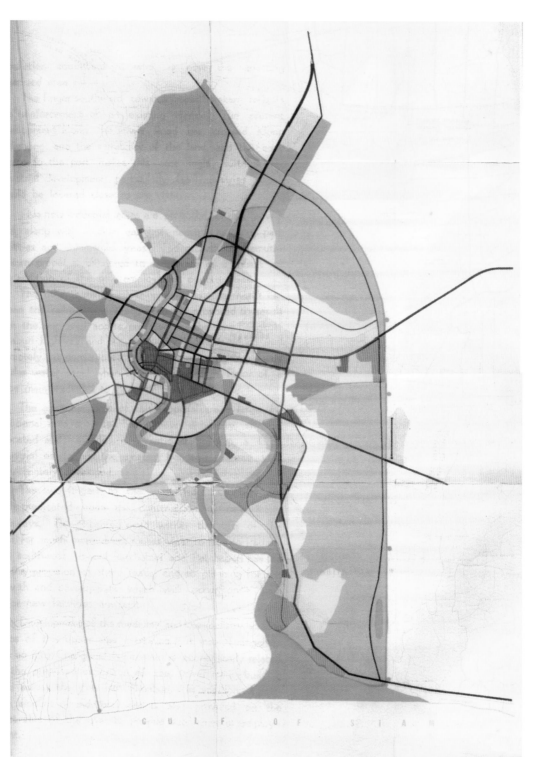

GREATER BANGKOK PLAN 2533

MINISTRY OF INTERIOR · GOVERNMENT OF THAILAND
BANGKOK-THONBURI CITY PLANNING PROJECT
LITCHFIELD WHITING BROWN & ASSOCIATES
INTERNATIONAL · ARCHITECTS ENGINEERS & CITY PLANNERS
ADAMS HOWARD & GREELEY CITY PLANNING CONSULTANTS

of small, efficient cities was more attuned to the needs of modern living, modern commerce, and modern industry and was less inviting as a military target.[43] He advocated a "cluster city" of some twenty units averaging about fifty thousand each and separated from one another by four to five miles of open country. While an atomic bomb would likely decimate a concentrated city, it would have only a one-in-five chance of a direct hit on urban territory in a cluster-form city.[44] Although overall distances in the cluster-form city were three times those in the concentrated form, Augur argued that this was offset by the fact that "at least two-thirds of the distance between points in different units was through open country, free of congestion."[45] Augur's vision placed an emphasis on the automobile as the primary mode of urban transportation.

The *Greater Bangkok Plan 2533* also emphasized urban automotive transportation as part of a larger national network. It noted that although historically the state had focused on railways to link Bangkok with the agricultural hinterland, in recent years major contributions from the United States had bolstered the government's large-scale highway construction program. "This program, plus the increase in vehicle use, particularly in the Bangkok Area, indicate that the highway traffic outside of the Bangkok Area will continue to increase as the population increases and the economy improves."[46] The implicit suggestion that the plan made was that the automobile was necessary for an improved economy. As a result, the plan also advocated for the removal of Bangkok's last remaining trams, which would interfere with free-moving automobile traffic.[47] The plan proposed thirty-two routes of various sizes, including large arterial roads that bisected the city (from Saraburi to Nakhon Pathom and from Nakhon Pathom to Chachoengsao) as well as a circumferential route (from the Rama VI Bridge to the Krung Thep Bridge) and routes that provided direct access for truck traffic between the Port Area and planned industrial areas to the south and the Bang Sue freight yards that bypassed the center of the city. It also proposed extending smaller commercial roads like Phetchaburi and Sukhumvit and improving smaller roads to relieve traffic on flanking arterial roads.[48] The proposed road system suggested the replacement of water-based transportation with land-based services but also acknowledged that this would be a long process, as

◀ **FIG. 8.1.** Map 13 of the Greater Bangkok Plan 2533, depicting proposed land-use zoning and new arterial roads. Concentric roads created an urban pattern that radiates outward from a square-shaped grid at the center, a ring surrounding that, and a large peri-urban area encircling both. Commercial areas are denoted by red, industrial zones by pink, stand-alone recreational spaces by dark green, institutional spaces by blue, waterways by light blue, and agricultural areas by green. Residential zones are denoted by varying shades of yellow. The darkest shade of yellow denotes high-density "fingers" proposed by the planning team. The smallest amount of space has been designated for recreational zones that are independent of the road network. Scale 1:100,000. Ministry of the Interior.

inland waterways had been an important part of the country's social and economic fabric for such a long time.[49]

In turn, the plan claimed that the faster pace and more rigid forms of life of motorized urban societies increased the need for recreational activities as a "well-spring of health, pleasure and self-development."[50] The plan advocated for the construction of recreational zones that could be scattered throughout the city, similar to the ways Augur's 1948 model of the cluster city emphasized the open country between clusters as "a place for active or passive relaxation from the increasing pace of city living."[51] It noted that while a large share of all recreational activity involved the use of open space, urban "pressures" diminished the private open space that was available to urban residents. This necessitated, in turn, the need to provide urban open spaces for "public and semi-public bodies." Such spaces also acted as "lungs" for the city, helping to cool the air of the tropical city and relieving the press of the city's buildings and pavement.

Notably, the plan did not acknowledge the ways such public spaces had become critical tools in the consolidation of military power under Sarit.[52] In the aftermath of the cremation of commoners on Sanam Luang discussed in chapter 5, the field became the site of mass demonstrations. On 8 December 1946, the Thai Communist Party used the field to stage a demonstration against France's annexation of four of Thailand's provinces. On 1 May 1947, the Central Labor Union organized the largest May Day celebrations in the history of the country.[53] After the Second World War, Sanam Luang became the site of the "Hyde Park rallies." These were a new type of public spectacle organized by then prime minister Phibun Songkhram after returning from a trip around the world in 1955. Based on the public speeches Phibun had witnessed in London's Hyde Park, the rallies were a forum every Saturday and were popular with urban and rural citizens, who would come to vent antigovernment sentiments.[54] The practice was initially used by Phibun to discredit his rivals, and was later banned when his rivals used it to attack him.[55] The park, however, would continue to figure in the politics of the period as a site where grievances were voiced. In a speech at Sanam Luang on 10 August 1957, Representative Bunkhong Bumpetch accused the government of catering to a few rich families and not fulfilling its promises of national development.[56] Just over a month later, on 15 September 1957, a gathering at Sanam Luang to attack the Phibun government grew into a mass demonstration that marched to Sarit's home and galvanized him into staging a coup on 17 September 1957.[57]

Instead of acknowledging the increasing political importance of Bangkok's open-air recreational spaces, the plan developed a politically neutral language and an accompanying metric for quantifying the city's existing spaces where public congress was possible and categorizing them as simply recreational spaces. It estimated that in addition to the 70-*rai* Sanam Luang, play facilities in the city consisted of about 500 *rai* (800,000 square meters) on public and private school sites, 150 *rai* on open land adjacent to school sites, and three small public playgrounds, as well as 360 wat. In addition to these, the plan noted the use of sitting areas and plazas along Ratchadamnoen Avenue and the partially developed boulevard connecting the Memorial Bridge to the King Taksin monument in Thonburi. It also identified the importance of the wat as a historic provider of recreation and community space. "Although the Metropolitan Area's 360 wats no longer perform as wide a range of services as are offered by the Kingdom's many thousands of rural wats—the various government agencies within the Metropolitan Area having taken over many of its services—the city wats still serve as play areas for children of all ages, and as sitting areas, general gathering places and community centers for adults."[58] A Ford Foundation report from 1974 noted the importance of the wat and *khlong* (canal), which had been "sources of relief, refuge, recreation, and fellowship for hundreds of years." Their importance was more than aesthetic or recreational, the report argued.[59] This suggested awareness of infrastructure space like the street and the *khlong,* as well as monastic complexes, as forms of public space that were markedly different from older, European-oriented understandings of open-air fields like Sanam Luang as public spaces.

The planners recommended 10 *rai* per thousand persons or 16 square meters per capita, more than ten times the prevailing ratio in Bangkok at the time, as the optimum amount of open recreation area for Bangkok, exclusive of the land used for boulevards.[60] This would be distributed mostly in playgrounds and playfields (22,000 *rai*) with an additional 5,800 *rai* in residential neighborhood parks, 200 *rai* in small, 1-*rai* nonresidential parks adjacent to markets and government buildings, 12,000 *rai* in district parks, and 5,000 *rai* in metropolitan parks and reservations.[61] It included allowances for recreational space along a recommended boulevard system of about 33 kilometers that included a renovated Ratchadamnoen and Memorial Bridge–Phra Chao Taksin Boulevards as well as the construction of three new boulevards: Ratchavithi, running from a newly proposed Thonburi circumferential road to the Victory Monument and then to the Bangkok-Saraburi highway; Ratchaprarop-Ratchadamri-Sathorn; and Rama VI Boulevard, running south from Bang Sue through the central business district and connected to the Ratchaprarop-Ratchadamri-Sathorn Boulevard.[62] It further recommended that existing wat be encouraged to expand their open spaces and that the neighborhood and small nonresidential park areas be devoted to this purpose, particularly in areas it had targeted for redevelopment. It also promoted the building of new wat in new urban areas and the provision of parkland for this purpose.[63] The plan thus established a viable metric for limiting large public spaces. It fragmented public space by distributing it in regulated parcels among the proposed residential zones of the city.

Although the plan was never implemented in its entirety and the US Operation Mission planning adviser to the Thai government, Cyrus Nims, was critical of the obstacles that prevented much of it from being realized, its ideas were gradually absorbed into traffic circulation plans.[64] In the intervening years, new suburbs emerged around the schools, shops, cinemas, and clubs that catered to Americans. Wealthy Thai families were drawn to them because of their status and rising property values.[65] Planners largely monitored and mapped the dynamic spaces of the city on paper, painting the colors of land uses that they could not control. However, a close reading of the Litchfield plan suggests that it provided an important conceptual framework for a city in transition from a period engaged in a project of modernization to one of development. It suggested that a successful master plan could not only reconcile the city's old and new morphologies but also coordinate commercial and recreational functions into a profitable organism within the world economy. The Sarit regime, through the National Economic Development Board, had opened up the city to the forces of the global market. International tourism would come to form an important cornerstone of the city's new economy.

THE VIRTUES OF TOURISM: REFORMATTING PUBLIC SPACE

Less than a year after Sarit staged his second coup, on 20 October 1958, he established the Tourist Organization of Thailand (TOT). The TOT was primarily interested in attracting American tourists to the country, but an unintended side effect of its campaigns was a marketing of the country, and particularly Bangkok, to its own citizens. In a speech marking the opening of the TOT, Sarit remarked, "The benefits that the state can gain from a tourist industry are not in the direct income received by the government but in an income that can't be seen. Moreover, what is important is that it allows us to display the culture and virtue of the Thai people for the world to see."[66]

Sarit's remark suggested that, like infrastructure, tourism would have both visible and invisible effects on the country's development. From its earliest conception in the early twentieth century, the project of tourism sought to produce a narrative about Thailand that was consistent with official historiography, which projected an imagined lineage from the polities of Sukhothai and Ayutthaya to Bangkok. For example, after completing a two-month tour of archaeological sites in the northern central plains and attempting to identify the monumental remains of Sukhothai based on the Ramkhamhaeng Inscription's description of the city, King Vajiravudh published *Thio muang phra ruang* (A Trip to the Land of Phra Ruang).[67] Primarily directed at a Thai audience, the book sought to promote a historical lineage as well as delineate a national topography. Vajiravudh wrote, "It is my hope that, as a result of this book, the Thai people will understand that this Thai nation of ours, is not a young nation, and that it is not a country of savages or to put it in English, uncivilized people."[68] The People's Party also sought to use tourism as a means of educating Thai citizens about the extent of the country's geo-body as well as its history through the publication of lavish pictorial magazines like *Muang thai* and the construction of modern hotels in Bangkok and Lopburi.[69] The establishment of the Rattanakosin Hotel at the end of Ratchadamnoen Avenue, for example, suggested the importance of tourism to the building program of the People's Party in its renovation of the royal thoroughfare. The Sarit regime's ideological basis for tourism was different in that it was rooted in what historian Matthew Phillips has identified as "a global consumer culture emanating from the United States that was concerned principally with the logic of the Cold War."[70]

The problem the TOT faced in marketing Thailand as a tourist destination was that the country was engulfed in political instability and violence. The TOT countered this by projecting an image of the country as a stable but exotic outpost of the "Free World" and emphasized that visitors would not be threatened by any harm. In a 1962 press release, the TOT stated in no uncertain terms that it was safe to visit Thailand, particularly its capital. "Bangkok—and all of Thailand is at PEACE," the document proclaimed. In case the reader was not persuaded, it continued, "Peace is the essence of Thailand. The alarms of Far-Eastern events in recent months will not disturb you. No evidence presents itself, in the form of military personnel or preparations, to disturb your PEACEFUL visit. Please come: traditional Thai hospitality and courtesy will make your visit to Thailand an event which will not dim in memory."[71]

The TOT sought to project an image of Thailand as an oasis of safety in a region wracked with political upheaval. It wanted to produce an image of a pastoral Thai identity, rooted in "traditional hospitality and courtesy," while appealing to the developed tastes of international tourists. Thai architects after World War II were already debating the characteristics of an architecture that could be both modern and Thai. In an article in the February 1951 issue of *ASA*, the journal of the Association of Siamese Architects, an anonymous editor reflected on "Problems in Architecture," namely, the question of which was the appropriate style for Thai architecture: "ultra-modernism" (*samai mai wu wa*) or "Thai style" (*baeb thai*).[72] The author conjured a debate among a group of fictional architects. One complained about a fad of copying the "West" and argued for the beauty inherent in Thai ornamentation, which could be adapted into something new and beautiful. Another rejoined that this was an outdated perspective. "This is the era of science (*witthaya-sat*) and engineered machinery (*khruang yon kon kai*). There are cold storage rooms, radios, televisions, electricity, airplanes and cars to take us around.

FIG. 8.2. Postcard depicting the Siam Intercontinental Hotel, designed by Joseph P. Salerno and constructed in 1966. Collection of author.

We have already taken everything from the West at this point. To blend into what we have already borrowed, we would have to take rectangular forms, square forms, flat, smooth surfaces, fins, cubic volumes, hooks, scaffolding. We could make these look as smart as we want!" The author quietly suggested in his head, "Whatever and however you people choose, do look at the environment. Go with the appropriateness of time and place (*khwam mosom tam kalathesa*) according to your own point of view." The author invoked the opinion of an anonymous but respected professor: "No matter how much we are bound to the artistic characteristics of our past, and do not want to lose them, we don't intend to head into designing housing like the *kuti* at Wat Pho or the kind of raised houses where the ground floor is used as a chamber pot. Our art must combine with up-to-date technology but maintain true Thai characteristics, which are not the same as in any other countries." The author concluded, "Therefore, beware of the day you will be forced to design an airplane hangar with Thai ornament or the time may come when you have to design a Thai pavilion as an experimental nuclear reactor." The article suggested that the seemingly irreconcilable polarities of "ultra-modernism" and "Thainess" could be adjusted if one adopted a balance between the two. An architecture that was appropriate to environment and time (*ru kalathesa*) looked back to the past even as it was propelled by modern technologies and geometric forms.

The transition from the basic, unadorned geometric forms of *samanchon* (commoner) architecture built under the auspices of the People's Party to a new image that was both self-consciously Thai and modern can be seen in the history of the Erawan Hotel, which opened its doors to full occupancy in 1957. Initially a government project, it was essentially a rectangular concrete box with muted ornamentation. At the end of 1960, however, the hotel underwent an interior "renovation" to provide a "revolution back to the past" and creating a "Thai atmosphere" for American tourists.[73] In addition to incorporating Thai dishes into its restaurant's menu, it would now dress its maids in "Chiang Mai styles" made with Thai silk, and its waiters would be outfitted like royal pages. This blatant signaling of a national identity was echoed in the heavily symbolic design of hotels like the Siam Intercontinental Hotel (figure 8.2). Located on the grounds of the Pathumwan Palace, the hotel was designed in the shape of King Mongkut's helmet (*phramalanip*), denoting the royal pedigree of the business venture on lands leased from the royal family. The Dusit Thani, designed by Yozo Shibata and built in 1970, resembled the *mongkut* (ceremonial crown) of King Vajiravudh (figure 8.3). Named after the miniature city discussed in chapter 4, the hotel stood opposite the statue of the king at the entrance to Lumpini Park. At the time of its construction, it was said to be the tallest building in the city, and in a symbolic reversal of scale, it now towered over the image of its founder.[74]

National symbolism could also be integrated into the city's hotel architecture in the form of abstracted motifs. The design of the Indra Regent Hotel, designed by Chira Silpakanok and built in 1970, consisted of a vertical

FIG. 8.3. Dusit Thani hotel (background), designed by Yozo Shibata and built in 1970, and the monument to King Vajiravudh, designed by Samaichaloem Kridakon and erected in 1942. Photo by author.

FIG. 8.4. The Indra Regent Hotel, designed by Chira Silpakanok and built in 1970, with Sukhothai-style palace replica by the rooftop pool. Photo by author.

FIG. 8.5. Postcard depicting the Sukhothai-style poolside restaurant at the Indra Regent Hotel. Collection of author.

rectangular slab that appeared to hover over a horizontal rectangular base. It incorporated a shopping arcade and cinema that were connected to the hotel rooms via an interior walkway. The most notable aspect of the facade was the brise-soleil, composed of multiple reproductions of fin-shaped aedicules that were based on a Thai geometric motif known as the *prachamyan* (figure 8.4). The brise-soleil not only masked the activities within the hotel from outside view; it gave the basic geometries of the hotel the look of an exotic destination in the tropics.[75] Barely noticeable from the street view was a gable-roofed replica of a thirteenth-century Thai palace that housed a poolside restaurant at the top of the rectangular base (figure 8.5).

The Erawan, the Siam Intercontinental, the Dusit Thani, and the Indra Regent were examples of the ways architects eventually interpreted this attitude into material form. Situated on some of the important new thoroughfares of the city, they served as highly visible symbols of the union between easily legible details of Thai art and architecture and modern technology. They also served as sites of socially acceptable congress between Thais and a primarily American foreign clientele. They were exceptional zones of refinement and exchange carved out of a city that was faced with problems of overcrowding, crime, drug abuse, and poverty. As the capital's center of gravity moved eastward away from the royal compounds and riverside trading centers to a new cosmopolitan zone dominated by hotels, banks, office buildings, and shopping plazas, an alternative city developed in its shadow. This shadow city was where more salubrious forms of social congress were accommodated in massage parlors (*ap op nuat*), gay bars, and love motels catering to what Benedict Anderson has called "the sleaziest aspects of American civilization."[76]

THE SHADOW CITY

One of the typologies that emerged during this period to accommodate the transition to a land-based city, the emphasis on the automobile, and the influx of labor without permanent settlement was the *rong raem man rud* (lit. "pull curtain hotel"). While there is little archival material available on the hotels, they proliferated in some of the new areas opened up by infrastructural development in the city, notably in the areas adjacent to Sukhumvit and New Phetchaburi Roads.[77] While hotels like the Dusit Thani and the Siam Intercontinental were highly visible on some of the main thoroughfares of the city, the *rong raem man rud* were concealed from casual view, exploiting odd parcels of real estate in the shadows of the city's narrow lanes, or *soi*, and sub-*soi*.

The hotels that emerged in these areas consisted of a series of bay-fronted rooms arranged around a courtyard. Each bay was screened off by a curtain that an assistant would pull to conceal the car once it drove into the bay (figure 8.6). The system afforded users a sense of privacy, allowing them to enter and exit the vehicles that brought them to the hotel, at least theoretically, without being seen by others. The automobile provided the basic unit from which the rest of the motel emerged. Contemporary Thai architects have remarked that the *rong raem man rud* could not be considered a true hotel because hotels are not primarily oriented toward automobile traffic.[78] In high-profile hotels like the Dusit Thani, the lobby was a key component of the composition and acted as a transitional space between the street and private rooms. In the *rong raem man rud*, the public program was accommodated by the courtyard and was not intended for individual pedestrian guests (figure 8.7). The brise-soleils, which figured so prominently in the Indra Regent and other commercial typologies on the city's main roads, were used in the *rong raem man rud* as well, but at a smaller scale and with less grandiose symbolism. The emphasis on the automobile as the primary unit of design was reinforced through the use of "Mercedes bricks" (figure 8.8), which transformed the automobile's corporate branding into a formal geometric design. The design of *rong raem man rud* privileged the private aspects of the hotel over its "public" spaces. There was little space in the new typologies for social gathering spaces outside of the rooms.

FIG. 8.6. Parking bay of a *rong raem man rud* on Soi Ruam Rudi. Photo by Timothy Gerken.

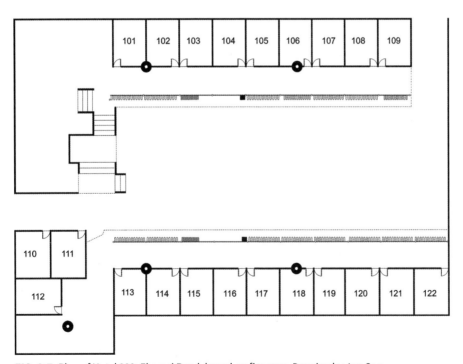

FIG. 8.7. Plan of Hotel 999, Ekamai Road, based on fire map. Drawing by Jun Cao.

FIG. 8.8. "Mercedes brick" ventilation device at former *rong raem man rud* on Sukhumvit Soi 1. Photo by author.

These rooms were sites of the kinds of encounter between rural and urban citizens and between foreign and native agents that proliferated in the Cold War era. Such encounters form the basis of the *Kai phi* and *Kai phi Bangkok* series by Ta Tha-it. The series is comprised of twelve collections of short stories that were published weekly from 1971 until just after the 1976 coup. Most of the stories appeared in *Fa muang thai rai sapda* (Thai Sky Weekly, 1969–1988), a popular weekly magazine with a primarily urban audience. The first-person narrator of the stories is Ta himself, a freelance guide who approaches atypical tourists who prefer not to go on package tours and offers specially catered to and unusual tours, although many of the sites are familiar sites in the tourist canon. As the *kai phi* narrator, Ta moves between historical anecdotes, English lessons (he defines the term "pimp," for instance, in fairly polite terms for a Thai readership), and background stories about his *farang* (white) clients. The stories introduce Thai readers to the city through *farang* eyes and encounters, simultaneously introducing cultural difference and cultural identity, describing both the importance of certain historical sites to a Thai reader as well as the foreigners' misunderstandings of them. The literary scholar Janit Feangfu has noted that in Ta's stories, Thailand becomes exotic to Thai readers.[79]

Indeed, Ta's stories are remarkable not only for their fusion of soft-core pornography, architectural and urban history, and tourist information, but also for the ways they perform a double dislocation, informing Thai readers of the city's emerging networks that were usually unseen by foreign tourists but also largely unknown to a broader Thai audience. For example, in the story "Wiman loi," the American tourists remark after their experience on the floating brothel that Vietnamese prostitutes are better and tell the story of one soldier who spent seven weeks on a brothel boat. When Ta, the ghost guide, suggests that the soldier was addicted to the skills of the woman, the Americans correct him: he was addicted to opium. The floating brothels in Vietnam serve opium as well as women. The ghost guide opines, as if to extol Thailand's advanced state of development over its neighbors, "I knew that if one wanted to find something like that here it wasn't difficult, but the whites would shudder to know that we don't serve opium. Rather, here in Thailand we've got heroin to welcome you on some of our play boats."[80]

His concluding observations to the story suggest that the guide is resigned to this encroaching seediness, which he describes as inevitable. By the late 1960s, an estimated three hundred thousand prostitutes worked in Bangkok. Then interior minister General Praphat Charusathian is said to have wanted even more because they attracted tourists and boosted the economy.[81] Against this backdrop, it is little wonder that Ta's guide saw the typology of the floating brothel as a permanent fixture of the urban landscape, even if its staff and clients change. "They came, they saw, and they did it. We Thai people—is there anyone taking a look at these ways of life? To this moment, to this day, the Floating Whore Boat still exists and I think it will continue on for a long time. No one would know when it will end. One after the other, the old ones leave, the young newly arrived ones will carry on their role. Rotating in cycles, forever and might continue to grow with Bangkok . . . who knows?"[82]

Ta treats the shadow city's floating brothels and gay bars as if they are another Thai attraction for foreign tourists, like the Floating Market.[83] However, there is also something foreign about these places, and Ta reports to his Thai readers as if he is describing customs and language that are unfamiliar to them. In the title story of *Talui ke khlap* (A Visit to the Gay Club), he recounts the inflated prices and overly fanciful menu descriptions of dishes in a restaurant where he meets his client, suggesting to his readers the ways Thai culture was repackaged for foreign consumption.[84] Throughout the story, Ta sees Bangkok in a new way as he tries to accommodate the needs of his gay client. He is initially confused by the terms the client uses ("trade," he learns, doesn't necessarily mean the work that a vendor does but rather, someone who can have sex with men but normally prefers women).[85] He is also confused by the presence of what appear to be female musicians in the club, although he later learns that these are men in wigs and women's clothing when they reveal themselves in a dramatic floor show at the end of the evening. Exiting the bar, the ghost guide waits for his client outside and reflects on the ways he has been tricked by the illusion of the female musicians. As he observes the first rays of light scattering the darkness in the early morning sky, he wistfully implores, "Oh Bangkok, City of Angels, why is your every street teeming with the stench of profane pleasures and lust (*khao lokki*) like these? Don't accuse me of excavating only profane stories to spread. I have already tried to filter my story to cleanse it. But real life is dirty. For me to paint and decorate it, to turn black into color, is difficult. I don't even know how to do that."[86]

As a participant in the shadow economy of official tourism, Ta's ghost guide is aware that the narrative he is constructing for Thai readers is very different from the sanitized version that the TOT was promoting to American tourists. However, the two could not exist without each other: the *wiman* of Ta's stories are the lurid shadows of the paradise that the TOT sought to narrate; so too were the *rong raem man rud* shadows of the Siam Intercontinental and Indra Regent Hotels. The shadow depended on the subject's form as well as actions and both reinforced the free-world consumerism of the Cold War and suggested the translatability of roles in both the official economy and its underbelly. However, a third, less stable narrative also accompanied this relationship, made by migrants who circulated within the infrastructural networks of the Cold War era.

THE PENUMBRA CITY

The circulation of labor, including sex labor, between the countryside and the city was supported by foreign loans, chiefly from the United States for highway construction and improvement.[87] American financial aid was initially focused on the construction of the Thanon Mitraphap (Friendship Highway). This highway linked Bangkok to Nong Khai, across the Mekong River from Vientiane, and crossed the northeastern region of the country. Major planning for the highways occurred in 1962 after the Rusk-Khoman agreement of 6 March 1962, which committed the United States to defend Thailand against possible aggression from Laos. Less than a month before, Sarit had mobilized troops on the Laos border during an offensive from communist forces there.[88] The Friendship Highway was the first trunk road in Thailand to use new technology (both asphalt and concrete) and apply international highway standards.[89] The post–World War II expansion of the provincial road network and the rise of truck and bus services encouraged labor mobility.[90] By 1950, the total number of national highways was close to four thousand miles, of which only five hundred, mostly within the vicinity of Bangkok, were paved. By 1966, however, more than half of the state highway network of seven thousand miles was paved, and a large network of feeder roads had been established.[91]

These new infrastructural standards provided not just a reorganization of territories heretofore peripheral to the state and a burgeoning neoliberal economy. They formed the penumbra to the shadow city and introduced new opportunities for populations to think of themselves as modern political subjects and, to borrow Marx and Engels's provocative phrase, escape "the idiocy of rural life."[92] The highway became not simply a conduit of labor and commodities into and out of the city, but also a means of expression for the migrants that it carried. In 1980, anthropologist Thawisak Pinthong and three of his students—Manot Phonthawi, Suphap Phuthawong, and Wutikrai Suwanwanich—published *Wannakam kep tok,* a collection of graffiti from restrooms, buses, and trucks plying routes across Thailand. The book offers a way to understand the truth claims of populations that have often been written out of official historical archives. The authors note that they view the graffiti as a kind of literature, composed by many people from different backgrounds. The title of the collection may be translated as *Literature That Has Been Gathered from What Is Left Behind* or *Recycled Literature* and is a term borrowed from scholar Chumdech Dechphimol to describe heartfelt literary expression that parodies (*lo lian*), satirizes (*siad si*), curses (*da tho*), critiques (*to wa to khan*), laments (*ramphueng ramphan*), and grieves (*alay awon*). The authors noted that these "scratchings" had been scattered and had never been collected and classified.[93] In addition to interviews with a driver of a *songthaew* (pickup truck fitted with two rows of benches for passengers) who plied the route from Tha Chang to Pak Soi Phrakhru, a delivery truck driver, and a security guard, the book is organized according to routes and periods and then further divided into types of transport and places as well as subject matter. The vast majority of entries have to do with love and longing, but a significant number are also concerned with social and political problems.

The authors discovered a sampling of political graffiti in toilets along the Friendship Highway. Some are familiar from the anti-dictatorship movements of the 1970s and 1980s: "Let / democracy bloom and let dictatorship wither," "Pay back the blood debt for justice," "Our comrades will come / the people will be happy / May all Thai sisters and brothers / unite in spirit to become a force," and "Leaders who think abnormally see us as pawns in their own survival scheme."

Others, however opted for a more complex perspective, for example: "Today's identity / ride a Benz / get on an airplane / gamble / smoke cigarettes, opium, heroin / pay no attention to studying / prevent money from going out of the country to save for big shots to embezzle inside the country."[94]

The cynical tone of the last poem belied a candid critique not only of the images of the floating paradise, but of the system that it represented as well. Sarit's *phatthana* deployed a familiar nationalist discourse but replaced the autarkic policies of the People's Party with a dependence on foreign capital. The graffito suggested a growing consciousness of the ways Cold War–era development benefited from not only legal enterprises like the automotive and air travel industries, but the informal economies of drug dealing and gambling as well. Together, the graffiti in *Wannakam kep tok* offered a different understanding of infrastructure space than histories of its development in the "American era" suggest. These poems offered an important counterpoint to the language of development and its promises of modernizing the country. They were a way of reclaiming the public nature of infrastructure as space. As literature, they connected reader and writer across time and space and served to remind readers, even in the isolated act of using the toilet, of the commonality of their experiences. They reframed public conveniences as political arenas in which it was possible to articulate a critique of the state and point further to the possibilities that exist beyond the limits of an imagination conditioned by consumer capitalism.

While early twentieth-century architects were interested in creating a "civilized" and "modern" nation, the Cold War emphasis on "development" decoupled state priorities from the concepts of democracy and social equality that had been associated with modernism. Utopianism and militarism had already made common cause during the tenure of the People's Party. Sarit's pastoral utopia moved even further to the right, demonstrating that individual happiness and fulfillment required not a democratic foundation but security and highways. As Thailand's military dictatorship concerned itself with national infrastructural projects, the architectural profession moved from "public" forms of architecture to new commercial typologies like office buildings, banks, and hotels that projected an image of a developed city that was consistent with the image of a safe yet exotic destination that the tourist industry sought to project to the world. The developmental utopia that the proposals of the National Economic Development Board, the Tourism Organization of Thailand, and the authors of the Litchfield plan celebrated can be seen in the hotels and commercial buildings of the period. The symbolism of the institution of the monarchy or of an imagined "traditional" past could be reimagined in the Cold War era as abstracted forms that gave the universal volumes of hotels like the Dusit Thani or the Siam Intercontinental a national character that was slightly out of sync with the rest of the ostensibly "developed" world. This disjuncture was enough to signal to international tourists that, although safe, they were no longer in the modern, democratic West.

The shadows of the floating paradise were exposed in the lurid narratives of the *Kai phi* series and experienced in the love motels that haunted the city of tourists and development specialists. This was a mimetic architecture that mirrored the forms of the floating paradise but drew its symbolism from the commodities of development, like ventilation devices fabricated from "Mercedes bricks." These motels accommodated intimate relations between different members of urban society but also took them out of the public realm. A third narrative, however, emerged in the penumbra of these shadows, along the roads that brought labor into and out of the city. Authored by the migrant laborers that were transported through the new infrastructure of roads that linked "strategic" provinces with the capital, the graffiti inscribed in public toilets and motor vehicles is evidence of the critical reception of the floating paradise. Collected by sociologists, the graffiti was framed as a form of literature that suggested the return to a moral and ethical utopia. It can best be understood within the context of the momentous changes that occurred in infrastructure space in 1973.

In October 1973, mass demonstrations erupted on Ratchadamnoen Avenue, the processional thoroughfare established by King Chulalongkorn to link the center of the concentric mandala with the grid of Dusit and which the People's Party sought to renovate into a "Thai Champs-Elysées."[95] The demonstrations were led by students associated with the National Student Center of Thailand who called on the military regime of Sarit's heirs, Field Marshals Thanom Kittikachorn and Praphat Charusathian to redraft the constitution that Thanom had abolished two years earlier when he seized power in a coup d'état. The demonstrations grew as the military regime closed schools and the demonstrators gained popular support among a large section of urban classes. On the morning of 14 October 1973, armed forces fired into demonstrators, killing 77 and wounding 857.[96] The dead body of a protestor was raised on top of the Democracy Monument to proclaim the fraudulence of the military government.[97] King Bhumibol, along with dissenting factions of the military, demanded that Thanom, Praphat, and Narong (Thanom's son who was married to Praphat's daughter) leave the country.[98] The demonstrations turned a symbolic urban thoroughfare into a commons and precipitated a three-year period of debate, conflict, experiment, and change across Thai society. Street protests and labor strikes became almost daily events and put pressure on the government to restore the project of democratization that had begun in 1932. Students, workers, peasants, and monks created political alliances to demand social and economic justice.[99]

In the intervening three-year experiment with popular democracy in Thailand, architectural education embraced new pedagogical strategies and moved away from passive models of education to foster critical exchanges between students and professors.[100] The curriculum also opened up, moving beyond teaching the mere design of buildings to include urban planning, landscape, investment, business administration, law, computer technology, and broader systematic thinking of architecture's role in society.[101] These years had little impact on the architectural profession, however, which continued to follow the private investment that had driven architectural production since the market was opened under the Sarit regime.[102] The profession thus abandoned the political implications of architecture to pursue the uncritical image of a laissez-faire utopia. The pursuit of this "floating paradise" resulted not in the smooth-functioning productive metropolis that was intended by Litchfield, Whiting, Bowne, and Associates, the World Bank, or the US Operation Mission, but in a city of congested infrastructure networks and broken social services.[103] In these moments of failure, or systemic "glitches," the contradictions of *phatthanakan* became legible.[104] Just as both mandala and grid could be sustained within the city plan, utopia and dystopia became entwined in the development of the city. But even as the attempt to create a developed city resulted in increased exploitation and repression, radical expressions of liberation persisted in the deepest shadows of the neoliberal *vimāna*.

CHAPTER NINE

EPILOGUE

The power of storytelling is one of the themes that runs throughout this book. According to a well-known refrain from the American novelist and essayist Joan Didion, "We tell ourselves stories in order to live."[1] Narrative, sociologist Vittoria Bonnel and historian Lynn Hunt have pointed out, is the arena in which meaning takes form, the connective tissue between individuals and the public and social world, and the site in which change becomes possible.[2] Nowhere has this been truer than in twentieth-century Bangkok, where the power of narration has both conjured national communities and exposed their frailties. Fiction has been described by its more thoughtful practitioners as a lie that reveals the truth, while politicians have historically fabricated stories as a way to conceal complex truths. Although functionally providing material shelter for human communities, architecture operates rhetorically as a narrative form. Victor Hugo famously polemicized the dramatic transformations brought about by new building technologies in the nineteenth century by observing, "Ceci tuera cela. Le livre tuera l'edifice."[3] Hugo—or, more precisely, his character Claude Frollo, the archdeacon of Notre-Dame cathedral—rued the changes that the printing press would bring to the social role of the cathedral that had long dominated the Parisian skyline. Buddhist sites in Southeast Asia long functioned in a similar way, narrating religious ideals not only through didactic murals and friezes but also with building forms that could be engaged through sensorial contact as complex representations and metaphors of the cosmos and the felicitous realms within it. As buildings, their technical production, and labor relations changed over the course of the twentieth century, so too did the narratives the buildings described.

In the beginning of the twentieth century, migrant laborers from the southern coast of China brought diagrams of a dynastic utopia, the City of

Willows, with them to Bangkok to map the future empire they sought to build. As the Chakri monarchy embarked on its own project of nation building, it too drew on images of a felicitous city, *nibbāna*, that were reproduced in building manuals. Vajiravudh, the last Siamese king to complete his reign as an absolute monarch, drew on both historicist architectural idioms and modern conceptions of governance when he constructed a model utopia in the gardens of his palaces to speculate on a possible democratic future for Siam. These imaginative speculations about the city were historically conditioned, on the one hand by capitalism and colonialism, and on the other by Buddhist felicities concerned with emancipation from suffering. Vajiravudh's crematorium, for example, reproduced the spatial dimensions of Mount Meru in lived, Euclidean space in order to announce his position not only as a *devaraja* but also as the righteous leader of a modern nation-state. When the absolute monarchy was overthrown, the new constitutionalist state also built a crematorium that conjured Mount Meru but used it to sacralize the nation-state itself. Throughout the twentieth century, Thai architects drew on modern building materials and technologies to narrate a new trajectory for the imagined community of the nation. M. C. Samaichaloem Kridakon, for example, used not only steel and concrete but air-conditioning as well to create a modern space in which the technology of the cinema could reinforce older approaches to political narrative, like the *Ramakian*. Although the architects of the People's Party sought to formulate a new aesthetic order through the use of concrete and purge Thai architecture of its hieratic royalist symbolism, they created a new architecture in which the felicitous spaces of the Buddha were linked to the territory of the nation-state. The relic *chedi* of Wat Phra Sri Mahathat created a space that was at once democratic and authoritarian, bringing the remains of commoners into unprecedented intimacy with the remains of the historic Buddha under the auspices of the state. The commonality between utopianism and militarism in the World War II era paved the way for the shift from narratives of modernization to those of "development." As the US-supported military dictatorship moved away from the mid-twentieth-century modernist project of social equality, the architectural profession in Thailand also turned its attention from "public" monuments, monastic complexes, schools, and stadia to commercial typologies that were integral to the image of a "developed" city: hotels, banks, and office buildings.

Bangkok's twentieth-century utopian projects suggest that capitalist development has been only one component of the historical process in regions like Southeast Asia, which have been peripheral to histories of the modern. In Bangkok, modernity was not merely imitative of the experience of urbanization, industrialization, and secularization in Europe and the United States. It was the heterogeneous product of an encounter between labor, materials, technologies, and, most important, ideas that circulated across diverse trade, migration, and intellectual networks. This encounter not only challenged and transformed older, Buddhist understandings of space and time but transformed modernism itself. Like all fictions, utopia and the felicitous realms of the Pali imaginaire were a powerful engine for the building of Bangkok as well as a mask for its internal contradictions. Utopian imagery became an important part of a nationalist ideology that disguised the dialectical nature of historical development but was also capable of motivating social and political change. In many respects, the formal, programmatic, and narrative expressions of utopia have always paradoxically expressed both hope and hegemony. A nightmare, after all, is also a kind of dream, and the two often visit our dormant consciousness intertwined. The literary, architectural, and political utopias that emerged in twentieth-century Bangkok offer a new way of understanding the dual character of modern relationships between the practice and representation of space. Buildings like the Sala Chaloem Krung, one of the first air-conditioned cinemas to be built in the world, rose anachronistically out of a city that was still developing roads, housing, and a modern public infrastructure. Plans, sections, and elevations of what the city and its architecture should look like emerged as temple murals and illustrated cosmological manuscripts continued to inform understandings of urban space. These built and unbuilt interventions were at once nowhere and somewhere, "dreamworld and catastrophe," and became important instruments not only of imagining abstract communities like the nation but also of inventing the urban spaces modern populations inhabited.[4]

The fraught relationship between utopia, Buddhist felicities, nationalist ideology, and urban space was vividly expressed on 24 June 1932 when leaders of the People's Party announced the arrival of the era of *sri ariya* for the people of Siam. This visionary declaration was made in the open Royal Plaza by the equestrian statue of King Chulalongkorn in front of the Ananta Samakhom Throne Hall. These sites, intended originally to aggrandize the monarchy and announce its place within a new modern world of nation-states, were commemorated as national sites for the Thai public by the installation of a plaque that read, "We the People's Party have birthed the Constitution for the nation's progress." It is today close to a century after the People's Party sought to usher in the era of *sri ariya*, and yet Bangkok has never been further from that felicitous state. In early April 2017, the plaque installed by the People's Party was mysteriously replaced by a new one that read, "Long live Siam forever! Happy, fresh-faced citizens build up the power of the land!" Surrounding this were slogans that proclaimed, "Loyalty and love for the Triple Gem, one's clan and having an honest heart for one's king is good. These are the tools to make one's state prosper!"[5] Other monuments to the People's Party era of *sri ariya* have also been under attack. The Supreme Court, designed by Sarot Sukhyang and built in 1939 as an imposing flat-roofed concrete monument to universal justice across from the royal parade ground of Sanam Luang, was destroyed in 2008 and replaced by a retrograde complex crowned with a gabled roof and *naga*-head finials. The Monument to the Defense of the Constitution, discussed in chapter 5, has been moved several times as part of a larger effort by ultraroyalist advocates to erase the legacy of the People's Party from public memory.[6] It remains, for the time being, dwarfed by new infrastructure projects that aim to expand the city's mass transit system in pursuit of a formal, developmental model of utopia.

These events can be understood as part of the continuing contradictions of utopian nationalism in Thailand. In the Cold War era, the political importance of the monarchy was revived and the king recast as a modern *chakravartin* whose sage generosity underwrote the happiness of his subjects. This "rebranding" of the monarchy took form through a US-backed military dictatorship and was enforced through both repressive and ideological means. The monarchy thus returned to the top of not only a sociopolitical hierarchy, but a moral one as well, in which the greatest merit makers (the monarchy, the titled bureaucracy, wealthy merchants, and even the urban bourgeoisie) were elevated above peasants and workers who lacked the material means to make merit.[7] If the image of utopia and the felicitous realms of the Pali imaginaire could be used by the ideologues of the People's Party as a model for justice and equality in 1932, they could also be deployed after 1957 to argue against a democratic system that sought to topple the moral hierarchy of capitalism.

In spite of the willful erasure of the era of the People's Party in the city, traces of *sri ariya* persist in Bangkok and remind us of the necessity of being able to step out of the certainty of the time and place of the present to insist on what the performance studies scholar José Esteban Muñoz has called "something else, something better, something dawning."[8] Throughout the twentieth century, utopia and the felicitous spaces of the Pali imaginaire have been a resource for the political imagination, offering up aesthetic and narrative practices that have allowed humans to plan for a collective becoming. Is it possible to recover such imagery from its use as a tool of cooptation and false consciousness and shape it into an instrument and method of emancipation? The ruins of *sri ariya* suggest that architecture's potential for enacting social change may not necessarily lie in *building* a better world but in demolishing the totalizing stranglehold late-stage capitalism places on the speculative imagination. The narratives architects and activists of the twenty-first century produce will only differ from the utopias of the past when they imagine the architectonics of an urban environment that is "ni le royaume de Dieu, ni le cloaque," but a city liberated from the conditions of suffering.[9]

NOTES

CHAPTER ONE: INTRODUCTION

1 "'Ja New' Assault Spurs Outcry," *Bangkok Post*, 29 June 2019; "Would Bangkok Tolerate a Vehicle Ban to Ease Toxic Haze?" *Bangkok Post*, 21 February 2018; Phanarat Thepgumpanat, "Pollution Prompts Bangkok to Close Schools for the Week," Reuters, 30 January 2019; "Floods Paralyze Bangkok Traffic after Downpour," *Bangkok Post*, 7 June 2019; "Inequality Exposed," *Bangkok Post*, 10 December 2018; "Thailand Most Unequal Country in 2018," *Bangkok Post*, 6 December 2018.

2 Thipakorawong, *Dynastic Chronicles, Bangkok Era, the First Reign, Volume One: Text*, trans. Thadeus and Chadin Flood (Tokyo: Centre for East Asian Cultural Studies, 1978), 58.

3 Nathaniel Coleman, *Imagining and Making the World: Reconsidering Architecture and Utopia* (Oxford: Peter Lang, 2011); Jane Alison, Frédéric Migayrou, and Neil Spiller, *Future City: Experiment and Utopia in Architecture* (London: Thames and Hudson, 2007); Peter Blake, *No Place Like Utopia: Modern Architecture and the Company We Kept* (New York: W.W. Norton, 1993); Manfredo Tafuri, *Architecture and Utopia: Design and Capitalist Development* (Cambridge, MA: MIT Press, 1976).

4 Because Collins's conception of the Pali imaginaire functioned as an ideal type, he also noted that it consisted of all Pali texts from the premodern period of which there is a "western edition." Steve Collins, *Nirvana and Other Buddhist Felicities: Utopias of the Pali Imaginaire* (Cambridge: Cambridge University Press, 1998), 78, 110. James Egge refined the term to mean those things about which the whole body of Pali texts, or at least most of them, agree. See James Egge, *Religious Giving and the Invention of Karma in Theravada Buddhism* (London: RoutledgeCurzon, 2002).

5 About felicities, Collins has written, "Perhaps one could speak of aspirations to comfort, of the modest and more ambitious kinds, and of the reassurance that the universe is such as to contain many kinds of comfort, including the pos-

sibility of one which is entirely secure from misfortune." Importantly, Collins reminds readers that the paradisiacal conditions of natural abundance, unlimited food, and palaces glittering with jewels spoke to the poverty in which most inhabitants of southern Asia historically lived. Collins, *Nirvana*, 93–95.

6 The length of the *yojana* varied depending on the different standards of various South Asian astronomers and generally ranged between 8 and 14.63 kilometers. Measuring the *yojana* against the Chinese *li* in historical accounts of Chinese pilgrims between the fourth and sixth centuries CE, nineteenth-century engineer and archaeologist Alexander Cunningham deduced the *yojana* as equivalent to variously 4.5, 8.5, 6.71, or 8.3 British miles. See *The Ancient Geography of India*, vol. 1, *The Buddhist Period, Including the Campaigns of Alexander and the Travels of Hwen-Thsang* (London: Trübner, 1876), 571–576. To further complicate matters, the *yojana* would have had denoted different distances depending on the worlds in which it was deployed. Craig Reynolds, "Buddhist Cosmography in Thai History, with Special Reference to 19th-Century Culture Change," *Journal of Asian Studies* 35, no. 2 (February 1976): 205. *The Royal Government Gazette* of Thailand records the distance as 16 kilometers. This is consistent with the calculations of Gerolamo Emilio Gerini, an Italian native who became a Siamese military official. G. E. Gerini, *Chūḷākantamaṅgala, or The Tonsure Ceremony as Performed in Siam* (Bangkok: Bangkok Times Office, 1893), 97, 102; Lithai, *Traibhumikatha* (Bangkok: ASEAN Committee on Culture and Information, 1985), 74, 248; *Ratchakitchanubeksa* 40 (27 December 1923), 183–218.

7 Charles Hallisey, "Nibbānasutta: An Allegedly Non-canonical Sutta on Nibbāna as a Great City," *Journal of the Pali Text Society* 18 (1993): 113.

8 Although differences between *nibbāna* and other felicitous states were more distinct in Buddhist systematic thought, in narrative thought—which is primarily the focus of this book—the distinction was not as pronounced. Collins, *Nirvana*, 121.

9 Collins, *Nirvana*, 77; Kevin S. Trainor, *Relics, Ritual, and Representation in Buddhism: Rematerializing the Sri Lankan Theravāda Tradition* (Cambridge: Cambridge University Press, 1997), 88–92, 96–117; Kevin S. Trainor, "Constructing a Buddhist Ritual Site: Stupa and Monastery Architecture," *Unseen Presence: The Buddha and Sanchi*, ed. Vidya Dehejia (Bombay: Mārg, 1996); Donald K. Swearer, *The Buddhist World of Southeast Asia* (Albany: State University of New York Press, 2010), 76–82; Donald K. Swearer, Sommai Premchit, and Phaithoon Dokbuakaew, *Sacred Mountains of Northern Thailand and Their Legends* (Chiang Mai, Thailand: Silkworm, 2004), 21–35; Edward Van Roy, "The Rise and Fall of the Bangkok Mandala," *Journal of Asian History* 45, nos. 1–2 (2011).

10 Collins, *Nirvana*, 291; Anne Ruth Hansen, *How to Behave: Buddhism and Modernity in Colonial Cambodia, 1860–1930* (Honolulu: University of Hawai'i Press, 2007), 19; Charles F. Keyes, "Millennialism, Theravāda Buddhism, and Thai Society," *Journal of Asian Studies* 36, no. 2 (1977): 283–302.

11 Bangkok is the capital of Thailand. Before 1939, the country was known as Siam.

12 No philosopher has observed this more astutely than Karl Marx, who, writing in the mid-nineteenth century, observed, "Was aber von vorn herein den schlechtesten Baumeister vor der besten Biene auszeichnet, ist, dass er die Zelle in seinem Kopf gebaut hat, bevor er sie in Wachs baut" (But what distinguishes the worst architect from the best bee is that the architect raises the structure in his imagination before he erects it in reality). Karl Marx, *Das Kapital: Kritik*

der politischen Ökonomie, erster Band, Buch 1: Der Produktionsprozeß des Kapitals (Hamburg: Otto Meißners Verlag, 1922), 140.

13 French philosopher Louis Althusser further developed an understanding of the importance of ideology as a state apparatus that ensured the continuity of the conditions of production. He identified a plurality of institutions known as "Ideological State Apparatuses" through which the state exerted its authority outside outright violent repression. While Althusser did not include architecture among the nonrepressive institutions that reproduce the labor force and its submission to the rules of the established order, his argument is key to understanding the political arrangements of architecture and urban design in early twentieth-century Siam. Louis Althusser, "Ideology and Ideological State Apparatuses (Notes Towards an Investigation)," *Lenin and Philosophy, and Other Essays* (London: New Left Books, 1971), 143.

14 The most prevalent conception of ideology comes from the writings of Marx and comes to the forefront of his thinking in *The German Ideology*. Following Ludwig Feuerbach, Marx saw religion as the first example of ideology as an inverted reflection of reality. Karl Marx, *The German Ideology* (New York: International Publishers, 1947), 47; Paul Ricouer, *Lectures on Ideology and Utopia* (New York: Columbia University Press, 1986), 4; Louis Althusser, "Ideology and Ideological State Apparatuses (Notes Towards an Investigation)," 143; James Duncan, *The City as Text: The Politics of Landscape Interpretation in the Kandyan Kingdom* (Cambridge: Cambridge University Press, 1990), 19; Collins, *Nirvana*, 77.

15 Bernard Philippe Groslier, "La cité hydraulique angkorienne: Exploitation ou surexploitation du soi?" *Bullete de l'École française d'Extrême-Orient* 66 (1979).

16 Swearer, *Buddhist World*, 208–210; J. G. De Casparis, "Inscripties uit de Cailendra-tijd," in *Prasati Indonesia diterbitkan oleh Djawatan Purbakala Republic Indonesia*, vol. 1 (Bandung: A.C. Nix, 1950), 193; H. G. Quaritch Wales, *The Making of Greater India* (London: B. Quaritch, 1961), 123; R. Soekmono, Jacques Dumarcay, and J. G. De Casparis, *Borobudur: Prayer in Stone* (London: Thames and Hudson, 1990), 32.

17 Anne Blackburn, "Writing Buddhist Histories from Landscape and Architecture," *Buddhist Studies Review* 24, no. 2 (2007): 194, 201.

18 Blackburn, "Writing Buddhist Histories"; Anne Blackburn, "Buddha-Relics in the Lives of Southern Asian Polities," *Numen* 57, nos. 3–4 (2010); Duncan, *City as Text*.

19 Maurizio Peleggi, *Monastery, Monument, Museum: Sites and Artifacts of Thai Cultural Memory* (Honolulu: University of Hawai'i Press, 2017), 2–3, 9–29.

20 "Utopia" and "eu-topia." See the poem "Anemolius: A Short Metre of Utopia, Written by Anemolius, Laureate and Nephew to Hythlodya, by His Sister," which was included in the front matter in the four original editions of *Utopia* that Thomas More was directly involved in publishing from 1516 to 1518. Thomas More, *Utopia* (Louvain: Arte Theoidorici Martini, 1516).

21 Although the dominant royalist narrative is that the country was never colonized, scholars of Thailand's political economy have argued that Siam's rulers collaborated with European colonial powers to produce a kind of surrogate colonialism that they could administer and profit from. Tamara Loos, *Subject Siam: Family, Law, and Colonial Modernity in Thailand* (Ithaca, NY: Cornell University Press, 2006), 17–18.

22 Keyes, "Millennialism," 283–302.

23 Benedict Anderson, *Imagined Communities: Reflections on the Origins and Spread of Nationalism* (London: Verso, 1983); Philip E. Wegner, *Imaginary Communities: Utopia, the Nation, and Spatial Histories of Modernity* (Berkeley: University of California Press, 2002).

24 Chit Phumisak, "Chomna khong sakdina thai nai patchuban" (The real face of Thai feudalism today), *Nitisat 2500 chabap rap sattawatmai* (The Faculty of Law yearbook 2500 to greet the new century) (Bangkok: Thammasat University Faculty of Law, 2007); Marc Léopold Benjamin Bloch, *Feudal Society*, vol. 1 (Chicago: University of Chicago Press, 1961), 170–173, 189; Seksan Prasertkul, "The Transformation of the Thai State and Economic Change (1855–1945)" (PhD diss., Cornell University, 1989), 453–459.

25 Marshall Berman, *All That Is Solid Melts into Air: The Experience of Modernity* (New York: Simon and Schuster, 1982), 16.

26 Berman, *All That Is Solid*, 16.

27 Hilde Heynen, *Architecture and Modernity: A Critique* (Cambridge, MA: MIT Press, 1999), 10–11.

28 Sibel Bozdoğan, *Modernism and Nation Building: Turkish Architectural Culture and the Early Republic* (Seattle: University of Washington Press, 2001), 9.

29 Chatri Prakitnontakan, *Khana ratsadorn chalong ratthamnun: Prawatisat kan mueang lang 2475 phan satthapatayagam "amnat"* (The People's Party celebrates the constitution: Political history after 1932 through the architecture of "power") (Bangkok: Matichon, 2005), 25–27.

30 Gyan Prakash, "Introduction," in *Spaces of the Modern City: Imaginaries, Politics, and Everyday Life*, ed. Gyan Prakash and Kevin M. Kruse (Princeton, NJ: Princeton University Press, 2008), 15; Jennifer Robinson, *Ordinary Cities: Between Modernity and Development* (New York: Routledge, 2006), 7.

31 Dipesh Chakrabarty, *Provincializing Europe: Postcolonial Thought and Historical Difference* (Princeton, NJ: Princeton University Press, 2000), 16.

32 Loos, *Subject Siam*; Arnika Fuhrmann, *Ghostly Desires: Queer Sexuality and Vernacular Buddhism in Contemporary Thai Cinema* (Durham, NC: Duke University Press, 2016), 5.

33 Robinson, *Ordinary Cities*, 28–30. "But precisely the modern, *la modernité*, is always citing primal history. Here, this always occurs through the ambiguity peculiar to the social relations and products of the time. Ambiguity is the manifest imaging of dialectic, the law of dialectics at a standstill. This standstill is utopia and the dialectical image, therefore, dream image." Walter Benjamin, *The Arcades Project* (Cambridge, MA: Belknap, 1999), 10.

34 Anne Blackburn, *Locations of Buddhism: Colonialism and Modernity in Sri Lanka* (Chicago: University of Chicago Press, 2010), xii.

35 Hansen, *How to Behave*, 12–13, 182.

36 Dell Upton, *Another City: Urban Life and Urban Spaces in the New American Republic* (New Haven, CT: Yale University Press, 2008), 122.

37 Anthony Cascardi and Michael Dear, "What Are the Urban Humanities?" *Boom: A Journal of California* (Fall 2016): 7.

38 Max Hirsh, *Airport Urbanism: Infrastructure and Mobility in Asia* (Minneapolis: University of Minnesota Press, 2016), 11; Swati Chattopadhyay, *Unlearning the City: Infrastructure in a New Optical Field* (Minneapolis: University of Minnesota Press), ix–xviii.

39 Christian F. Otto has noted that the recording of architects' conversations of the 1920s into a series of publications began with Adolf Bruno Behne's *Der moderne Zweckbau* (1926) and continued with texts such as Gustav Adolf Platz's *Die Baukunst der neuen Zeit* (1927), Sigfried Giedion's *Bauen in Frankreich: Eisen, Eisenbeton* (1928), and Henry Russel Hitchock's *Modern Architecture: Romanticism and Reintegration* (1929); Otto, "Program and Programs," in *Rethinking Architectural Historiography*, ed. Dana Arnold, Elvan Altan Ergut, and Belgini Turan Özkaya (London: Routledge, 2006), 56, 59n.

40 Thongchai Winichakul, "The Changing Landscape of the Past: New Histories in Thailand Since 1973," *Journal of Southeast Asian Studies* 26, no. 1 (March 1995): 99.

41 Donald K. Swearer, "The Northern Thai City as a Sacred Center," in *The City as a Sacred Center: Essays on Six Asian Contexts*, ed. Bardwell Smith and Holly Baker Reynolds (Leiden: Brill, 1987), 104.

42 Swearer, "Northern Thai City," 104.

43 Pridi Phanomyong, "Announcement of the People's Party, No. 1 (1932)," in *Pridi by Pridi: Selected Writings on Life, Politics, and Economy* (Chiang Mai, Thailand: Silkworm, 2000), 72.

44 Mark Fisher, *Capitalist Realism: Is There No Alternative?* (London: Zero Books, 2009), 80.

CHAPTER TWO: A HISTORICAL AND COSMOLOGICAL FRAMEWORK

1 Before his coronation, Phuttayotfa was known as Chao Phraya Chakri (Thong Duang) and ruled as Ramathibodi, after the founder of Ayutthaya. It was only posthumously that he was given the title of Phra Phuttayotfa Chulalok. This book uses this title for the founder of the dynasty and the title given upon coronation rather than the regnal name (Rama) or the full Thai title.

2 The jewel of Kosindra refers to the palladium of the Emerald Buddha, brought to Bangkok by Phuttayotfa and installed within its own chapel on the grounds of the Grand Palace in 1784.

3 Translation by the author, based on Thipakorawong, *Phraratchaphongsawadan krung rattanakosin ratchakan thi 1–2* (Dynastic chronicles of Rattanakosin, First and Second Reigns) (Bangkok: Khlingwitthaya, 1963), 84–85. The name was amended during the reign of King Phra Chomklao from "Bawonrattanakosin" to the present-day "Amonrattanakosin."

4 Neither, however, was descended from the royal family of Ayutthaya. Taksin was the son of a Teochew father and Siamese mother who was adopted into a noble family and served as the governor of Tak Province. Phuttayotfa was the son of a middle-level Ayutthayan official and related to important noble families of the polity. David Wyatt, *Thailand: A Short History* (New Haven, CT: Yale University Press, 1984), 140, 142.

5 Maurizio Peleggi, *Lords of Things: The Fashioning of the Siamese Monarchy's Modern Image* (Honolulu: University of Hawai'i Press, 2002), 78; Thipakorawong, *Dynastic Chronicles, Bangkok Era, the First Reign, Volume One: Text,* trans. Thadeus and Chadin Flood (Tokyo: Centre for East Asian Cultural Studies, 1978), 58–59.

6 Thipakorawong, *Dynastic Chronicles, Bangkok Era, First Reign,* 59.

7 Thipakorawong, *Dynastic Chronicles, Bangkok Era, First Reign,* 1.

8 Peleggi, *Lords of Things*, 78.

9 Phra Sumen refers to the center of the Indic/Buddhist cosmos, Mount Meru, and Mahakan is the Indic/Buddhist deity who is beyond time. Sujit Wongthes, *Krungthep ma jak nai* (Bangkok: A historical background) (Bangkok: Dream Catcher, 2005), 118–120; Udomporn Teeraviriyakul, *Bangkok Modern* (Bangkok: Institute of Asian Studies, Chulalongkorn University, 2014), 73.

10 Nidhi Eoseewong, *Pen and Sail: Literature and History in Early Bangkok,* trans. Chris Baker et al. (Chiang Mai, Thailand: Silkworm, 2005), 131.

11 Wyatt, *Thailand,* 154.

12 Wyatt, *Thailand,* 147.

13 Sawan Tangtrongsitthikun, "Kan sang 'lak chai kaen muang' mua raek sathabana krung rattanakosin in ayutthaya" (The building of the "Victory Monument in the Center of the City" at the establishment of the city of Rattanakosin), *Silpawatthanatham* 36, no. 6 (April 2015): 112.

14 The exact origins of the city pillar are uncertain but are likely indigenous and predate Indic influence in the region. B. J. Terwiel, "The Origin and Meaning of the City Pillar," *Journal of the Siam Society* 66, no. 2 (1978): 167.

15 There is some discrepancy in the dynastic chronicles regarding the exact year. *The Dynastic Chronicles, Version of the Royal Secretary* records the year as the dynastic year of 860 (2041 BE / 1498 CE) while the *Dynastic Chronicles of the Old Capital, Luang prasoet aksorn version* lists the dynastic year as 880 (2061 BE / 1518 CE). *Phraratchaphongsawadan chabap phraratchahatlekha* (Bangkok: Krom silpakorn, 1973), 125; *Phraratchaphongsawadan chabap luangprasoetaksorn* (Bangkok: Krom silpakorn, 1972), 453; *Tamra phra maha phichai songkhram chabap wat kuaninniimitr amphoe muang phattalung changwat phattalung* (Songkhla: Sathaban Taksinkhadisuksa, Mahawittayalai Thaksin, 1998), 5–6.

16 *Tamra phichai songkhram khong krom silpakorn: Phim pen anuson nai ngan chapon kit sop Nang Sanitiaronarot (Tlap Bunratphan)* (Bangkok: Krom Silpakon, 1969), 1–6; Craig Reynolds, *Seditious Histories: Contesting Thai and Southeast Asian Pasts* (Seattle: University of Washington Press, 2006), 229–230.

17 H. G. Quaritch Wales, *Divination in Thailand: The Hopes and Fears of a Southeast Asian People* (London: Curzon, 1983), 132–133; *Tamra phichai songkhram khong krom silpakorn,* ก.

18 Reynolds, *Seditious Histories,* 229–230.

19 Vinayak Bharne, Krupali Krusche, and Leon Krier, *Rediscovering the Hindu Temple: The Sacred Architecture and Urbanism of India* (Newcastle upon Tyne, UK: Cambridge Scholars, 2012), 33; Sheldon Pollock, "The Theory of Practice and the Practice of Theory in Indian Intellectual History," *Journal of the American Oriental Society* 105, no. 3 (1985): 501.

20 Kautalya, *The Arthashastra,* ed. L. N. Rangarajan (New Delhi: Penguin, 1992).

21 Pasuk Phongpaichit and Chris Baker, *A History of Ayutthaya: Siam in the Modern World* (Cambridge: Cambridge University Press, 2017), 100–101; Pasuk Phongphaichit and Chris Baker, "The Spirits, the Stars, and Thai Politics" (talk at the Siam Society, Bangkok, 2 December 2008), 7.

22 Paul Wheatley, "The Suspended Pelt: Reflections on a Discarded Model of Spatial Structure," in *Geographic Humanism, Analysis and Social Action: Proceedings of Symposia Celebrating a Half Century of Geography at Michigan,* ed. Donald Deskins Jr., George Kish, John Nystuen, and Gunnar Olson (Ann Arbor: Department of Geography, University of Michigan, 1977), 52–54.

202

NOTES TO PAGES 14–16

23 Naengnoi Suksri and Michael Freeman, *Palaces of Bangkok: Royal Residences of the Chakri Dynasty* (Bangkok: River Books, 1996), 12–16; *Tamra phichai song-khram* illustrated manuscript, Or 15760, British Library.

24 *Tamra phichai songkhram chabap ratchakan thi neung* (Bangkok: Krom Silpakon, 2002), 59.

25 Sawan, "Kan sang 'lak chai kaen muang' mua raek sathabana krung rattanako-sin in ayutthaya," 107.

26 Thipakorawong, *Phraratchaphongsawadan krung rattanakosin ratchakan thi 1-2*, vol. 1, 43.

27 Krom Silpakon, *Chotmai het kan anurak krung rattanakosin* (Bangkok: Krom Sil-pakon, 1982), 372–374.

28 Sawan, "Kan sang 'lak chai kaen muang' mua raek sathabana krung rattana-kosin in ayutthaya," 104. The *mangkon phayu kham nam* was in the form of a *yantra*, or linear representation consisting of letters, numbers, syllables, or mantras. For further reading on the dynamics of the *yantra*, see Thomas Pat-ton, "In Pursuit of the Sorcerer's Power: Sacred Diagrams as Technologies of Potency," *Contemporary Buddhism* 13, no. 2 (2012); Catherine Becchetti-Bizot and François Bizot, *Le mystère dans les lettres: Étude sur les yantra bouddhiques du Cambodge et de la Thaïlande* (Bangkok: Edition des cahiers de France, 1991).

29 Sawan, "Kan sang 'lak chai kaen muang' mua raek sathabana krung rattanako-sin in ayutthaya," 110.

30 Wyatt, *Thailand*, 139–140.

31 The wars between the Kongbaung dynasty and the polities of Ayutthaya, Thon-buri, and Bangkok were fought between 1751 and 1855. Wyatt, *Thailand*, 149–152.

32 Paul Wheatley, "Suspended Pelt," 52–54.

33 Edward Van Roy, "The Rise and Fall of the Bangkok Mandala," *Journal of Asian History* 45, nos. 1–2 (2011): 86; Frank E. Reynolds and Mani B. Reynolds, "Trans-lators' Introduction," *Three Worlds According to King Ruang*, by Lithai, trans. Frank E. Reynolds and Mani B. Reynolds (Berkeley: Regents of the University of California, 1982), 3.

34 Van Roy, "Rise and Fall," 85; See also Stanley Tambiah, "The Galactic Polity: The Structure of Traditional Kingdoms in Southeast Asia," *Annals of the New York Academy of Sciences* 293 (1977): 69–97; Diana Eck, "The City as a Sacred Center," in *The City as Sacred Center: Essays on Six Asian Contexts*, ed. Bardwell Smith and Holly Baker Reynolds (Leiden: Brill, 1987).

35 Sunait Chutintaranond, "Mandala, Segmentary State and Politics of Central-ization in Medieval Ayudhya," *Journal of the Siam Society* 78, no. 1 (1990): 90; O. W. Wolters, *History, Culture and Religion Southeast Asian Perspectives* (Ithaca, NY: SEAP Publications/Institute of Southeast Asian Studies, 1999), 25.

36 Michael Aung-Thwin, *Pagan: The Origins of Modern Burma* (Honolulu: Univer-sity of Hawai'i Press, 1985), 164.

37 The Thai term *yan* is also used to describe a kind of mandala, although it is derived from the Pali *yanta*, a means of holding or an instrument. Ratchabandit-tayasathan, *Photchananukrom chabap ratchabandiuttayasathan pho so 2525* (Dictionary of the Royal Institute of Thailand, 1996 version) (Bangkok: Ratcha-bandittayasathan, 1996).

38 Wheatley, "Suspended Pelt," 52–54.

39 Eck, "City as Sacred Center," 6; Donald K. Swearer, "The Northern Thai City as a Sacred Center," in Smith and Reynolds, *City as a Sacred Center*, 112.

40 Wheatley, "Suspended Pelt," 52–54.

41 Peleggi, *Lords of Things,* 78.

42 This may have also been related to Phuttayotfa's concern that linga worship would displace reverence for Buddhist teachings. He originally ordered all linga to be collected and burned, but as there were some references to guardian spirits in Pali texts, he relented and allowed them to remain on condition that they not be revered more than the Three Jewels (the Buddha, the dhamma, and the sangha). Nidhi, *Pen and Sail,* 329; D. B. Bradley, ed., *Kotmai muang thai* (Thai law) (Bangkok: Rim pom phak khlong bangkok yai, 1873), 503.

43 Marc Askew, *Bangkok: Place, Practice, and Representation* (London: Routledge, 2002), 17; Van Roy, "Rise and Fall," 99; Wyatt, *Thailand,* 147.

44 I offset the term "recension" because although the text commissioned by Phuttayotfa had several notable differences from earlier versions of the *Traiphum,* it still claimed ancestry—like the new Chakri monarchs—to the royalty of earlier Tai-speaking polities in the central plains.

45 A revised copy already existed in the royal library, but for unknown reasons this version did not meet with the king's approval. Nidhi, *Pen and Sail,* 326.

46 Craig Reynolds, "Buddhist Cosmography in Thai History," 207; Wheatley, "Suspended Pelt," 55.

47 Wheatley, "Suspended Pelt," 55.

48 Lithai, *Traibhumikatha* (Bangkok: ASEAN Committee on Culture and Information, 1985), 66.

49 In addition to these three universes and their heavens and hells was a Hell between the Universes (Lokantra), which was located at the interstices of these three disks.

50 Lithai, *Traibhumikatha,* 74, 248.

51 Lithai, *Traibhumkatha,* 376.

52 The palace of Indra that sat at the center of the city has also been called the Vejayanta castle. Lithai, *Three Worlds,* 223; H. G. Quartich Wales, *The Mountain of God: A Study in Early Religion and Kingship* (London: B. Quaritch, 1953), 163.

53 Satapatha Brahmana V.4.3.7, in Stanley Tambiah, *World Conqueror and World Renouncer* (Cambridge: Cambridge University Press, 1976), 98; Nidhi, *Pen and Sail,* 251.

54 Barbara Andaya, "Statecraft in the Reign of Lu Tai of Sukhodaya," *Cornell Journal of Social Relations* 1 (Spring 1971): 61–83.

55 Anne Blackburn has noted the strong affinity of the exordium and colophon of the *Traiphum* (in English and French translations) with the inscriptions and footprint installations of Lithai. See Anne Blackburn, "Writing Buddhist Histories from Landscape and Architecture," *Buddhist Studies Review* 24, no. 2 (2007): 208n34.

56 Michael Vickery, "A Note on the Date of the Traibhumikatha," *Journal of the Siam Society* 62, no. 2 (July 1974): 284; Barend Jan Terwiel, "On the Trail of King Taksin's *Samutphāp Traiphūm*," *Journal of the Siam Society* 102 (2014): 43–49.

57 Frank Reynolds has pointed out that only three *Traiphum* manuscripts survived the sacking of Ayutthaya; of these, two contain little written material and the third contains only about one-tenth of the full work. Lithai, *Three Worlds,* 38; Peter Jackson, "Thai-Buddhist Identity: Debates on the Traiphum Phra Ruang," in *National Identity and Its Defenders: Thailand, 1939–1989,* ed. Craig Reynolds (Victoria, Australia: Centre of Southeast Asian Studies, Monash University,

1991), 199; Somphong Chaulaem suggests that the lack of an original text that could be traced back to the fourteenth century led to the compilation of the second version of the *Traiphum* only sixteen years after Phuttayotfa's recension. Somphong Chaulaem, *Traiphumikatha chabap khoi yang chua* (Traiphum, simplified version) (Bangkok: Suan Aksorn Sakhaburi, 1985), 1.

58 Although Nidhi Eoseewong has pointed out that the text was originally called the *Trailokawinitchai*, I use the title given to it by the National Library, *Traiphum lokwinitchai*, to avoid confusion for future researchers trying to locate it. Nidhi, *Pen and Sail*, 324–325; Phuttayotfa Chulalok, *Traiphum lokwinitchai* (Treatise on the three worlds) (Bangkok: Rōngphim Sōphonphiphatthanākōn, 1912); *Traiphum lokwinitchai* (National Library of Thailand, manuscript division, religious records, cupboard 107, no. 1).

59 Lithai, *Traibhumikhatha: The Story of the Three Planes of Existence*, trans. Thai National Team (Bangkok: Amarin Printing Group, 1987), 13.

60 Anne Blackburn, "Buddhist Technologies of Statecraft and Millennial Movements," *History and Theory* 56, no. 1 (March 2017): 71–79.

61 Namphueng Padamalangula, "Framing the Universe: Cosmography and the 'Discourse on the Frame,'" *Rian Thai: International Journal of Thai Studies* 1, no. 1 (2008): 72; Tambiah, *World Conqueror*, 97; Georges Coedès, *The Indianized States of Southeast Asia* (Honolulu: East West Center, 1968), 221.

62 Nidhi, *Pen and Sail*, 325.

63 Sombat Jantharawong and Chai-anan Samudavanija, *Khwamkit thang kanmuang lae sangkhom thai* (Thai political and social thought) (Bangkok: Thammasat University, Thai Khadi Institute, 1980), 93; Jackson, "Thai-Buddhist Identity," 163.

64 The geo-body of a nation refers not only to its territory but also to the image of the territory that is recognizable to its citizens. Thongchai Winichakul, *Siam Mapped: A History of a Geo-Body of a Nation* (Honolulu: University of Hawai'i Press, 1994).

65 Dell Upton, *Another City: Urban Spaces and Urban Life in the New American Republic* (New Haven, CT: Yale University Press, 2008), 122–123.

66 Reynolds, "Buddhist Cosmography," 211.

67 Thipakhorawong, *Nangsu sadaeng kitchanukit* (Book showing work to be done) (Bangkok: Nai Thep, 1872), 110; Reynolds, "Buddhist Cosmography," 216.

68 Reynolds, "Buddhist Cosmography," 220.

69 Thipakhorawong, *Kitchanukit*, 14–16; Reynolds, "Buddhist Cosmography," 215–216.

70 Although the grid has its own cosmological foundations, similarly rooted in divination and the organization of the gods according to the cardinal directions, by the nineteenth century it had come to signify a modern, rational approach to urban planning thanks to its systematic deployment in the curriculum of the École des Beaux-Arts. See Joseph Rykwert, *The Idea of a Town* (Cambridge, MA: MIT Press, 1988), 41–43; O. A. W. Dilke, *The Roman Surveyors: An Introduction to the Agrimensores* (Newton Abbot, UK: David and Charles, 1971), 32–38, 61–63.

71 Peleggi, *Lords of Things*, 85.

72 Later, the school would become the Polytechnic Institute. Vilma Fasoli and Francesca B. Filippi, "The Penetration of Italian Professionals in the Context of the Siamese Modernization," *Architecture Beyond Europe*, 5 (2014): 4.

CHAPTER THREE: DIAGRAMMING UTOPIAN NATIONALISM

1 Though the elimination of slavery began in 1874, the practice was not fully dispensed with until 1905. Pasuk Phongpaichit and Christopher John Baker, *Thailand, Economy and Politics* (Kuala Lumpur: Oxford University Press, 1995), 25; William G. Skinner, *Chinese Society in Thailand: An Analytical History* (Ithaca, NY: Cornell University Press, 1957), 115.

2 "Chotmai rachahatlekha phra rachawang suan dusit ruang anuyat hai nerathet jin tai sen jin tan chiang" (Letter to Chao Phraya Yommaraj, Ministry of the Interior, from the Royal Secretary, Suan Dusit, regarding permission to exile Jin Tai Sen and Jin Tan Chiang), 10 June 1910, Ministry of the Capital 16–11/168, Archives of the Fifth Reign, National Archives of Thailand. Siam and France concluded a treaty that transferred jurisdiction over French Asiatic subjects and protégés to Siamese courts of law in 1907. Francis Sayre, "The Passing of Extraterritoriality in Siam," *American Journal of Law* 22, no. 1 (1928): 78.

3 "Banchi phuak jin thi go gan wun wai kan tai suan dai khwam jing khuan nerathet" (Index of the group of Chinese who had created violence, interrogation and testimony, recommendation for deportation), 1910, Ministry of the Capital 168, Archives of the Fifth Reign, National Archives of Thailand.

4 The Thai word used is *chat* ชาติ, or "life," which originates from the Pali-Sanskrit word *jati,* meaning "birth." In turn-of-the-century Siam, the word came to mean "a community of people who shared a cultural commonality particularly defined by being the subjects of the same monarch," but in this context the term may also be understood as part of the compound *cheua chat* เชื้อชาติ, or "race." See Thongchai Winichakul, *Siam Mapped: A History of the Geo-Body of a Nation* (Honolulu: University of Hawai'i Press, 1994), 134–135.

5 "Banchi phuak jin thi go gan wun wai kan tai suan dai khwam jing khuan nerathet."

6 Rulers of premodern Southeast Asian polities had long ruled over heterogeneous populations, but in the late nineteenth century, large-scale intraregional migration coupled with the expansion of European colonialism made legal identification with a particular state increasingly salient to Bangkok's ruling class.

7 Craig Reynolds notes that the term *tamrap tamra* has its origins in Khmer and can be found in eighteenth- and nineteenth-century Thai materials to refer to "all kinds of information, schema, procedures, and rules." It was often used synonymously with the term *sat.* Prince Wan, the twentieth-century diplomat and president of the Ratchabandittayuasapha (Royal Society of Thailand), defined the term as "authoritative text" and declared it a Thai translation of the Sanskrit term *śāstra.* As referenced earlier, the *śāstra* were paradigmatic formats for the codification of rules, whether of divine or human provenance. Craig Reynolds, *Seditious Histories: Contesting Thai and Southeast Asian Pasts* (Seattle: University of Washington Press, 2006), 217–218.

8 Benedict R.O'G. Anderson, *Imagined Communities: Reflections on the Origins and Spread of Nationalism* (London: Verso, 1983), 184.

9 The Song dynasty scholar Zheng Qiao used the character *wen* 文 as a metaphor for the ways that early Chinese manuals (*tu* 圖) operated. The character can mean both "fabric" and "text." In the same ways that the warp and weft alternate to form a fabric pattern, so too do images and written word alternate to form a text. "To see the writing without the image is like hearing a voice with-

out seeing the form; to see the image without the words is like seeing a person but not hearing his words." See Zheng Qiao, "Tupu lüe" 圖譜略, in *Tongzhi* 通志 j. 71:837–840 (Taipei: Xin Xing Shuju, 1968); and Francesca Bray, Vera Dorofeeva-Lichtmann, and Georges Métailié, eds., *Graphics and Texts in the Production of Technical Knowledge in China: The Warp and the Weft* (Leiden: Brill, 2007).

10 Reynolds, *Seditious Histories*, 214.

11 Reynolds, *Seditious Histories*, 235, 237–238.

12 Lewis Flint Anderson, *History of Manual and Industrial Education* (New York: Appleton, 1926); Charles Alpheus Bennett, *History of Manual and Industrial Education up to 1870* (Peoria, IL: Manual Arts, 1926); Charles Alpheus Bennett, *History of Manual and Industrial Education 1870–1917* (Peoria, IL: Manual Arts, 1937).

13 Samuel Swinton Jacob, *Jeypore Portfolio of Architectural Details Prepared under the Supervision of S. S. Jacob* (London: B. Quaritch, 1890).

14 Although Siam's sovereignty was qualified by European imperial powers active in the region, its leaders adopted European colonial strategies to subjugate not only Bangkok but its surrounding areas, including the Muslim south, the Lao northeast, and the north. See Tamara Loos, *Subject Siam: Family, Law, and Colonial Modernity in Thailand* (Ithaca, NY: Cornell University Press, 2006), 14; Aran Phrommachomphu [Udom Srisuwan], *Thai kung-muang-kheun* (Thailand: A semicolonial country) (Bangkok: Mahachon, 1950); Chit Phumisak, "Chomna khong sakdina thai nai patchuban" (The real face of Thai feudalism today), *Nitisat 2500 chabap rap sattawatmai* (The Faculty of Law yearbook 2500 to greet the new century) (Bangkok: Thammasat University Faculty of Law, 2007); Thongchai Winichakul, "Siam's Colonial Conditions and the Birth of Thai History," in *Southeast Asian Historiography, Unravelling the Myths: Essays in Honour of Barend Jan Terwiel*, ed. Volker Grabowsky (Bangkok: River Books, 2011), 23–45.

15 Although the character *tu* 圖 meaning "to order" or "to position in space" has been traced back to inscribed bronzes in the early Zhou period (ca. 1000–800 BCE), it is not clear what materials the term referred to. By the Song dynasty, the term identified maps, charts, and other technical graphics. See Bray, Dorofeeva-Lichtmann, and Métailié, *Graphics and Texts*, 13.

16 Lit. "Lu Ban's manual." Klaas Ruitenbeek, *Carpentry and Building in Late Imperial China: A Study of the Fifteenth-Century Carpenter's Manual Lu Ban Jing*, Sinica Leidensia, vol. 23 (Leiden: Brill, 1993).

17 Joseph Needham described the scientific and technological pursuits of early Chinese history as undertaken by "technician-magicians." Joseph Needham and Wang Ling, *Science and Civilization in China*, vol. 2 (Cambridge: Cambridge University Press, 1954), 134. Ronald Knapp has also noted the importance of ritual to Chinese building practice, particularly in domestic architecture. Ronald Knapp, "Siting and Situating a Dwelling," in *House, Home, and Family: Living and Being Chinese*, ed. Ronald Knapp (Honolulu: University of Hawai'i Press, 2005), 117–121.

18 It is possible that the tradition predates the seventeenth century, but no manuscripts from earlier periods have survived. Henry Ginsburg, *Thai Art and Culture: Historic Manuscripts from Western Collections* (London: British Library, 2000), 7.

19 Reynolds, *Seditious Histories*, 221.

20 Barend Jan Terwiel, "On the Trail of King Taksin's *Samutphāp Traiphūm*," *Journal of the Siam Society* 102 (2014): 42.

21 A northern Thai map in the Cornell University Library collection combines an itinerary relating to Indian religious sites with cosmological concepts. Another well-known example is the 1776 *Traiphum* manuscript in the collection of the Staatliche Museen zu Berlin-Preußischer Kulturbesitz Museum für Indische Kunst, which combines the coastline of Asia with the cosmology of the *Traiphum* and places Ayutthaya at the center of a coastline that extends from China to Arabia. See Thomas Suárez, *Early Mapping of Southeast Asia* (Hong Kong: Periplus, 1999), 26–27. Thongchai, *Siam Mapped*, 24–30; Terwiel, "On the Trail," 43.

22 Lithai, *Traiphum phra ruang* (The Three Worlds of Phra Ruang), cremation volume for Phra Chao Boromawongthoe Phra Ong Chao Prasansrisa Phra Ong Chao Praphai Sri Saad (Bangkok, 1912); Ginsburg, *Thai Art and Culture*, 7–8; Lithai, *Three Worlds According to King Ruang: A Thai Buddhist Cosmology*, trans. Frank E. Reynolds and Mani B. Reynolds (Berkeley: Regents of the University of California, 1982), 24.

23 Reynolds, *Seditious Histories*, 216, 219.

24 Pirasri Povatong, *Chang farang nai krung sayam* ช่างฝรั่งในกรุงสยาม (Foreign craftsmen in Siam) (Bangkok: Faculty of Architecture, Chulalongkorn University, 2003); Phusadi Thipthat, *Chang farang nai krung sayam* (Foreign craftsmen in Siam) (Bangkok: Chulalongkorn University, 1998).

25 Philip E. Wegner, *Imaginary Communities: Utopia, the Nation, and Spatial Histories of Modernity* (Berkeley: University of California Press, 2002); Anderson, *Imagined Communities*.

26 The *sakdina* system has been compared to the European feudal system, most notably by Chit Phumisak. Unlike the European feudal system, however, Siamese *khunnang* (local lords) were not independent and permanent owners of the traditional means of production: the land. Under the European feudal system, meanwhile, lords granted lands to vassals, who in turn rented them to peasants. By the twelfth century, these estates became permanent and hereditary property. Under the *sakdina* system, control of manpower, ranks, and administrative positions were not entrusted to the *khunnang* hereditarily but were granted to them by the Crown. The *khunnang* had no independent existence outside the state, and the political power attached to their office was vital to their economic gains and their survival as a class. In the mid-nineteenth century, as the old system collapsed and merchant capitalism expanded in Siam, the power of the *khunnang* decreased because they remained tied to old production relations. The monarchy, on the other hand, benefited from capitalism, allowing the Siamese state to centralize and, in turn, establish royal absolutism. Chit, "Chomna khong sakdina thai nai patchuban"; Marc Léopold Benjamin Bloch, *Feudal Society*, vol. 1 (Chicago: University of Chicago Press, 1961), 170–173, 189; Seksan Prasertkul, "The Transformation of the Thai State and Economic Change (1855–1945)," (PhD diss., Cornell University, 1989), 453–459.

27 In 1899, compulsory male corvée was converted to a head tax, effectively "freeing" Thai labor to open up new lands and expand rice cultivation. Few Thais entered the wage-labor market, except in agriculture. A surplus of land created opportunities for Thais to become independent farmers and sell their surplus rice at favorable prices to a world market. However, the expanding economy left a vacuum for infrastructure construction labor, which was filled largely by unskilled migrants from five Chinese provinces. See Bevars Mabry, *The Development of Labor Institutions in Thailand* (Ithaca, NY: Southeast Asia Program,

Department of Asian Studies, Cornell University, 1979), 35; Edward Van Roy, "Sampheng: From Ethnic Isolation to National Integration," *Sojourn: Journal of Social Issues in Southeast Asia* 22, no. 1 (2008): 18; Virginia Thompson, *Labor Problems in Southeast Asia* (New Haven, CT: Yale University Press, 1947), 215.

28 "Proclamation," *The Siam Repository: Containing a Summary of Asiatic Intelligence* (Bangkok: S.J. Smith's Office, 1873), 65.

29 Early nineteenth-century Thai sources referred to the secret societies as *tua hia* ตั๋วเฮีย, or "big brother" 大哥 in Teochew. The term *ang yi* อั้งยี่ (the Teochew term for *hong zi* 洪字) came into official usage to describe the societies during the Fifth Reign. Jeffery Sng and Pimpraphai Bisalputra, *A History of the Thai-Chinese* (Singapore: Editions Didier Millet, 2015), 192.

30 Skinner, *Chinese Society in Thailand*, 139–140.

31 Skinner, *Chinese Society in Thailand*, 168; James McCarthy, *Surveying and Exploring in Siam* (London: John Murray, 1902), 3.

32 Sng and Pimpraphai, *History of the Thai-Chinese*, 200; Supharat Loedphanichkul, "Samakhom lap ang yi nai prathet thai, 2367–2453" (Secret societies in Thailand, 1824–1910) (PhD diss., Chulalongkorn University, 1981), 58.

33 The Dutch sinologist and naturalist Gustaaf Schlegel made perhaps the earliest study of the Tiandihui in Southeast Asia. Gustaaf Schlegel, *Thian ti hwui: The Hung-League, or Heaven-Earth League, a Secret Society with the Chinese in China and India* (Batavia: Lenge, 1866). The anthropologist J. S. M. Ward, who had no experience in Asia, would later revise some of Schlegel's translations of society rituals and materials in collaboration with the colonial civil servant and protector of Chinese in Malaya, William Stirling. J. S. M. Ward and William George Stirling, *The Hung Society, or the Society of Heaven and Earth* (London: Baskerville, 1925). An account of the activities of the Tiandihui in French colonial Indochina is offered by Georges Coulet, *Les sociétés secrètes en terre d'Annam* (Saigon: n.p, 1927). Two early Chinese-language studies are Xiao Yishan, *Jin dai bi mi she hui shi liao* 近代秘密社會史料 (History of modern secret societies) (Beiping: Guo Li Beiping Yan Jiu Yuan Zong Ban Shi Chu Chu Ban She, 1935); and Hirayama Shu, *Zhongguo mi mi she hui shi* 中國秘密社會史 (History of China's secret societies) (Shanghai: Shang Wu Yin Shu Guan, 1912).

34 The northern temple is the earlier one, founded in 490 CE in Henan Province. The southern temple was founded in 557 CE. "Tamra ang yi ekasan yep lem chut tamra ang yi" (Secret society handbook: Collected documents on secret societies), 44, Ministry of the Capital, National Archives of Thailand.

35 See Tai Hsuan-Chih and Ronald Suleski, "Origin of the Heaven and Earth Society," *Modern Asian Studies* 11 (1977): 423.

36 Adriana Proser, Cathy Dorsey, and the Asia Society Museum, *Pilgrimage and Buddhist Art* (New York: Asia Society, 2010); Toni Huber, *The Holy Land Reborn: Pilgrimage and the Tibetan Reinvention of Buddhist India* (Chicago: University of Chicago Press, 2008).

37 The Ghee Hin were active throughout Southeast Asia, including in Bangkok, Chanthaburi, and Phuket. Their Chanthaburi lodge was in Tambon Bang Kaja, Amphoe Ploywaen, in Chanthaburi Province. Sakhonkhotkhet (Pratuan Sakhrikanont), *Chotmaihet khwam trong jam samai thi farangset yeud chanthaburi, pi po so 2436–2447* (Memorial archives of the period that France occupied Chanthaburi 1893–1904 CE) (Bangkok: Phraephithya, 1972); Ward and Stirling, *Hung Society*, 18, 24.

38 Schlegel, *Thian ti hwui*, 26.

39 Damrong Rachanuphap noted the influence of *hongmen* in the area around Charoenkrung Road near Wat Yannawa as well as on the periphery of the city. Damrong Rachanuphap, "Ruang ang yi," *Phraratcha phongsawadan krung rattanakosin ratchakan thi 5* (Royal chronicles of the Fifth Reign of Rattanakosin) (Bangkok: Khrusupha, 1961), 344–366.

40 Schlegel, *Thian ti hwui*, xxiii.

41 北方王癸水連天 /雲南四川有路个行; "Tamra ang yi," 68.

42 Nancy Shatzman Steinhardt, "The Tang Architectural Icon and the Politics of Chinese Architectural History," *Art Bulletin* 86, no. 2 (June 2004): 228–254.

43 Schlegel understands the city as the capital of a non-Han polity that was brought under the rule of the Tang emperor Taizong 太宗. Schlegel, *Thian ti hwui*, 92–93.

44 Ward and Stirling, *Hung Society*, 110.

45 Ward and Stirling point out that these were the political characteristics of the Qing Empire. Ward and Stirling, *Hung Society*, 94.

46 慈雲廣濟. Schlegel understands this to mean the coming of the Buddha into the world as if he were a great cloud, whose charitable heart overshadowed the whole universe. Ward and Stirling read it to mean simply, "God who sends rain which feeds the earth." Schlegel's interpretation is probably more likely, given Ward and Stirling's sometimes strained ambition of understanding the society as a Chinese version of the Freemasons. Schlegel, *Thian ti hwui*, 94; Ward and Stirling, *Hung Society*, 94.

47 In the origin story of the Tiandihui, the nine-story pagoda was erected over one of the martyred monks. Ward and Stirling believed that the pagoda represented the nine lower heavens in "Chinese Buddhism." In fact, the nine "lands" 九地 refer to the realm of desire 欲界, the four realms of form 色界, and the four formless realms 無色界. Ward and Stirling, *Hung Society*, 97, book 2, 20; Irene Lim, *Secret Societies in Singapore: Featuring the William Stirling Collection* (Singapore: Singapore History Museum, 1999), 49; William Edward Sopothjill and Lewis Hodous, *A Dictionary of Chinese Buddhist Terms with Sanskrit and English Equivalents and a Sanskrit-Pali Index* (London: Kegan Paul, Trunch, Tubner, 1937), 16–17.

48 Ward and Stirling, *Hung Society*, 97.

49 Schlegel, *Thian ti hwui*, 92–105; Jean Chesneaux, *Secret Societies in China in the Nineteenth and Twentieth Centuries* (Ann Arbor: University of Michigan Press, 1971), 17, 19–21, 95–96, 104–105; Ward and Stirling, *Hung Society*, 95–96.

50 Ward and Stirling, *Hung Society*, 3.

51 James H. Billington, *Fire in the Minds of Men: Origins of the Revolutionary Faith* (New York: Basic Books, 1980), 86–123; Gerard Gayot, *La Franc-maçonnerie française: Textes et pratiques (XVIII–XIX siècles)* (Paris: Archives Gallimard Juilliard, 1980).

52 J. S. M. Ward, Stirling's coauthor, was also a Freemason, but not a colonial civil servant. L. F. Comber, *Chinese Secret Societies in Malaya: A Survey of the Triad Society from 1800 to 1900* (Locust Valley, NY: J.J. Augustin, 1959), 3.

53 Ward notes in his preface to their collaboration that the *hongmen* and the Freemasons are both descendants of the "Ancient Mysteries" and understands the induction ritual as an attempt not only to teach morality and brotherly love but also to indicate what happens after death and to give instruction in the "mysti-

cal journey" that unites one with the "Supreme Being, by whatsoever name we may call Him." Ward and Stirling, *Hung Society*, i–iii.

54 Stanford Lyman, "Chinese Secret Societies in the Occident: Notes and Suggestions for Research in the Sociology of Secrecy," *Canadian Review of Sociology and Anthropology* 1, no. 2 (1964): 82–84, 105; Dian Murray and Qin Baoqi, *The Origins of the Tiandihui* (Stanford, CA: Stanford University Press, 1994), 90–91.

55 Susan Buck-Morss, *Hegel, Haiti, and Universal History* (Pittsburgh, PA: University of Pittsburgh Press, 2009), 123.

56 Samson Lim, *Siam's New Detectives: Visualizing Crime and Conspiracy in Modern Thailand* (Honolulu: University of Hawai'i Press, 2016), 7–8, 66.

57 Anderson, *Imagined Communities*, 185.

58 Immanuel Wallerstein and Etienne Balibar, *Race, Nation, and Class* (London: Verso, 1991), 79, 83.

59 Santi Leksukhum, *Khwam samphan jin-thai yong yai nai luad lai pradap* (Sino-Thai relations in ornamental patterns) (Bangkok: Muang Boran, 2007), 96–98.

60 Nidhi Eoseewong, *Pen and Sail: Literature and History in Early Bangkok*, trans. Chris Baker et al. (Chiang Mai, Thailand: Silkworm, 2005), 79.

61 Arjun Subrahmanyan, "Buddhism, Democracy and Power in the 1932 Revolution," *Asian Studies Review* 41, no. 1 (2017): 42.

62 Worrasit Tantinipankul, "Modernization and Urban Monastic Space in Rattanakosin City: Comparative Study of Three Royal Wats" (PhD diss., Cornell University, 2007), 348.

63 Translation by the author. Prince Wachirayan, *Baeb nawakam, phra nawakam kowit* (The styles of Phra Nawakam Kowit) (Bangkok: Ongkankha khong khru supha, 1985), ก.

64 Worrasit notes that this "curtailed architectural creativity and the syncretistic amalgamation that had been the paragon of Thai architecture in the past." Worrasit, "Modernization," 352–353.

65 "Dhammasangani illustrations, one large illustration of the different levels of the world and heavens covering 30 folios," Or 15245, *Dhammasangani/Traiphum* illustrated manuscript attributed to Nai Sun, fol. 1r., British Library.

66 Ginsburg, *Thai Art and Culture*, 60.

67 See, for instance, *Milindapañha* (London: Pali Text Society, 1880), 330–345; "Buddhavamsa-a.t.thakathaa," in *Buddhavamsa and Cariyapitaka* (London: Pali Text Society, 1974), 155–156; *Sumangalavilasini III* (London: Pali Text Society, 1932), 881.

68 Dharmasēna Thera, *Jewels of the Doctrine: Stories of the Saddharma Ratnāvaliya*, trans. Ranjini Obeyesekere (Albany: State University of New York Press, 1991), x, 207; *Saddharmaratnāvaliya* (Colombo: Sri Lanka Oriental Studies Society, 1985), I.126; Charles Hallisey, "Nibbānasutta: An Allegedly Non-Canonical Sutta on Nibbāna as a Great City," *Journal of the Pali Text Society* 18 (1993): 106.

69 "The Blessed One's City of Dhamma," from the *Milindapañha, Based on the Translation by I.B. Horner* (Kandy: Buddhist Publication Society, 1993), 2–3.

70 Hallisey, "Nibbānasutta," 110.

71 Hallisey, "Nibbānasutta," 128–129.

72 Leon Battista Alberti, *On the Art of Building in Ten Books*, trans. Joseph Rykwert et al. (Cambridge, MA: MIT Press, 1988), 34.

73 Worrasit, "Modernization," 353.

74   *ASA: Journal of the Association of Siamese Architects* 3 (1963): n.p.; Phusadi Thip-
      that, *Satthapok sathapatayakam* (Architect architecture) (Bangkok: Chulalong-
      korn University, 1999), 17.

75   See V. Ganapathi, *Building Architecture of Sthāpatya Veda* (Chennai: Dakshinaa,
      2001); V. Banapatii, *Sthapatya Veda: The Science of Technology of Vaastu Sahstra—
      Re-defined, Re-interpreted and Its Relevance and All Time Universal Applicability
      Re-established. Archetypal Building Forms Illustrated and Punctuated with Apt Quo-
      tations* (New Delhi: Munshiram Manoharlal, 2005).

76   Vinayak Bharne, Leon Krier, and Krupail Krusche, *Rediscovering the Hindu
      Temple: The Sacred Architecture and Urbanism of India* (Newcastle upon Tyne:
      Cambridge Scholars, 2012), 33.

77   The scrap of paper with these words found its way into the earliest Thai-language
      lexicon published by the Ministry of Education (Krasuang Thammakan) in 1927.
      Ithithepsan Kridakon, *Ruang kiokap sathapatayakam* (On architecture) (Bang-
      kok: Rongphim Phra Chan, 1935), 14–15.

78   Ithithepsan, *Ruang kiokap sathapatayakam*, 8.

79   Ithithepsan, *Ruang kiokap sathapatayakam*, 8.

80   Ithithepsan, *Ruang kiokap sathapatayakam*, 9.

81   The first generation of Siamese architects emerged during the reign of King
      Vajiravudh. *ASA: Journal of the Association of Siamese Architects* 3 (1963); Phu-
      sadi, *Sathapok sathapatayakam*, 17.

82   Worrasit, "Modernization," 348.

83   The extent to which this racialized understanding of architecture has perme-
      ated the ordering of the past can be discerned in the work of the cultural histo-
      rian Phya Anuman Rajadhon, writing in the post–World War II era:

      When the Thai came within the orbit of Hinduism and Buddhism as already
      mentioned, it is easy to imagine that the Khmer art in relation to these two
      great religions was gradually transfused into the spirit of the Thai people,
      and through their inborn aesthetic sense for art and racial characteristics
      the Thai were able to create their own personality in art, quite distinct from
      that of the old background. Although the Thai people intermingled freely for
      centuries with other races in the Peninsula of Indo-China, they nevertheless
      maintained their own identity of racial character. In fact, if one looks at the
      various examples of Thai art such as sculpture, painting and architecture, one
      will be able to see at a glance that Thai art has an artistic expression quite
      peculiar to the race.

          Anuman Rajadhon, *Popular Buddhism in Siam and Other Essays on Thai Stud-
      ies* (Bangkok: Thai Inter-Religious Commission for Development and Sathira-
      koses Nagapradipa Foundation, 1986), 16.

84   Thomas Metcalf, *An Imperial Vision: Indian Architecture and Britain's Raj* (New
      Delhi: Oxford University Press, 2002), 34.

85   Samuel Swinton Jacob, *Jeypore Portfolio of Architectural Details, Prepared under
      the Supervision of S.S. Jacob* (Varanasi: Indological Book House, 1977).

86   The identification, measurement, recording, and display of monuments under-
      taken by colonial archaeological services in the later part of the nineteenth
      century were part of the warp and weft of the colonial state's domain. Ander-
      son, *Imagined Communities*, 36, 178, 184.

87   Bert S. Hall, "The Didactic and the Elegant: Some Thoughts on Scientific and
      Technological Illustrations in the Middle Ages and Renaissance," in *Picturing*

Knowledge: Historical and Philosophical Problems Concerning the Use of Art in Science, ed. Brian S. Baigrie (Toronto: University of Toronto Press, 2016), 9.

88 The architect and intellectual historian Pier Vittorio Aureli has argued that diagrams are a form of language and in the same way that languages can camouflage reality, diagrams can appear as a form of "value-free nihilism," in which the things and ideas they represent are without value, or "nothing." Pier Vittorio Aureli, "After Diagrams," *Log* 6 (Fall 2005): 5.

CHAPTER FOUR: MODELING QUEERTOPIA

1 Chaem Sunthonwet, *Dusit thani muang prachathipatai khong phrabat somdet phra mongkut klao chao yu hua* (Dusit Thani: The democratic city of King Rama VI) (Bangkok: National Library, 1970), 34–36.

2 "Dusit Thani: Muang chamlong prachathipatai khong phrabat somdet phra mongkut klao chao yu hua" (Dusit Thani: The democratic city of King Rama VI), *Sakul thai* 45, no. 2332 (29 June 1999): 111.

3 There is a strong parallel between the ways that the term was deployed in nineteenth-century Victorian culture and turn-of-the-century Siamese culture. Scholars of nineteenth-century English literature have used "queer" and postcolonial frameworks to explore the ways that Victorian cultural expressions like the Gothic simultaneously explored anxieties about "foreigners," racial miscegenation, gender identity, and sexual practices alongside normative iterations of sexuality, gender identity, race, nation, and class. Duc Dau and Shale Preston, eds., *Queer Victorian Families: Curious Relations in Literature* (London: Routledge, 2015); Ardel Haefele-Thomas, *Queer Others in Victorian Gothic: Transgressing Monstrosity* (Cardiff: University of Wales, 2012).

4 Chaem, *Dusit thani muang prachathipatai khong phrabat somdet phra mongkut klao jao yu hua*, 78.

5 Tamara Loos, "Sex in the Inner City: The Fidelity between Sex and Politics in Siam," *Journal of Asian Studies* 64, no. 4 (November 2005): 901–902.

6 "Ruang rai kan khwam hen ruang kan jad kan sukhaphiban" (Correspondence regarding views on the organization of the municipal government of Bangkok), July 10, R.S., 125, Ministry of the Capital, 5.1/120, Archives of the Fifth Reign, National Archives of Thailand.

7 Thamora V. Fishel, "Romances of the Sixth Reign: Gender, Sexuality, and Siamese Nationalism," in *Genders and Sexualities in Modern Thailand*, ed. Peter Jackson and Nerida Cook (Chiang Mai, Thailand: Silkworm, 1999), 163.

8 Chaem, *Dusit thani muang prachathipatai khong phrabat somdet phra mongkut klao chao yu hua*, 41.

9 Chaem, *Dusit thani muang prachathipatai khong phrabat somdet phra mongkut klao chao yu hua*, 45.

10 The crown prince was privately tutored upon his arrival in England, then went to Sandhurst Military Academy and then Oxford. He spent a total of nine years as a student in England.

11 Ramachitti, *Heart of a Young Man* (originally published as *Hua chai chai num*), trans. Ted Strehlow (Melbourne: n.p., 1989), 8.

12 Ramachitti, *Heart of a Young Man*, 4.

13 Bureau of the Royal Household, *Chotmaihet kankosang lae somsaem Phrathinang Wimanmek Phutthasakkarat 2443-2518* (Chronicles of the construction

and renovation of Wimanmek Mansion, 1900–1975) (Bangkok: Bureau of the Royal Household, 1990); Pirasri Povatong, "Building Siwilai: Transformation of Architecture and Architectural Practice in Siam during the Reign of Rama V, 1868–1910" (PhD diss., University of Michigan, 2011), 190.

14 Maurizio Peleggi, *Lords of Things: The Fashioning of the Siamese Monarchy's Modern Image* (Honolulu: University of Hawai'i Press, 2002), 87.

15 "Ruang rai kan khwam hen ruang kan jad kan sukhaphiban"; Pirasri, "Building Siwilai," 199.

16 The Public Works Department was established under the reign of King Chulalongkorn in 1889. After Vajiravudh ascended the throne, he reformed the Public Works Department and split the staff into two groups in 1912. One group of painters, sculptors, and some architects was sent to the newly established Department of Fine Arts. The rest of the architects and engineers, including Mario Tamagno, went to the Local Sanitation Department of the Ministry of the Capital (Nakhonaphiban).

17 Ministry of Justice 1/32, Archives of the Fifth Reign, National Archives of Thailand, quoted in Pirasri, "Building Siwilai," 187.

18 Pirasri, "Building Siwilai."

19 Originally the commission was given to German architect Carl Sandreczki, but the two Italians took over most of the work during construction. Rigotti would work in Bangkok for two years, return to Italy in 1909, and then return to Bangkok in 1923 for another three years. Although technically only in Bangkok for five years, he left an indelible impression on the city, largely through projects like Villa Norasingh (1923–1925) and the Siam Commercial Bank (1916–1926). "Farewell Dinner to Prof. Arch. Rigotti," *Bangkok Times*, 12 July 1909.

20 Udomporn Teeraviriyakul, "Bangkok Modern: Singapore and Batavia as Models," *Rian Thai: International Journal of Thai Studies* 5 (2012).

21 "Visakhuposatha Sutta: The Discourse to Visakha on the Uposatha with the Eight Practices" (AN 8.43), translated from the Pali by Bhikkhu Khantipalo. Access to Insight (Legacy Edition), 30 November 2013, http://www.accesstoinsight.org/tipitaka/an/an08/an08.043.khan.html.

22 Stanley Tambiah has noted that Uttarakuru is one of three kinds of Buddhist utopias articulated in the *Traiphum*. The other two utopias were the paradisiacal realms of the *devadatas*, Brahma kings, and Phra Sri Ariya Metteya, the Buddha of the next millennium, and the righteous realm of the *chakkrawadirat* monarch in the world of mortal humans. Stanley J. Tambiah, "The Buddhist Cosmos: Paradise Lost, Gained, and Transcended," *History of Religions* 24, no. 1 (August 1984): 78–79.

23 Vajiravudh, *Uttarakuru: Phra ratcha niphon phra bat somdet phra mongkut klao jao yu hua* (Uttarakuru: The royal opinion of His Majesty King Rama VI) (Bangkok: Wat Bowornivet, 1965), 1.

24 Vajiravudh, *Uttarakuru*, 19.

25 Kasian Tejapira, *Commodifying Marxism: The Formation of Modern Thai Radical Culture* (Kyoto: Kyoto University Press, 2001), 17.

26 Vajiravudh, *Uttarakuru*, 3.

27 Kang Youwei believed that "if there are Families, then there is Selfishness, which Injures [Human] Nature and Injures the Species." He advocated replacing the traditional Chinese family structure with "womb-teaching institutions," nurseries, and schools. He believed contemporary marriage was too

oppressive and should be replaced by one-year contracts between men and women. Kang Youwei, *Ta T'ung Shu: The One-World Philosophy of K'ang Yu-wei*, trans. Laurence G. Thompson (London: George Allen and Unwin, 1958), 180–182, 194–200. Hsiao Kung-chuan suggests that the Buddha's leave-taking of his family may have been an influence on Kang's idea that the family was detrimental to happiness. Hsiao Kung-chuan, *A Modern China and a New World: K'ang Yu-Wei, Reformer and Utopian, 1858-1927* (Seattle: University of Washington Press, 1975), 15. He was also an advocate of eugenics and argued for a transformation of the human race into a fair-skinned homogeneous race where everyone would be the same appearance, intelligence, and size. Kang, *Ta T'ung Shu*, 140–148.

28 Worachat Meechubot, *Kret phonsawadan rachakan thi 6* (Historical anecdotes from the Sixth Reign) (Bangkok: Sansan Buk, 2010), 61.

29 Worachat, *Kret phonsawadan rachakan thi 6*, 61.

30 Loos, "Sex in the Inner City," 888.

31 Vajiravudh's father, King Chulalongkorn, had 152 wives; King Mongkut had 54 (Loos gives 153 and 50). Loos, "Sex and the Inner City," 883; Chanan Yothong, *Nai nai samai ratchakan thi hok* (Men of the inner palace during the sixth reign) (Bangkok: Matichon, 2013), 7.

32 Chanan, *Nai nai*, 216–218.

33 Loos, "Sex in the Inner City," 901–902.

34 In similar fashion, contemporary residents of Bangkok were renting out shop houses built by the Privy Purse Bureau along the new roads that had been laid by the Ministry of the Capital. "Letter from King Chulalongkorn to Prince Naresworarit, November 4, 1901," Office of the Prime Minister, *A Collection of King Chulalongkorn's Manuscripts*, vol. 3:1 (Bangkok: n.p., 1970), 129.

35 Chaem, *Dusit thani muang prachathipatai khong phrabat somdet phra mongkut klao chao yu hua*, ข, 45.

36 Chanan, *Nai nai*, p. 127.

37 Phaetying Kannika Tanprasoet, *Phrarachawang phya thai nai wan wan ha phaen din* (Phyathai royal palace on its centennial anniversary) (Bangkok: Matichon, 2010), 171.

38 Kannika, *Phrarachawang phya thai nai wan wan ha phaen din*, 176.

39 Kannika, *Phrarachawang phya thai nai wan wan ha phaen din*, 171.

40 Henry A. Millon and Vittorio Magnago Lampugnani, eds., *The Renaissance from Brunelleschi to Michelangelo: The Representation of Architecture* (New York: Rizzoli, 1994), 21n9.

41 Karen Moon describes the architectural model as a "princely toy," given the historical relationships between the architectural profession and political patrons during the Italian Renaissance. See Karen Moon, *Modeling Messages: The Architect and the Model* (New York: Moncaelli Press, 2005), 30.

42 King Prasat Thong reigned from 1629 to 1636 CE. David K. Wyatt, ed., *The Royal Chronicles of Ayutthaya*, trans. Richard Cushman (Bangkok: Siam Society, 2000), 216; Chris Baker and Pasuk Phongpaichit, *A History of Ayutthaya: Siam in the Early Modern World* (Cambridge: Cambridge University Press, 2017), 145–146.

43 Thipakorawong, *The Dynastic Chronicles, Bangkok Era, the Fourth Reign: BE 2394–2411*, trans. Kanjanavit Flood (Tokyo: Center for East Asian Cultural Studies, 1965), 222, 376.

44 Thipakorawong, *Dynastic Chronicles*, 226–227.

45   Bua Sochisewi, "Dusit Thani: Muang prachathipatai samai rachakan thi hok" (Dusit Thani: The democractic city of the Sixth Reign), *Silpawatthanatham* 9, no. 3 (January 1988): 25.

46   Chaem Sunthonwet, *Phra rachakoranikit samkhan nai phra bat somdet phra mong-kut klao chao yu hua ruang het pol thi rachakan hok song prakat songkhram dusit thani* (Important activities of King Rama VI regarding the events of World War I and Dusit Thani) (Bangkok: Ongkanha khong khurusupha, 1969), 159.

47   Chaem, *Dusit thani muang prachathipatai khong phrabat somdet phra mongkut klao chao yu hua*, 45.

48   The eighteenth-century French priest and architectural theorist the abbé Marc-Antoine Laugier, for example, remarked that whoever knew how to design a park would know how to design a city, with attention to "un grand ordre dans les détails, de la confusion, du fracas, du tumulte dans l'ensemble." Marc-Antoine Laugier, *Observations sur l'architecture* (La Haye: Desaint, 1765), 312–313; Manfredo Tafuri, *Architecture and Utopia* (Cambridge, MA: MIT Press, 1977), 7.

49   The throne hall was built in "the American style," although what this meant to the writer is not clear. *Dusit samai*, 20 May 1919; Chaem, *Dusit Thani muang prachathipatai khong phrabat somdet phra mongkut klao chao yu hua*, 154.

50   *Dusit sakkhi/Dusit Recorder*, March 1918/2461, 1.

51   A fuller gloss on the imperial use of the Gothic is in Thomas Metcalf, *An Impe-rial Vision: Indian Architecture and Britain's Raj* (New Delhi: Oxford University Press, 2002), 243.

52   Benedict R. O'G. Anderson, *Imagined Communities: Reflections on the Origins and Spread of Nationalism* (London: Verso, 1983), 35.

53   Chaem, *Dusit thani muang prachathipatai khong phrabat somdet phra mongkut klao chao yu hua*, 132–134.

54   Chanan, *Nai nai*, 122.

55   It is not entirely clear whether these were life-size exhibitions. *Dusit sakkhi/ Dusit Recorder*, 3 September 1920, 4 September 1920, and 28 September 1920.

56   Chaem, *Dusit thani muang prachathipatai khong phrabat somdet phra mongkut klao chao yu hua*, 45, 111.

57   *Dusit sakkhi/Dusit Recorder*, 18 March 1918.

58   *Phra ratchawong phya thai: Wan wan lae wan ni* (Phya Thai Palace: Days gone by and today) (Bangkok: Chomrom khon rak wang nai phra ubtham somdet phra chao phakhinitoe chao fa phecharatanasuda sirisophaphannawadi, 2010), 51.

59   Chaem, *Dusit thani muang pratchatiptai khong phrabat somdet phra mongkut klao chao yu hua*, 56.

60   The parliament was inaugurated with a speech by Vajiravudh in which he called on civil servants to attend to their responsibilities in the real world as efficiently as they had in Dusit Thani. Chaem, *Dusit thani muang pratchatiptai khong phrabat somdet phra mongkut klao chao yu hua*, 78–79.

61   In one respect, however, Dusit Thani might be understood as the fulfillment of one of Chulalongkorn's last wishes, that his son give the people of Siam "a parliament and a constitution." Mattana Ketkamon, "Kan muang lae kan pok-khrong nai rachakan phrabat somdet phra mongkut klao phra chao yu hua" (Politics and administration in the reign of King Rama VI), *Sangkomsat paritat* 14, nos. 3–4 (1975): 71; Scot Barmé, *Luang Wichit Wathakan and the Creation of a Thai Identity* (Singapore: Institute of Southeast Asian Studies, 1993), 21.

62 The term *sakdina* (lit. "power over fields") may have originally referred to some kind of land grant and defined social hierarchy in the polity of Ayutthaya and the early Bangkok period. In the late Ayutthaya period, it had become a numerical ranking attached to each official post. Pasuk Phongphaichit and Chris Baker, *A History of Thailand* (Cambridge: Cambridge University Press, 2005), 266.

63 Kullada Kesbonchoon-Mead, *The Rise and Decline of Thai Absolutism* (London: Routledge-Curzon, 2004), 118n26.

64 Patrick Jory, "Thailand's Politics of Politeness: Qualities of a Gentleman and the Making of 'Thai Manners,'" *Southeast Asia Research* 23, no. 3 (2015), 363.

65 The concern with modern manners and Buddhist morality preoccupied intellectuals in neighboring Cambodge during this period, as Anne Hansen has shown in her thoughtful study of Khmer Buddhist modernism. Anne Ruth Hansen, *How to Behave: Buddhism and Modernity in Colonial Cambodia, 1860–1930* (Honolulu: University of Hawai'i Press, 2007).

66 This estimate is based on the 1929–1930 census and supported by a survey undertaken by the Department of Revenue's census, which numbers the population at 687,966. Ministry of Finance 0301.1.1/13, 1931, National Archives of Thailand; Constance Wilson, *Thailand: A Handbook of Historical Statistics* (Boston: G.K. Hall, 1983), 32; Porphant Ouyyanont, "Bangkok's Population and the Ministry of the Capital in Early 20th Century Thai History," *Southeast Asian Studies* 35, no. 2 (September 1997): 248. "Revision of the 1910 Census, Undertaken in 1913," R6, Ministry of the Capital, 27/8, 1920–1921, National Archives of Thailand.

67 "Ruang sang tao phao tham lai khaya mun foi lamrap krom sukhaphiban lae ruang wat kan sukhaphiban hai pen miunisipaelitti," 12 January 2460 to 14 August 2465, Ministry of the Capital, 1/23, Archives of the Sixth Reign, National Archives of Thailand.

68 Chaem, *Dusit thani muang prachathipatai khong phrabat somdet phra mongkut klao chao yu hua*, 78.

69 David Harvey, *Spaces of Hope* (Berkeley: University of California Press, 2000), 160.

70 Porphant Ouyyanont, "Physical and Economic Change in Bangkok," *Southeast Asian Studies* 36, no. 4 (March 1999): 451.

71 A possible rationale for his comparative neglect of urban investment may have been Vajiravudh's preoccupation with distancing himself from the older aristocratic families that had profited from Crown investments in the city during the nineteenth century. Vajiravudh's focus, instead, was on creating a new ruling class who would become *phu di* (refined people), with good manners, taste, and comportment befitting the members of a modern urban society. Chanan, *Nai nai*, 216–218.

72 After the throne hall was damaged during the renovation of Phya Thai Palace into a hotel, the Fine Arts Department stored it on the third floor of the Vajiravudh Hall in the National Library Complex, unsure of when they could repair it. The throne hall and other buildings from Dusit Thani are currently part of a permanent exhibition at the Vajiravudh Hall that is open by special appointment. The Baan Mahithon is on display at the Phya Thai Palace museum. Bua Sochisewi, "Dusit Thani: Muang prachathipatai samai ratchakan thi hok"

(Dusit Thani: The democratic city of the Sixth Reign), *Silpawatthanatham* 9, no. 3 (January 1988): 25.

73 The members of the initial People's Assembly were all commoners. Kenneth Landon, *Siam in Transition: A Brief Survey of Cultural Trends in the Five Years since the Revolution of 1932* (New York: Greenwood, 1968), 17.

CHAPTER FIVE: PLANNING KAMMATOPIA

1 "Cremation of King Rama VI: A Stately Pageant, the Capital in Mourning," *Bangkok Times Weekly Mail*, 25 March 1926, 20.

2 The terms *phra merumat* and *phra men* refer to royal crematoria. The term *phra men* also refers to the sacred mountain the crematorium is named after. Both derive from the words *meru* and *men*, which refer generally to both the crematorium and the sacred mountain.

3 One of the chief differences in the development of the conception of the Three Worlds from its Indic origins to its Buddhist iteration was that in Hindu kingdoms, Mount Meru was represented as a temple, whereas Buddhist kingdoms used the palace to represent the sacred mountain. Stanley Tambiah, *World Conqueror and World Renouncer* (Cambridge: Cambridge University Press, 1976), 97.

4 *Sri ariya metteya* and *sri ariya* are the name, realm, and epoch associated with the next incarnation of the Buddha, Metteya. Although more familiar in Mahayana Buddhist imagery as Maitreya (Sanskrit), Metteya and *sri ariya* play an important role in the Thai Phra Malai narrative, in which the monk Phra Malai encounters Maitreya on his journeys through the realms of heaven and hell. Pridi Phanomyong, *Pridi by Pridi: Selected Writings on Life, Politics, and Economics,* trans. and intro. Chris Baker and Pasuk Phongphaichit (Chiang Mai, Thailand: Silkworm, 1989), 15–19, 68–85.

5 See chapter 2 of this book. The Sanskrit term "mandala," meaning "circle," has come to be associated with premodern Southeast Asian polities, most notably through the work of O. W. Wolters. It denotes an organization of land and power based on a cyclical conception of history focused on the present with relatively flexible boundaries that expand and contract around shifting power centers. It stands in contrast to a Cartesian, cadastral concept of the modern nation-state. Each mandala is centered on a "man of prowess" (*phu mi bun*) and typically involves the ritual divination of ancestors. See, O. W. Wolters, *History, Culture and Religion in Southeast Asian Perspectives* (Ithaca, NY: SEAP Publications/Institute of Southeast Asian Studies, 1999).

6 Namphueng Padamalangula, "Framing the Universe: Cosmography and the 'Discourse on the Frame,'" *Rian Thai: International Journal of Thai Studies* 1, no. 1 (2008): 72.

7 King Lithai, *Traibhumikatha* (Bangkok: ASEAN Committee on Culture and Information, 1985), 159, 179.

8 Chatri Prakitnontakan, *Kanmuang lae sangkhom nai silpasathapatayakam: Sayam samai thai prayuk chat niyom* (Politics and society in architecture: Siam in the era that Thailand adopted nationalism) (Bangkok: Matichon, 2004), 40.

9 Chatri, *Kanmuang lae sangkhom nai silpasathapatayakam*, 396–397.

10 Department of Fine Arts, *Thānānusak nai ngān sathāpattayakam Thai* (Bangkok: Krom Silapākǫrn, 2008).

11 Pirasri Povatong, "Building Siwilai: Transformation of Architecture and Architectural Practice in Siam during the Reign of Rama V, 1868–1910" (PhD diss., University of Michigan, 2011), 36–37.

12 During the reign of Mongkut, for example, the *uparaja* (viceroy) wanted to construct a new throne hall and crown it with a *prasat* roof. Mongkut pointed out that only the abode of the king could be graced with such a roof, and the *uparaja* had to donate the spire to a nearby temple. Damrong Rachanuphap, *Tamnan wang na* (History of the Front Palace) (Bangkok: Sophonphiphatthanakon, 1925).

13 Pirasri, "Building Siwilai," 107.

14 Craig Reynolds, "Buddhist Cosmography in Thai History, with Special Reference to 19th-Century Culture Change," *Journal of Asian Studies* 35, no. 2 (February 1976): 211.

15 Woraphorn Phupongsaphan, "Ngan phramen: Phra rachaphiti satorn thipphawa haeng ong phra mahakastri nai samai Ayutthaya" (The cremation pyre: The royal ceremony reflecting the heavenly status of the monarchy in the Ayutthaya period), in *Ngan phramen: Silpasathapatayakam prawatisat lae watthanatham kieo neuang* (The cremation pyre: The history of its architecture and related culture) (Bangkok: Ministry of Culture, 2009), 131; Sirot Phinanrachatorn, "Mohorosop somphot lae kan len nai ngan phramen" (Ritual entertainment and play in the funeral pyre) in *Ngan phramen*, 283.

16 The custom of acrobatic performances at funerals may have derived from older Chinese practices appropriated by the royal court at Ayutthaya. Medieval Chinese translators and commentators of Buddhist sutras used acrobatics to describe the festivities of Buddhist celestial deities in the upper realms of the cosmos. A northern Wei Buddhist stela from 529 CE depicts the integration of these performances into sixth-century ritual ceremonies. Eugene Y. Wang, *Shaping the Lotus Sutra: Buddhist Visual Culture in Medieval China* (Seattle: University of Washington Press, 2005), 62.

17 *Nang utai klon suat* (Bangkok: Department of Fine Arts, 2004), 20; Sayam Phatranuprawati, "Kan sadaeng mohorosop somphot nai ngan phramen: Kan rap ru phan wannakhadi," in *Ngan phramen*, 196.

18 *Ruang khlong phra phloeng phra boromati phrachaoluang phra niphon phra chao borom wongtoe korom mun sri surenot lae tamnak phae* (Regarding the poem on lighting the pyre of Phra Boromati Phra Chao Luang Phra Niphon Phrachao Boromwongtoe krom munsri surenot and the residential building in the royal compound) (Bangkok: Khuanpim, 1963); Sayam, "Kan sadaeng mohorosop somphot nai ngan phramen Kan rap ru phan wannakhadi," 196.

19 Nidhi Eoseewong, *Pen and Sail: Literature and History in Early Bangkok Including the History of Bangkok in the Chronicles of Ayutthaya*, trans. Chris Baker et al. (Chiang Mai, Thailand: Silkworm, 2005), 100, 114, 144.

20 Nidhi, *Pen and Sail*, 51–56, 164.

21 Sirot Phinanrachton, "Mohorosop somphot lae kan la len nai ngan phramen" (Entertainments and games at the cremation ceremony), in *Ngan phramen*, 291.

22 Sangaroon Kanokpongchai, *Wat Thongthammachat* (Bangkok: Muang Boran, 1982), 25.

23 Sangaroon, *Wat Thongthammachat*, 27.

24 Nidhi Eoseewong, *Pha khaw ma pha sin kang gaeng nai lae un un: Wa duay phrapheni khwam plian plaeng lae ruang sapsara* (Loincloth, sarong, underwear,

etc.: On customs, changes, and interesting stories) (Bangkok: Matichon, 2004), 143.

25 Robin Evans has noted the crucial though underexamined role that parallel projection played in the development of orthographic projection in architectural drawing. Robin Evans, *Translations from Drawing to Building and Other Essays* (Cambridge, MA: MIT Press, 1997), 164.

26 Choti Kalyanamitra, *Phon ngan hok satthawat khong chang thai* (Six hundred years of work by Thai artists and architects) (Bangkok: Fine Arts Commission of the Association of Siamese Architects, 2003), 112–113; "Cremation of King Rama VI," 20.

27 Choti, *Phon ngan hok satthawat khong chang thai*, 114–115.

28 Prior to the nineteenth century, architectural production was the work of *nai chang* (master craftsmen or master builders) in the employ of the court. The historian Pirasri Povatong points out that the term "architect" was transliterated as *akhitek* in the late nineteenth century, but it was not until King Vajiravudh coined the term *sathapanik* in the 1920s and the Association of Siamese Architects was founded in 1933 that a professional class of Thai architects emerged. Pirasri, "Building Siwilai," 29; Wimonsit Horayangkura et al., *Phattanakan naeo khwamkhit lae rupbaep khong ngan sathapatayakam* (Concepts and forms of architecture) (Bangkok: Association of Siamese Architects, 1993), x; Phuttsadi Thipphathat, *Sathapok sathapatayakam* (Architect architecture) (Bangkok: Chulalongkorn University, 1999), 17; *ASA: Journal of the Association of Siamese Architects* 3 (1963): n.p.; Ithithepsan Kridakon, *Ruang kio kap sathapatayakam* (On architecture) (Bangkok: Krom Silpakon, 1935), ฆ.

29 In the late nineteenth century, a significant number of Italian architects and engineers found employment in the recently formed Siamese Public Works Department. Many of these architects and engineers trained at the Accademia Albertina di Belle Arti in Turin and worked not only in Bangkok but in the royal courts of czarist Moscow and Ottoman Istanbul as well, employed by modernizing rulers to create a Europeanized public image. In Bangkok, they worked under the authority of Siamese princes such as Prince Naris and That Hongsakul (the father of Kon Hongsakul). Pirasri Povatong, *Chang farang nai krung sayam: Ton phaendin Phraphutthachao luang* (European builders in the kingdom of Siam during the early years of the Fifth Reign) (Bangkok: Faculty of Architecture, Chulalongkorn University, 2005); Maurizio Peleggi, *Lords of Things: The Fashioning of the Siamese Monarchy's Modern Image* (Honolulu: University of Hawai'i Press, 2002); International Conference on Italian-Thai Studies, *Italian-Thai Studies from the Nineteenth Century to the Present to Commemorate the Centennial of King Rama V's First Visit to Europe* (Bangkok: National Museum, 1997).

30 M. L. Chittawadi Chitrabongs, *Prince Naris: A Siamese Designer* (Bangkok: Naris Foundation, 2016), 21.

31 State-of-the-art industrial furnaces would later be imported from Golders Green Crematorium in London at the order of King Vajiravudh and installed at Wat Saket. These were said to be based on the Indian funeral pyre. Chittawadi, *Prince Naris*, 35–43.

32 Sited between the king's palace and the viceroy's palace soon after Bangkok's founding, the field became a political stage early in the city's history when tensions between the soldiers for the two leaders threatened to erupt in armed

conflict. See Wora Rochnawiphat, "Thong snam luang," *Muang boran* 42, no. 4 (October–December 2016): 121. *Phrai* were corvéed freemen under the *sakdina* social system, described briefly in chapter 4.

33 Chulada Phakdiphumintr, "Thung phra sumeru," *Sakul thai* 49, no. 3538 (10 June 2003): 29.

34 *Jotmaihet kan prab prung phumi that phun thi thong phra rong klang jaeng sanam luang phutthasakrat 2554* (Archives of the renovation of the central announcement hall of Sanam Luang, 2554 BE) (Bangkok: Amarin, 2011), 36–39.

35 The renovation of the field took place after Chulalongkorn's state visits to Singapore and Batavia. Historian Udomporn Teeraviriyakul suggests that Singapore's Padang and Batavia's Konigsplein served as models for the oval shape ringed with tamarind trees that Prince Naris designed. Udomporn Teeraviriyakul, *Bangkok Modern* (Bangkok: Institute of Asian Studies, Chulalongkorn University, 2014), 260–261.

36 Peleggi, *Lords of Things*, 138–142.

37 Chatri, *Kanmuang lae sangkhom nai silpasathapatayakam*, 74.

38 If commoners died within the walls of the royal precinct, Rattanakosin, their bodies had to be removed through the Pratu Phi (Gate of Ghosts), which lay west of the city (in the present-day area of Wat Thepthidaram). Chatri, *Kanmuang lae sangkhom nai silpasathapatayakam*, 79.

39 Wales noted that these towers had been elevated in previous *phra men* but does not give any symbolic reason why they were built at ground level for Vajiravudh's funeral. H. G. Quaritch Wales, *Siamese State Ceremonies: Their History and Function* (London: Curzon, 1992), 145.

40 Phra Saroj Ratanimman, "The Golden Meru," *Journal of the Siam Society* 26 (December 1947): 110; Wales, *Siamese State Ceremonies*, 145.

41 "Cremation of King Rama VI," 20.

42 Wales, *Siamese State Ceremonies*, 146.

43 Phra Saroj, "Golden Meru," 112.

44 Kullada Kesbonchoo Mead, *The Rise and Decline of Thai Absolutism* (London: RoutledgeCurzon, 2004), 136.

45 Vajiravudh, *Pluk chai sua pa* (Instilling the wild tiger spirit) (Bangkok: Khrusupha, 1943), 61; Mead, *Rise and Decline*, 137.

46 Vajiravudh, *Pluk chai sua pa*, 72.

47 Vajiravudh, *Pluk chai sua pa*, 67–69.

48 Eva Neumaier-Dargyay, "Buddhism," in *Life after Death in World Religions*, ed. Harold Coward (Maryknoll, NY: Orbis, 1997), 92.

49 Buddhaghosa, *Visuddhimagga: The Path of Purification*, trans. Bhikkhu Ñāṇamoli (Kandy: Buddhist Publication Society, 1975), chap. 19, pt. 22, 628.

50 Sorasan Phaengsopha, *Baan ya phai* (Granny Phai's house) (Bangkok: Sarakhadi, 2002), 164, 166, 168; Wales, *Siamese State Ceremonies*, 151.

51 Wales referred to this as the *brah peñca*, or the "pyre proper." However, Thai manuals refer to it as the *phra benjajitdatan*. Wales, *Siamese State Ceremonies*, 146.

52 "Cremation of King Rama VI," 18.

53 While the custom had been to preserve the fire from any building that had been struck by lightning, the fire for Vajiravudh's pyre was created from the sun by means of a magnifying glass and was considered ceremonially pure. Wales, *Siamese State Ceremonies*, 144.

54 Some of them would be interred at Wat Boworniwes, while others were interred at the great *chedi* at Nakhon Pathom. Wales, *Siamese State Ceremonies,* 154.

55 Woraphorn Phuphongsphan, "Ngan phra men: Phra rachaphithi sathon thip phawa hang ong phra mahakasatri nai samai ayuthaya" (The funeral pyre: The royal rituals reflecting the divine status of the monarchy in the Ayutthaya period), in *Ngan phramen,* 128.

56 Woraphon, "Ngan phra men," 132.

57 Wales, *Siamese State Ceremonies,* 166.

58 Pierre Fistié, *Sou-développement et utopie au Siam: Le programme de reeformes présenté en 1933 par Pridi Phanomyong* (Paris: Mouton, 1969), 60–71.

59 By June 1932, the People's Party had around a hundred members. Just over half of them were in the military. Within three hours on 24 June 1932, this small group captured the commander of the royal guard, arrested members of the royal family and their aides, and announced the overthrow of the absolute monarchy. The event was widely hailed by business and labor groups, and people queued up to join the People's Party. The event was marred only by a minor shooting incident, but there were no deaths. Pasuk Phongpaichit and Chris Baker, *A History of Thailand* (Melbourne: Cambridge University Press, 2014), 115–119.

60 Pridi, *Pridi by Pridi,* 72.

61 Although Theravada Buddhist text and practices underscore the importance of the historic Buddha, Gautama, they also delineated eonic schemes that adumbrated the five Buddhas of the present age with between twenty-five and twenty-eight Buddhas, including Gautama and Metteya. Donald K. Swearer, *Becoming the Buddha: The Ritual of Image Consecration in Thailand* (Princeton, NJ: Princeton University Press, 2004), 176–178, 179; Jana Igunma, "A Buddhist Monk's Journey to Heaven and Hell," *Journal of International Association of Buddhist Universities* 6, no. 1 (2013): 65; Bonnie Pacala Brereton, *Thai Tellings of Phra Malai: Texts and Rituals Concerning a Popular Buddhist Saint* (Tempe: Program for Southeast Asian Studies, Arizona State University, 1995).

62 A detailed illustration of this tree appears in a manuscript in the collection of the British Library. Or 14115, fol. 75, British Library.

63 Pasuk and Baker, *History of Thailand,* 121.

64 Pasuk and Baker, *History of Thailand,* 119.

65 This was the first time lèse-majesté was used as a political tool in Siam. Chatri Prakitnontakan, *Silpasathapatayakam khana ratsadon* (The art and architecture of the People's Party) (Bangkok: Matichon, 2009), 689.

66 Chatri, *Silpasathapatayakam khana ratsadon,* 71.

67 The bodies of the rebel soldiers who lost their lives were cremated at Nakhon Ratchasima. Office of the Prime Minister to the Palace Secretary, "Ruang phloeng sop tahan lae tham khuan meuang nakhon ratchasima" (Memo on the cremation ceremonies of soldiers at Nakhon Ratchasima), Cabinet Secretary, 0201.26/5, National Archives of Thailand.

68 Office of the Prime Minister to the Palace Secretary, "Chotmai ratamontri wa kan krasuang wang rian nayok ratamontri" (Letter from the prime minister's office to the Ministry of the Palace), 6 January 1934, Cabinet Secretary, 0201.26/6, National Archives of Thailand.

69 Office of the Prime Minister to the Palace Secretary, "Chotmai ratamontri wa kan krasuang wang rian nayok ratamontri."

70 Office of the Prime Minister to the Palace Secretary, "Chotmai ratamontri wa kan krasuang wang rian nayok ratamontri."

71 Sibel Bozdoğan, *Modernism and Nation Building: Turkish Architectural Culture and the Early Republic* (Seattle: University of Washington Press, 2001), 10–11.

72 In fact, between 1932 and 2017, the country had twenty-one constitutions or charters.

73 Thawat Mokarapong, *History of the Thai Revolution: A Study in Political Behavior* (Bangkok: Thai Watana Panich, 1972), 124; Pasuk Phongphaichit and Chris Baker, *Thailand: Economy and Politics* (Kuala Lumpur: Oxford University Press, 2005), 253.

74 Kompong Noobanjong has noted that the Democracy Monument on which the *phan ratthathammanun* rested was an example of "polar binarism" signifying military and civilian, liberation and repression, and inherited power and meritocracy. Kompong Noobanjong, "Power, Identity, and the Rise of Modern Architecture from Siam to Thailand" (PhD diss., University of Colorado at Denver, 2003), 260. Malinee Khumsupha, *Anusawari prachathiptai kap khwam mai thi mong mai hen* (Democracy Monument and its hidden meanings) (Bangkok: Wiphasa, 2005).

75 Chatri Prakitnontakan, *Khana ratsadon chalong ratthathammanun: Prawatisat kan mueang lang 2475 phan satthapatayagam "amnat"* (The People's Party celebrates the constitution: Political history after 1932 through the architecture of "power") (Bangkok: Matichon, 2005), 49, 151, 153, 155, 159, 165, 167, 169, 182.

76 Chatri, *Khana ratsadon chalong ratthathammanun*, 74, 89; "Kamnot kan bumphen kuson nai ngan phra rachathan phloeng sop tahan sia chiwit pai nai kan prop kabot" (Schedule of the cremation ceremony of the soldiers who sacrificed their lives to suppress the revolt), *Thai kasem khao* 291 (25 February 1934), 6.

77 Office of the Prime Minister, "Kamnot kan bumphen kuson nai ngan phra rachathan phloeng sop tahan sia chiwit pai nai kan prap kabot" (Schedule of the cremation ceremony of the soldiers who sacrificed their lives suppressing the revolt), Cabinet Secretary, 0201.26/7, National Archives of Thailand.

78 Tony Day, *Fluid Iron: State Formation in Southeast Asia* (Honolulu: University of Hawai'i Press, 2002), 236–237.

79 Day, *Fluid Iron*, 256.

80 Kompong Noobanjong, "Forgotten Memorials," in *Southeast Asia's Modern Architecture*, ed. Jiat-Hwee Chang and Imran bin Tajudeen (Singapore: NUS Press, 2018), 196; *San anuson ngan phraratthan phloengsop Luang Naramitr Laekhakarn* (Cremation volume for Lieutenant Colonel Naramitr Laekhakarn) (Bangkok: Taikasem, 1957), 20.

81 The poem, later set to music, is based on a World War I–era English slogan, "What stands if freedom falls? Who dies if England lives?"

82 A corollary in European thought is suggested by Georg Wilhelm Friedrich Hegel's invocation of the Greek myth of Zeus, the father of the gods, and his establishment of the state in order to counter the destructive forces of Chronos, or time, as change. The modern nation-state thus imagined itself as a complete and changeless entity. Georg Wilhelm Friedrich Hegel, *Lectures on the Philosophy of World History: Introduction*, trans. H. B. Nisbet (Cambridge: Cambridge University Press, 1975), 145; Harry Harootunian, "'Memories of Underdevelopment' after Area Studies," *Positions* 20, no. 1 (Winter 2012): 20;

Benedict Anderson, *Imagined Communities: Reflections on the Origin and Spread of Nationalism* (London: Verso, 1983), 9.

CHAPTER SIX: ORDER AND ODOR

1 In retrospect, Prajadhipok is remembered as wanting to improve the face of the country (*choed na chu ta khong prathet*). Romnichatr Kaewkiriya, *Sala-chalo-em-krung* (Bangkok: Chaloem krung manithat, 1995), 39.

2 The area is part of the administrative *khet*, or district, of Phra Nakhon today.

3 Sibel Bozdoğan has pointed to architectural history's tendency to focus on buildings as "visible politics," or the highly visible and politicized images of power. Sibel Bozdoğan, *Modernism and Nation Building: Turkish Architectural Culture in the Early Republic* (Seattle: University of Washington Press, 2001). For a different approach to governmentality and technoscientific knowledge in nineteenth- and twentieth-century architecture, see Jiat-Hwee Chang, *A Genealogy of Tropical Architecture: Colonial Networks, Nature, and Technoscience* (London: Routledge, 2016), 10.

4 Sophia Siddique Harvey, "Sensuous Citizenship in Contemporary Singapore Cinema," in *Singapore Cinema: New Perspectives,* ed. Liew Kai Khiun and Stephen Teo (London: Routledge, 2017), 84.

5 Davide Panagia, *The Political Life of Sensation* (Durham, NC: Duke University Press, 2009), 5.

6 Panagia, *Political Life of Sensation,* 12.

7 Laura Marks, *The Skin of the Film: Intercultural Cinema, Embodiment, and the Senses* (Durham, NC: Duke University Press, 2000), xvi.

8 Constance Classen, "The Deodorized City: Battling Urban Stench in the Nineteenth Century," in *Sense of the City: An Alternate Approach to Urbanism,* ed. Mirko Zardini (Montréal: Canadian Center for Architecture and Lars Müller Publishers, 2005), 292–299.

9 Sirichai Sirikaya, *Nang thai* (Thai movies) (Bangkok: Communications Division, Faculty of Communication Arts, Chulalongkorn University, 1988), 41.

10 Scot Barmé, *Woman, Man, Bangkok: Love, Sex, and Popular Culture in Thailand* (Lanham, MD: Rowman and Littlefield, 2002), 45.

11 Thanathip Chattraphuti, *Tamnan rong nang* (History of movie theaters) (Bangkok: Weladi, 2004), 14–15.

12 Thanathip, *Tamnan rong nang,* 20.

13 Mattani Mojdara Rutnin, *Dance, Drama, and Theater in Thailand: The Process of Development and Modernization* (Chiang Mai, Thailand: Silkworm, 1996), 181.

14 Chamreanrak Tanawangnoi, *Thai Film History from the Beginning to the End of World War II* (Bangkok: Thammasat University, 2001), 39.

15 Patsorn Sungsri, *Thai National Cinema: The Three Potent Signifiers of Thai Identity, Nation, Religion, and Monarchy, Their Interrelationship and Influence in Thai National Cinema* (Saarbrucken: VDM Verlag, 2000), 36.

16 *Siam Rat,* 12 April 1923, quoted in Sirichai, *Nang thai,* 57.

17 Examining the changing modes of courtly consumption in the nineteenth century, Maurizio Peleggi argues that the consumer behavior of Siam's modernizing "elite" was a key part of the self-creation of their social identity as both a national ruling class and a part of an enduring world aristocracy. Maurizio

Peleggi, *Lords of Things: The Fashioning of the Siamese Monarchy's Modern Image* (Honolulu: University of Hawai'i Press, 2002), 20.

18 *Bangkok Daily Mail,* 21 October 1930, quoted in H. G. Quaritch Wales, *Siamese State Ceremonies: Their History and Function* (London: Curzon, 1992), 6.

19 Sirichai, *Nang thai,* 42.

20 The cheapest ticket might have cost the average coolie two-thirds of his daily wage. Average daily wages for coolies in 1914 were 3 *saleung,* or 0.75 baht. By 1935, two years after the change in government, wages for coolies rose to 0.80 baht. However, in 1928, office workers made between 50 and 200 baht a day, and their wages stabilized to 65.42 baht in 1935. Sirichai, *Nang thai,* 42; figures from the Department of General Statistics, *Statistical Yearbook of the Kingdom of Siam, 1929–1930* (Bangkok: Ministry of Finance, 1930), 446. See also C. C. Zimmerman, *Siam: Rural Economic Survey* (Bangkok: Bangkok Times Press, 1931), 48.

21 Barmé, *Woman, Man, Bangkok,* 69.

22 Barmé, *Woman, Man, Bangkok,* 73–76.

23 Barmé, *Woman, Man, Bangkok,* 70–73.

24 David Howe, "Architecture of the Senses," in Zardini, *Sense of the City,* 322.

25 Phaphayon Sayam Paliment, *Phaphayon sayam* 1, no. 49 (9 March 1922), 14.

26 Phaphayon Sayam Paliment, *Phaphayon sayam* 2, no. 15 (13 July 1923), 15.

27 Phaphayon Sayam Paliment, *Phaphayon sayam* 1, no. 49 (9 March 1922), 15.

28 The first Thai-produced feature, *Nang sao suwan,* was made in 1923. S. Bangjaeng, "67 pi phaphayon thai 2466–2533," *Khana anukam kan jad ngan chaloem chalong 67 pi phaphayon thai* (Bangkok: Samaphan phaphayon haeng chat, 1990), 8. Scot Barmé notes that an obscure 1912 production advertised in English as *A Siamese Elopement* is actually the first commercial, narrative motion picture produced in Siam. Barmé, *Woman, Man, Bangkok,* 52. Most films, however, were collections of twelve to thirteen short films placed on one reel and projected. C. Euabamrungjit, "100 pi phaphayon nai prathet thai," *Sarakhadi* 150, no. 13 (August 1997): 91.

29 Mangkon Thong, "Rong nang pho kho than reu?" Phaphayon Sayam Paliment, *Phaphayon sayam,* 2 March 1922.

30 Phaphayon Sayam Paliment, *Phaphayon sayam* 2, no. 21 (August 1923).

31 Phaphayon Sayam Paliment, *Phaphayon sayam* 2, no. 23 (7 September 1923), 11.

32 Phaphayon Sayam Paliment, *Phaphayon sayam* 2, no. 24 (14 September 1923).

33 Phaphayon Sayam Paliment, *Phaphayon sayam* 2, no. 25 (21 September 1923), 15–16.

34 Chatri Prakitnontakan, *Silpasatthapatayagam khana ratsadon* (The art and architecture of the People's Party) (Bangkok: Matichon, 2009), 22–23.

35 Benjamin Batson, *The End of the Absolute Monarchy in Siam* (Singapore: Oxford University Press, 1984), 188.

36 Batson, *End of the Absolute Monarchy,* 58.

37 Romnichatr, *Sala-chaloem-krung,* 35.

38 The steel is the same material used on the Phuttayotfa Bridge. "Chaloemkrung royal thiatoe di oldsayam phlasa" (Chaloem Krung Royal Theater and the Old Siam Plaza), *ASA: Journal of the Association of Siamese Architects* (January–February 1995): 51.

39 "Chaloemkrung royal thiatoe di oldsayam phlasa," 51. The use of air-conditioning in other Southeast Asian cities was becoming more popular during

this period as well. The New Alhambra Theatre was the first cinema to acquire air-conditioning in Singapore, in 1938. "Mountain-Air Climate in Singapore," *Singapore Free Press,* 27 July 1938, 4; "Alhambra to Reopen in October," *Singapore Free Press,* 17 September 1947, 5; Chang Jiat-Hwee and Tim Winter, "Thermal Modernity and Architecture," *Journal of Architecture* 20, no. 1 (2015): 97.

In his memoir, Vicha Dhitavadha remarked that the air-conditioning in the special bus that took him from Kuala Lumpur to Singapore in 1939 was "just like in the Chaloem Krung." Vicha Dhitavadha, *Khon thai nai gong thap nasi* (A Thai in the Nazi army) (Bangkok: Sarakhadi, 2004), 39.

40 Marsha Ackerman, *Cool Comfort: America's Romance with Air-Conditioning* (Washington, DC: Smithsonian Institution Press, 2002), 47.

41 Barry Donaldson and Bernard Nagengast, *Heat & Cold: Mastering the Great Indoors* (Atlanta, GA: American Society of Heating, Refrigerating and Air-Conditioning Engineers, 1994), 286.

42 "His Majesty, the King of Siam, Visits Carrier," *Carrier Courier* 3, no. 4 (August 1931): 15.

43 Margaret Ingels, *Willis Haviland Carrier: Father of Air Conditioning* (Garden City, NY: Country Life Press, 1952), 64.

44 Ingels, *Willis Haviland Carrier,* 65. Grauman's Metropolitan Theater in Los Angeles, however, opened in 1922 with a traditional ammonia refrigeration system. Donaldson and Nagengast, *Heat & Cold,* 286.

45 Salvatore Besso, *Siam and China* (London: Simpkin, Marshall, Hamilton, Kent, 1914), 23.

46 N. A. McDonald, *Siam: Its Government, Manners, Customs, &c.* (Philadelphia: A. Martien, 1871), 13.

47 H. Campbell Highet, "Health and Hospitals: Climate and Health of Bangkok," *20th Century Impressions of Siam: Its History, Peoples, Commerce, Industries, and Resources with Which Is Incorporated an Abridged Edition of 20th Century Impressions of British Malaya* (London: Lloyds Greater Britain Publishing, 1908), 129.

48 Wilhelm, Prince of Sweden, *In the Lands of the Sun: Notes and Memories of a Tour in the East* (London: E. Nash, 1915), 46.

49 S. C. GilFillan, "The Coldward Course of Progress," *Political Science Quarterly* 35, no. 3 (September 1920): 393–410.

50 GilFillan, "Coldward Course of Progress," 396.

51 Ackerman, *Cool Comfort,* 30.

52 Rudolf Mrázek, *Engineers of Happy Land: Technology and Nationalism in a Colony* (Princeton, NJ: Princeton University Press, 2002), 79.

53 "Regulating Tropical Weather," *Straits Times,* 22 March 1929, 5, quoted in Chang Jiat-Hwee and Tim Winter, "Thermal Modernity and Architecture," *Journal of Architecture* 20, no. 1 (2015): 96.

54 Thongchai Winichakul, "The Quest for 'Siwilai,'" *Journal of Asian Studies* 59, no. 3 (August 2000): 529.

55 Thongchai, "Quest for 'Siwilai,'" 528.

56 Bhidayalongkorn, "Phawa yangrai no thi riak wa siwilai" (What is the condition of the thing called "civilization"?), *Prachum pathokatha khong kromamun phitthayalongkon* (Collected lectures by Prince Bhidayalongkorn) (Bangkok: Ruamsan, 1970), 433.

57 Bhidayalongkorn, "Phawa yangrai no thi riak wa siwilai," 443.

58 Bhidayalongkorn, "Phawa yangrai no thi riak wa siwilai," 470–471.

59 Samaichaloem Kridakon, *Ngan sathapatayakam khong mom chao samaichaloem kridakon* (The architectural work of Mom Chao Samaichaloem Kridakon) (Bangkok: Phrachan, 1967), 16.

60 Tamara Loos, *Subject Siam: Family Law and Colonial Modernity in Thailand* (Ithaca, NY: Cornell University Press, 2006), 14; Aran Phrommachomphu [Udom Sri-suwan], *Thai kung-muang-khun* (Thailand: A semi-colonial country) (Bangkok: Mahachon, 1950); Chit Phumisak, "Chomna khong sakdina thai nai pajjuban" (The real face of Thai feudalism today), *Nitisat 2500 chabap rap sattawat mai* (The Faculty of Law yearbook 2500 to greet the new century) (Bangkok: Thammasat University Faculty of Law, 2007).

61 Samaichaloem, *Ngan satthapatayakam khong mom chao samai chaloem kridakon*, 142.

62 "Kan poet 'sala chaloem krung' pen ngan moholan prachachon nen khanat rot rang tong yud cha ngat," *Sri krung*, 5 July 1933, n.p.; Samaichaloem, *Ngan sathapatayakam khong mom chao samai chaloem kridakon*, 39.

63 There is some discrepancy about the number of original seats in the theater. Its original capacity was reportedly 2,000 people, although photographs of the interiors make this figure an unlikelihood if it reflects seating arrangements. An interview with the general manager of the theater in 1994 in *Silpawatthana-tham* indicates that of the original 900 seats, only 600 were left, but in an article in *Sarakhadi*, the writer says that there are altogether 619 seats from an original 400. The latter figure is supported by the current administration of the theater and is reported on the theater's website. Tri Ratonruchi, "Chaloem krung royan tiato silpakam khrung satthawat" (The mid-century art of the Chaloem Krung Royal Theatre), *Silpawatthanatham* 15, no. 4 (February 1994): 130; Kittiphong Kirotthamakun, "Yon ramluk chet sip pi sala chaloem krung" (Seventy years of memories of the Sala Chaloem Krung), *Sarakhadi* 19, no. 222 (August 2003): 146.

64 "Chaloemkrung royal thiatoe di oldsayam phlasa," 54.

65 "Chaloemkrung royal thiatoe di oldsayam phlasa," 58; Chamnon Saengwi-chian, ed., *Khon sala chaloem krung* (Sala Chaloem Krung khon theater) (Bangkok: Crown Property Bureau, 2006), 108.

66 Kittiphong, "Yon ramluk chet sip pi sala chaloem krung," 145; Thanathip, *Tam-nan rong nang*, 44.

67 The original seal derives from the king's precoronation name, Chao Fa Pracha-thipok Sakdi Dech. The word *dech* เดช means "arrow" or "person who directs power." Kitthipong, "Yon ramluk chet sip pi sala chaloem krung," 145.

68 พระเทวาภินิมมิต, *Muang boran* 3, no. 1 (October–December 1976), 122.

69 The story of Rama, which has hundreds of versions, can best be understood as a South and Southeast Asian narrative that crystalized in the context of a variety of different religious traditions, including Hinduism, Buddhism, and Jainism. Frank Reynolds has noted that the *Ramakian* versions of the Rama story do not exhibit full-fledged Buddhist structural characteristics of earlier Buddhist tellings of the story but that they set the story in explicitly Buddhist contexts, giving it a Buddhist significance. A. K. Ramanujan, "Three Hundred Rāmayanas: Five Examples and Three Thoughts on Translation," *The Collected Essays of A. K. Ramanujan* (New Delhi: Oxford University Press, 1999); Frank E. Reynolds, "Ramayana, Rama Jataka, and Ramakien: A Comparative Study of Hindu and Buddhist Traditions," in *Many Rāmayaṇas: The Diversity of a Narra-*

tive Tradition in South Asia, ed. Paula Richman (Berkeley: University of California Press, 1999), 89.

70 Edward Van Roy, *Siamese Melting Pot: Ethnic Minorities in the Making of Bangkok* (Singapore: ISEAS, 2017), 14.

71 The three deities are Phra Prathontham พระประโทนธรรม, the patron of dance; Phra Wisnukam พระวิษณุกรรม, the patron of crafts or building; and Phra Paññasangkhorn พระปัญญสังขรณ์, the patron of music.

72 Thanathip, *Tamnan rong nang,* 44.

73 The annual income of a rural farmer was estimated at 184.56 baht in 1934. James M. Andrews, *Siam: Second Rural Economic Survey 1934–1935* (Hong Kong: Bangkok Times Press, 1935), 13.

74 Nimitmongkol Navarat, *The Dreams of an Idealist,* trans. David Smyth (Chiang Mai, Thailand: Silkworm, 2009), 11.

75 Phaphayon Sayam Paliment, *Phaphayon sayam* 1, no. 48 (2 March 1922), no. 49 (9 March 1922); *Phaphayon sayam* 2, no. 16 (20 July 1923).

76 "Bantuk chak sut thai sala chaloem krung kon plian hua khon" (Remembering the last scene before the Sala Chaloem Krung became a *khon* theater), *Reality Forum,* October 2000, 114.

77 Thanathip, *Tamnan rong nang,* 41.

78 Thanathip, *Tamnan rong nang,* 46.

79 The new renovations were undertaken by interior designer Wipwan Singhakowin. "Banthuek chak sut thai sala chaloem krung kon plian hua khon," *Reality Forum* (October 2000), 118.

80 Martin Loeperdinger and Bernd Elzer, "Lumiere's Arrival of the Train: Cinema's Founding Myth," *Moving Image* 4, no. 1 (Spring 2004): 89–118.

81 Flat roofs, which would become an important feature of many new government buildings after 1932, were said to have intrigued some residents, who wondered how square buildings with flat roofs could be built and continue to stand. Chatri Prakitnontakan, *Khana ratsadon chalong ratthathammanun* (The People's Party celebrates the constitution) (Bangkok: Matichon, 2005), 94.

82 Romnichatr, *Sala-chaloem-krung,* 35.

83 Chang and Winter, "Thermal Modernity and Architecture," 93.

CHAPTER SEVEN: CONCRETOPIA

1 Pridi Phanomyong, *Pridi by Pridi: Selecting Writings on Life, Politics, and Economics,* trans. and intro. Chris Baker and Pasuk Phongphaichit (Chiang Mai, Thailand: Silkworm, 1989), 15–19, 72.

2 Oliver Pye, *Khor Jor Kor: Forest Politics in Thailand* (Bangkok: White Lotus Press, 2005), 43. Perhaps ironically, Danes invested considerably in the Siam Cement Company throughout the twentieth century.

3 One exceptional example of pre-1932 ferroconcrete construction in Siam is the *uposot* hall of Wat Phrapatom Chedi (Prince Naris, Nakhorn Pathom, 1928–1932). Chatri Prakitnontakan, *Kanmuang lae sangkhom nai silpasathapatayakam: Sayam samai thai prayuk chat niyom* (Politics and society in architecture: Siam in the era that Thailand adopted nationalism) (Bangkok: Matichon, 2004), 362.

4 Louis Renou has noted that the word *stupa* appears in the Pāraskara Gṛhyasūtra, the Śāṅkhāyana Śrautasūtra, and the Markandyea Purāna. Louis Renou, "The Vedic House," *RES: Anthropology and Aesthetics* 34 (Autumn 1998): 151.

5　"Anagatavamsa," *Journal of the Pali Text Society* (1886): 33–42; "Dasabodhisatta uddesa," trans. François Martini, *Bulletin de l'École française d'Extreme-Orient* 36, no. 2 (1936): 299; Saya U Chit Tin, *The Coming Buddha Ariya Metteyya* (Kandy: Buddhist Publication Society, 1992), 44.

6　Bonnie Bereton, "The Phra Malai Legend in Thai Buddhist Literature: A Study of Three Texts" (PhD diss., University of Michigan, 1992), 15.

7　The *Phra Malai* texts served a political purpose even earlier. Literary scholar Bonnie Bereton has argued that *Phra Malai* texts from the northern region of Thailand and the recitation of the Vessantara Jataka enhanced the kingdom's spiritual and political potency. Bonnie Bereton, *Thai Tellings of Phra Malai: Texts and Rituals Concerning a Popular Buddhist Saint* (Tempe: Arizona State University, Program for Southeast Asian Studies, 1995), 79.

8　Pierre Fistié, *Sou-développement et utopie au Siam: Le programme de réformes présenté en 1933 par Pridi Phanomyong* (Paris: Mouton, 1969), 60–71.

9　The earliest proposal for a Siamese company to produce cement dates back to 1908. Archives of the Fifth Reign, "Prospectus and Documents Related to the Founding of the Siam Portland Cement Company, 1909," Ministry of Agriculture 12.2/16, National Archives of Thailand, in Porphant Ouyyanont, "The Foundation of the Siam Commercial Bank and the Siam Cement Company," *Sojourn: Journal of Social Issues in Southeast Asia* 30, no. 2 (2015): 482.

10　Although Siam did not participate in any of the exhibitions held in England during the period of the grandest international exhibitions (1851–1911), it regularly attended exhibitions in Paris and began to exhibit in other expositions in the late nineteenth and early twentieth centuries. Maurizio Peleggi, *Lords of Things: The Fashioning of the Siamese Monarchy's Modern Image* (Honolulu: University of Hawai'i Press, 2002), 145.

11　Kukrit Pramoj, *Anuson nai ngan chalong 50 pi haeng kitchakan khong borisat pun siment thai jamkat pho so 2456–2506* (Commemorative volume in celebration of 50 years of the Siam Cement Company, 1913–1963) (Bangkok: Siam Cement Company, 1963), 125.

12　Xian jing Guangzhou hui guan, "Xian luo Guangzhou shu zhi jianzhu ye" (The construction business of the Cantonese in Siam), *Xianluo Guangzhou hui guan qi shi zhou nian ji nian te kan* (Seventieth anniversary publication of the Cantonese Association in Bangkok) (Bangkok: Guangzhou hui guan, 1947), 12–13.

13　Scattered records show an increase in real estate transactions between 1890 and 1910. Porphant Ouyannont, "Physical and Economic Change in Bangkok, 1851–1925," *Southeast Asian Studies* 36, no. 4 (March 1999): 489.

14　In 1936, the Crown Property Bureau was separated from the royal household, and while its income was still used for royal household expenses, it was also used for entertainment for private and state visitors, donations for charitable purposes, and the support of pensions for members of the royal family. The Crown Property Bureau remained one of the largest asset holders in Thailand, with shares in a number of businesses, including banks, hotels, insurance, and construction. It was also the largest landowner in Bangkok. Before the Second World War, the Crown Property Bureau owned almost one-third of the land in the city. Porphant Ouyannont, "The Vietnam War and Tourism in Bangkok's Development, 1960–1970," *Southeast Asian Studies* 39, no. 2 (2001): 181–182. *Investor*, February 1971, 124.

15 Boonma Wongswan, *Siam Cement Company: 1913–1983* (Bangkok: Siam Cement Company, 1983), 70.

16 Porphant, *Regional Economic History*, 458.

17 Archives of the Sixth Reign, "Chaophraya yommarat krap bangkhom tun phra bat somdet phra mongkut klao chao yu hua, 8 maesayon 2462" (Chao Phraya Yommarat to King Vajiravudh), 8 April 1919, R1.20/13, National Archives of Thailand, in Chatthip Nartsupha, Suthy Prasartset, and Montri Chenvidya-karn, *The Political Economy of Siam, 1910–1932* (Bangkok: Social Science Association of Thailand, 1978), 136–140.

18 David G. Kohl, *Chinese Architecture in the Straits Settlements and Western Malaya: Temples, Kongsis and Houses* (Singapore: Heinemann Asia, 1984), 54.

19 These smaller firms concentrated on locating high-value timber that was scattered throughout the forests. See Pasuk Phongpaichit and Christopher John Baker, *Thailand: Economy and Politics* (Kuala Lumpur: Oxford University Press, 1995), 60; Phinai Sirikiartikul points out that revenues from the logging industry still went to European-owned companies well after 1932, however. See Phinai Sirikiatiul, "Na thi ni mai mi khwam seuam: Thanon ratchadamnoen po so 2484–2488" (Here there is no decline: Ratchadamnoen Avenue, 1941–1945), *Na jua: History of Architecture/Thai Architecture* 6 (September 2009–August 2010): 41.

20 *Thi raluk nai kan thi than dai karuna pai ruam ngan phiti poet khun mo phao pun met khrung thi si na rong ngan tha luang* (Commemorative volume for the opening ceremony of the Tha Luang clinker factory) (Bangkok: Siam Cement Company, 1960), 12.

21 The company's shareholders included the leader of the militarized youth movement Yuwachon, Prayun Phamonmontri; head of the Department of Public Relations, Wilat Osathanon; director-general of the Crown Property Division of the Finance Ministry, Chin Phinthanon; and the Sino-Thai businessman Chulin Lamsam. *Bangkok Times Weekly Mail*, 26 July 1940, in Scot Barmé, *Luang Wichit Wathakan and the Creation of a Thai Identity* (Singapore: Institute of Southeast Asian Studies, 1993), 154.

22 The text refers to "companies that were not owned by Thai people" (*borisat chon tang dao*). While seemingly vague, the context makes it clear that the term refers to the company's Chinese- and Sino-Thai-owned competitors, particularly as it refers to another category of businesses, "stores that are owned by foreigners" (*hang ran nai tang prathet*). The company argued that they were the first company established in the country and had the objective of establishing a business that was a commercial agent for the government of all kinds of goods, and conducted activities that supported the Thai people and nation. "Banthuek ruang borisat thai niyom phanit chamkat kho khwam sanap sanun khwam chuai lua chak ongkan tang tang khong rathaban" (Memo regarding the Thai Panit Niyom Company's request of support from various government bureaus), 40, Ministry of Education, 0701.41/6, National Archives of Thailand.

23 "Banthuek ruang borisat thai niyom phanit chamkat kho khwam sanap sanun khwam chuai lua chak ongkan tang tang khong rathaban," 40.

24 "Banthuek ruang borisat thai niyom phanit chamkat kho khwam sanap sanun khwam chuai lua chak ongkan tang tang khong rathaban," 40.

25 "Banthuek ruang borisat thai niyom phanit chamkat kho khwam sanap sanun khwam chuai lua chak ongkan tang tang khong rathaban," 40.

26 "Kio kap borisat pun siment thai niyom panit" (Memo regarding Siam Cement Thai Niyom Panit), dated 1/27/2483 BE, 60, Ministry of Education, 0701.41/4, National Archives of Thailand.

27 Worrasit Tantinipankul, "Modernization and Urban Monastic Space in Rattanakosin City: Comparative Study of Three Royal Wats" (PhD diss., Cornell University, 2007), 348–349.

28 Phra Phromphichit, *Phutta silpasathapatayakam phak ton* (Buddhist art, architecture) (Bangkok: Rong phim phra chan, 1952), 1.

29 Association of Siamese Architects, *Roi pi Phraphromphichit* (100 Years of Phra Phromphichit) (Bangkok: ASA, 1990), n.p.

30 The architect Amnuay Suwanaphong has noted that when the *prang* was appropriated by Tai-speaking polities like Sukhothai and Ayutthaya, it was not the Mahayana Buddhist *prang* of the Bayon ornamented with the four faces of Lokesvara, but the Brahmanic *prang* of Angkor Wat. It is likely that the geometries of the Brahmanic *prang* lent themselves more easily to Theravadan imagery or simply that they were easier to construct. Amnuay Suwanaphong, *Thananusak haeng sathapatayakam thai: Anusorn nai ngan phrarachthan phloeng sop* (Hierarchy in Thai architecture: Commemorative funeral volume) (Bangkok: Wat Makukasatriaram, 1984), 27.

31 Amnuay, *Thananusak haeng sathapatayakam thai*, 27.

32 Amnuay, *Thananusak haeng sathapatayakam thai*, 33.

33 "Ruang anusawari thai" (Letter from Luang Wichit Wathakan to the prime minister regarding Anusawari Thai), 18 February 1939, 12, Ministry of Education, 0701.41.1/26, National Archives of Thailand.

34 "Ruang anusawari thai," 11.

35 In December 1940, the Phak Khmer Issarak (Free Khmer Party) was established in Bangkok to overthrow the French. The party's leader, an expatriate Khmer named Phra Bhises Panich (Phra Phiset Phanit), claimed that the Issarak were established, funded, and supervised by the Thai. Barmé, *Luang Wichit Wathakan*, 168.

36 Interestingly, architect Miw Aphaiwong's family were nobles in Battambang, one of the contested Cambodian provinces. The family remained a strong social and political presence in the city up until the People's Republic of Kampuchea forces overthrew Democratic Kampuchea in 1978. See Michael Vickery, *Cambodia, 1975–1982* (Boston: South End Press, 1984), 159.

37 Wichit Wathakan, *Luat suphan, ratchamanu, phrachao krung thon, suk Thailand* (Four plays) (Bangkok: Commemoration volume for Khunying Chan Thepprachum, 17 October 1937), 71; Barmé, *Luang Wichit Wathakan*, 125.

38 Wichit, *Luat suphan, ratchamanu, phrachao krung thon, suk Thailand*, 30; Barmé, *Luang Wichit Wathakan*, 125.

39 Wichit Wathakan, *Thailand's Case* (Bangkok: Thanom Punnahitananda, 1941), 130.

40 Wichit, *Thailand's Case*, 125.

41 Foreign Office, FO 371/22207, 6 May 1938, National Archives of Thailand; Barmé, *Luang Wichit Wathakan*, 126.

42 *Prachamit*, May 6, 1938.

43 Barmé, *Luang Wichit Wathakan*, 167.

44 Chatri Prakitnontakan, *Khana ratsadon chalong ratthathammanun: Prawatisat kan mueang lang 2475 phan sathapatayakam "amnat"* (The People's Party celebrates

the constitution: Political history after 1932 through the architecture of "power") (Bangkok: Matichon, 2005), 81.

45 Maurizio Peleggi, *Thailand: The Worldly Kingdom* (London: Reaktion, 2007), 189.

46 Phiphat Phongraphiphon, "Sastracharn Silpa Bhirasri sinlap lae mahawithayalai Silpakorn" (Professor Silpa Bhirasri, art and Silpakorn University), *Bulletin of the Art Gallery of Silpakorn University* 1 (September 1984): 27; Apinan Poshyananda, *Modern Art in Thailand* (Oxford: Oxford University Press, 1992), 46.

47 *Patokatha lae kham banyai khong phontri luang wichit watthakan pheua rong amnat-tho khunchitrakankhamni* (Speeches and talks by Major General Luang Wichit Watthakan: Funeral volume for Rongamnattho khunchitrakankhamni) (Bangkok: Wat Mokutkasatriyaram, 1966), 116.

48 Barmé, *Luang Wichit Wathakan*, 154.

49 *Patokatha lae kham banyai khong phontri luang wichit watthakan pheua rong amnat-tho khunchitrakankhamni*, 120.

50 Sitthidet and Phiman were among the first graduates of the art school that Silpa helped to found, Silpakorn University, and upon graduation worked as assistants for Silpa in the Department of Fine Arts. Silpakorn University, *"Rakngao" mahawitthayalai sinlapakopn: Nithatsakan phon ngan khong "sit" rongrian pranit sinlapakam-rongrian sinlapakorn phanaek chang* ("Roots" of Silpakorn University: Exhibition of "disciples" from Silpakorn Art Academy) (Bangkok: Amarin, 1993), 18; Thanavi Chotpradit, "Revolution versus Counter-Revolution: The People's Party and the Royalist(s) in Visual Dialogue" (PhD diss., Birkbeck, University of London, 2016), 111.

51 A series of twelve mandates issued by the government of Phibun Songkhram between 1939 and 1942, the *rathaniyom* sought to create a "civilized" Thai culture through changes in the dress, decorum, language, national and royal anthems, national flag, and name of the country.

52 "Banthuek ruang wat phra sri mahathat" (Memo on Wat Phra Sri Mahathat), 1, Ministry of Education, 2.3.6.7/4, National Archives of Thailand.

53 "Banthuek ruang wat phra sri mahathat," 6.

54 Rajabhat University Bangkok, *Anusawari phithak ratthathammanun wat phra sri mahathat maha vihan sathaban rachaphatphranakhon* (Laksi monument, Wat Phra Sri Mahathat, and the Rajabhat University) (Bangkok: Sathaban Rachaphat-phranakhorn, 2000), 116–117.

55 Donald Swearer, "Signs of the Buddha in Northern Thai Chronicles," in *Embodying the Dharma: Buddhist Relic Veneration in Asia*, ed. David Germano and Kevin Trainor (Albany: State University of New York Press, 2004), 158.

56 Steve Collins, *Nirvana and Other Buddhist Felicities: Utopias of the Pali Imaginaire* (Cambridge: Cambridge University Press, 1998), 19.

57 Although an important reference for Asian modernism, the École occupied a disreputable place in the history of European modernist architecture. In 1928, Siegfried Giedion wrote that "even today the academy des Beaux-Arts proves itself to be a most distressing drag on active development." Siegfried Giedion, *Building in France, Building in Iron, Building in Ferro-concrete* (Santa Monica, CA: Getty Center for the History of Art and the Humanities, 1995), originally published as *Bauen in Frankreich, Bauen in Eisen, Bauen in Eisenbeton* (Leipzig: Klinkhardt and Biermann, 1928), 100.

58 Sakchai Saising, *Chedi nai prathet thai* (Stupas in Thailand) (Bangkok: Matichon, 2017), 688.

59 Peter Williams-Hunt (or William Hunts, or William Hunt) was a British photographer who was a reader, translator, and aerial photographer for the Royal Air Force. In the beginning of the Second World War, he was stationed in the north of Italy and began to study and write articles about ancient Roman places and used aerial photographs to help him analyze them. After the German surrender, he went to Asia, first to Saigon, then Bangkok, and then Kuala Lumpur. He married a Senoi woman and wrote books of anthropology on the Orang Asli. Williams-Hunt's photographs were commissioned by a British government that ostensibly sought agricultural information after World War II, although it is likely an interest in security was part of their surveying project. Williams-Hunt died of injuries following an accident in 1953. These photographs, and Williams-Hunt's biographical information, were found in the National Archives of Thailand.

60 Karl Döhring calls these discs *luk keo,* but Choti Kalyanamitra defines *luk keo* ลูกแก้ว as simply the round ornament on the end of the *yod.* Karl Döhring, *Buddhist Stupa Architecture of Thailand* (Bangkok: White Lotus, 2000), 69; Choti Kalyanamitra, *Phochananukrom satthapatayagam lae silp kio nuang* (Dictionary of architecture and applied arts) (Bangkok: Muang Boran, 2005), 445.

61 "Ruang kho khwam damri ruang chai chong nai chedi phra sri mahathat" (Regarding information for the use of the passage in the chedi of Wat Phra Sri Mahathat), 58–62, Ministry of Education, 0701.46/1, National Archives of Thailand. Originally intended as a church dedicated to the patron saint of Paris, St. Geneviève, the Panthéon was transformed into a mausoleum for the remains of distinguished citizens of the Republic in 1791, after construction was completed.

62 Chatri, *Kanmuang lae sangkhom nai silapa satthapatayagam,* 305.

63 Phraya Satjphirom Udomrachaphakdi, *Thewakamnot* (Origin of heavenly deities) (Bangkok: Thammasat University, 1964), 35; Chatri, *Kanmuang lae sangkhom nai silpasathapatayakam,* 397.

64 Namphueng Padamalangula, "Framing the Universe: Cosmography and the 'Discourse on the Frame' in *Traiphum Phra Ruang,*" *Rian Thai: International Journal of Thai Studies* 1, no. 1 (2008): 72.

65 Chatri, *Kanmuang lae sangkhom nai silpasathapatayakam,* 40.

66 Chatri, *Kanmuang lae sangkhom nai silpasathapatayakam,* 396–397.

CHAPTER EIGHT: THE FLOATING PARADISE

1 The canal was excavated in 1837 to facilitate the movement of troops and supplies to Cambodian territory during Siam's war with Annam. Chao Phraya Thipakorawong, *Phraratchaphongsawadan krung rattanakosin, chabap ho samut haeng chat ratchakan thi sam, ratchakan thi si* (Royal dynastic chronicles of Rattanakosin, National Library edition, Third and Fourth Reigns) (Bangkok: Khlingwitthaya, 1963), 179; Chao Phraya Wongsanupraphat, *Ruangprawat krasuangkasethrathikan* (History of the ministry of agricultural works) (Bangkok, 2484 BE), 133, cited in Shigeharu Tanabe, "Historical Geography of the Canal System in the Chao Phraya River Delta: From the Ayutthaya Period to the Fourth Reign of the Rattanakosin Dynasty," *Journal of the Siam Society* 65, no. 2 (1977): 44.

2 Ta Tha-it, *Talui ke khlap: Kai Bangkok chut 7* (A visit to the gay club: Bangkok guide series 7) (Bangkok: Joralsanitwong, 1975), 125–126.

3   In the story from which the collection takes its name, "Talui ke khlap" (A Visit to the Gay Club), it's used to describe the gay bar to which he takes a gay American doctor. After using his connections to gain admission to the club, a shop house on New Phetchaburi Road, the narrator opines, "Wiman khong phuak ke yu thi ni aeng khrap" (The paradise of gays is right here). Ta, *Talui ke khlap*, 7.

4   The *Vimāna-vatthu* is part of the *Khuddaka Nikāya*, the last of the five collections in the *Sutta Pitaka*, one of the three "baskets" of the *Tipitaka*. It is a collection of eighty-five "stories" in verse. Steve Collins, *Nirvana and Other Buddhist Felicities: Utopias of the Pali Imaginaire* (Cambridge: Cambridge University Press, 1998), 312.

5   King Lithai, *Three Worlds According to King Ruang: A Thai Buddhist Cosmology,* trans. Frank E. Reynolds and Mani B. Reynolds (Berkeley: Regents of the University of California, 1982), 223.

6   This is consistent with Partha Chatterjee's observation that the debate over social transformation in the colonial period was that of modernity, whereas in political society of the postcolonial period, the framing question is that of democracy. It departs slightly from his thesis that in the latest phase of the globalization of capital, there is an emerging opposition between modernity and democracy. Partha Chatterjee, "On Civil and Political Society in Postcolonial Democracies," in *Civil Society: History and Possibilities,* ed. Sudipta Kaviraj and Sunil Khilnani (Cambridge: Cambridge University Press, 2001), 178.

7   Phusadi Thipthat, *Sathapok sathapatayakam* (Architect architecture) (Bangkok: Faculty of Architecture, Chulalongkorn University, 1999), 114.

8   Theorist Pier Vittorio Aureli has noted that since at least the 1970s, a failure to understand the political project of the city has made architects comfortable with staying within the limits of their profession. See Pier Vittorio Aureli, "Means to an End: The Rise and Fall of the Architectural Project of the City," in *The City as a Project,* ed. Pier Vittorio Aureli (Berlin: Ruby Press, 2016), 14.

9   Manuel Castells, *The Rise of the Network Society* (Oxford: Blackwell, 2000).

10 Lauren Berlant, "The Commons: Infrastructure for Troubling Times," *Environment and Planning D: Society and Space* 34, no. 3 (2016): 393.

11 Maurizio Peleggi, *Lords of Things: The Fashioning of the Siamese Monarchy's Modern Image* (Honolulu: University of Hawai'i Press, 2002), 78; Porphant Ouyyanont, "Physical and Economic Change in Bangkok, 1851–1925," *Southeast Asian Studies* 36, no. 4 (March 1999): 437; Tomas Larsson, *Land and Loyalty: Security and the Development of Property Rights in Thailand* (Ithaca, NY: Cornell University Press, 2012), 31–34.

12 Porphant Ouyyanont, *A Regional Economic History of Thailand* (Bangkok: Chulalongkorn University Press; Singapore: Institute of Southeast Asian Studies-Yusof Ishak Institute, 2017), 37.

13 Although Thompson's book is filled with many factual errors, her observation on the state of the city's roads is supported by other scholars. Virginia Thompson, *Thailand: The New Siam* (New York: Macmillan, 1967), 507.

14 Office of the Prime Minister 02066.5/5 (1934–1953), National Archives of Thailand, cited in Porphant, *Regional Economic History,* 38.

15 Benedict Anderson and Ruchira Mendiones, *In the Mirror: Literature and Politics in Siam in the American Era* (Bangkok: Editions Duang Kamoi, 1985); Pasuk Phongphaichit and Chris Baker, *Thailand: Economy and Politics* (Kuala Lumpur: Oxford University Press, 2002), 140–167.

16 Most of the migrants came at first from the central plains region, but by the 1980s, northeasterners also joined the flow. Chris Baker and Pasuk Phongphaichit, *A History of Thailand* (Melbourne: Cambridge University Press, 2017), 162.

17 Thak Chaloemtiarana, *Thailand: The Politics of Despotic Paternalism* (Ithaca, NY: Cornell Southeast Asia Program Publications, 2007), 151.

18 Sarit Thanarat, "Khamklao nai kanpredprachum phu waratchakan changwat lae phubankhaphkan tramruad phutonhkhet," 16 March 1960, in Sarit Thanarat, *Pramuan suntharaphot khong chomphon Sarit Thanarat I* (Bangkok: n.p., 1964), 146; Thak, *Thailand*, 151.

19 Amanda Kay McVetty, "Wealth and Nations," in *The Development Century: A Global History*, ed. Stephen J. Macekura and Erez Manela (Cambridge: Cambridge University Press, 2018), 23.

20 Thak, *Thailand* (2007), xxvi.

21 The National Economic Development Board would later become the National Economic and Social Development Board, as it is still known today, in 1972, under the office of the prime minister. "Phraratchabanyat sapha phatthanakn setthakit haeng chat, pho so 2502" (National Economic Development Council Act, 1959), in *Ratchakitcha* 76, sec. 69, 1; Thak, *Thailand* (2007), 151, 184.

22 International Bank of Reconstruction and Development, *A Public Development Program for Thailand* (Baltimore: Johns Hopkins, 1959). Thak noted that the NEDB plan allotted more funding for irrigation than the World Bank report had recommended, suggesting that the Thai government was more interested in irrigation and social welfare than in strategic roads. Thak, *Thailand* (2007), 151, 168–169.

23 National Economic Development Board, *National Economic Development Plan, 1961–1966, Second Phase 1964–1966* (Bangkok, January 1964), 9, cited in Thak Chaloemtiarana, *Thailand: The Politics of Despotic Paternalism* (Bangkok: Social Science Association, Thai Kadi Institute, Thammasat University, 1979), 228.

24 National Economic Development Board, *National Economic Development Plan*, 9.

25 Thak, *Thailand* (1979), 230; Chatthip Nartsupha, *The Economic Development of Thailand 1956–1963* (Bangkok: Phrae Phitthaya, 1970), 50.

26 Thak, *Thailand* (2007), 168–169.

27 Pasuk and Baker, *Thailand*, 188.

28 Thomas Robertson, "New Frontiers," in *The Development Century: A Global History*, ed. Stephen J. Macekura and Erez Manela (Cambridge: Cambridge University Press, 2018), 108–109.

29 Benedict Anderson cited three interrelated factors that made Bangkok a nexus: the post-1945 end of European colonial powers' hegemony in Southeast Asia, American regional expansionism centered on Thailand, and the technological revolution that made tourism a major industry in East and Southeast Asia after World War II. Benedict Anderson, "Withdrawal Symptoms: Social and Cultural Aspects of the October 6 Coup," *Bulletin of Concerned Asian Scholars* 9, no. 3 (1977): 14.

30 Thak Chaloemtiarana noted that the orientation of national development shifted from "welfare" to "security." Thak, *Thailand* (2007), 155.

31 Thak, *Thailand* (2007), 239.

32 Krom Thang Luang (Royal Highways Department), *Thang luang nai prathet thai, 2527/1984,* (Bangkok: Krom Thang Luang, 1984), 8.

33 Litchfield, Whiting, Bowne, and Associates and Adams, Howard, and Greeley, *Greater Bangkok Plan 2533* (Bangkok: Ministry of the Interior, 1960), 92.

34 Sarit Thannarat, "Khamprasai nuang nai wan khroprop pi haeng kantang khanaratthamontri" (Cabinet anniversary speech), 10 February 1960, in *Pramuan Sunthoraphot*, I, 127–128, cited in Thak, *Thailand* (2007), 164.

35 Litchfield et al., *Greater Bangkok Plan 2533*, 92.

36 They were eventually replaced with motorized *samlor*, which still presented many of the same problems, but at a slightly faster speed. Thak, *Thailand* (1979), 164.

37 Cyrus Nims, *City Planning in Thailand* (Bangkok: Ministry of the Interior, 1963), 4–6.

38 Robert A. Heinlein, *Expanded Universe* (New York: Simon and Schuster, 2003), 326.

39 Litchfield, Whiting, Bowne, and Associates, *Technical Monograph: Travel Time* (Bangkok: Ministry of the Interior, 1959), 3; Litchfield et al., *Greater Bangkok Plan 2533*, 89.

40 Litchfield et al., *Greater Bangkok Plan 2533*, 70.

41 Apiwat Ratanawaraha, "From Boston to Bangkok: How American Cold-War Urbanism Shaped Thailand's Current Urban Plans" (lecture, Southeast Asia Program, Cornell University, 3 October 2019).

42 Michael Quin Dudley, "Sprawl as Strategy: City Planners Face the Bomb," *Journal of Planning Education and Research* 21 (2001): 54.

43 Tracy B. Augur, "The Dispersal of Cities as a Defense Measure," *Journal of the American Institute of Planners* 14, no. 3 (1948): 31.

44 Augur, "Dispersal of Cities," 33.

45 Augur, "Dispersal of Cities," 33.

46 Litchfield et al., *Greater Bangkok Plan 2533*, 90.

47 Litchfield et al., *Greater Bangkok Plan 2533*, 93.

48 Litchfield et al., *Greater Bangkok Plan 2533*, 101–107.

49 In fact, the plan suggested that although dependence on the waterways would decrease because of the growth of highway transport, the communities that had developed along the canals would continue to rely on them for personal transportation as well as commerce, suggesting that these communities would be marginalized from the main roads it proposed. Litchfield et al., *Greater Bangkok Plan 2533*, 112.

50 Litchfield et al., *Greater Bangkok Plan 2533*, 126.

51 Augur, "Dispersal of Cities," 34.

52 Augur, however, believed that the cluster-form city would be effective in preventing internal unrest. Augur, "Dispersal of Cities," 35.

53 Kasian Tejapira, *Commodifying Marxism: The Formation of Modern Thai Radical Culture* (Kyoto: Kyoto University Press, 2001), 97.

54 Thak Chaloemtiarana has noted that while the practice in London's Hyde Park was really intended to give eccentrics the opportunity to "let off steam," Bangkok's Hyde Park was taken seriously as a "legitimate source of interest articulation," and Phibun even ordered officials to pay attention to the suggestions of its speakers. Thak, *Thailand* (1979), 104–105.

55 Thak, *Thailand* (1979), 105.

56 *Sayam nikon*, 11 August 1957, cited in Thak, *Thailand* (1979), 111.

57 Thak, *Thailand* (1979), 119–120.

58 Litchfield et al., *Greater Bangkok Plan 2533*, 129.

59 Jeff Romm, *Urbanization in Thailand* (New York: Ford Foundation, 1974), 91.

60 Litchfield et al., *Greater Bangkok Plan 2533*, 130.

61 Litchfield et al., *Greater Bangkok Plan 2533*, 130.

62 Litchfield et al., *Greater Bangkok Plan 2533*, 132.

63 Litchfield et al., *Greater Bangkok Plan 2533*, 133.

64 By 1963, street construction and widening had taken place in many parts of the city; slaughterhouses, tanneries, and other heavy industries were moved out of the city; a new airport site was selected near the site that the plan recommended; and industrial land-use classification was adopted in accordance with the planning principle. However, it was not until 1992 that a master plan for Bangkok would finally be adopted. Nims, *City Planning*, 5; Romm, *Urbanization in Thailand*, 89.

65 Baker and Pasuk, *A History of Thailand*, 148–149.

66 Matthew Phillips, *Thailand in the Cold War* (London: Routledge, 2017), 158.

67 Maurizio Pellegi, *Monastery, Monument, Museum: Sites and Artifacts of Thai Cultural Memory* (Honolulu: University of Hawai'i Press, 2018), 100.

68 Vajiravudh, *A Trip to Muang Phra Ruang* (n.p., [1967?]); Vajiravudh, King of Siam, *Thio muang phra ruang* (Bangkok: Thaikhasem, 1978).

69 Chatri Prakitnontakan, *Khana ratsadon chalong ratthathammanun: Prawattisat kan muang lang 2475 phan sathapattakaykam "amnat"* (The People's Party celebrates the constitution: Political history after 1932 through the architecture of "power") (Bangkok: Matichon, 2005).

70 The Intercontinental Hotels group sent promotional material to the Thai government in 1960 that argued profits from American tourism in Europe could be translated into the "Far East." Not long after, American visitors constituted the largest number of arrivals. In 1962, the Pacific Area Travel Association named the United States as the most important tourist market. Phillips, *Thailand in the Cold War*, 150–151.

71 "Khao san chak OST" (News from the TOT), July 1962, 121, Ministry of Education 0701.9.10.9/3, National Archives of Thailand, cited in Phillips, *Thailand in the Cold War*, 152.

72 "Kho khit nai panha sathapatayakam," *ASA: Journal of the Association of Siamese Architects* (3 February 1951): 36–37.

73 "Erawan Hotel a 'Thai Treat' for Tourists Expanding," *Bangkok Post*, 20 December 1960, 2; "Erawan hai phanakngan taeng chutmaithai roem patiwat khrueang baep chut kao phua dudut chai chao tangprathet" (The Erawan makes its employees wear Thai costumes for a revolution back to old-style uniforms in order to appeal to foreigners), *San Seri*, 15 December 1960, 5, cited in Phillips, *Thailand in the Cold War*, 159.

74 The design of both hotels is indicative of the general tendency toward symbolism in the commercial architecture of the period, which often indulged in a kind of *architecture parlante:* the Rong Rian Triam Tahan (Military School) was in the shape of a battleship, and the Thanakan Kasikorn (Thai Farmer's Bank) was in the shape of a rice stalk. Phusadi, *Sathapok sathapatayakam*, 66–67.

75 Suphawadi Ratanamat, Parinya Chukaew, et al., *Kan jat tang klum anurak ngan sathapatayakam samai modoen nai prathet thai* (Activities of the preservation group, modern architectural works in Thailand) (Bangkok: Docomomo Thailand, 2003), 100–101.

76 Anderson and Mendiones, *In the Mirror*, 23.

77 Phetchaburi Road was one of fourteen roads originally laid in the nineteenth century during the Fifth Reign and was named Prajaejin Road, after a Chinese teapot design manufactured by the Kim Tung company and collected during that period by members of the royal family and titled bureaucracy. King Vajiravudh changed the names of the streets to something people would remember for a long time: the names of the provinces that comprised the new geo-body of the nation. Sukhumvit Road crosses four provinces and the capital and was named in honor of Phra Phisansukhumvit (né Prasop Sukhum), third son of Chao Phraya Yomarat and Than Phuying Tlap, whose official career was primarily concerned with building an infrastructural network of roads in Thailand during the tenure of Phibun Songkhram. Sansoni Wirasinchai, *Roi raek nai muang thai* (Bangkok: Matichon, 1994), 67–68.

78 "Yak sap kotmai nai kan ok baeb rong raem man rud (Khuan cha rap ngan ru mai)" (Curious about official laws designing a pull-curtain motel [Should I take the job or not?]), Association of Siamese Architects Web Board, http://www.asa.or.th/th/node/92649.

79 Janit Feangfu, "(Ir)resistably Modern: The Construction of Modern Thai Identities in Thai Literature during the Cold War Era, 1958–1976" (PhD diss., University of London, School of Oriental and African Studies, 2011), 125.

80 Ta, *Talui ke khlap*, 137.

81 Baker and Pasuk, *A History of Thailand*, 148.

82 Ta, *Talui ke khlap*, 138.

83 There is evidence to suggest that brothels in Bangkok catering to men who were interested in the same sex predated the Cold War. A report of a police raid on a brothel staffed by ten- to twelve-year-old boys was reported in 1935. "Tang song sopheni thuan yang witthan doi chai dek chai pen phu rap chang gratham chamrao" (A bogus and peculiar brothel that uses boys to hire for rape), *Sri Krung*, 20 June 1935, *Sayam sanuk khao*, n138; cited in Wirayut Pisali, *Krungthep yamaratri* (Bangkok at midnight) (Bangkok: Matichon, 2014), 198–202.

84 Ta, *Talui ke khlap*, 2.

85 Ta, *Talui ke khlap*, 5.

86 Ta, *Talui ke khlap*, 15.

87 According to the Royal Highways Department, between 1963 and 1984, a total of 558.4 million US dollars in foreign loans supplemented the national budget and produced a total length of ninety-three hundred kilometers of highways. Krom Thang Luang, *Thang luang nai prathet thai*, 63.

88 Thak, *Thailand* (1979), 151.

89 Krom Thang Luang, *Thang luang nai prathet thai*, 7.

90 Porphant Ouyyanont, "Transformation of Bangkok and Concomitant Changes in Urban-Rural Interaction in Thailand in the 19th and 20th Centuries," in *The Chao Phraya Delta: Historical Development, Dynamics and Challenges of Thailand's Rice Bowl* (Bangkok: Kasetsart University, 2000), 27.

91 Porphant, "Transformation of Bangkok," 28.

92 Karl Marx and Friedrich Engels, *The Communist Manifesto* (Beijing: Foreign Languages Press, 1975).

93 Thawisak Pinthong et al., *Wannakam kep tok* (Bangkok: Odian Sato, 1980), ข.

94 Thawisak et al., *Wannakam kep tok*, pp. 65–66.

95 The demonstrations began in November 1972 as a student-led protest against Japanese goods. Once the students grasped their effectiveness, they began to focus on restoring the constitution. Baker and Pasuk, *A History of Thailand*, 186.

96 Charnvit Kasetsiri and Thamrongsak Phetloetanan, eds., *14 tula 2516 thung 6 tula 2519* (14 October 1973 to 6 October 1976) (Bangkok: Foundation for the Promotion of Social Sciences and Humanities Textbook Project, 2006), 19; Baker and Pasuk, *A History of Thailand*, 186.

97 Malini Khumsupha, *Anusawari prachatipatai kap khwam mai thi mong mai hen* (The Democracy Monument and the meaning of things that can't be seen) (Bangkok: Wiphasa, 2005), 290; *Prawatsat chut prachatipatai* (Bangkok: Samnak pimp Siam, 1974), n.p.

98 The king appointed a new prime minster, Sanya Thammasak, and initiated the process for writing a new constitution. Pasuk and Baker note that this event not only marked the political ascendance of the students, but also elevated the king as a "supra-constitutional force arbitrating the conflicts of a deeply divided nation." Baker and Pasuk, *A History of Thailand*, 186.

99 At a rally of the newly formed Peasants Federation of Thailand in Bangkok in late 1974, monks occupied the front ranks. Baker and Pasuk, *A History of Thailand*, 189.

100 Phusadi, *Sathapok sathapatayakam*, 39.

101 Phusadi, *Sathapok sathapatayakam*, 35.

102 Phusadi, *Sathapok sathapatayakam*, 125.

103 Paul N. Edwards, "Infrastructure and Modernity: Force, Time, and Social Organization in the History of Sociotechnical Systems," in *Modernity and Technology*, ed. Thomas J. Misa, Philip Brey, and Andrew Feenberg (Cambridge, MA: MIT Press, 2003), 188.

104 Berlant, "The Commons," 393.

CHAPTER NINE: EPILOGUE

1 Joan Didion, *The White Album* (New York: Simon and Schuster, 1979), 11.

2 Vittoria Bonnel and Lynn Hunt, eds., *Beyond the Cultural Turn: New Directions in the Study of Society and Culture* (Berkeley: University of California Press, 1999), 17.

3 "This will kill that. The published book will kill the edifice." Victor Hugo and A. J. Krailsheimer, *Notre-Dame de Paris* (Oxford: Oxford University Press, 1999), 192.

4 Susan Buck-Morss, "The City as Dreamworld and Catastrophe," *October* 73 (Summer 1995): 9.

5 It is likely that the plaque was removed with state support. Todd Ruiz, "1932 Democratic Revolution Plaque Removed," *Khaosod English*, 14 April 2017; Koompong Noobanjong, "Forgotten Memorials: The Constitutional Defense Monument and the Democracy Temple in Bangkok, Thailand," in *Southeast Asia's Modern Architecture: Questions of Translation, Epistemology and Power*, ed. Jiat-Hwee Chang and Imran bin Tajudeen (Singapore: NUS Press, 2018), 211–216.

6 Koompong, "Forgotten Memorials," 213.

7 Patrick Jory, *Thailand's Theory of Monarchy: The Vessantara Jataka and the Idea of the Perfect Man* (Albany: State University of New York Press, 2016), 187.

8 José Esteban Muñoz, *Cruising Utopia: The Then and There of Queer Futurity* (New York: New York University Press, 2009), 189.

9 "Neither the kingdom of God, nor the cloaca." Paul B. Preciado, *Un appartement sur Uranus: Chroniques de la traversée* (Paris: Bernard Grasset, 2019), 30; Buddhadasa Bhikkhu, "Towards a Dictatorial Dhammic Socialism," in *Me and Mine: Selected Essays of Bhikkhu Buddhadasa*, ed. Donald K. Swearer (Albany: State University of New York Press, 1989), 184–185.

BIBLIOGRAPHY

ARCHIVAL MATERIAL

BRITISH LIBRARY

Or 15245, *Dhammasangani/Traiphum* illustrated manuscript attributed to Nai Sun.
Or 15760, *Tamra phichai songkhram* illustrated manuscript.
Or 6630, *Phra Malai* illustrated manuscript.

MUSEUM FÜR ASIATISCHE KUNST, BERLIN

Mss II 650. "Traiphum phra ruang," ca. 1776.

NATIONAL ARCHIVES OF THAILAND

Archives of the Fifth Reign (ร.๕)

Ministry of Justice (ยธ). 1/32 "Chotmai Koed Bunnag ruang kan ko sang phra thi nang Ananta samakhom (Ministry of Public Works: Correspondence of Koed Bunnag regarding the construction of the Ananata Samakhom Throne Hall).

Ministry of the Capital (น). 5.1/120 "Ruang rai kan khwam hen ruang kan jad kan sukhaphiban" (Correspondence regarding views on the organization of the municipal government of Bangkok), July 10, R.S. 125.

Ministry of the Capital. 16–11/168 "Chotmai ratchahatlekha phra ratchawang suan dusit ruang anuyat hai nerathet jin tai sen jin tan chiang" (Letter to Chao Phraya Yommaraj, Ministry of the Interior from the Royal Secretary, Suan Dusit, regarding permission to exile Jin Tai Sen and Jin Tan Chiang), 10 June 1910.

Ministry of the Capital. 168 "Banchi phuak jin thi go gan wun wai kan tai suan dai khwam jing khuan nerathet" (Index of the group of Chinese who had created violence, interrogation and testimony, recommendation for deportation), 1910.

Ministry of the Capital. "Tamra ang yi ekasan yep lem chut tamra ang yi" (Secret society manual: Collected documents on secret societies), 1910.

Archives of the Sixth Reign (ร.๖)

Ministry of the Capital (น). 27/8, 1920–1921, "Revision of the 1910 Census, Undertaken in 1913."

Ministry of the Capital. 7.1/23, "Ruang sang tao phao tham lai khaya mun foi lamrap krom sukhaphiban lae ruang wat kan sukhaphiban hai pen miunisi-paelitti," (Correspondence regarding establishing a municipal incinerator by the Ministry of the Capital), 12 January 2460 BE to 14 August 2465 BE.

Ministry of Finance (ค)

0301.1.1/13 (1931), Report of the Ministry of Finance.

Cabinet Secretary (สร)

0201.26/5. Office of the Prime Minister to the Palace Secretary, "Ruang phloeng sop tahan lae tham khuan meuang nakhon ratchasima" (Memo on the cremation ceremonies of soldiers at Nakhon Ratchasima).

0201.26/6. Office of the Prime Minister to the Palace Secretary, "Chotmai rata-montri wa kan krasuang wang rian nayok ratamontri" (Letter from the prime minister's office to the Ministry of the Palace), 6 January 1933.

0201.26/7. Office of the Prime Minister, "Kamnot kan bumphen kuson nai ngan phra ratchathan phloeng sop tahan sia chiwit pai nai kan prap kabot" (Schedule of the cremation ceremony of the soldiers who sacrificed their lives suppressing the revolt).

Ministry of Education (ศธ)

0701.41/4. Kio kap borisat pun siment thai niyom panit (Memo regarding Siam Cement Thai Niyom Panit), 27 January 1940.

0701.41/6. Banthuek ruang borisat thai niyom phanit chamkat kho khwam sanap sanun khwam chuai lua chak ongkan tang tang khong rathaban (Memo regarding the Thai Panit Niyom Company's request of support from various government bureaus).

0701.41.1/26. Ruang anusawari thai (Letter from Luang Wichitwathakan to the Prime Minister regarding Anusawari Thai), 18 February 1939.

0701.46/1. Ruang kho khwam damri ruang chai chong nai chedi phra sri maha-that (Regarding information for the use of the passage in the chedi of Wat Phra Sri Mahathat).

2.3.6.7/4. Banthuek ruang wat phra sri mahathat (Memo on Wat Phra Sri Mahathat).

0701.9.10.9/3. "Khao san chak Oo So Tho" (News from the TOT), July 1962.

NATIONAL LIBRARY OF THAILAND RELIGIOUS MANUSCRIPT DIVISION (ธรรมคดี)

Cupboard 107, no. 1. *Traiphum lokwinitchai.*

Newspapers and Periodicals

Bangkok Daily Mail
Bangkok Post
Bangkok Times
Bangkok Times Weekly Mail
Dusit sakkhi/Dusit Recorder
Dusit samai
Dusit samit
Phaphayon sayam
Prachamit
Reality Forum
Sakul Thai
San Seri
Siam Repository
Singapore Free Press
Sri Krung
Thai kasem khao

SECONDARY SOURCES

Ackerman, Marsha. *Cool Comfort: America's Romance with Air-Conditioning.* Washington, DC: Smithsonian Institution Press, 2002.

Alberti, Leon Batista. *On the Art of Building in Ten Books.* Translated by Joseph Rykwert et al. Cambridge, MA: MIT Press, 1988.

Althusser, Louis. "Ideology and Ideological State Apparatuses (Notes Towards an Investigation)." In *Lenin and Philosophy and Other Essays.* New York: Monthly Review Press, 1972.

Amnuay Suwanaphong. *Thananusak haeng sathapatayakam thai: Anusorn nai ngan phrarachthan phloeng sop* (Hierarchy in Thai architecture: Commemorative funeral volume). Bangkok: Wat Makukasatriaram, 1984.

"Anagatavamsa." *Journal of the Pali Text Society* (1886): 33–42.

Andaya, Barbara. "Statecraft in the Reign of Lu Tai of Sukhodaya." *Cornell Journal of Social Relations* 1 (Spring 1971).

Anderson, Benedict R. O'G. *Imagined Communities: Reflections on the Origins and Spread of Nationalism.* London: Verso, 1983.

———. "Withdrawal Symptoms: Social and Cultural Aspects of the October 6 Coup." *Bulletin of Concerned Asian Scholars* 9, no. 3 (1977).

Anderson, Benedict R. O'G., and Ruchira Mendiones. *In the Mirror: Literature and Politics in Siam in the American Era.* Bangkok: Editions Duang Kamoi, 1985.

Anderson, Lewis Flint. *History of Manual and Industrial Education.* New York: Appleton, 1926.

Andrews, James M. *Siam: Second Rural Economic Survey 1934–1935.* Hong Kong: Bangkok Times Press, 1935.

Anuman Rajadhon. *Popular Buddhism in Siam and Other Essays on Thai Studies.* Bangkok: Thai Inter-Religious Commission for Development and Sathira-koses Nagapradipa Foundation, 1986.

Apinan Poshyananda. *Modern Art in Thailand.* Oxford: Oxford University Press, 1992.

Araŋ Phrommachomphu [Udom Srisuwan]. *Thai kung-muang-kheun* ไทยกึ่งเมือง ขึ้น (Thailand: A semicolonial country). Bangkok: Mahachon, 1950.

Augur, Tracy B. "The Dispersal of Cities as a Defense Measure." *Journal of the American Institute of Planners* 14, no. 3 (1948).

Aung-Thwin, Michael. *Pagan: The Origins of Modern Burma.* Honolulu: University of Hawai'i Press, 1985.

Aureli, Pier Vittoro. "After Diagrams." *Log* 6 (2005).

——. "Means to an End: The Rise and Fall of the Architectural Project of the City." In *The City as a Project.* Edited by Pier Vittorio Aureli. Berlin: Ruby Press, 2016.

Baker, Chris, and Pasuk Phongphaichit. *A History of Ayutthaya: Siam in the Early Modern World.* Cambridge: Cambridge University Press, 2017.

"Banthuek chak sut thai sala chaloem krung kon plian hua khon" (Remembering the last scene before the Sala Chaloem Krung became a khon theatre). *Reality Forum* (October 2000).

Barmé, Scot. *Luang Wichit Wathakan and the Creation of a Thai Identity.* Singapore: Institute of Southeast Asian Studies, 1993.

——. *Woman, Man, Bangkok: Love, Sex, and Popular Culture in Thailand.* Lanham, MD: Rowman and Littlefield, 2002.

Batson, Benjamin. *The End of the Absolute Monarchy in Siam.* Singapore: Oxford University Press, 1984.

Becchetti-Bizot, Catherine, and François Bizot. *Le mystère dans les lettres: Étude sur les yantra bouddhiques du Cambodge et de la Thaïlande.* Bangkok: Edition des cahiers de France, 1991.

Benjamin, Walter. "Paris—Capital of the 19th century." *New Left Review* 1, no. 48 (March–April 1968).

Bennett, Charles Alpheus. *History of Manual and Industrial Education up to 1870.* Peoria, IL: Manual Arts, 1926.

——. *History of Manual and Industrial Education 1870-1917.* Peoria, IL: Manual Arts, 1937.

Bereton, Bonnie. "The Phra Malai Legend in Thai Buddhist Literature: A Study of Three Texts." PhD diss., University of Michigan, 1992.

——. *Thai Tellings of Phra Malai: Texts and Rituals Concerning a Popular Buddhist Saint.* Tempe: Arizona State University, Program for Southeast Asian Studies, 1995.

Berlant, Lauren. "The Commons: Infrastructure for Troubling Times." *Environment and Planning D: Society and Space* 34, no. 3 (2016).

Berman, Marshall. *All That Is Solid Melts into Air: The Experience of Modernity.* New York: Simon and Schuster, 1982.

Besso, Salvatore. *Siam and China*. London: Simpkin, Marshall, Hamilton, Kent, 1914.

Bharne, Vinayak, Krupali Krusche, and Leon Krier. *Rediscovering the Hindu Temple: The Sacred Architecture and Urbanism of India*. Newcastle upon Tyne: Cambridge Scholars, 2012.

Bhidayalongkorn. "Phawa yangrai no thi riak wa siwilai" (What is the condition of the thing called "civilization"?) in *Prachum pathokatha khong kromamun phitthayalongkon* (Collected lectures by Prince Bhidayalongkorn). Bangkok: Ruamsan, 1970.

Billington, James H. *Fire in the Minds of Men: Origins of the Revolutionary Faith*. New York: Basic Books, 1980.

Blackburn, Anne. "Buddhist Technologies of Statecraft and Millennial Moments." *History and Theory* 56 (2017).

———. *Locations of Buddhism: Colonialism and Modernity in Sri Lanka*. Chicago: University of Chicago Press, 2010.

Bloch, Ernst. *Literary Essays*. Stanford, CA: Stanford University Press, 1998.

Bloch, Marc Léopold Benjamin. *Feudal Society*. Vol. 1. Chicago: University of Chicago Press, 1961.

Bonnel, Vittoria, and Lynn Hunt, eds. *Beyond the Cultural Turn: New Directions in the Study of Society and Culture*. Berkeley: University of California Press, 1999.

Boonma Wongswan. *Siam Cement Company: 1913–1983*. Bangkok: Siam Cement Company, 1983.

Bozodğan, Sibel. *Modernism and Nation Building: Turkish Architectural Culture and the Early Republic*. Seattle: University of Washington Press, 2001.

Bray, Francesca, Vera Dorofeeva-Lichtmann, and Georges Métailié, eds. *Graphics and Texts in the Production of Technical Knowledge in China: The Warp and the Weft*. Leiden: Brill, 2007.

Brun, Viggo. "Traditional Manuals and the Distribution of Knowledge in Thailand." In *The Master Said: To Study and . . . To Soren Egerod on the Occasion of His Sixty-Seventh Birthday*. Edited by Simon B. Heilesen and Jens Østergård Petersen. Copenhagen: East Asian Institute, University of Copenhagen, 1990.

Bua Sochisewi. "Dusit Thani: Muang prachathipatai samai ratchakan thi hok (Dusit Thani: The democractic city of the Sixth Reign). *Silpawatthanatham* 9, no. 3 (January 1988).

Buck-Morss, Susan. "The City as Dreamworld and Catastrophe." *October* 73 (Summer 1995).

———. *Hegel, Haiti, and Universal History*. Pittsburgh, PA: University of Pittsburgh Press, 2009.

Buddhadassa Bhikkhu. *Me and Mine: Selected Essays of Bhikkhu Buddhadassa*. Edited by Donald K. Swearer. Albany: State University of New York Press, 1989.

———. *Teaching Dhamma with Pictures*. Bangkok: Social Science Association Press, 1968.

Buddhaghosa. *The Sumaṅgala-vilāsinī.* Edited and translated by Wilhelm Stede, T. W. Rhys Davids, and J. Estlin Carpenter. London: Published for the Pali Text Society by Luzac, 1968.

———. *Visuddhimagga: The Path of Purification.* Translated by Bhikkhu Ñāṇamoli. Kandy: Buddhist Publication Society, 1975.

Bureau of the Royal Household. *Chotmaihet kankosang lae somsaem Phrathinang Wimanmek Phutthasakkarat 2443-2518* (Chronicles of the construction and renovation of Wimanmek Mansion, 1900–1975). Bangkok: Bureau of the Royal Household, 1990.

C. Euabamrungjit. "100 pi phaphayon nai prathet thai." *Sarakhadi* 150, no. 13 (August 1997).

Castells, Manuel. *The Rise of the Network Society.* Oxford: Blackwell, 2000.

Chaem Sunthonwet. *Dusit thani muang prachathipatai khong phrabat somdet phra mongkut klao chao yu hua* (Dusit Thani: The democratic city of King Rama VI). Bangkok: National Library, 1970.

———. *Phra ratchakoranikit samkhan nai phra bat somdet phra mongkut klao chao yu hua ruang het pol thi ratchakan hok song prakat songkhram dusit thani* (Important activities of King Rama VI regarding the events of World War I and Dusit Thani). Bangkok: Ongkanha khong khurusupha, 1969.

Chakrabarty, Dipesh. *Provincializing Europe: Postcolonial Thought and Historical Difference.* Princeton, NJ: Princeton University Press, 2000.

"Chaloemkrung royal thiatoe di oldsayam phlasa" (Chaloem Krung Royal Theater and the Old Siam Plaza). *ASA: Journal of the Association of Siamese Architects* (January–February 1995).

Chamnon Saengwichian, ed. *Khon sala chaloem krung* (Sala Chaloem Krung khon theatre). Bangkok: Crown Property Bureau, 2006.

Chamreanrak Tanawangnoi. *Prawatisat phapphayon thai tangtae raek roem chon sin samai songkhramlok khrang thi song* (Thai cinema history from the beginning to the end of World War II). Bangkok: Thammasat University, 2001.

Chanan Yothong. *Nai nai ratchakan thi hok* (Men of the inner palace during the sixth reign). Bangkok: Matichon, 2013.

Chang, Jiat-Hwee, and Tim Winter. "Thermal Modernity and Architecture." *Journal of Architecture* 20, no. 1 (2015).

Charnvit Kasetsiri and Thamrongsak Phetloetanan, eds. *14 tula 2516 thung 6 tula 2519* (14 October 1973 to 6 October 1976). Bangkok: Foundation for the Promotion of Social Sciences and Humanities Textbook Project, 2001.

Chatri Prakitnontakan. *Kanmuang lae sangkhom nai silpasathapatayakam: Sayam samai thai prayuk chat niyom* (Politics and society in architecture: Siam in the era that Thailand adopted nationalism). Bangkok: Matichon, 2004.

———. *Khana ratsadon chalong ratthathammannun: Prawatisat kan mueang lang 2475 phan sathapatayakam "amnat"* (The People's Party celebrates the constitution: Political history after 1932 through the architecture of "power"). Bangkok: Matichon, 2005.

———. *Silpasathapatayakam khana ratsadon* (The art and architecture of the People's Party). Bangkok: Matichon, 2009.

Chatterjee, Partha. "On Civil and Political Society in Postcolonial Democracies." In *Civil Society: History and Possibilities.* Edited by Sudipta Kaviraj and Sunil Khilnani. Cambridge: Cambridge University Press, 2001.

Chatthip Nartsupha. *The Economic Development of Thailand 1956–1963.* Bangkok: Phrae Phitthaya, 1970.

Chatthip Nartsupha, Suthy Prasartset, and Montri Chenvidyakarn. *The Political Economy of Siam, 1910–1932.* Bangkok: Social Science Association of Thailand, 1978.

Chit Phumisak. "Chomna khong sakdina thai nai patchuban" (The real face of Thai feudalism today). In *Nitisat 2500 chabap rap sattawatmai* (The Faculty of Law yearbook 2500 to greet the new century). Bangkok: Thammasat University Faculty of Law, 2007.

Chit Tin. *The Coming Buddha Ariya Metteyya.* Kandy: Buddhist Publication Society, 1992.

Chittawadi Chitrabongs. *Prince Naris: A Siamese Designer.* Bangkok: Naris Foundation, 2016.

Choti Kalyanamitra. *Phochananukrom sathapatayakam lae silp kio nuang* (Dictionary of architecture and applied arts). Bangkok: Muang Boran, 2005.

———. *Phon ngan hok satthawat khong chang thai* (Six hundred years of work by Thai artists and architects). Bangkok: Fine Arts Commission of the Association of Siamese Architects, 2003.

Chotmaihet kan prab prung phumi that phun thi thong phra rong klang jaeng sanam luang phutthasakrat 2554 (Archives of the renovation of the central announcement hall of Sanam Luang, 2554BE). Bangkok: Amarin, 2011.

Chulada Phakdiphumintr. "Thung phra sumeru." *Sakul thai* 49, no. 3538 (10 June 2003).

Classen, Constance. "The Deodorized City: Battling Urban Stench in the Nineteenth Century." In *Sense of the City: An Alternate Approach to Urbanism.* Edited by Mirko Zardini. Montréal: Canadian Center for Architecture and Lars Müller Publishers, 2005.

Coedès, Georges. *The Indianized States of Southeast Asia.* Honolulu: East West Center, 1968.

Collins, Steve. *Nirvana and Other Buddhist Felicities.* Cambridge: Cambridge University Press, 1998.

Comber, L. F. *Chinese Secret Societies in Malaya: A Survey of the Triad Society from 1800 to 1900.* Locust Valley, NY: J.J. Augustin, 1959.

Coulet, Georges. *Les sociétés secrètes en terre d'Annam.* Saigon: n.p., 1927.

Cunningham, Alexander. *The Ancient Geography of India.* Vol. 1, *The Buddhist Period, Including the Campaigns of Alexander and the Travels of Hwen-Thsang.* London: Trübner, 1876.

Cushman, Richard, and David K. Wyatt, eds. *The Royal Chronicles of Ayutthaya: A Synoptic Translation.* Bangkok: Siam Society, 2000.

Damrong Rachanuphap. "Ruang ang yi." In *Phraratcha phongsawadan krung rattanakosin ratchakan thi 5* (Royal chronicles of the Fifth Reign of Rattanakosin). Bangkok: Khrusupha, 1961.

———. *Tamnan wang na* (History of the Front Palace). Bangkok: Sophonphiphat-thanakon, 1925.

"Dasabodhisatta uddesa." Translated by François Martini. *Bulletin de l'École française d'Extreme-Orient* 36, no. 2 (1936).

"Das Auswanderungsplan des Bürgers Cabet." *Kommunistische Zeitschrift* (1847).

Day, Tony. *Fluid Iron: State Formation in Southeast Asia.* Honolulu: University of Hawai'i Press, 2002.

Department of General Statistics. *Statistical Yearbook of the Kingdom of Siam, 1929–1930.* Bangkok: Ministry of Finance, 1930.

Dharmasēna Thera. *Jewels of the Doctrine: Stories of the Saddharma Ratnāvaliya.* Translated by Ranjini Obeyesekere. Albany: State University of New York Press, 1991.

Didion, Joan. *The White Album.* New York: Simon and Schuster, 1979.

Dilke, O. A. W. *The Roman Surveyors: An Introduction to the Agrimensores.* Newton Abbot, UK: David and Charles, 1971.

Dirlik, Arif. *The Postcolonial Aura: Third World Criticism in the Age of Global Capitalism.* Boulder, CO: Westview Press, 1997.

Döhring, Karl. *Buddhist Stupa (Phra Chedi) Architecture of Thailand.* Bangkok: White Lotus, 2000.

Donaldson, Barry, and Bernard Nagengast. *Heat & Cold: Mastering the Great Indoors.* Atlanta, GA: American Society of Heating, Refrigerating and Air-Conditioning Engineers, 1994.

Duc Dau and Shale Preston, eds. *Queer Victorian Families: Curious Relations in Literature.* London: Routledge, 2015.

Dudley, Michael Quin. "Sprawl as Strategy: City Planners Face the Bomb." *Journal of Planning Education and Research* 21 (2001).

Edwards, Paul N. "Infrastructure and Modernity: Force, Time, and Social Organization in the History of Sociotechnical Systems." In *Modernity and Technology.* Edited by Thomas J. Misa, Philip Brey, and Andrew Feenberg. Cambridge, MA: MIT Press, 2003.

Evans, Robin. *Translations from Drawing to Building and Other Essays.* Cambridge, MA: MIT Press, 1997.

Fasoli, Vilma, and Francesca B. Filippi. "The Penetration of Italian Professionals in the Context of the Siamese Modernization." *Architecture Beyond Europe* 5 (2014).

Fishel, Thamora V. "Romances of the Sixth Reign: Gender, Sexuality, and Siamese Nationalism." In *Genders and Sexualities in Modern Thailand.* Edited by Peter Jackson and Nerida Cook. Chiang Mai, Thailand: Silkworm, 1999.

Fisher, Mark. *Capitalist Realism: Is There No Alternative?* London: Zero Books, 2009.

Fistié, Pierre. *Sou-développement et utopie au Siam: Le programme de reeformes présenté en 1933 par Pridi Phanomyong.* Paris: Mouton, 1969.

Fourier, Charles. "New Material Conditions." In *The Utopian Vision of Charles Fourier: Selected Texts on Work, Love, and Passionate Attraction.* Edited and translated by Jonathan Beecher and Richard Bienvenu. Boston: Beacon Press, 1971.

Fuhrmann, Arnika. *Ghostly Desires: Queer Sexuality and Vernacular Buddhism in Contemporary Thai Cinema.* Durham, NC: Duke University Press, 2016.

Gayot, Gerard. *La Franc-maçonnerie française: Textes et pratiques (XVIII–XIX siècles).* Paris: Archives Gallimard Juilliard, 1980.

Geohegan, Vincent. "Ideology and Utopia." *Journal of Political Ideologies* 9, no. 2 (2004).

Gerini, G. E. *Chūḷākantamaṅgala, or The Tonsure Ceremony as Performed in Siam.* Bangkok: Bangkok Times Office, 1893.

Giedion, Siegfried. *Building in France, Building in Iron, Building in Ferro-concrete.* Santa Monica, CA: Getty Center for the History of Art and the Humanities, 1995.

Ginsburg, Henry. *Thai Art and Culture: Historic Manuscripts from Western Collections.* London: British Library, 2000.

Haefele-Thomas, Ardel. *Queer Others in Victorian Gothic: Transgressing Monstrosity.* Cardiff: University of Wales, 2012.

Hall, Bert S. "The Didactic and the Elegant: Some Thoughts on Scientific and Technological Illustrations in the Middle Ages and Renaissance." In *Picturing Knowledge: Historical and Philosophical Problems Concerning the Use of Art in Science.* Edited by Brian S. Baigrie. Toronto: University of Toronto Press, 2016.

Hallisey, Charles. "Nibbānasutta: An Allegedly Non-canonical Sutta on Nibbāna as a Great City." *Journal of the Pali Text Society* 18 (1993).

Hansen, Anne Ruth. *How to Behave: Buddhism and Modernity in Colonial Cambodia, 1860–1930.* Honolulu: University of Hawai'i Press, 2007.

Harootunian, Harry. "'Memories of Underdevelopment' after Area Studies." *Positions* 20, no. 1 (Winter 2012).

Harvey, David. *Spaces of Hope.* Berkeley: University of California Press, 2000.

Harvey, Sophia Siddique. "Sensuous Citizenship in Contemporary Singapore Cinema." In *Singapore Cinema: New Perspectives.* Edited by Liew Kai Khiun and Stephen Teo. London: Routledge, 2017.

Hegel, Georg Wilhelm Friedrich. *Lectures on the Philosophy of World History: Introduction.* Translated by H. B. Nisbet. Cambridge: Cambridge University Press, 1975.

Heinlein, Robert A. *Expanded Universe.* New York: Simon and Schuster, 2003.

Heynen, Hilde. *Architecture and Modernity: A Critique.* Cambridge, MA: MIT Press, 1999.

Highet, H. Campbell. "Health and Hospitals: Climate and Health of Bangkok." In *Twentieth Century Impressions of Siam: Its History, Peoples, Commerce, Industries, and Resources with Which Is Incorporated an Abridged Edition of 20th Century Impressions of British Malaya.* London: Lloyds Greater Britain Publishing, 1908.

"His Majesty, the King of Siam, Visits Carrier." *Carrier Courier* 3, no. 4 (August 1931).

Howe, David. "Architecture of the Senses." In *Sense of the City: An Alternate Approach to Urbanism.* Edited by Mirko Zardini. Montréal: Canadian Center for Architecture and Lars Müller Publishers, 2005.

Hsiao Kung-chuan. *A Modern China and a New World: K'ang Yu-Wei, Reformer and Utopian, 1858–1927.* Seattle: University of Washington Press, 1975.

Huber, Toni. *The Holy Land Reborn: Pilgrimage and the Tibetan Reinvention of Buddhist India.* Chicago: University of Chicago Press, 2008.

Hugo, Victor, and A. J. Krailsheimer. *Notre-Dame de Paris.* Oxford: Oxford University Press, 1999.

Igunma, Jana. "A Buddhist Monk's Journey to Heaven and Hell." *Journal of International Association of Buddhist Universities* 6, no. 1 (2013).

———. "Meditations on the Foul in Thai Manuscript Art." *Journal of the International Association of Buddhist Universities* 8, no. 1 (2015).

Ingels, Margaret. *Willis Haviland Carrier: Father of Air Conditioning.* Garden City, NY: Country Life Press, 1952.

International Conference on Italian-Thai Studies. *Italian-Thai Studies from the Nineteenth Century to the Present to Commemorate the Centennial of King Rama V's First Visit to Europe.* Bangkok: National Museum, 1997.

Ithithepsan Kridakon. *Ruang kiokap sathapatayakam* (On architecture). Bangkok: Rongphim Phra Chan, 1935.

Jackson, Peter. "Thai-Buddhist Identity: Debates on the Traiphum Phra Ruang." In *National Identity and Its Defenders: Thailand, 1939–1989.* Edited by Craig Reynolds. Victoria, Australia: Centre of Southeast Asian Studies, Monash University, 1991.

Jacob, Samuel Swinton. *Jeypore Portfolio of Architectural Details Prepared under the Supervision of S. S. Jacob.* London: B. Quaritch, 1890.

Janit Feangfu. "(Ir)resistably Modern: The Construction of Modern Thai Identities in Thai Literature during the Cold War Era, 1958–1976." PhD diss., University of London, School of Oriental and African Studies, 2011.

Jory, Patrick. "Thailand's Politics of Politeness: Qualities of a Gentleman and the Making of 'Thai Manners.'" *Southeast Asia Research* 23, no. 3 (2015).

———. *Thailand's Theory of Monarchy: The Vessantara Jataka and the Idea of the Perfect Man.* Albany: State University of New York Press, 2016.

Kang Youwei. *Ta T'ung Shu: The One-World Philosophy of K'ang Yu-wei.* Translated by Laurence G. Thompson. London: George Allen and Unwin, 1958.

Kannika Tanprasoet, Phaetying. *Phraratchawang phya thai nai wan wan ha phaen din* (Phyathai royal palace on its centennial anniversary). Bangkok: Matichon, 2010.

Kasian Tejapira. *Commodifying Marxism: The Formation of Modern Thai Radical Culture.* Kyoto: Kyoto University Press, 2001.

Kautalya. *The Arthashastra.* Edited by L. N. Rangarajan. New Delhi: Penguin, 1992.

Keyes, Charles. "Millenialism, Theravada Buddhism, and Thai Society." *Journal of Asian Studies* 36, no. 2 (February 1977).

King, Ross. *Reading Bangkok.* Singapore: NUS Press, 2001.

Kittiphong Kirotthamakun. "Yon ramluk chet sip pi sala chaloem krung" (Seventy years of memories of the Sala Chaloem Krung), *Sarakhadi* 19, no. 222 (August 2003).

Knapp, Ronald. "Siting and Situating a Dwelling." In *House, Home, and Family: Living and Being Chinese.* Edited by Ronald Knapp. Honolulu: University of Hawai'i Press, 2005.

Kohl, David G. *Chinese Architecture in the Straits Settlements and Western Malaya: Temples, Kongsis and Houses.* Singapore: Heinemann Asia, 1984.

Koompong Noobanjong. "Forgotten Memorials: The Constitutional Defense Monument and the Democracy Temple in Bangkok, Thailand." In *Southeast Asia's Modern Architecture: Questions of Translation, Epistemology and Power.* Edited by Jiat-Hwee Chang and Imran bin Tajudeen. Singapore: NUS Press, 2018.

Krom Silpakorn (Department of Fine Arts). *Chotmai het kan anurak krung rattanakosin* (Archives of the preservation of Rattanakosin city). Bangkok: Krom Silpakon, 1982.

———. *Thānānusak nai ngān sathāpattayakam Thai* (Hierarchy in architectural work). Bangkok: Krom Silapakorn, 2008.

Krom Thang Luang (Royal Highways Department). *Thang luang nai prathet thai* (Royal highways in Thailand). Bangkok: Krom Thang Luang 1971.

———. *Thang luang nai prathet thai, 2527* (Royal highways in Thailand, 1984). Bangkok: Krom Thang Luang, 1984.

Kukrit Pramoj. *Anuson nai ngan chalong 50 pi haeng kitchakan khong borisat pun siment thai jamkat pho so 2456–2506* (Commemorative volume in celebration of 50 years of the Siam Cement Company, 1913–1963). Bangkok: Siam Cement Company, 1963.

Kullada Kesbonchoon-Mead. *The Rise and Decline of Thai Absolutism.* London: RoutledgeCurzon, 2004.

Landon, Kenneth. *Siam in Transition: A Brief Survey of Cultural Trends in the Five Years since the Revolution of 1932.* New York: Greenwood, 1968.

Larsson, Tomas. *Land and Loyalty: Security and the Development of Property Rights in Thailand.* Ithaca, NY: Cornell University Press, 2012.

Laugier, Marc-Antoine. *Observations sur l'architecture.* La Haye: Desaint, 1765.

Lim, Irene. *Secret Societies in Singapore: Featuring the William Stirling Collection.* Singapore: Singapore History Museum, 1999.

Lim, Samson. *Siam's New Detectives: Visualizing Crime and Conspiracy in Modern Thailand.* Honolulu: University of Hawai'i Press, 2016.

Lindquist, John. "Borobudur: The Top Plan and the Upper Terraces." *East and West* 45, nos. 1–4 (December 1995).

Litchfield, Whiting, Bowne, and Associates. *Technical Monograph: Travel Time.* Bangkok: Ministry of the Interior, 1959.

Litchfield, Whiting, Bowne, and Associates and Adams, Howard, and Greeley. *Greater Bangkok Plan 2533.* Bangkok: Ministry of the Interior, 1960.

Lithai. *Three Worlds According to King Ruang: A Thai Buddhist Cosmology.* Translated by Frank E. Reynolds and Mani B. Reynolds. Berkeley: Regents of the University of California, 1982.

———. *Traibhumikatha.* Bangkok: ASEAN Committee on Culture and Information, 1985.

———. *Traiphum phra ruang* (The Three Worlds of Phra Ruang). Cremation volume for Phra Chao Boromawongthoe Phra Ong Chao Prasansrisa Phra Ong Chao Praphai Sri Saad. Bangkok, 1912.

Loeperdinger, Martin, and Bernd Elzer. "Lumiere's Arrival of the Train: Cinema's Founding Myth." *Moving Image* 4, no. 1 (Spring 2004).

Loos, Tamara. "Sex in the Inner City: The Fidelity between Sex and Politics in Siam." *Journal of Asian Studies* 64, no. 4 (November 2005).

———. *Subject Siam: Family Law and Colonial Modernity in Thailand.* Ithaca, NY: Cornell University Press, 2006.

Lyman, Stanford. "Chinese Secret Societies in the Occident: Notes and Suggestions for Research in the Sociology of Secrecy." *Canadian Review of Sociology and Anthropology* 1, no. 2 (1964).

Mabry, Bevars. *The Development of Labor Institutions in Thailand.* Ithaca, NY: Southeast Asia Program, Department of Asian Studies, Cornell University, 1979.

Malinee Khumsupha. *Anusawari prachathipatai kap khwam mai thi mong mai hen* (Democracy Monument and its hidden meanings). Bangkok: Wiphasa, 2005.

Mannheim, Karl. *Ideology and Utopia: An Introduction to the Sociology of Knowledge.* London: Routledge and Kegan Paul, 1960.

Marks, Laura. *The Skin of the Film: Intercultural Cinema, Embodiment, and the Senses.* Durham, NC: Duke University Press, 2000.

Marx, Karl. *The German Ideology, Part I.* New York: International Publishers, 1947.

Marx, Karl, and Friedrich Engels. *Manifesto of the Communist Party* (Beijing: Foreign Languages Press, 1972).

Mattana Ketkamon. "Kan muang lae kan pokkhrong nai ratchakan phrabat somdet phra mongkut klao phra chao yu hua" (Politics and administration in the reign of King Rama VI). *Sangkhomsat paritat* 14, nos. 3–4 (1975).

Mattani Mojdara Rutnin. *Dance, Drama, and Theater in Thailand: The Process of Development and Modernization.* Chiang Mai, Thailand: Silkworm, 1996.

Mbembe, Achille. *Critique of Black Reason.* Chicago: University of Chicago Press, 2017.

McCarthy, James. *Surveying and Exploring in Siam.* London: John Murray, 1902.

McDonald, N. A. *Siam: Its Government, Manners, Customs, &c.* Philadelphia: A. Martien, 1871.

McVetty, Amanda Kay. "Wealth and Nations." In *The Development Century: A Global History.* Edited by Stephen J. Macekura and Erez Manela. Cambridge: Cambridge University Press, 2018.

Metcalf, Thomas. *An Imperial Vision: Indian Architecture and Britain's Raj.* New Delhi: Oxford University Press, 2002.

Mignolo, Walter. *Local Histories / Global Designs: Coloniality, Subaltern Knowledges, and Border Thinking.* Princeton, NJ: Princeton University Press, 2000.

Milindapañha. Based on the translation by I. B. Horner. Kandy: Buddhist Publication Society, 1993.

Millon, Henry A., and Vittorio Magnago Lampugnani, eds. *The Renaissance from Brunelleschi to Michelangelo: The Representation of Architecture.* New York: Rizzoli, 1994.

Moon, Karen. *Modeling Messages: The Architect and the Model.* New York: Moncaelli Press, 2005.

More, Thomas. *Utopia.* Louvain: Arte Theoidorici Martini, 1516.

Mrázek, Rudolf. *Engineers of Happy Land: Technology and Nationalism in a Colony.* Princeton, NJ: Princeton University Press, 2002.

Muang boran 3, no. 1 (October–December 1976).

Muñoz, Jose Esteban. *Cruising Utopia: The Then and There of Queer Futurity.* New York: New York University Press, 2009.

Murray, Dian, and Qin Baoqi. *The Origins of the Tiandihui.* Stanford, CA: Stanford University Press, 1994.

Naengnoi Suksri and Michael Freeman. *Palaces of Bangkok: Royal Residences of the Chakri Dynasty.* Bangkok: River Books, 1996.

Namphueng Padamalangula. "Framing the Universe: Cosmography and the 'Discourse on the Frame.'" *Rian Thai: International Journal of Thai Studies* 1, no. 1 (2008).

Nang utai klon suat. Bangkok: Fine Arts Department, 2004.

National Economic Development Board. *National Economic Development Plan, 1961–1966, Second Phase 1964–1966.* Bangkok, January 1964.

Needham, Joseph. *Science and Civilization in China.* Vol. 3. Cambridge: Cambridge University Press, 1954.

Neumaier-Dargyay, Eva. "Buddhism." In *Life after Death in World Religions.* Edited by Harold Coward. Maryknoll, NY: Orbis, 1997.

Nidhi Eoseewong. *Pen and Sail: Literature and History in Early Bangkok Including the History of Bangkok in the Chronicles of Ayutthaya.* Translated by Chris Baker, Benedict Anderson, Craig J. Reynolds, Hong Lysa, Pasuk Phongpaiichit, Patrick Jory, and Ruth McVey. Chiang Mai, Thailand: Silkworm, 2005.

———. *Pha khaw ma pha sin kang gaeng nai lae un un: Wa duay phrapheni khwam plian plaeng lae ruang sapsara* (Loincloth, sarong, underwear, etc.: On customs, changes, and interesting stories). Bangkok: Matichon, 2004.

Nimit Mongkol Navarat. *The Dreams of an Idealist.* Translated by David Smyth. Chiang Mai, Thailand: Silkworm, 2009.

Nims, Cyrus. *City Planning in Thailand.* Bangkok: Ministry of the Interior, 1963.

Office of the Prime Minister. *A Collection of King Chulalongkorn's Manuscripts,* 3:1. Bangkok: n.p., 1970.

O'Neil, Marvelma. *Bangkok: A Cultural History.* Oxford: Oxford University Press, 2008.

Panagia, Davide. *The Political Life of Sensation.* Durham, NC: Duke University Press, 2009.

Parry, Benita. *Postcolonial Studies: A Materialist Critique.* London: Routledge, 2004.

Pasuk Phongpaichit and Christopher John Baker. *A History of Ayutthaya: Siam in the Modern World.* Cambridge: Cambridge University Press, 2017.

———. *A History of Thailand*. Melbourne: Cambridge University Press, 2014.

———. *Thailand: Economy and Politics*. Kuala Lumpur: Oxford University Press, 2002.

Patsorn Sungsri. *Thai National Cinema: The Three Potent Signifiers of Thai Identity, Nation, Religion, and Monarchy, Their Interrelationship and Influence in Thai National Cinema*. Saarbrucken: VDM Verlag, 2000.

Patton, Thomas. "In Pursuit of the Sorcerer's Power: Sacred Diagrams as Technologies of Potency." *Contemporary Buddhism* 13, no. 2 (2012).

Peleggi, Maurizio. *Lords of Things: The Fashioning of the Siamese Monarchy's Modern Image*. Honolulu: University of Hawai'i Press, 2002.

———. *Monastery, Monument, Museum: Sites and Artifacts of Thai Cultural Memory*. Honolulu: University of Hawai'i Press, 2018.

———. *Thailand: The Worldly Kingdom*. London: Reaktion, 2007.

Phillips, Matthew. *Thailand in the Cold War*. London: Routledge, 2017.

Phiphat Phongraphipon. "Sastracharn Silpa Bhirasri sinlap lae mahawithayalai Silpakorn" (Professor Silpa Bhirasri, art and Silpakorn University). *Bulletin of the Art Gallery of Silpakorn University* 1 (September 1984).

Phra Phrombhicitr (Phra Phromphichit). *Phutta silpasathapatayakam phak ton* (Buddhist art, architecture). Bangkok: Rong phimp Phra Jan, 1952.

Phraratchaphongsawadan chabap luangprasoetaksorn (Royal dynastic chronicles: Luang Prasoet Aksorn version). Bangkok: Krom silpakorn, 1972.

Phraratchaphongsawadan chabap phraratchahatlekha (Royal dynastic chronicles: Version of the royal secretary). Bangkok: Krom silpakorn, 1973.

Phra ratchawong phya thai: Wan wan lae wan ni (Phya Thai Palace: Days gone by and today). Bangkok: Chomrom khon rak wang nai phra ubtham somdet phra chao phakhinitoe chao fa phecharatanasuda sirisophaphannawadi, 2010.

Phusadi Thipthat. *Chang farang nai krung sayam* (Foreign craftsmen in Siam). Bangkok: Chulalongkorn University, 1998.

———. *Sathapok sathapatayakam* (Architect, architecture). Bangkok: Chulalongkorn University, 1999.

Phuttayotfa Chulalok. *Traiphum lokwinitchai* (Treatise on the Three Worlds). Bangkok: Rōngphim Sōphonphiphatthanākǭn, 1912.

Pirasri Povatong. "Building Siwilai: Transformation of Architecture and Architectural Practice in Siam during the Reign of Rama V, 1868-1910." PhD diss., University of Michigan, 2011.

———. *Chang farang nai krung sayam* (Foreign craftsmen in Siam). Bangkok: Faculty of Architecture, Chulalongkorn University, 2003.

Pollock, Sheldon. "The Theory of Practice and the Practice of Theory in Indian Intellectual History." *Journal of the American Oriental Society* 105, no. 3 (1985).

Porphant Ouyyanont. "Bangkok's Population and the Ministry of the Capital in Early 20th Century Thai History." *Southeast Asian Studies* 35, no. 2 (September 1997).

———. "Physical and Economic Change in Bangkok, 1851-1925." *Southeast Asian Studies* 36, no. 4 (March 1999).

———. *A Regional Economic History of Thailand.* Bangkok: Chulalongkorn University Press; Singapore: ISEAS Yusof Ishak Institute, 2017.

———. "Transformation of Bangkok and Concomitant Changes in Urban-Rural Interaction in Thailand in the 19th and 20th Centuries." *Proceedings of the International Conference: The Chao Phraya Delta: Historical Development, Dynamics and Challenges of Thailand's Rice Bowl.* Bangkok: Kasetsart University, 2000.

Prabhu, Anjali. *Hybridity: Limits, Transformations, Prospects.* Albany: State University of New York Press, 2007.

Preciado, Paul B. *Un appartement sur Uranus: Chroniques de la traversée.* Paris: Bernard Grasset, 2019.

Pridi Phanomyong. *Pridi by Pridi: Selected Writings on Life, Politics, and Economy.* Chiang Mai, Thailand: Silkworm, 2000.

Proser, Adriana, Cathy Dorsey, and the Asia Society Museum. *Pilgrimage and Buddhist Art.* New York: Asia Society, 2010.

Pye, Oliver. *Khor Jor Kor: Forest Politics in Thailand.* Bangkok: White Lotus Press, 2005.

Rajabhat University Bangkok. *Anusawari phithak ratthathammanun wat phra sri mahathat maha vihan sathaban rachaphatphranakhon* (Laksi monument, Wat Phra Sri Mahthat, and the Rajabhat University). Bangkok: Sathaban Rachaphatphranakhorn, 2000.

Ramachitti [Vajiravudh]. *Heart of a Young Man.* Originally published as *Hua chai chai num.* Translated by Ted Strehlow. Melbourne: n.p., 1989.

Ramanujan, A. K. "Three Hundred Rāmayanas: Five Examples and Three Thoughts on Translation." In *The Collected Essays of A.K. Ramanujan.* New Delhi: Oxford University Press, 1999.

Ratchabandittayasathan. *Photchananukrom chabap ratchabandiuttayasathan pho so 2525* (Dictionary of the Royal Institute of Thailand, 1996 version). Bangkok: Ratchabandittayasathan, 1996.

Reynaud, Dominique. *A Critical Edition of Ibn al-Haytham's "On the Shape of the Eclipse": The First Experimental Study of the Camera Obscura.* Cham, Switzerland: Springer, 2016.

Reynolds, Craig. "Buddhist Cosmography in Thai History, with Special Reference to 19th-Century Culture Change." *Journal of Asian Studies* 35, no. 2 (February 1976).

———. *Seditious Histories: Contesting Thai and Southeast Asian Pasts.* Seattle: University of Washington Press, 2006.

Reynolds, Frank E. "Ramayana, Rama Jataka, and Ramakien: A Comparative Study of Hindu and Buddhist Traditions." *Many Rāmayaṇas: The Diversity of a Narrative Tradition in South Asia.* Edited by Paula Richman. Berkeley: University of California Press, 1999.

Ricouer, Paul. *Lectures on Ideology and Utopia.* New York: Columbia University Press, 1986.

Robertson, Thomas. "New Frontiers." In *The Development Century: A Global History.* Edited by Stephen J. Macekura and Erez Manela. Cambridge: Cambridge University Press, 2018.

Romm, Jeff. *Urbanization in Thailand.* New York: Ford Foundation, 1974.

Romnichatr Kaewkiriya. *Sala-chaloem-krung.* Bangkok: Chaloem krung manithat, 1995.

Ruang khlong phra phloeng phra boromati phratchaoluang phra niphon phra chao borom wongtoe korom mun sri surenot lae tamnak phae (Regarding the poem on lighting the pyre of Phra Boromati Phra Chao Luang Phra Niphon Phrachao Boromwongtoe krom munsri surenot and the residential building in the royal compound). Bangkok: Khuanpim, 1963.

Ruitenbeek, Klaas. *Carpentry and Building in Late Imperial China: A Study of the Fifteenth-Century Carpenter's Manual Lu Ban Jing.* Leiden: Brill, 1993.

Rykwert, Joseph. *The Idea of a Town.* Cambridge, MA: MIT Press, 1988.

S. Bangjaeng. "67 pi phaphayon thai 2466–2533" (67 years of Thai cinema). *Khana anukam kan jad ngan chaloem chalong 67 pi phaphayon thai.* Bangkok: Samaphan phaphayon haeng chat, 1990.

Sakchai Saising. *Chedi nai prathet thai* (Stupas in Thailand). Bangkok: Matichon, 2017.

Sakhonkhotkhet (Pratuan Sakhrikanont). *Chotmaihet khwam song jam samai thi farangset yeud chanthaburi, pi po so 2436–2447* (Memorial archives of the period that France occupied Chanthaburi 1893–1904). Bangkok: Phraephithya, 1972.

Samaichaloem Kridakon. *Ngan sathapatayakam khong mom chao samai chaloem kridakon* (The architectural work of Mom Chao Samaichaloem Kridakon). Bangkok: Phrachan, 1967.

Samakhom sathapanik sayam (Association of Siamese Architects). *Roi pi Phraphromphichit* (100 years of Phraphromphichit). Bangkok: ASA, 1990.

Sangaroon Kanokpongchai. *Wat Thongthammachat.* Bangkok: Muang Boran, 1982.

Santi Leksukhum. *Khwam samphan jin-thai yong yai nai luad lai pradap* (Sino-Thai relations in ornamental patterns). Bangkok: Muang Boran, 2007.

Santikaro Bhikkhu. "Buddhadassa Bhikkhu: Life and Society through the Natural Eyes of Voidness." In *Engaged Buddhism: Buddhist Liberation Movements in Asia.* Edited by Christopher Queen and Sallie King. Albany: State University of New York Press, 1996.

Sansoni Wirasinchai. *Roi raek nai muang thai* (100 firsts in Thailand). Bangkok: Matichon, 1994.

Sarit Thanarat. *Pramuan Suntharaphot Khǫng Čhǫmphon Sarit Thanarat I* (Collection of speeches of Field Marshal Sarit Thanarat I). Bangkok: n.p., 1964.

Sarot Rattananimman. "The Golden Meru." *Journal of the Siam Society* 26 (December 1947).

Satchaphirom Udomrachaphakdi. *Thewkamnoet* (Origin of heavenly deities). Bangkok: Thammasat University, 1964.

Sawan Tangtrongsitthikun. "Kan sang 'lak chai kaen muang' mua raek sathabana krung rattanakosin in ayutthaya" (The building of the "Victory Monument in the center of the city" at the establishment of the city of Rattanakosin). *Silpawatthanatham* 36, no. 6 (April 2015).

Sayre, Francis. "The Passing of Extraterritoriality in Siam." *American Journal of Law* 22, no. 1 (1928).

Schlegel, Gustaaf. *Thian ti hwui. The Hung-League, or Heaven-Earth League, a Secret Society with the Chinese in China and India.* Batavia: Lenge, 1866.

Seksan Prasertkul. "The Transformation of the Thai State and Economic Change (1855–1945)." PhD diss., Cornell University, 1989.

Shu, Hirayama. *Zhongguo mi mi she hui shi* (History of China's secret societies). Shanghai: Shang Wu Yin Shu Guan, 1912.

Siam Cement Company. *Thi raluk nai kan thi than dai karuna pai ruam ngan phithi poet khun mo phao pun met khrung thi si na rong ngan tha luang* (Commemorative volume for the opening ceremony of the Tha Luang clinker factory). Siam Cement Company: Bangkok, 1960.

Silpakorn University. *Rakngao mahawitthayalai sinlapakopn: Nithatsakan phon ngan khong "sit" rongrian pranit sinlapakam-rongrian sinlapakorn phanaek chang* ("Roots" of Silpakorn University: Exhibition of "disciples" from Silpakorn Art Academy). Bangkok: Amarin, 1993.

Sirichai Sirikaya. *Nang thai* (Thai movies). Bangkok: Communications Division, Faculty of Communication Arts, Chulalongkorn University, 1988.

Skinner, William G. *Chinese Society in Thailand: An Analytical History.* Ithaca, NY: Cornell University Press, 1957.

Snellgrove, David. "Borobudur: Stūpa or Mandala?" *East and West* 46, nos. 3–4 (December 1996).

Sng, Jeffery, and Pimpraphai Bisalputra. *A History of the Thai-Chinese.* Singapore: Editions Didier Millet, 2015.

Snodgrass, Adrian. *The Symbolism of the Stupa.* Ithaca, NY: Cornell University Southeast Asia Program Publications, 1985.

Sombat Jantharawong and Chai-anan Samudavanija. *Khwamkit thang kanmuang lae sangkhom thai* (Thai political and social thought). Bangkok: Thammasat University, Thai Khadi Institute, 1980.

Somphong Chaulaem. *Traiphumikatha chabap khoi yang chua* (Traiphum, simplified version). Bangkok: Suan Aksorn Sakhaburi, 1985.

Sopothjill, William Edward, and Lewis Hodous. A *Dictionary of Chinese Buddhist Terms with Sanskrit and English Equivalents and a Sanskrit-Pali Index.* London: Kegan Paul, Trunch, Tubner, 1937.

Sorasan Phaengsopha. *Ban ya phai* (Granny Phai's house). Bangkok: Sarakhadi, 2002.

Steinahrdt, Nancy Shatzman. "The Tang Architectural Icon and the Politics of Chinese Architectural History." *Art Bulletin* 86, no. 2 (June 2004).

Suárez, Thomas. *Early Mapping of Southeast Asia.* Hong Kong: Periplus, 1999.

Subrahmanyan, Arjun. "Buddhism, Democracy and Power in the 1932 Revolution." *Asian Studies Review* 41, no. 1 (2017).

Sudara Seriwat. *Wiwathanakam khong ruang san nai muang thai tangtae raek jon pho so 2475* (Evolution of Thai short stories from the beginning until 1932 CE). Bangkok: Ministry of Education, 1977.

Sujit Wongthes. *Krungthep ma jak nai* (Bangkok: A historical background). Bangkok: Dream Catcher, 2005.

Sunait Chutintaranond. "Mandala, Segmentary State and Politics of Centralization in Medieval Ayudhya." *Journal of the Siam Society* 78, no. 1 (1990).

Supharat Loedphanichkul. "Samakhom lap ang yi nai prathet thai, 2367–2453" (Secret societies in Thailand, 1824–1910). PhD diss., Chulalongkorn University, 1981.

Suphawadi Ratanamat, Parinya Chukaew, et al. *Kan jat tang klum anurak ngan sathapatayakam samai modoen nai prathet thai* (Activities of the preservation group, modern architectural works in Thailand). Bangkok: Docomomo Thailand, 2003.

Swearer, Donald K. *Becoming the Buddha: The Ritual of Image Consecration in Thailand.* Princeton, NJ: Princeton University Press, 2004.

———. "Signs of the Buddha in Northern Thai Chronicles." *Embodying the Dharma: Buddhist Relic Veneration in Asia.* Edited by David Germano and Kevin Trainor. Albany: State University of New York Press, 2004.

Ta Tha-it. *Talui ke khlap: Kai Bangkok chut 7* (A visit to the gay club: Bangkok guide series 7). Bangkok: Joralsanitwong, 1975.

Tafuri, Manfredo. *Architecture and Utopia: Design and Capitalist Development.* Cambridge, MA: MIT Press, 1979.

Tai Hsuan-Chih and Ronald Suleski. "Origin of the Heaven and Earth Society." *Modern Asian Studies* 11, no. 3 (1977).

Tambiah, Stanley J. "The Buddhist Cosmos: Paradise Lost, Gained, and Transcended." *History of Religions* 24, no. 1 (August 1984).

———. "The Galactic Polity: The Structure of Traditional Kingdoms in Southeast Asia." *Annals of the New York Academy of Sciences* 293 (1977).

Tamra phichai songkhram chabap ratchakan thi neung (Manual of the art of war: First Reign version). Bangkok: Krom Silpakon, 2002.

Tamra phichai songkhram khong krom silpakorn: Phim pen anuson nai ngan chapon kit sop Nang Sanitiaronarot (Tlap Bunratphan) (Manual of the art of war of the Department of Fine Arts: Cremation volume of Nang Sanitiaronarot [Tlap Bunratphan]). Bangkok: Krom Silpakon, 1969.

Tamra phra maha phichai songkhram chabap wat kuaninniimitr amphoe muang phattalung changwat phattalung (Manual of the art of war: Wat Kuan in nimitr, Phattalung version). Songkhla: Sathaban Taksinkhadisuksa, Mahawittayalai Thaksin, 1998.

Tanabe, Shigeharu. "Historical Geography of the Canal System in the Chao Phraya River Delta: From the Ayutthaya Period to the Fourth Reign of the Rattanakosin Dynasty." *Journal of the Siam Society* 65, no. 2 (1977).

Terwiel, B. J. "On the Trail of King Taksin's *Samutphāp Traiphūm.*" *Journal of the Siam Society* 102 (2014).

———. "The Origin and Meaning of the City Pillar." *Journal of the Siam Society* 66, no. 2 (1978).

Thai National Team. *Traibhumikhatha: The Story of the Three Planes of Existence.* Bangkok: Amarin Printing Group, 1987.

Thak Chaloemtiarana. *Thailand: The Politics of Despotic Paternalism.* Bangkok: Social Science Association, Thai Kadi Institute, Thammasat University, 1979.

Thanathip Chattraphuti. *Tamnan rong nang* (History of movie theaters). Bangkok: Weladi, 2004.

Thanavi Chotpradit. "Revolution versus Counter-Revolution: The People's Party and the Royalist(s) in Visual Dialogue." PhD diss., Birkbeck, University of London, 2016.

Thawat Mokarapong. *History of the Thai Revolution: A Study in Political Behavior.* Bangkok: Thai Watana Panich, 1972.

Thawisak Pinthong et al. *Wannakam kep tok* (Literature of what's left behind). Bangkok: Odian Sato, 1980.

Thipakorawong. *Dynastic Chronicles, Bangkok Era, the First Reign, Volume One: Text.* Translated by Thadeus and Chadin Flood. Tokyo: Center for East Asian Cultural Studies, 1978.

———. *Nangsu sadaeng kitchanukit* (Book showing work to be done). Bangkok: Nai Thep, 1872.

———. *Phraratchaphongsawadan krung rattanakosin, chabap ho samut haeng chat ratchakan thi sam, ratchakan thi si* (Royal dynastic chronicles of Rattanakosin, National Library edition, Third and Fourth Reigns). Bangkok: Khlingwitthaya, 1963.

Thompson, Virginia. *Labor Problems in Southeast Asia.* New Haven, CT: Yale University Press, 1947.

———. *Thailand: The New Siam.* New York: Macmillan, 1967.

Thongchai Winichakul. "The Quest for 'Siwilai,'" *Journal of Asian Studies* 59, no. 3 (August 2000).

———. *Siam Mapped: A History of a Geo-Body of a Nation.* Honolulu: University of Hawai'i Press, 1994.

———. "Siam's Colonial Conditions and the Birth of Thai History." In *Southeast Asian Historiography, Unravelling the Myths: Essays in Honour of Barend Jan Terwiel.* Edited by Volker Grabowsky. Bangkok: River Books, 2011.

Tri Ratonruchi. "Chaloem krung royan thiato silpakam khrung satthawat" (The mid-century art of the Chaloem Krung Royal Theater), *Silpawatthanatham* 15, no. 4 (February 1994).

Udomporn Teeraviriyakul. *Bangkok Modern.* Bangkok: Institute of Asian Studies, Chulalongkorn University, 2014.

Upton, Dell. *Another City: Urban Spaces and Urban Life in the New American Republic.* New Haven, CT: Yale University Press, 2008.

Vajiravudh. *Pluk chai sua pa* (Instilling the wild tiger spirit). Bangkok: Khrusupha, 1943.

———. *Thio Muang Phra Ruang* (A trip to Muang Phra Ruang). Bangkok: Thaikhasēm, 1978.

———. *A Trip to Muang Phra Ruang.* N.p., 1967.

———. *Uttarakuru: Phra ratcha niphon phra bat somdet phra mongkut klao jao yu hua* (Uttarakuru: The royal opinion of His Majesty King Rama VI). Bangkok: Wat Boworniwet, 1965.

Van Roy, Edward. "Rise and Fall of the Bangkok Mandala." *Journal of Asian History* 45, nos. 1–2 (2011).

———. "Sampheng: From Ethnic Isolation to National Integration." *Sojourn: Journal of Social Issues in Southeast Asia* 22, no. 1 (2008).

———. *Siamese Melting Pot: Ethnic Minorities in the Making of Bangkok.* Singapore: ISEAS, 2017.

Vicha Dhitavadha. *Khon thai nai kong thap nasi* (A Thai in the Nazi army). Bangkok: Sarakhadi, 2004.

Vickery, Michael. *Cambodia, 1975–1982.* Boston: South End Press, 1984.

———. "A Note on the Date of the Traibhumikatha." *Journal of the Siam Society* 62, no. 2 (July 1974).

Wachirayanwararot (Prince Wachirayan). *Baeb Nawakam, phra nawakam kowit* (The styles of Phra Nawakam Kowit). Bangkok: Ongkankha khong khru supha, 1985.

Wales, H. G. Quartich. *Divination in Thailand: The Hopes and Fears of a Southeast Asian People.* London: Curzon, 1983.

———. *The Mountain of God: A Study in Early Religion and Kingship.* London: B. Quaritch, 1953.

Wallerstein, Immanuel, and Etienne Balibar. *Race, Nation, and Class.* London: Verso, 1991.

Walshe, Maurice O'C., ed. *The Long Discourses of the Buddha: A Translation of the Dīgha Nikāya.* Boston: Wisdom Publications, 1995.

Wang, Eugene Y. *Shaping the Lotus Sutra: Buddhist Visual Culture in Medieval China.* Seattle: University of Washington Press, 2005.

Ward, J. S. M., and William George Stirling. *The Hung Society, or the Society of Heaven and Earth.* London: Baskerville, 1925.

Warren, William. *Bangkok.* London: Reaktion Books, 2002.

Wegner, Philip E. *Imaginary Communities: Utopia, the Nation, and Spatial Histories of Modernity.* Berkeley: University of California Press, 2002.

Wheatley, Paul. "The Suspended Pelt: Reflections on a Discarded Model of Spatial Structure." In *Geographic Humanism, Analysis and Social Action: Proceedings of Symposia Celebrating a Half Century of Geography and Michigan.* Edited by Donald Deskins Jr., George Kish, John Nystuen, and Gunnar Olson. Ann Arbor: Department of Geography, University of Michigan, 1977.

Wichit Wathakan. *Luat suphan rathcamanu phrachao krung thon suk thailand* (Four plays). Commemoration volume for Khunying Chan Thepprachum. Bangkok, 17 October 1937.

———. *Patokatha lae kham banyai khong phontri luang wichit watthakan pheua rong amnattho khunchitrakankhamni* (Speeches and talks by Major General Luang Wichit Watthakan: Funeral volume for Rongamnattho khunchitrakankhamni). Bangkok: Wat Mokutkasatriyaram, 1966.

———. *Thailand's Case.* Bangkok: Thanom Punnahitananda, 1941.

Wilhelm, Prince of Sweden. *In the Lands of the Sun: Notes and Memories of a Tour in the East.* London: E. Nash, 1915.

Wilson, Constance. *Thailand: A Handbook of Historical Statistics*. Boston: G.K. Hall, 1983.

Wirayut Pisali. *Krungthep yamaratri* (Bangkok at midnight). Bangkok: Matichon, 2014.

Wolters, O. W. *History, Culture and Religion: Southeast Asian Perspectives*. Ithaca, NY: SEAP Publications/Institute of Southeast Asian Studies, 1999.

Wongsanupraphat. *Ruangprawat krasuangkasethrathikan* (History of the Ministry of Agricultural Works). Bangkok: n.p., 1941.

Woodard, Hiram. "The Thai Čhêdî and the Problem of Stūpa Interpretation." *History of Religions* 33, no. 1 (August 1933).

Woodward, F. L., Caroline A. F. Rhys Davids, and E. M. Hare. *The Book of the Gradual Sayings (Anguttara-Nikāya) or More-Numbered Suttas*. London: Published for the Pali Text Society by Luzac and Company, 1960.

Wora Rochnawiphat. "Thong sanam luang." *Muang Boran* 42, no. 4 (October–December, 2016).

Worachat Meechubot. *Kret phonsawadan ratchakan thi 6* (Historical anecdotes from the Sixth Reign). Bangkok: Sansan Buk, 2010.

Woraphorn Phupongsaphan. "Ngan phramen: Phra rachaphithi satorn thipphawa haeng ong phra mahakastri nai samai Ayutthaya" (The cremation pyre: The royal ceremony reflecting the heavenly status of the monarchy in the Ayutthaya period). In *Ngan phramen: Silpasathapatayakam prawatisat lae watthanatham kieo neuang* (The cremation pyre: The history of its architecture and related culture). Bangkok: Ministry of Culture, 2009.

Worrasit Tantinipankul. "Modernization and Urban Monastic Space in Rattanakosin City: Comparative Study of Three Royal Wats." PhD diss., Cornell University, 2007.

Wright, Arnold, and Oliver T. Breakspear. *Twentieth Century Impressions of Siam*. London: Lloyd's Greater Britain Publishing, 1908.

Wyatt, David. *Thailand: A Short History*. New Haven, CT: Yale University Press, 1984.

Xian jing Guangzhou hui guan. "Xian luo Guangzhou shu zhi jianzhu ye" (The construction business of the Cantonese in Siam). In *Xianluo Guangzhou hui guan qi shi zhou nian ji nian te kan* (Seventieth anniversary publication of the Cantonese Association in Bangkok). Bangkok: Guangzhou hui guan, 1947.

Xiao Yishan. *Jin dai bi mi she hui shi liao* (History of modern secret societies). Beiping: Guo Li Beiping Yan Jiu Yuan Zong Ban Shi Chu Chu Ban She, 1935.

Zheng Qiao. "Tupu lüe." In *Tongzhi* (Comprehensive records). Taipei: Xin Xing Shuju, 1965.

Zimmerman, C. C. *Siam: Rural Economic Survey*. Bangkok: Bangkok Times Press, 1931.

INDEX

Page numbers in **boldface** refer to illustrations.

center of the mandala polity, 2–3, 63, 79; Vajiravudh's displacement of the meaning of, 62, 88, 194

Didion, Joan, 193

Döhring, Karl, 233n60

Duncan, James, 4

Dusit Thani, Muang Prachathipatai (miniature city): dismantling of, 75, 217n72; eclectic historicism of, 65–68; Khonthapnatsala Theater at Dusit Thani, 70, **70**; location in the Dusit Palace, 53, **54**; Phra Ratchawang Angkrit (English Palace), 68, **70**; Royal Palace at, 65–66, **66**; speculative play toy for Vajiravudh, 54, 62, 215n41; Theoatchamthan Throne Hall at, 66, **67**, 68; Wat Thammathipatai at, 65–66, **65**, 67

—as political tool: failure of, 72–75; Vajiravudh's modeling of a modern ruling class, 10, 50, 54–55

—queerness of: homosocial relations it cultivated in, 55, 62–63, 74; and the inversion of social reality, 55–56, 74–75

—Royal Palace, 66, **66**

Dusit Thani Hotel: and the linking of legible details of Thai art with modern technology, 183; and the shape of the *mongkut* (ceremonial crown) of King Vajiravudh, 181, **181**

dynastic chronicles: on the compilation of the *Tamra phichai songkhram*, 202n15; on the naming of Bangkok, 13–14, 201n3

Egge, James, 197n4

Engels, Friedrich, 189

Evans, Robin, 219n25

exhibitions and exhibition spaces: entertainment halls and exhibition spaces as political spaces, 69–71; public exhibition of the "permanent" constitution in front of the Ananta Samakhom Throne Hall, 96, **97**; Siam's participation in international exhibitions, 133,

229n10. *See also* Dusit Thani; funeral pyres

—recreational spaces: and the *Greater Bangkok Plan 2533,* 177–178; and the *vimāna* of Indra on the summit of Mount Meru, 166. *See also* Sanam Luang (royal field)

family ties: birth and childrearing responsibilities in Uttarakuru, 59; the ideal of the nuclear family identified with the nation-state, 148, 151, **152**, **153**; Kang Youwei's view that it was detrimental to happiness, 214n27; model family depicted on the Monument for the Defense of the Constitution, 99; and Vajiravudh's queer formulation, 60–61

funeral pyres: imagined community of the nation linked to the afterlife by, 89–92, 97–101; the *Traiphum* as a cremation volume, 33. *See also* Vajiravudh, King—cremation

garuda: on the entrance of Sala Chaloem Krung, 121, **123**; on the facade of the General Post Office, 151, **152**; and legitimation of the monarchy, 80; and Wat Phra Sri Mahathat, 159, **159**

Gerini, Gerolamo Emilio, 198n6

graffiti: and "spatial imagination," 8, 24, 167, 189–191; *Wannakam kep tok,* 189–191

Grand Palace (Phra Borom Maha Ratchawong): palladium of the Emerald Buddha (Phra Kaew Morakot) installed on the grounds of, 13, 18–19, 201n2; Sawasdisopha gate at, 139–141, **140**, 162; scale model of Angkor Wat displayed in, 62; and the state display of relics of former kings, 91; and the symbolic plan of Bangkok, 20, 23–24, **25**, 173; and the Thai sumptuary code, 130; Thung Phra Men open area outside the walls of (*see* Sanam Luang)

the Pali imaginaire, 2, 4; and Phra
Phromphichit's conflation of
commercial and political programs
within a religious typology, 139,
146; the *Tamra ang yi* as a model
for its serial reproduction across
diasporic networks, 37–38, 42.
See also *kamma*; Mount Meru;
urban planning—mandala-based
planning
Laugier, Marc-Antoine, 216n48
Lim, Samson, 41–42
Litchfield plan. See *Greater Bangkok
Plan 2533*
Lithai, Phya. *See* Sukhothai—Lithai,
king
Loos, Tamara, 7, 60, 215n31

magic: "building magic" associated
with Chinese building practices,
3, 32–33, 207n17; and the sacred,
almost magical value of technical
knowledge, 3, 33; of the structural
and ventilation systems of the
Sala Chaloem Krung Cinema, 11,
115–120, 127
Marks, Laura, 107
Marx, Karl, 189, 199n12, 199n14
Metteya (Skt. Maitreya). See *sri ariya
metteya* and *sri ariya*
Mongkut, King (Rama IV): and
Angkor Wat, 62; grandson Prince
Boworadet (*see* Boworadet,
Prince); the Siam Intercontinental
Hotel designed in the shape
of his helmet, **180**, 181; son
Prince Narisara (*see* Narisara
Nuwattiwong, Prince)
Monument to the Defense of the
Constitution, 97, **98**, 196; and the
architectural reconciliation of
seemingly contradictory impulses,
98–100
Moon, Karen, 215n41
More, Thomas, 4–5, 59, 100n20
Mount Meru: diagram of the *Triaphum*
of, 20, **21**; and the sacralized
nation-state in the form of
Vajiravudh's crematorium, 194;

and the symbolic plan of Bangkok,
14, 19; and the symbolism of the
phra men, 76–80; *vimāna* of Indra
(Phaichayon Prasat or Vejayanta
castle) at the peak of, 20, 166,
204n52. *See also* Uttarakuru
Muñoz, Jose Esteban, 196

Nangklao, King (Rama III), 141
Narisara Nuwattiwong, Prince (Prince
Naris): and the crematorium
for soldiers who died defending
the constitution, 98; Soldier's
Memorial designed by, 94;
Vajirvudh's *phra men* designed by,
86–92, **90**
Needham, Joseph, 207n17
nibbāna (nirvana): Buddhist felicities
expressed by, 2, 197n5, 198n8; and
the Chakri monarchy's national
building project, 194; floating
paradise of a modern *vimāna*
contrasted with, 166
—City of Nibbāna: and the City
of Willows, 46; in Nai Sun's
Dhammasangani/Traiphum
manuscript, 43–44, **45**, 46–47; as
a Theravada Buddhist metaphor,
44–46; utopian nationalist ideology,
4–5
Nidhi Eoseewong, 14, 205n58; on
premodern ideas of space in Thai
Culture, 85
Nimitmongkol Navarat, M. R., 126
Nims, Cyrus, 178

Pali imaginaire: and the building
of Bangkok, 195–196;
Collins's conception of, 2, 197n4;
and the political imagination
of the People's Party, 196;
and the urban organization
of Bangkok, 2–3, 4, 18–19;
and the use of the *naganam* as
a template for urban organization,
18. See also *sri ariya metteya*
and *sri ariya*
Panagia, Davide, 106–107
Peleggi, Maurizio, 4, 14, 18, 224–225

268

Siam Cement Company: assets of, 134, 136, 228n2, 230n21; steel-reinforced concrete produced by, 11; Vajiravudh's founding of, 47, 65, 129, 133–134

Silpa Bhirasri (né Corrado Feroci): assistants Bunchua (né Sitthidet) and Phiman, 151, 232n50; and concrete as symbolic of the idealized character of the masses, 148–149; Democracy Monument designed with Jitrasen Miw Aphaiwong, 148, **149**; *garuda* on the facade of the General Post Office designed by, 151, **152**; glorification of the bodies of laboring Thai citizens, 151

Sitthidet Saenghiran, 151, **153**

slaves and slavery: abolition of slavery and the repeal of corvée labor, 29, 34, 206n1. See also *sakdina system*

sri ariya metteya and *sri ariya*: floating paradise of a modern *vimāna* contrasted with, 166; and the narrative of Phra Malai, 93, 131–132, **132**; and the next incarnation of the Buddha, Metteya (Skt. Maitreya), 93, 129, 222n61; and the Pali imaginaire, 2; and the People's Party overthrow of the monarchy (23 June 1932), 11, 78–79, 93, 160, 195–196; and the Phra Malai narrative, 93, 218n4; and the Phra Sri Ariya Metteya articulated in the *Traiphum*, 214n22

storytelling: and graffiti, 8, 24, 167, 189–191; and the People's Party's exploitation of the Pali imaginaire, 196; and religious contextualization of the Ramayana epic throughout South and Southeast Asia of, 227n69; and the Thai film industry, 126. *See also* Pali imaginaire; *Phra Malai* texts; Ramakian; *sri ariya metteya* and *sri ariya*

—architecture as a narrative form: *architecture parlante* symbolism of commercial architecture and,

237n74; and Bangkok's twentieth-century utopian projects, 193–196; and images of *nibbāna*, 194; and murals as a medium for mediating and broadcasting ideas about power, 85; and premodern ideas about space in Thai culture, 85; and the role of the wat in making religious discourse tangible, 153–154; and twentieth-century urban development, 8–9

—Thai historical writing: and the naming of Bangkok, 13–14, 201n3; *phongsawadan* dynastic chronicles, 9; *prawatisat* narrative tradition, 9; *tamnan* prehistorical narratives, 9

Sukhothai: and mandala geometries, 63; poolside restaurant at the Indra Regent Hotel, 183, **183**; *prang* (towerlike spires) appropriated by, 231n30; sacred Buddhist landscapes recreated by the fourteenth-century kings of, 4; and the *Traiphum phra ruang*, 20–22

—Lithai, king (Maha Dhammaraja I): on re-birth in the continents surrounding Mount Meru, 59; *Traiphum phra ruang* composed by (*see Traiphum phra ruang*)

Swearer, Donald K., 9, 153

Ta Tha-it: *Kai phi* and *Kai phi Bangkok* series, 165, 167, 186–188, 191; "Talui ke khlap" (A Visit to the Gay Club), 187, 234n3; "Wiman loi" (The Floating Paradise), 165–167, 187–188

Taksin, King: and Ayutthaya's cosmopolitan ruling class, 13, 201n4; capital of Thonburi, 13, 14, 15, 80; fifteen-year reign of, 14; monument in Thonburi, 177; Phuttayotfa's overthrowing of, 13; Thonburi *Traiphum* commissioned by, 44, **46**

Tamagno, Mario, 57, **58**, 154, 214n16

Tambiah, Stanley J., 214n22

Tamra ang yi (Secret Society Manual): the meaning of the

nation-state, 51–52; and the serial reproduction of the City of Willows across diasporic networks, 37–40, **38**, **40**, 42; and utopian nationalism, 30–31, 32, 33–34

Tamra phichai songkhram (Manual of the art of war): compilation and revision of, 15–16; diagram of the *naganam* mandala, 16–17, **17**; and the Indic *śāstra* tradition, 16; mandalas identified for strategic defense in, 16

Teochew: and Taksin's family background, 201n4; and the terms for secret societies, 209n29

Teochew craftsmen: and the general strike of Bangkok's migrant labor force (May 1910), 29–30; influence on the construction of *chedi* (pagodas) and *sum* (entrance arches), 42; and the language of architecture, 51–52

Thawisak Pinthong, *Wannakam kep tok*, 189–191

Theravada Buddhism: and Bangkok as terrestrial realm of the king in the Theravada Buddhist cosmos, 1–4, 7, 10; the Buddha and Buddhas in, 222n61; Buddhaghosa on reincarnation and *kammic* inheritance, 89; the City of Nibbāna as a Theravada Buddhist metaphor, 44–46; definitive version of the *Tipitaka* established by Phuttayotfa, 15; and *prang* (towerlike spires), 231n30; and the symbolism of the *wat,* 153–154. See also *devaraja*; Pali *imaginaire*; *sri ariya metteya* and *sri ariya*; *Traiphum phra ruang*

Thompson, Virginia, 168, 234n13

Thonburi: Memorial Bridge connecting it with Bangkok, 115, 177; as Taksin's capital, 13, 14, 15, 80; and the *Traiphum phra ruang,* 22, 44. *See also* Wat Thongthammachat in Thonburi

Thongchai Winichakul, 9, 205n64

Tiandihui (Heaven and Earth Society): founding by Hong Er, 35; origin story of, 210n47

Tourist Organization of Thailand (TOT), marketing of Thailand as an oasis of safety, 178–179, 188

Trailokya (Three Worlds) cosmology: earliest history of, 19. See also *Traiphum phra ruang*

Traiphum phra ruang (Three Worlds According to King Ruang): Buddhist utopias articulated in, 214n22; diagrams of the material characteristics of the Theravadan Buddhist cosmos, 31–32; Hell between the Universes (Lokantra), 204n49; *kammaphum* (world of desire) visualized in, 19–20, **21**, 58; and the legitimation of the monarchy, 80, 159; Phuttayotfa's revision of, 19, 21; and Phya Lithai's composition of, 20, 59, 204n55; and the spatial organization of the *phra men,* 79–80; and the symbolic plan of Bangkok, 19–24; texts emerging after the 1767 sacking of Ayutthaya, 21; and Thipakhorawong's *Kitchanukit,* 23; Universal Monarch of, 22, 159; *vimāna* of Indra on the summit of Mount Meru in, 166

Upton, Dell, 22–23

urban planning: City Planning Section established in Bangkok, 172; cluster-form city advocated by Augur (Tracy), 173, 175, 176, 236n52; and the cosmological view of the *Traiphum,* 79–80; emphasis on the automobile as the primary unit of design, 184; integration with astrological study, 15–17; "Mercedes brick" ventilation, 184, **186**, 191; *rong raem man run* ("pull curtain hotels"), 184–185, **185**, 188. See also *Greater Bangkok Plan 2533*

—mandala-based planning: and the *devaraja* (celestial monarch,

Th. *thewarat*) at the center of the mandala polity, 3, 22, 62, 63, 194; and the political organization of Southeast Asian polities, 15, 18–23, 79, 218n5

utopia and utopian order: and graffiti, 189–191; and the *Greater Bangkok Plan 2533* (Litchfield plan), 173, 190; and militarism, 194; as a motivator for social change, 11–12; and the mythic and historical past, 7, 200n33; and the sensorial experience of the Sala Chaloem Krung Cinema, 106, 108, 113–114, 126; and the Thai language, 4; and Tourist Organization of Thailand's marketing of Thailand as an oasis of safety, 178–179, 188

utopian nationalism: and the architectural forms of the *Baeb nawakam* and *Tamra ang yi*, 30–34, 49–52; and the Chakri dynasty's project of nation building, 194–195; and homosocial relationships at Dusit Thani, 55, 62–63, 74; and the ideal of the nuclear family, 151, **152, 153**; and Siam's adjustment to merchant capitalism, 5, 33–35; and *sri ariya metteya* and *sri ariya*, 2, 11, 78–79, 93, 195–196; and the story of Phra Malai, 132; urban conflict as a challenge to, 30–31, 194–196

Uttarakuru (continent surrounding Mount Meru): birth and childrearing responsibilities in, 59; floating paradise of a modern *vimāna* contrasted with, 166; Kalpapreuk (inexhaustible wishing tree) on, 59, 93; and utopias articulated in the *Traiphum*, 214n22; and Vajiravudh's vision of utopia, 58–60

Vajiravudh, King (Rama VI, r. 1910–1925): Ananta Samkhom Throne Hall built by, 142–143; miniature city constructed by (*see* Dusit Thani, Muang Prachathipatai); Public Works Department

reformed by, 214n16; and the shift from *nai chang* (craftsman) to *sathapanik* (architect), 24, 47–48, 86, 220n28; Siam Cement Company established by, 47, 65, 129, 133–134; studies in England, 213n10; *Thio muang phra ruang* (A Trip to the Land of Phra Ruang), 178–179

—cremation: creation of fire for, 221n43; Mount Meru conjured to sacralize the nation-state, 194; Prince Naris's plan of the *phra men*, 86–92, **90**; tricolor national flag reflecting triple values of, 91

Van Roy, Edward, 18–19

Victorian culture: and etiquette, 73; and queerness, 213n3; Vajiravudh's redefinition of heteronormative domestic conventions of, 62, 74

Victory Monument: concrete construction of, 133; Pum Malakun's design of, 147–148, **148**

vimāna (mythical flying palaces or chariots): and the projection of Bangkok as "floating paradise," 11, 23–24, 165–167, 192; and Ta Tha-it's writing about Bangkok, 165–167, 187

Vimāna-vatthu, 166, 234n4

Wachirayan, Prince: and the *Baeb nawakam* construction manual, 43, 49–52, 138–139; Chinese craftsmen employed to restore monastic complexes, 43

Wales, H. G. Quartich, 92, 221n39, 221n51

Wallerstein, Immanuel, 42

Wat Phra Chetuphon (Wat Pho): *jian nian* technique applied to *prang* (towerlike spires) of, 42–43, 141, **142**; the structure of the Panthéon compared with, 158, 233n61

Wat Phra Sri Mahathat: *chedi* at, 155–158, **155, 156, 157**; crypts of leaders in the wall of the *chedi* of, 158, **158**, 194; gable end of the *uposot* hall at, 159; light as a feature in the design of, **157**, 159;

and the new aesthetic order of the nation state envisioned by the People's Party, 99, 153, 194; plan and elevation drawing of, 154–155, **154**

Wat Thongthammachat in Thonburi, 82; scenes of the life of the historic Buddha Sakyamuni in the *uposot* of, 82–85, **83**, **84**

Wheatley, Paul, 17

Wichit Wathakan, Luang: on the Ananta Samakhom Throne Hall, 142–143; and the Anusawari Thai (Thai Monument), 141–143, 146; on building of a monument to celebrate Thai values of democracy and progress, 141–146, 148;

and the dissemination of a new national blueprint for monastic architecture, 138–139; "Human Revolution" lecture on Thai culture, 149–151; views on race, 147

Williams-Hunt, Peter, 155, **155**, 233n59

Wolters, O. W., 218n5

Wren, Christopher, Sir, 48

yojana: Buddhist felicities measured in terms of, 2, 20; length of, 198n6

Yommarat, Chao Phraya (Pan Sukhum), 57, 73–74, 134–135, 230n17

Zheng Qiao, 206–207n9

ABOUT THE AUTHOR

A historian of the modern built environment with a focus on transregional histories of Asian architecture and urbanism, Lawrence Chua is assistant professor in the School of Architecture at Syracuse University. His writing has appeared in the *Journal of the Society of Architectural Historians,* the *Journal of Urban History,* อ่าน, and the *Journal of Architecture.*